COMPOSERS OF THE TWENTIETH CENTURY

ALLEN FORTE, General Editor

THE MUSIC OF ALEXANDER SCRIABIN

JAMES M. BAKER

Yale University Press
New Haven and London

To Nancy, Christopher,
and Elizabeth

Designed by Nancy Ovedovitz and set in Baskerville type by Graphic Composition, Inc. Printed in the United States of America by Vail-Ballou Press, Binghamton, N.Y.

Library of Congress Cataloging in Publication Data

Baker, James M., 1948–
The music of Alexander Scriabin.
(Composers of the twentieth century)
Includes index.
1. Scriabin, Aleksandr Nikolayevich, 1872–1915—
Criticism and interpretation. I. Title. II. Series.
ML410.S5988B33 1985 786.1′092′4 85-2494
ISBN 0-300-03337-0

The paper in this book meets the guidelines for permanence and durability of the Committee on Production Guidelines for Book Longevity of the Council on Library Resources.

10 9 8 7 6 5 4 3 2 1

CONTENTS

MUSICAL EXAMPLES

Musical illustrations are listed according to example number. Those examples containing voice-leading sketches of entire compositions are indicated in italics.

PREFACE

Alexander Scriabin would have resented being remembered merely as a composer. Born in 1872, he was raised in the tradition of European keyboard music, and his career began conventionally enough with the composition of works for the piano in the same genres as those of Chopin. As he matured, however, he came increasingly under the influence of diverse aesthetic, philosophical, and mystical doctrines which impelled him toward an artistic vision of unprecedented grandiosity. Around the turn of the century he was impressed with Wagner's conception of a *Gesamtkunstwerk*, and this influence is strongly felt in the *Divine Poem* Op. 43 (1903), Scriabin's third symphony, which is based on a Nietzschean program. His later orchestral works, the *Poem of Ecstasy* Op. 54 (1905–07) and *Prometheus* Op. 60 (1909–10), reflect other influences as well. By the time these works were written, Scriabin had admitted many of the tenets of Theosophy into his own highly idiosyncratic philosophy, and he had also assimilated many ideas which originated in the symbolist movement in Russian poetry. At the time of his premature death in 1915, he was at work on a gigantic multimedia composition, the *Mysterium*, through which he believed all of humanity would be transcendentally united.

In view of his extraordinary career, there can be little wonder that Scriabin is generally remembered today not as a practitioner of the craft of composition in the traditional sense, but rather as an eccentric visionary whose mission led him so far afield that he lost touch with conventional musical structures as they were evolving. It is widely believed that he made a complete and abrupt break with traditional tonal structures and procedures around 1910, adopting totally novel methods of structure in *Prometheus* and later works. It is, however, difficult to imagine how any composer firmly grounded in the craft of tonal composition could suddenly and completely escape his musical past. Actually, Scriabin was one of the very few composers thoroughly trained and experienced in conventional tonality who ultimately succeeded in breaking out of the tonal system. Nonetheless, his departure from tonality was not sudden; rather, he made a gradual transition to atonality over a period of years, beginning as early as 1903.[1]

Those whose attention is focused solely on the mystical aspirations of Scriabin's large works lose sight of an equally important aspect of his career: even when his harmonic practice was quite advanced and he was striving for magnificent ecstatic effects in his sonatas and orchestral works, Scriabin remained at heart a confirmed formalist. His compositions consistently reflect both his sensitivity to the finest detail and his interest in subtle, complex relationships worked out with meticulous precision. His biographer, Leonid Sabaneiev, says of Scriabin's compositional method:

> A great deal in his creative work seems to be not the result of intuition, of inspiration that had suddenly illumined him, but the result of stubborn "research" work, that possessed, if you will, a mathematical character to some extent. The traits of the ecstatic visionary in Skryabin lived side by side with traits of the rational research scholar, and the schematism which is so clear in his philosophic concepts of the universe manifests itself no less strikingly also in his music, in the structure of his compositions which are so harmonious, so "rationalised" in their harmony that occasionally their form appears to be some logical conclusion rather than the creative work of their author.[2]

By all accounts, Sabaneiev's evaluations are accurate. Viktor Delson states that Scriabin concentrated his efforts on "constructing edifices of different proportions and symmetries, first counting out the number of measures in a work, the Seventh and Eighth Sonatas, for examples."[3] Evidently Scriabin often composed around certain sections of a work, specifying only the exact number of measures of material to be inserted at a later time.[4] The composer himself characterized his method as a "strict style," saying, "There's nothing by accident. . . . I compose according to definite principle." Unfortunately, he never spelled out the operations and premises of his system.[5]

Scriabin was one of the few composers to bridge the gap between conventional tonality and genuine atonality, so it is altogether appropriate that an examination of his music be included in a series of analytical studies of twentieth-century composers. Because his early music continues the late romantic tradition and bears no direct relation to his highly innovative later work, this book treats only the music written in the twentieth century, with special attention to Scriabin's transition to atonality.[6] It is not a chronological survey or a comprehensive companion to the music, nor is it a biography or a study of the composer's mystical or aesthetic beliefs; rather, it is a treatise on the structure of Scriabin's music.[7] Accordingly, the discussion progresses from details of structure at the surface of the music to fundamental structures of entire compositions, and from small forms to large. The tonal music is generally considered before the atonal, but a thoroughly chronological approach is taken only within certain chapters.

Chapters 1 through 6 are based upon nineteen short compositions, each analyzed as a complete structural entity, though on occasion only excerpts are discussed. Each work is thoroughly examined in terms of both tonal and atonal aspects of structure. Chapters 1 through 3 deal with tonality in Scriabin's transitional music, chapters 4 and 5 with atonality. In particular, chapter 5 involves a statistical survey of Scriabin's use of novel structural components throughout the transitional music. In chapter 6, two especially problematic structures are analyzed with respect to both tonal and atonal structure.

It should be emphasized that Scriabin's small pieces stand in a special relationship to his larger works. In few cases, if any, are they mere trifles tossed off for a few extra rubles. On the contrary, some were to be incorporated into larger works which never got off the ground,[8] and many others were in effect studies for completed larger works (for example, the "Feuillet d'album" Op. 58, in which Scriabin exploits the potential of the mystic chord of *Prometheus* Op. 60). Nearly every short piece is devoted to the exploration of the compositional possibilities of some novel component or procedure or to the working out of a particular technical problem.

In short, these pieces are of primary importance in Scriabin's transition to atonality. Because they concentrate heavily on innovative structural procedures, they are ideal source material for the study of that evolution. Only three larger works—the *Poem of Ecstasy* Op. 54, the Fifth Sonata Op. 53, and *Prometheus* Op. 60—were involved directly in the transition. Without the smaller works, therefore, the exact progress of Scriabin's development would be unclear, for the chronological gaps between the large works are filled only by his collections of small piano pieces. For instance, the Four Pieces Op. 56, the two *Morceaux* Op. 57, and the "Feuillet d'album" Op. 58 are links between the *Poem of Ecstasy* and *Prometheus*.

In order to provide a context for the study of Scriabin's transition to atonality, it is essential to look beyond the transitional works to those which are unequivocally atonal. Chapter 7 therefore provides a statistical survey, parallel to that in chapter 5, of the structural components of the atonal works.

Having examined Scriabin's creative evolution from the perspective of the shorter compositions, we shall shift focus in the later chapters to his extended forms. Chapter 8 concentrates on the Fifth Sonata Op. 53 (1907), Scriabin's last large tonal composition and thus a pivotal work in his career. As in preceding chapters, a tonal analysis of the entire piece is presented, and the atonal structure is considered as well. The evolutionary significance of the Fifth Sonata will become evident in subsequent analytical discussions comparing it with the Fourth Sonata Op. 30 (1903) and the Tenth Sonata Op. 70 (1913), which represent respectively the beginning and the completion of Scriabin's transition to an atonal idiom.

This volume culminates, in chapter 9, with discussions of Scriabin's two most grandiose and complex compositions, the *Poem of Ecstasy* and *Prometheus: The Poem of Fire*. The analytic observations and procedures of preceding chapters are applied in extensive analyses focusing on factors of structural coherence, especially motivic relations, thematic transformation, and underlying harmonic progressions, both tonal and atonal.

In the literature on Scriabin's compositional innovations, there has been no thorough study of his evolution from conventional tonality to his later system. Scholars have generally subscribed to one of two viewpoints. A small group, including Kurt Westphal and Paul Dickenmann, has considered Scriabin's novel harmonies to be derived from traditional harmonic components structured of superposed thirds.[9] These scholars have been unable to explain the tonality of the less conventional works—especially those composed after 1910—although generally they have assumed that the individual components in these works somehow still have tonal functions. A larger group of analysts, whose most prominent spokesman is Varvara Dernova, has been concerned almost solely with tracing unconventional harmonic components and nontonal procedures in Scriabin's music—even in those works which clearly possess a type of tonal coherence.[10] In many cases, scholars in this group, including Zofia Lissa, have been preoccupied with locating chords of superposed fourths.[11] Some authors have wavered between these views, explaining Scriabin's transition to atonality in terms of his use of harmonies which may be interpreted as either tonal or nontonal.[12]

Those scholars who have dealt with Scriabin's transitional works as tonal structures have pointed to some important procedures operating at the surface of the music. Yet in every study to date the analytical orientation has been consistently, rigidly vertical. No explanation of these works as coherent integral structures is offered in the existing literature. No one has examined voice leading in Scriabin's transitional works in light of the theories of Heinrich Schenker, which are now widely accepted as a basis for demonstrating structural coherence in tonal music. As stated previously, an important aim of this book is to deal with each transitional composition as a unified whole. To this end, Schenkerian techniques are employed extensively in the analysis of tonal structure. One of the main purposes here is to determine the applicability of Schenkerian notions of tonal structure to the analysis of music which lies on the borderline between tonality and atonality. There has not previously been a thorough and conclusive examination of the problems of dealing with structural hierarchies in unconventional yet (possibly) tonal music.[13]

Transitional works, whose structures may often seem vague or even indeterminate, pose immense difficulties for the analyst who wishes to use Schenkerian techniques to disclose prolongations and structural levels. The Schenkerian method is employed here in accordance with the following premise: If one is to discover the extent to which a structure is determined by tonal procedures, one must begin as a strict constructionist, examining every possibility for interpreting the structure in conventional terms. In the absence of any such possibility, the analyst must nevertheless compare the structure of the problematic piece to those found in conventional tonality. He may then ascertain whether it is a derivation or extension of a normal tonal structure, or whether it projects a conventional structure implicitly. If no relation to traditional tonality is discovered, then the composition may not be considered tonal. Because prolongations are effected by operations on functions of varying structural weights, the analyst must also establish the existence of a closed system of such operations and functions in order to posit a multileveled structure. To date, no closed system has been discovered for any corpus of posttonal music.

With regard to aspects of atonality in Scriabin's transitional works, the literature contains only one particularly noteworthy contribution—the discovery of a fundamental chord whose pitch content is retained completely when transposed up six half steps.[14] However, the discussion of this basic chord has generally become entangled with misleading and erroneous theories of Scriabin's atonal system, such as the theory of polytonality. Furthermore, concentration on this basic chord has impeded adequate consideration of the great variety of sonorities in Scriabin's music. A much more complete and accurate view of his exploitation of novel structural components is possible within the framework of the theory of set relations and complexes of relations. This analytic framework, set forth most comprehensively in Allen Forte's *Structure of Atonal Music* (1973), is adopted in the chapters on aspects of atonality in the transitional works.[15] Ultimately, the question of the relation between tonal and atonal aspects of Scriabin's music must be resolved, for that relation is surely the basis for the composer's transition to atonality.

The research for this book has been motivated by a strong conviction that a correct and complete understanding of principles of musical structure can be obtained only through a thorough analysis of complete compositions; accordingly, many analyses of entire works are included. Wherever possible, complete scores or significant excerpts accompany the discussion; for the extended compositions treated in chapters 8 and 9, however, such a practice has not been possible. The reader is therefore urged to have scores on hand when reading those chapters.

Although each piece treated in this study is analyzed as a complete entity, the discussion has been organized so that specific structural features and analytical procedures are fully explained only once in the course of the argument. For the sake of brevity, discussion is based on the assumption that the reader has read the preceding chapters. No analysis in this book is intended to be completely self-contained.

Portions of chapters 1 and 2 as well as passages in the preface and afterword have been adapted from my article "Scriabin's Implicit Tonality," *Music Theory Spectrum* 2 (1980): 1–18. Permission to include this material is gratefully acknowledged. Several remarks have been adapted from my article "Schenkerian Analysis and Post-Tonal Music" in *Aspects of Schenkerian Theory*, ed. David Beach (New Haven: Yale University Press, 1983), 153–86.

I wish to comment briefly on the history of my research and to express my gratitude to those who have influenced or helped me along the way. My first exposure to Scriabin's music was Vladimir Horowitz's performance of the Poem Op. 32/1 and the Ninth Piano Sonata, recorded at the famous Carnegie Hall recital of 9 May 1965 (Columbia M2L 328). The exotic colors and textures, the profoundly expressive harmonies, the dazzling rhythmic complexity of this music were a source of endless fascination. Through the years, Horowitz's interpretations of Scriabin have continued to amaze and inspire me. During my undergraduate years, I became familiar with other works of Scriabin through my piano teacher, Francis Whang, whose performance of the Fifth Sonata made a special impact. As a graduate student, I made preliminary attempts at analysis of the Fifth Sonata as well as "Vers la flamme" Op. 72 and the Preludes Op. 74 in seminars with Thomas Clifton and Allen Forte. This work led eventually to the research for my Ph.D. dissertation, "Alexander Scriabin: The Transition from Tonality to Atonality" (Yale University, 1977), in which I traced Scriabin's evolution through thirty-six short works composed from 1903 to 1914, developing the concepts and analytical methods upon which this book is based.

While teaching at Barnard College, Columbia University, I started the book by revising the dissertation. At the same time I began to work on Scriabin's extended forms, in particular the Fourth, Fifth, and Tenth piano sonatas analyzed in chapter 8. I took leaves as a Mellon Special Assistant Professor at Barnard in the fall of 1981 and as a Fellow of the American Council of Learned Societies in 1982–83, and some of my research on the sonatas was conducted as part of the projects sponsored by these grants. I am extremely grateful for this support, without which completion of the book would have been delayed. I wish to thank my Barnard colleagues Patricia Carpenter, Hubert Doris, Charles Olton, and James Crawford for their interest in my research and their support of my fellowship applications. Barnard College also generously covered the cost of photocopying much of the final typescript.

In the fall of 1983, when I joined the Brown University Department of Music, I began analysis of the *Poem of Ecstasy* and *Prometheus* for the final chapter, completed the following spring. I thank all of my colleagues at Brown for their sympathy and support during the final phases of publication.

My debt to Allen Forte is evident throughout. For the challenge and inspiration of his teaching and scholarship and for his generosity and concern as friend and advisor I shall always be grateful. Without his steadfast support this book might not have been completed. To my copyeditor, Channing Hughes, go my special thanks for an exceptionally thorough and discriminating reading. His judicious changes have improved the text considerably. I am indebted to the artistry of Melvin Wildberger in rendering the musical examples.

My wife Nancy has lived through the vagaries of this project with patience and equanimity. I have relied on her for solace and encouragement and have benefited on countless occasions from her scholarly expertise. Finally, thanks are due to Christopher and Elizabeth, who never allowed their father to become totally preoccupied with his work or to take himself too seriously.

SPECIAL ANALYTIC NOTATIONS

Many of the musical examples include sketches of voice-leading structure. In these sketches, the following special notations are employed:

An overlapping is shown by a dotted arrow pointing to the pitch in the more important register.

[ ] Brackets enclose an implicit harmony.

( ) Parentheses indicate a pitch crucial for strict voice leading which is not explicitly stated.

Dotted slurs indicate displacement of a pitch from its expected occurrence in strict voice leading—either by anticipation or by delay.

A horizontal bracket between two bass notes indicates a tritone bass progression which prolongs a dominant function (either secondary or primary) at a given level of structure.

A solid slur with an arrow points to an important element to which another element refers.

ONE
TONALITY IN THE TRANSITIONAL WORKS I
General Considerations

It is difficult to trace Scriabin's path to atonal music, for he traversed regions which even today remain largely uncharted. This chapter surveys features peculiar to Scriabin's late tonal style which may serve as milestones in exploring his transitional music.

HARMONIC COMPONENTS

The most important harmonic function in Scriabin's tonal music, aside from those of tonic and dominant, is ♭II—the major triad constructed on the lowered second scale degree. Occasionally this chord is a traditional Neapolitan sixth chord preparing the dominant. More often ♭II occurs in root position in its dominant-preparing role, as in the final cadential progression of the Prelude Op. 45/3 (example 1a).[1] This progression has two important effects. First, an exotic juxtaposition of chords separated by a tritone (♭II and V) is achieved. Second, the root of ♭II serves as a chromatic upper auxiliary note to the tonic root. This chromatic connection is of particular importance in the bass of the highly linear opening progression of Op. 45/3 (example 1b). In example 1a the

Example 1a Prelude Op. 45/3

Example 1b Prelude Op. 45/3

harmonization of F♭ as the root of ♭II enables Scriabin to close with a conventional cadential progression while retaining clear reference to the original linear opening.

The harmonic function ♭II is often the point of reference for harmonies only distantly related to the tonic. In example 1a, ♭II is preceded by its own secondary dominant, which might also be understood as ♭VI in the overall tonality.[2] There is no better example of ♭II as a secondary tonal reference than in "Nuances" Op. 56/3 (examples 2a–c). In this eighteen-measure piece, mm. 3, 11, and 14 contain exactly the same material (although with varying dynamic levels). This material, a chord built on D♭ (the lowered second scale degree in the key of C), is ultimately a ♭II^{7} harmony in the overall tonality of C major, although this function is concealed by the "nuances" created by unresolved unessential dissonances.[3] Harmonies distant from C major are, however, introduced into the composition by virtue of their direct relation to the chord on D♭. Measure 3 and the first two beats of m. 4 contain an exact repetition, transposed up one half step, of the corresponding material in the opening measures, which stated a progression from I to V.[4] In m. 4 V/♭II might thus be understood to follow ♭II in m. 3 (example 2a). When the material of m. 3 is repeated in m. 11, it is treated as the dominant of G♭ (♭V in the overall tonality), which arrives in m. 12 (ex-

Example 2a "Nuances" Op. 56/3

Example 2b "Nuances" Op. 56/3

Example 2c "Nuances" Op. 56/3

ample 2b). With a further repetition in m. 14, the D♭ chord ultimately assumes its true role, preparing the dominant in the next measure (example 2c). The more interesting and structurally important nuances in the composition are created not by the characteristic dissonant voice-leading inflections, but rather by the subtle recurrences of the same harmony (built on the lowered scale degree 2) in a variety of contexts.

Augmented sixth chords are important sonorities in Scriabin's compositions and play the traditional role of preparing the dominant. In the Poem Op. 32/2, for example, a French sixth chord (m. 11) prepares the dominant (m. 12), followed by the return of the opening material (example 27). In the Prelude Op. 51/2, the only readily identifiable tonal progression in the composition is found in m. 21. Here a linear $^4_2$ harmony (which behaves like a German sixth chord in third inversion) progresses to the dominant of the A minor tonic (example 3a).[5] In characteristic fashion for this opus, a strong consonant tonic triad does not immediately ensue. At the very end of the piece, however, when the tonic is heard in pure form for the first time, it is preceded—in a type of plagal cadence—by the auxiliary chord which is in fact the same linear $^4_2$ heard in m. 21 (example 3b).

Scriabin often employs chords which sound like augmented sixths but do not serve a dominant-preparing function. For instance, the final cadence of the Etude Op. 49/1 closely resembles that of Op. 51/2 in that an auxiliary chord, which sounds like a French sixth, precedes the tonic (example 4). In this instance, however, the "French sixth" has no explicit function in the E♭ tonality of the piece (it would prepare instead the dominant of D♭, as indicated in the sketch beside the score); it exists for purely linear reasons. Similarly, in Scriabin's tonal music, as in most late nineteenth-century music, many familiar sonorities,

Example 3a Prelude Op. 51/2

Example 3b Prelude Op. 51/2

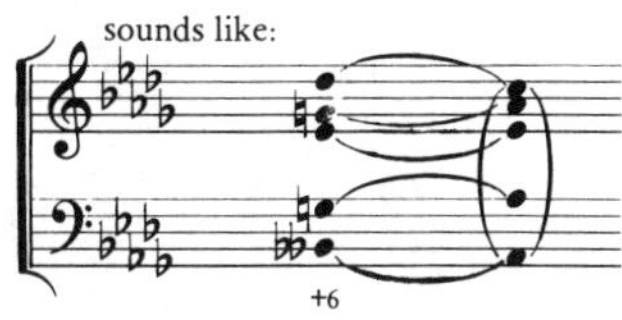

Example 4 Etude Op. 49/1

such as seventh chords, often arise from voice-leading (connecting or embellishing) procedures and so are not in themselves discernible harmonic functions.

The French sixth sonority also functions as a dominant seventh chord with lowered fifth. This $V^{7}_{\flat 5}$ is the basic component of Varvara Dernova's theory of dual modality in Scriabin's music, set forth in her *Garmoniia Skriabina*.[6] Dernova's "dual modality" is a type of bitonality made possible by the special properties of the basic chord. For when $V^{7}_{\flat 5}$ is transposed up six half steps, the resulting chord contains the same pitches but functions as the dominant of a tonic a tritone above the original tonal center.[7] The most problematic aspect of Dernova's work is the fundamental assumption that in a single composition two different tonics may act simultaneously as primary structural referents. Indeed, this concept of "polytonality" has long been questioned and even dismissed as an auditory possibility by many theorists, including Paul Hindemith and Milton Babbitt.[8]

Without a doubt, the potential for enharmonic reinterpretation of $V^{7}_{\flat 5}$ is exploited in many of Scriabin's tonal compositions. For example, in the progression from "Fragilité" Op. 51/1 shown in example 5, a dominant chord on G (m. 16) is approached via its own secondary dominant. Where one might expect to continue around the circle of fifths, the bass progresses up a tritone to a dominant chord on D♭, which progresses to its tonic on G♭ (m. 17). The dominants on G and D♭ would represent for Dernova the two forms (which she labels Da and Db) of the basic harmony. This chord has the potential, as a *dual dominant* (my own term), to cadence to either C or G♭. However, the connection of these two dominants is much less strongly represented in this passage than would ideally occur according to Dernova's theory. The $V^{7}_{\flat 5}$ on G does not actually contain a ♭5 (D♭), and therefore only three pitches are retained when it is transposed with t = 6. In addition, two other pitches (A and E) which occur over G in the bass do not occur over D♭, whereas three new pitches (B♭, A♭, and E♭) are introduced over the latter bass tone. One may just as satisfactorily explain, in terms of traditional theories of modulation, that the chord on G serves as a pivot,

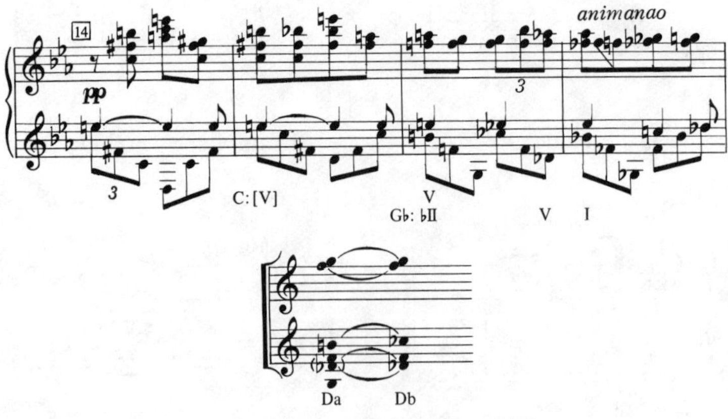

Example 5 "Fragilité" Op. 51/1

V^7/C becoming ♭II/G♭. Finally, the events described here are of purely passing and local significance in terms of both the E♭ tonality and the important goals of motion in the composition.

In exceptional cases in Scriabin's tonal works, the exploitation of the "dual modality" property is a real structural basis for a composition. Such a work is the Etude Op. 56/4, which opens with a sequence arriving at a $V^{7}_{\flat 5}$ in m. 3. This chord is formed most clearly as a combination of the two left-hand chords in this measure (example 6a). (Each individually is a V^7 lacking a fifth, and they are a tritone apart.) In m. 5 the G assumes priority by being the lower bass tone and an element of the sforzando chord, and the harmony on G progresses as a dominant to a C major tonic (mm. 7–8). The opening progression is repeated in mm. 13–16 but is followed by new material in which the dominant on D♭ is allowed to progress to its tonic on G♭ (example 6b). This passage is then immediately repeated with rhythmic variations, the most important result of which is the arrival of the G♭ chord on the downbeat of m. 24. A comparison of the cadences on C and G♭ leaves no doubt that the latter possesses far greater structural weight. The C major (local) tonic arrives on the weak beat of m. 7 but is not immediately heard as a consonance for notes from the preceding V^9 are suspended over the tonic bass note. Consonant resolution occurs only at the beginning of m. 8, where the low bass note has ceased to sound, so that one probably hears the chord in its weaker first inversion. The chord member in the melody, G, is itself displaced by the chromatic passing tone, A♭. As soon as the C major chord has been completely realized, it is displaced by a sforzando seventh chord which is apparently unrelated to the C major goal. This chord combines the chord tone C with the neighbor notes to G heard earlier in the measure, A♭ and F♯ (now spelled G♭). Thus the sforzando chord is a type of auxiliary chord, with the notes distributed and spelled misleadingly.

Example 6a Etude Op. 56/4

Example 6b Etude Op. 56/4

The cadence to G♭ is altogether different. Beginning in m. 17, the harmonies progress around the circle of fifths to a straightforward arpeggiation of the G♭ triad in m. 20. The passage is then repeated (with the variations described above) to stabilize the G♭ tonic. After a variation on the opening three measures in mm. 25–27, G♭ is reaffirmed as the ultimate goal. This goal is never fully attained, however, for Scriabin suspends notes from the preceding dominant (which itself contains unresolved unessential dissonances) over the tonic root and never resolves them (example 6c).[9] It is clear that the tonics indicated by the two enharmonically equivalent versions of the $V^{7}_{\flat 5}$ chord are not weighted equivalently. Rather, C major is in the larger view a secondary function (♭II) in the tonal area of the subdominant, which arrives in m. 11 (examples 6d and 8). "Dual modality" is therefore a misleading term, for it implies an equal weighting of two tonal centers within a single tonal structure. It actually involves the use of a dominant chord (either primary or secondary in the overall tonal scheme) as the pivot in a modulation—a technique already observed in the use of ♭II as a secondary point of reference for harmonies only distantly related to the tonic.

The harmony $V^{7}_{\flat 5}$ is a subset of the whole-tone scale. Scriabin had a predilection for other whole-tone sonorities as well. Although he rarely introduced a pure, complete whole-tone scale without accompanying inflection from notes outside the scale, four- and five-note whole-tone subsets are frequent. A single complete whole-tone scale underlies the opening of the "Poème fantasque" Op. 45/2 (example 10). All four-note simultaneities in m. 1 and its upbeat are subsets of the scale, as is the five-note chord in the first two beats of m. 1. The complete scale occurs in the initial upbeat and again in the third beat of m. 1, but in each case a note from the complementary whole-tone scale is introduced significantly in a clearly passing, connecting capacity. In an analogous manner, complementary underlying whole-tone scales are found in mm. 1–2 of Op. 56/4 (example 6a).

It should now be evident that many chords in Scriabin's music, sometimes even those most characteristic of his harmonic practice, are unessential in that they are by-products of a more important linear motion. These linear chords are therefore best analyzed in terms of their voice-leading contexts. On occasion it is useful to characterize harmonies resulting from short-term voice-leading procedures according to their contrapuntal origins. Suspension chords are frequent in Scriabin's music, and in the works composed in 1907–09 provide a

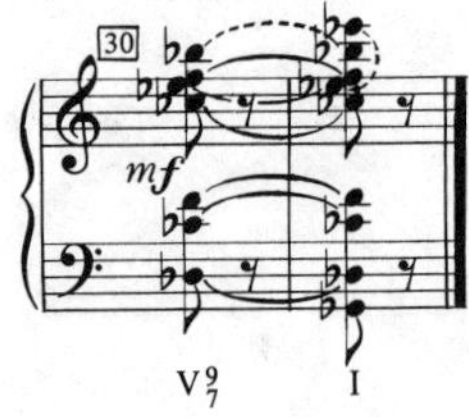

Example 6c Etude Op. 56/4

Example 6d Etude Op. 56/4

means of achieving dissonant conclusions, as in the close of Op. 56/4 (example 6c). Anticipation chords are also found; for example, the dominant in the final cadence of the Prelude Op. 48/4 contains an E whose arrival was expected only with the tonic chord (example 7). This harmony is technically an anticipation chord, but the A in the dominant chord is a passing note between B of the preceding chord and G of the tonic, and thus the chord might be even more precisely described as an anticipation-passing dominant chord! Such cumbersome terminology points to the necessity of examining directly the voice leading of even the simplest of Scriabin's harmonic progressions.

COMPOSITIONAL PROCEDURES

Repetition of musical material, either at the same pitch level (which shall be termed *exact* repetition) or at another level (*transposed literal* repetition), is basic to the organization of most of Scriabin's compositions. Exact repetition often calls attention to a particular harmony in order to emphasize its changing meaning. In "Nuances" Op. 56/3 (examples 2a–c), as we have seen, three identical statements of a harmony on D♭ initiate three different harmonic progressions, and the effect of surprise results largely from the thwarting of expectations aroused by the repetitions. In the same manner, the opening progression of the Etude Op. 56/4 (example 6a) is repeated twice in the composition (beginning in m. 13 and m. 25) to call attention to the dual interpretation of $V^{7}_{\flat 5}$, which is its goal.

These repeated passages are distributed strategically throughout the composition; occasionally, however, an exact repetition of material occurs immediately following the initial statement. For example, in the Prelude Op. 45/3 the final phrase cadencing to an E♭ tonic (mm. 13–16) is immediately followed by a repetition which preserves the pitch-class content but introduces a composed-in ritardando (extending the phrase to five measures instead of the previous four) as well as the lowest notes in the piece. (The repeated phrase is shown in ex-

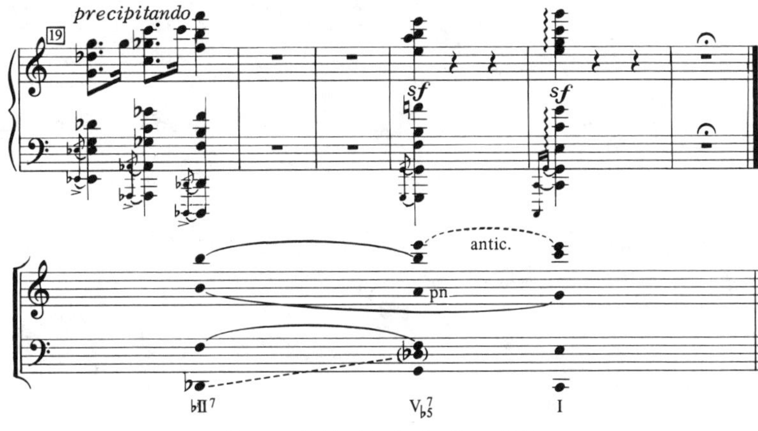

Example 7 Prelude Op. 48/4

ample 1a.) The work thus attains a sense of finality which is lacking the first time the phrase is heard, for we first encounter a pure and simple tonic triad in m. 16 just before the repetition.

Most repetitions in Scriabin's music involve a literal restatement of a passage, but transposed to another pitch level—one of the composer's primary means of reaching the main harmonic goals of his tonal schemes. Transposition up seven or five half steps indicates motion around the circle of fifths, the former usually involving motion from a tonic to a dominant, the latter from a dominant to a tonic. For example, the "Poème fantasque" Op. 45/2 opens with a progression (at least implicit) to the tonic in mm. 2–3 (example 10), immediately followed by a literal transposition, with $t = 7$, effecting the simplest possible shift to the dominant (m. 5).[10]

In many compositions, Scriabin returns to the tonic by transposing up five half steps a phrase which originally opened from tonic to dominant. Examples include the Prelude Op. 45/3 and the opening sixteen-measure period of "Caresse dansée" Op. 57/2. Another typical maneuver is the transposition to T_4 of a phrase which closes in the tonic in order to reach the mediant. This progression takes place at the opening of the Poem Op. 32/2. (For a discussion of this passage see pp. 51–55.)

Although large phrases are most frequently transposed up four, five, or seven half steps (effecting I–III, V–I, and I–V progressions respectively), other transpositions may be associated with ingenious large-scale harmonic maneuvers. Such is the transposition in mm. 5–12 of the Etude Op. 56/4 (example 8). The cadence to C in mm. 7–8 (discussed in conjunction with example 6a) is further weakened by the immediate transposition of the material in mm. 5–8 down a half step in mm. 9–12, achieving a cadence to B major, which in the tonality of G♭ is the enharmonic equivalent of the subdominant. In m. 12 the transposition of the sforzando auxiliary chord from m. 8 forms, with the addition of D♭, $V^{7}_{\flat 5}$ in the overall tonality. Thus before the opening material (which also progresses to $V^{7}_{\flat 5}$) is repeated at the original pitch level in mm. 13–16, the harmony

Example 8 Etude Op. 56/4

has progressed—in an obscure and deceptive fashion—via the subdominant (m. 11) to the dominant, pointing to G♭ as the tonic and strongly displacing C major as a goal in the piece.

So far this discussion has been limited to transpositional repetitions of large phrases or periods, but smaller musical gestures may be treated similarly. In many cases a small phrase will be repeated several times, each time transposed to a different level. The term *sequence* denotes multiple, transposed repetitions, a procedure by which a single harmonic-melodic progression is carried forward from the beginning of a pattern to the goal achieved when that pattern is broken. The values of the individual harmonic and melodic events in the sequence are diminished because they are subsumed within the patterned progression. Sequential repetitions fall within the broader category of linear intervallic patterns, which frequently do not entail literal repetition yet still effect large gestures by means of patterned voice leading. Because linear intervallic patterns can produce large-scale harmonic progressions, they will be discussed in the next chapter, on prolongational procedures.

One further purpose of literal transpositions deserves mention. When the whole-tone scale or one of its subsets underlies a span of music, transposing the material up an odd number of half steps will produce a maximum change in pitch-class content; if it is transposed up an even number of half steps, the original pitches will be retained. Scriabin often exploits this property in his literal transpositions. For example, m. 1 of Op. 56/4 (example 6a) contains an entire whole-tone scale (plus one pitch, D). This idea is repeated three half steps higher in m. 2, introducing six new pitches (five of which belong to the other whole-tone scale, plus E♯), thus providing maximum pitch-class contrast within the limitations of literal repetition.

The literal sequence from "Ironies" Op. 56/2 (mm. 25–28) in example 9 demonstrates transpositional repetition of whole-tone sets and its effects on pitch retention. Measure 25 contains an entire whole-tone scale plus two pitches—C and F♭, the first two pitches in the right hand. This material is repeated at T_2, T_4, and T_6—retaining the same whole-tone scale all the while. At the same time, all of the tones of the complementary whole-tone scale have been systematically introduced (two per measure). Most important, the large chord formed by the two three-note chords in the left-hand part of m. 25 is $V^7_{\flat 5}$ (of D). The literal se-

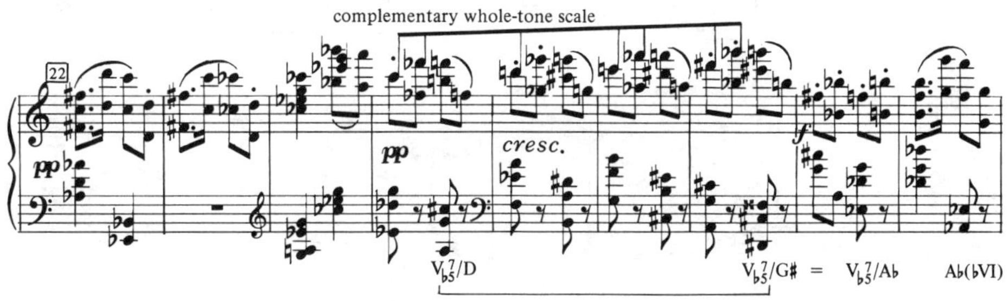

Example 9 "Ironies" Op. 56/2

quence achieves a chord with exactly the same pitch-class content in the left-hand part of the last measure of the sequence (m. 28), but with the crucial difference that the chord now occurs as V/G♯, with the bass tone a tritone away from that of the original chord. The sequence is thus designed to achieve the transpositional level at which the pitch content of the original chord is retained, and it uses an exceptional third repetition to attain that goal within the 2 + 2 + 2 pattern.

Scriabin typically exploits the properties of his whole-tone structures so that important tonal cadences coincide with a shift in the underlying sonority from one whole-tone scale to its complement. For example, when the opening measures of the "Poème fantasque" Op. 45/2 (example 10), which contain a whole-tone dominant chord progressing to the tonic, are literally transposed up seven half steps, not only is a modulation to the dominant accomplished, but also a maximum contrast is obtained by using the complementary whole-tone scale. The shift actually occurs gradually and before the transposition, for in m. 2, when the tonic enters in the bass, notes from the preceding dominant are suspended over it, effectively mingling elements of both whole-tone sonorities. A "resolution" of the suspension occurs at the beginning of m. 3, however—not to a consonance but to a full-fledged whole-tone chord, a subset of the complement of the original whole-tone scale. The effect is an almost coloristic shift of tonal planes. A return to the original whole-tone plane occurs in mm. 5–6, of course,

Example 10 "Poème fantasque" Op. 45/2

for the opening progression is transposed up an odd number of half steps. More sudden shifts occur in the B section of the piece (mm. 7–12), but they effect smooth transitions between adjacent two-measure phrases. For example, the phrase in mm. 7–8 (which is the basis for a sequence in subsequent measures) begins on the same whole-tone plane as the cadence on the dominant in the preceding measure. The phrase has a dynamic quality due in large part to the dramatic whole-tone shift which reinforces the accented melodic high point at the beginning of m. 8. A sequential repetition then begins on the same plane, and so forth. Measure 9 does not contain the entire whole-tone scale; rather, the aggregate is formed only by mm. 8 and 9 together. The whole-tone shifts may be summarized as follows (with overlappings indicating transitions):

WT I (C♯, D♯, F, G, A, B) mm. 0–2	5–7		10–14
WT II (C, D, E, F♯, G♯, A♯)	2–5	8–9	14–(15)

Whole-tone planes are not primary determinants of structure in this composition. This is especially clear at the end, when the whole-tone harmony on the second beat resolves to a first inversion of the C major tonic. Some notes in the whole-tone chords are basic to the tonal structure; others are unessential and therefore dissonant. The whole-tone scale is established beyond a doubt, however, as a characteristic focal sonority which reinforces the tonal scheme as well as the phrasing and periodic structure.

Many procedures used by Scriabin do not deviate significantly from the standard practice of his contemporaries and therefore need no explanation: invertible counterpoint in Op. 32/1, for example, and pedal-point passages in that work and others such as Op. 32/2 and Op. 51/1. One distinctive procedure should be explained, however: the equal or symmetrical divisions of intervals often effected by bass progressions. For example, the sequence in Op. 56/2 (example 9) creates a large-scale progression by tritone achieved by three successive transpositions of identical material with $t = 2$. Here the A of the A–D♯ tritone is the symmetrical midpoint of an E♭ octave which, though not stated explicitly, can be found between E♭ in m. 25 and D♯ in m. 28. (The D♯ in m. 28 is an enharmonic equivalent which refers to the low-register E♭ in m. 22.) As an interval of bass progression, the tritone is often divided symmetrically as well. The Prelude Op. 48/4 features a large-scale bass progression from V to ♭II, divided by the temporary harmonic goal of the mediant (example 35).

HARMONIC PLANS

In Scriabin's works of 1903 and later, consonant openings on the tonic triad are rare.[11] The tonic root occurs frequently at the beginning, but as the bass of a dissonant chord, often V⁷/IV. For instance, the E♭ tonic of the Prelude Op. 56/1 is a complete consonance only at the end of the first phrase (example 16). At first one might not even surmise that E♭ is the tonic note, for it progresses to the bass of a $V^{\flat 7}_{\flat 5}$ of A♭ (IV) in m. 2. The harmonic strategy in the opening phrase of the Etude Op. 49/1 (in E♭) is essentially the same, although harmonic functions are rendered less clear by unessential dissonances (example 17). The Prelude Op. 48/4 (in C) employs the same type of opening progression, but this phrase opens to the dominant, and no clear tonic is heard until the final chord (example 35). These examples point to the importance of the bass as an indicator of tonality, even in the absence of traditional consonant harmonic components.

Many of Scriabin's tonal works open with phrases which have indefinite initial harmonies but which become gradually more determinate as they move toward an important harmonic function established by a culminating cadence. An excellent example is the opening phrase of the Poem Op. 32/2, which begins with the startling dissonance of a false French sixth but closes in m. 4 on the tonic (see the discussion of example 27 on p. 24). The dominant as well is frequently the goal of an initially indeterminate phrase. The Etude Op. 56/4 (example 6a) begins with a four-measure phrase opening to a "dual dominant"; this chord first cadences on C major but ultimately proves to be the structural dominant of G♭.

As in the "Feuillet d'album" Op. 45/1 and the Prelude Op. 51/2, an unequivocal statement of a complete tonic triad is frequently avoided until the end of a composition. In the former work, the tonality is not in doubt previous to the close: the tonic occurs as a unison and as a first-inversion chord in the opening phrase, and during the piece there are several weak cadences to the tonic (example 25). The first, in mm. 8–9, progresses from a complete V^7 to a tonic unison as a repetition of the opening phrase begins. In mm. 15–16, V^7 cadences to a complete tonic triad which is not yet fully stable, weakened by displacement of the triadic notes by unessential dissonances until the triad is heard in pure form but in first inversion at the end of the measure. The closing cadence (mm. 23–24)—comparable especially to that in mm. 8–9—is relatively stable. Opus 51/2 is entirely different, for the A minor tonic, stated in root position at the beginning, is distorted by an ever-present upper auxiliary to the fifth scale degree. Here, the tonic is never allowed to follow V immediately and thus the strongest possible stabilization of I is skirted, even at the very end (examples 3a–b).

In other works, the tonic chord may occur in similar fashion occasionally throughout the piece, but devitalized by unresolved unessential dissonances. For instance, in Op. 45/2 (example 10) the tonic is present in mm. 2–3, first as a suspension chord (m. 2) and then as a linear chord (m. 3). Only when this passage is repeated at the end (mm. 14–15) are A♭ and F♯ of the linear chord allowed to resolve to the G of the tonic triad. Here the tonic is weakened not only by the *smorzando* but especially by the fact that it occurs in first inversion—the tonic root losing its effect in the bass if the rest in m. 15 is taken literally.[12]

Many of Scriabin's compositions approach the area of the tonic only at the conclusion. For example, the Prelude Op. 45/3 contains only one consonant statement each of the dominant and tonic harmonies, in mm. 8 and 16 respectively (example 31). Elsewhere the tonic and dominant roots do not support clear statements of important harmonies at the surface of the music (except for

V in m. 15). A similar situation exists in the Prelude Op. 48/4, where a consonant C major tonic triad occurs only as the final chord (example 7). (Curiously, a root-position C *minor* chord occurs in m. 14, but there it is actually a passing harmony controlled by the low bass A♭ and thus part of a ♭VI^7 chord.)

It is not a large leap from these compositions in which the explicit statement of the tonic is postponed until the end to those works in which the tonic is never stated directly. The simplest of these pieces have conclusions constructed over the tonic root with one or more dissonant (nontriadic) notes—which often result from suspensions—remaining unresolved. The Etude Op. 56/4 (example 6c) ends in this way. By contrast, the final chord of "Nuances" Op. 56/3 contains only one dissonance, an unresolved leading tone which is actually a passing tone from the melodic A to an expected C which is never realized (example 2c). The suspension harmony which concludes "Désir" Op. 57/1 is especially significant, for it is a clear and poignant statement of the mystic chord (example 67a). "Enigme" Op. 52/2, the "Feuillet d'album" Op. 58, and the Prelude Op. 59/2, among others, feature dissonant finales whose structural significance is more difficult to discern. The latter two works will be examined in chapter 6.

In discussing the harmonic schemes of Scriabin's tonal compositions, we should avoid a limited categorization of his tonal plans. Each harmonic goal in a composition is attained by progressions unique to particular contexts, and the structural weights of harmonic goals are balanced differently in each work. It is useful, however, to consider the harmonic functions typically encountered at points of stability in Scriabin's tonal structures. Compositions in which frequent reference is made to the tonic are unusual, even though several have been discussed above. Other such works are the Poem Op. 45/1 and "Caresse dansée" Op. 57/2. As discussed above, there are a few more compositions which never actually state the tonic explicitly. Most of the tonal works possess a structural tension dependent upon the delay, for as long as possible, of a strong cadence to the tonic. However, each of Scriabin's tonal structures establishes a definite dominant. In "Désir" Op. 57/1, where no consonant tonic chord occurs, the dominant seventh occurs clearly—although somewhat blurred by melodic motion—in the second beat of m. 1 (example 59) and at the beginning of m. 13 (example 67a). In Op. 51/2, where the dominant never cadences directly to the tonic, a linear $^4_2$ preparation nevertheless strongly establishes the dominant (example 3a). In Op. 45/3 the dominant is the only major harmonic goal established before the tonic at the conclusion (example 31).

Most secondary functions which serve as the goals of progressions have already been discussed as characteristic harmonies. The Neapolitan (in root position) is an important goal in Op. 48/4 (example 35) and in m. 5 of Op. 48/2 (example 18).[13] (In Op. 48/2, ♭II does not have the same durational weight as the more fundamental V [m. 2] and I [m. 7], which are extended over two measures.) The harmony constructed on the lowered scale degree 2 often functions as a secondary dominant, stabilizing ♭V as a goal of progression, as in "Nuances" Op. 56/3 (mm. 11–12) (example 2b).[14] In the larger view, however, ♭V is a dead end—a chord which does not carry the progression further. Continuity is achieved instead by backtracking to V/♭V and reinterpreting it as ♭II in the overall tonality. In Op. 56/4 (example 8), however, ♭V is itself reinterpreted, becoming ♭II of the next harmonic goal, the subdominant. Due to transpositional repetition of the phrase leading to ♭V, this function is not a significant goal in the larger view. Rather, at the end of the repeated passage, IV culminates the large gesture created by the original phrase and its repetition; IV then progresses immediately to V before the return of the opening material. In general, progression to ♭V is a digression within a large-scale motion to the dominant.

The subdominant often occurs as a harmonic goal but ultimately prepares a structural dominant, as in Op. 56/4 and in mm. 21–25 of the Poem Op. 32/2 (example 27). The harmony ♭VI may also be the goal of harmonic progression, but likewise it always prepares the dominant. A case in point is Op. 56/2, where the dominant of ♭VI concludes the sequence in example 9. There follows a cadence to ♭VI (m. 30), but in mm. 35–37 the dominant is restored by an exact repetition of the opening material.

The mediant, which appears typically as a major chord, is a goal frequently approached immediately after the tonic has been established at the beginning of a piece. In this context, the mediant is usually the midpoint of a large-scale progression from tonic to dominant. In Op. 49/1 the mediant is reached at m. 8, and the next clear harmonic goal is the dominant in m. 14, which eventually cadences to the tonic in m. 24 (example 24).

As the goal of his harmonic progression, Scriabin preferred major triads to the almost total exclusion of minor chords as stabilized functions. The dominant is strongly articulated in every tonal structure, and any function (except the dissonant VII) may be the subsidiary goal preceding this strong dominant. The submediant and supertonic almost always occur in chromatically lowered forms as ♭II$^{\flat 5}$ and ♭VI$^{\flat 5}$ (functions belonging to the parallel minor mode), and the mediant usually occurs with a raised third, yielding a major chord. The natural diatonic counterparts of II, III, and VI—all minor triads—are unusual.

Harmonic goals are often concealed by enharmonic spellings. For example, in the Etude Op. 56/4 (example 8) the subdominant in m. 11 is spelled as a B major chord. Scriabin's main motivation here was probably the convenience of a spelling with five sharps instead of seven flats. (An analysis according to spelling would yield ♯III, which does not conform to Scriabin's general harmonic practice, whereas the equivalent spelling as IV does.) The unexpected spelling nevertheless creates an exotic, even indeterminate effect.

Occasionally, however, enharmonic spelling, though not affecting harmonic function, may indicate the direction of a progression. For example, in the Poem Op. 32/2 in D, III♯ in m. 7 is spelled not as an F♯ major chord but rather as G♭ (example 27). Because both spellings require six accidentals and are thus equally convenient (or inconvenient!), we must seek another explanation for the enharmonic change. When the mediant is reached, it becomes the starting point (in

m. 8) of a sequence leading to the dominant in m. 12. The sequential pattern actually breaks down at the arrival of a French sixth chord preparing the dominant. As the French sixth resolves to V, the crucial bass progression is B♭–A. Scriabin probably opted for a spelling of the mediant which would incorporate B♭, foreshadowing the pitch's importance in preparing the dominant. (The natural spelling of III♯ would involve A♯, but voice-leading considerations necessitate a change to B♭ before or at the arrival of the French sixth. Scriabin actually anticipates this change in the melody in mm. 5–6.) Later events therefore justify the change in spelling.

Again in this case no true change of harmonic function results from the use of another spelling. The occurrence of the mediant here conforms with Scriabin's standard procedures, whereas a true lowered IV is not typical. Earlier romantic composers would usually have retained a natural spelling as long as possible to convey the true harmonic function. Chopin, for example, would probably have allowed the progression to cadence to F♯ major in m. 7, with an enharmonic switch to G♭ at the beginning of the next measure. (Consider for instance Chopin's enharmonic shifts in the Prelude in A♭ Op. 28/17.) Scriabin, on the other hand, takes every opportunity to shift enharmonic planes early and attempts deliberately to achieve something new and exotic. His striving for these effects might explain in part not only the use of mixed mode functions (♭II, ♭VI) as harmonic goals, but also his choice of keys—for either factor creates situations calling for enharmonic respelling, if only for convenience.

That Scriabin's enharmonic spellings are often used for out-and-out deception is amply demonstrated in "Ironies" Op. 56/2. This relatively extended piece contains many local points of harmonic arrival, with spellings so varied that it is virtually impossible to determine at first a logical connection among these goals (example 11a). The tonic (in first inversion) is the goal of the first phrase at m. 4 (slightly concealed by unessential dissonances), and the next goal, the major mediant, is achieved in m. 8 by the typical transposing of the opening phrase up four half steps. This progression is repeated in mm. 9–16. The harmony then progresses to a C♯ major chord (mm. 18–20), whose relation to the foregoing progression is uncertain. (Is it ♯I? A respelled ♭II seems more likely, but perhaps its spelling relates it to the major mediant as VI/III♯.)

The next surprise occurs as this latest progression is literally transposed up two half steps, cadencing in m. 22 to an E♭ major chord whose function it is impossible to discern right away. There ensues the sequence (mm. 25–28) discussed as example 9, which ends on a D♯ chord (m. 28). This D♯ harmony is reconverted to an E♭ major chord in m. 29, where it is clearly the dominant of A♭, to which it cadences in m. 30. The A♭ chord itself is ♭VI in the overall C tonality and prepares the dominant in m. 36. A contrasting B section (mm. 50–82) follows, but at the return of the A section, this same V/♭VI–♭VI–V progression occurs (mm. 83–88), reestablishing the dominant. Only the C♯ major triad has not received a functional explanation. In light of the fact that it directly

Example 11a "Ironies" Op. 56/2

precedes a V–I cadence in the tonal area of ♭VI, however, it is best understood as IV/♭VI preparing V/♭VI. In the B section, the IV–V–I progression in the area of A♭ is the main subject and receives a very ironic treatment (example 11b).

Only one chord connection now lacks a logical rationale—that between III♯ and IV/♭VI (E major and C♯ [D♭] major). Because III♯ is not a harmonic referent after the C♯ chord, the explanation of C♯ as VI/III♯ is not adequate. However, it is possible to interpret E major in light of the important referent ♭VI—as a respelled ♭VI/♭VI. Thus the mediant is actually a pivot chord in a large-scale modulation from the tonic to ♭VI in m. 30, a goal which ultimately functions as a dominant preparation by the end of the A section. A summary of the tonal plan is offered in example 11c. This extraordinarily complicated scheme, further obscured by enharmonic deception, is in keeping with the ironic mood of the work and may in fact embody the irony.

Example 11b "Ironies" Op. 56/2

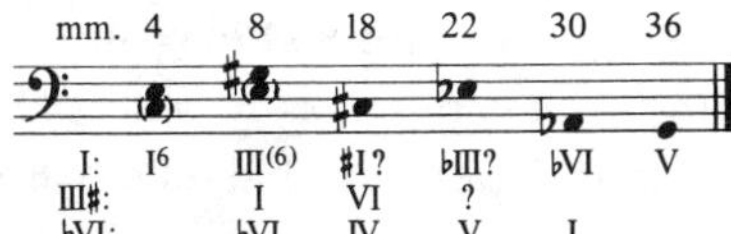

Example 11c "Ironies" Op. 56/2: Modulatory Scheme

PERIODIC STRUCTURES

The short works reveal Scriabin's predilection for regular and even symmetrical apportionment of subject matter. Their thematic content may consist of contrasting ideas (usually two) or may be relatively undifferentiated, yielding an essentially through-composed work. Whether or not the musical ideas are highly contrasted, there is generally a return to the opening material before the conclusion, even in Scriabin's most through-composed forms. The Prelude Op. 45/3 exemplifies that formal balance. (For the complete score see example 31.) Two types of subject matter are contrasted harmonically. The A idea, which appears in mm. 1–2, involves a chromatic bass progression culminating in the wispy arpeggiation of an apparently indeterminate harmony. The B idea (mm. 5–8) is related melodically to A but employs harmonies which progress by fifths in the bass and which effect a tonal cadence. The A material, although a two-measure unit, is always repeated at T_7 to form a four-measure phrase. There is a weaker 2 + 2 subdivision of the B phrase based on harmonic progression and the contour of the bass: [V]–♭II/V–[V]–V. Section B follows A as a consequent phrase, and A and B thus form an eight-measure period. This first period cadences to V and is balanced by a similar period (A + B) which cadences to the tonic. Section B is then repeated with a composed-in ritardando (mm. 17–21) to give weight to the final cadence. The form of Op. 45/3 is displayed graphically in example 12. Most important here is the balance achieved by similarly structured eight-measure phrases cadencing to the harmonies of the tonal axis. The internal structure of these phrases has a similar symmetrical balance at several levels (2 + 2, 4 + 4). The essential structure is contained in the first sixteen

Example 12 Prelude Op. 45/3: Periodic Structure

mm. 1–2	3–4	5–8	9–10	11–12	13–16	17–21
A	A′ (t = 7)	B	A	A′	B′ (t = 5)	B′
2	+ 2	(2+2)	2	+ 2	(2+2)	
4	+	4	4	+	4	5
	8			8		5
(?)		V	(?)		V–I	

measures. The repetition of B in mm. 17–21, in reality an appendix, serves an important harmonic purpose, for the tonic, heard for the first time in m. 16, is not adequately stabilized until the cadence is repeated.[15]

Although square phrasing and periodic balance are structural norms in his tonal music, Scriabin never adheres to them rigorously. On the contrary, musical motion is enhanced by subtle deviations from established patterns which usually affect periodic structure. In the "Feuillet d'album" Op. 45/1, for instance, the four-measure phrase length is retained throughout (with the exception of the final measures), but the phrases are grouped into periods of different sizes. (The complete score is included in example 25.) An initial period of eight measures consists of four-measure antecedent and consequent phrases. A twelve-measure middle period (mm. 9–20) is a single through-composed gesture, with individual four-measure phrases (all related to the original subject matter) linked on the basis of harmonic, rhythmic, and textural continuity. The piece concludes with the initial four-measure phrase overlapped with a four-measure melodic appendix, yielding a final period of seven measures instead of the expected eight.

The Poem Op. 32/1 balances two ten-measure phrases which are the contrasting A and B materials of the piece, but expands the size of the large period they constitute by inserting between them four measures of new material as a transition. (The score of Op. 32/1 is included in example 29.) The A phrase (mm. 1–10) is composed of two identical four-measure phrases which cadence respectively to the tonic and to the subdominant. The A phrase would normally take up eight measures but is extended to ten by the repetition of the final measure of each four-measure phrase. The transitional material (mm. 11–14), marked *con affetto*, extends by sequential motion the progression from IV to V. The entire B section (mm. 15–24) takes place over a dominant pedal. It too might be considered a basic eight-measure phrase expanded by the insertion of the material in mm. 21–22, which gives weight to the pure dominant chord. In the second half of the piece, which closely resembles the first, the A section is varied at the original pitch level. A modified transition connects A to B, which is transposed to take place over a tonic pedal. Here the transition is crucial, for it effects a cadence to the tonic. The periodic structure of the first half is graphed in example 13, indicating a 2:1 ratio between basic and transitional or extending material. This subsidiary material clearly reinforces harmonic goals and creates a smooth link between them.

The individual composition always establishes a norm for periodic structure, and on occasion the four-measure unit does not prevail. In the "Poème fantasque" Op. 45/2 (example 10) the basic unit is three measures. A six-measure period is composed of the opening three-measure phrase followed by its literal repetition at T_7. There follows immediately a contrasting section, also of six measures, and then the opening phrase is repeated (mm. 13–15) to close the piece. The contrasting central section features the sequential repetition of a two-measure phrase, creating a marvelous hemiola effect. The periodic structure of Op. 45/2 is shown in example 14. Note the odd effect of the final measure, which contains nothing but sustained silence. It ironically places the self-sufficient fifteen-measure structure within a sixteen-measure context where one would expect four-measure phrasing to apply.

Periodic structure and harmony generally coincide in Scriabin's music so that important harmonic goals are reached on the downbeat of the final measure of a phrase or period. When harmonic progression and periodicity are out of synchrony, a disorienting effect results. In the Etude Op. 56/4 the cadences to C major and B major in mm. 7–8 and 11–12 respectively are not obvious and thus are less important in comparison with the more regular cadence to G$\flat$ in m. 24 (see the discussion of examples 6a–c).

Harmony occasionally defines its own periodicity, at odds with that created by

Example 13 Poem Op. 32/1:
Periodic Structure

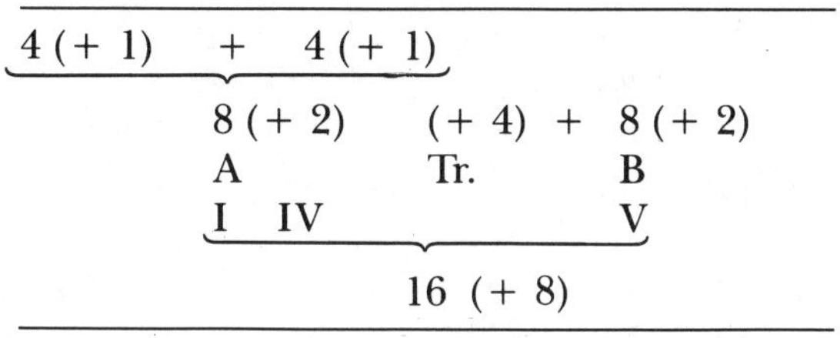

4 (+ 1) + 4 (+ 1)

8 (+ 2) (+ 4) + 8 (+ 2)
A Tr. B
I IV V

16 (+ 8)

Example 14 "Poème fantasque" Op. 45/2:
Periodic Structure

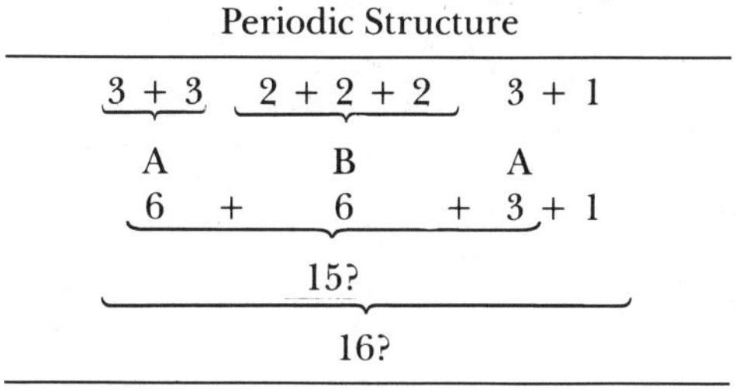

3 + 3 2 + 2 + 2 3 + 1

A B A
6 + 6 + 3 + 1

15?

16?

regular groupings of musical material. In the Prelude Op. 48/4 the opening phrase cadences to the dominant in m. 4, a harmony which is not reestablished until m. 16. (For the complete score see example 35.) In the interim the harmony progresses via III♯ in m. 8 to ♭II in m. 10, at which point a sequence is initiated leading back to the dominant. The twelve measures separating the dominants may ostensibly be divided into four-measure phrases corresponding to the opening phrase. However, another division is defined by ♭II, which divides the twelve measures into two six-measure phrases (in the same way that D♭ divides the G octave symmetrically). Thus a large-scale hemiola is created in which the periodicities of harmony and subject matter play complementary roles.

The periodic structure of the Poem Op. 32/1 (example 13) has been discussed. On the basis of surface harmonic events, one might divide the first twenty-four-measure period into two equal sections, because the dominant arrives in the bass at m. 13. But this division conflicts with the analysis in example 29, where m. 13 is part of a transition to a B section which begins in m. 15 with contrasting material over a dominant pedal. In terms of subject matter, a new section clearly does not begin in m. 13, yet the placement of the dominant in the bass here seems deliberate and strategic. The sequence beginning in m. 11 speeds up in m. 12, passing quickly over V/V, which was expected to arrive in and occupy m. 13. The C♯ in the bass at m. 13 may properly be heard as an anticipation of the real structural dominant in m. 15, especially in view of the initiation of the new material of the actual pedal-point passage two measures later. This anticipation is subsidiary to the structural bass tone and thus defines a periodicity secondary to that in example 13. The symmetrical division it defines is nevertheless important for the temporal experience of the piece.

Of the components and procedures examined here, none stands out as extraordinarily innovative in the context of late nineteenth-century practice. Some of Scriabin's devices, especially the use of periodic phrasing, even seem surprisingly conservative. Yet from these elements emerged a strikingly original compositional method with tremendous potential for development of novel atonal techniques as well as extension of traditional tonal procedures. The following chapters examine how Scriabin discovered and tapped these compositional resources.

TWO
TONALITY IN THE TRANSITIONAL WORKS II
Prolongational Procedures

INCOMPLETE SPANS AND IMPLICIT PROLONGATIONS

The harmonies and progressions characteristic at the surface of Scriabin's tonal compositions also exist in expanded forms controlling longer spans. These expansions, or prolongations, are achieved by procedures which are essentially the same as those first described by Heinrich Schenker in reference to music of the eighteenth and nineteenth centuries—although in Scriabin's twentieth-century music they are seldom straightforward. Instead of summarizing Schenker's approach, with which I assume most readers are familiar, I shall discuss the prolongational forces in a passage from one of Scriabin's more conventional pieces, the "Feuillet d'album" Op. 45/1.

Even in the unusually simple opening phrase of the "Feuillet d'album" (example 15), there are significant deviations from standard tonal procedures. This passage constitutes a circular progression opening from the tonic unison at the beginning to the dominant at the end of m. 8, and cadencing immediately back to the tonic with the return of the opening material. Such circular progressions always prolong a simple harmony—in this case the tonic—but here the presentation of the tonic triad is deliberately more tentative than in similar unfoldings in most of the strongly tonal works treated by Schenker.

The opening four measures entail an incomplete arpeggiation of the tonic triad, certain intervals of which are connected by passing notes (both diatonic and chromatic). Sketch 15a uses slurs to show the connecting function of these passing notes; sketch 15b reduces the passage to the arpeggiations which underlie the voice leading.[1] The clearest arpeggiation descends from the tonic root at the beginning to B♭ in mm. 1–2 and then to G which supports I^6 in m. 4. The B♭ is embellished by chromatic upper and lower auxiliary notes (the latter receiving metrical emphasis) before the diatonic A♭ connects it with G. At the same time an arpeggiation rises from the initial tonic unison, moving to G (m. 1) and eventually to B♭ (m. 4). This motion to B♭ is much less explicit because the G is retained, almost as a pedal tone, through the phrase—but in a middle voice, not

Example 15 "Feuillet d'album" Op. 45/1

in the melody. The melodic B♭ (m. 4) is the goal of an important linear motion from above. Beginning with D in m. 1, this line is interrupted, but hardly concealed, by leaps up to the chord tones E♭ and G. These pitches, also sustained in middle voices, may be said to *overlap* the main melodic motion.

Listeners familiar with tonal voice leading will recognize a significant deviation: D, the leading tone, would not ordinarily initiate such a melodic motion. Rather, it would typically occur as a passing note connecting two chord tones. In this case E♭ would normally precede the D in a line spanning an interval of the tonic triad. Here the span is incomplete, although not much tension is generated because the expected E♭ is present at the beginning in another voice. Ironically, E♭ occurs in the proper melodic register in m. 2, but only after the descending motion from D has begun, and it is therefore only a reminder of the lapse from conventional voice leading at the beginning of the phrase. A contrast is provided in a middle voice as well, where D is resolved properly as the lower auxiliary to the tonic root. The *incomplete span* is one of Scriabin's most characteristic prolongational procedures, but it often occurs without the missing elements being supplied in other voices. Even when the implicit completion is obvious, as in this example, incomplete spans attenuate the tonal strength of prolongations.

The opening phrase in mm. 1–4 of the "Feuillet d'album" contains only one real harmony—the tonic triad. It begins as a unison but is inverted as the bass arpeggiates the triad downwards so that by the end of the phrase the chord occurs in first inversion. Any other harmonies here, characteristic though they may be, are simply the results of linear or embellishing motions which expand the tonic triad. In contrast, the consequent phrase in mm. 5–8 contains definite harmonies which prepare an authentic cadence (sketches 15a–b): I^6 (m. 5), V^7/V (mm. 6–7), V (m. 8), and I (m. 9).

The material in m. 5 continues the harmony of the preceding measure, but melodic events sustain the interest here. The melody fills in chromatically the span between the third and fifth of the triad and thus makes explicit the arpeggiation from the root to the fifth in m. 4. The bass motion is similar to that of m. 1, but here C♭ may only be assumed to resolve to B♭ in the same register, with the note of resolution actually supplied only in the melody. (In the conventional voice leading shown in sketch 15a, the implicit note of resolution is in parentheses.) The V^7/V (m. 6), the first real harmonic change, occurs at the climax of the phrase and is made more poignant by unessential dissonances which resolve only after the downbeat of m. 7. The most crucial dissonance is the high D, unprepared and approached by leap, which is clearly related motivically to the D in m. 1. The other dissonance is B♮, a chromatic passing tone which connects B♭ of I^6 with C of V^7/V. The B♭ (m. 5) also resolves to A♮ of V^7/V, which moves to A♭ of V^7 (m. 8). The A♭ actually occurs only in the tenor register, shifting back to the original point of departure of a single line, C–C♭–B♭–A♮–A♭, which would hypothetically occur in a single register but actually is divided between two. Sketch 15b shows the descent from B♭ to A♭ (and on to G) in a single voice (the tenor, where it seems more permanently established), with pitches occurring in other registers shown in parentheses. The melody of m. 7 arpeggiates the underlying harmony, but this arpeggiation is incomplete in the uppermost register, where G (which would ordinarily connect A♮ with F) is momentarily unresolved. The expected F in the proper register is conspicuous in the next measure as a member of V^7. This interrupted linear connection is indicated by a slur. The melodic motion which interrupts this line is yet another line from a dissonant D (m. 7) to a consonant B♭ (m. 8) in the register of the primary melodic line. By the end of m. 8 the melody has descended into the middle-voice region, ready to recommence the initial material as the harmony cadences back to the tonic.

Several important melodic gestures are left dangling at the end of the opening eight-measure phrase. The melodic F in the upper voice of m. 8 does not resolve to E♭ as expected (though it does in a middle voice). Similarly, the A♭ in the tenor (m. 8) does not resolve to G in the same register. Perhaps most important, the expected E♭ is withheld in the bass at m. 9. Not only would this E♭ have been an effective resolution of the dominant bass note (m. 8), but it would also have completed a bass arpeggiation of the tonic triad. This arpeggiation had proceeded as far as the third of the triad (G) by m. 4. The line descended to F (the bass of V^7/V) in mm. 6–7, but then the F dropped out of the lower register in m. 8, leaving the span from G to E♭ incomplete in the bass. (Again, the complete span occurs in the middle-voice range.)

Thus the circular progression of the opening eight-measure phrase and its return to the tonic is an artful expansion of the tonic triad. Even V^7/V and V^7, the most conspicuous other harmonies in the basic progression, support notes which connect intervallic spans of the underlying tonic harmony. The sense of never having progressed far from the tonic is strongly confirmed by the return of the initial material (m. 9). Tensions have been created by the end of the opening phrase, but these result not from having traversed any great harmonic distance, but rather from the expectations thwarted by melodic spans left incomplete in various registers.

These incomplete spans in Op. 45/1 are easily understood because the missing elements are supplied by other voices in other registers, and thus the spans do not deviate much from voice-leading procedures involving registral transfers in traditional tonal music. The "Feuillet d'album" is an unusually straightforward piece, yet its voice leading nevertheless points to procedures in Scriabin's more dissonant, complicated works. For example, the typical dissonant opening which progresses to a definite harmony is almost always the result of a prolongation of that harmony—but one which is incomplete because one or more voices begin midspan.

The opening of the Poem Op. 32/2 (example 27) provides a good example whose structure incidentally bears a strong resemblance to that of the opening of Op. 45/1. The passage begins with a false French sixth chord which progresses through V/V at the beginning of m. 3 to V in the second half of the measure. The dominant then cadences to I (m. 4), heard first as a suspension chord but by the end of m. 4 as a simple consonant triad. The sketches in example 27 reveal direct linear connections for voices in several registers.[2]

Here, in contrast to the opening of Op. 45/1, the piece begins with several incomplete spans in a dissonant context which resists immediate interpretation. As harmony becomes more definite, however, we can easily surmise that the implicit origin of these lines is a tonic triad which is the conceptual beginning of the composition. In this analysis, as graphed in example 27, voice leading is ordinary in every respect. This reading is confirmed later in the piece. In mm. 12–13 the dominant arrives and is sustained after an extended preparation. It then progresses in m. 14 not to a clear tonic triad but rather to a repetition of the opening material. This cadential progression, admittedly deceptive, depends on the close relation of the dissonant chord (m. 1) to the expected tonic, a relation that is astonishingly clear at the end of the piece, when the entire opening occurs over a tonic pedal as a triumphant culmination. Here A♮ replaces A♭ and the bass C♮ is clearly a passing tone (see the accented bass notes), all within a forthright tonic prolongation. The final chord even resolves in the proper register the leading tone from the incomplete span beginning with C♯ in m. 27.

Direct linear progressions underlying a passage may often be concealed by rapid changes of register which overlap the basic melodic motion. In such passages as the opening of the Prelude Op. 56/1 (example 16), the analyst must determine the main register for each line and trace the line's progress as it would conform to normal voice-leading procedures. Usually the lower voices contain the most direct linear motion, whereas upper voices may be replete with overlappings, as in sketches 16a–c. The bass, an E♭ tonic pedal point, is most obvious, and the tenor voices are also fairly direct. One begins on D♭ and descends chromatically in the same register, reaching B♭ by the end of the passage. Another voice in the lower register (played at first by the thumb of the right hand) begins on B♭♭ and moves to A♭ in m. 2. The A♭ resolves to G by the end of the phrase, not in the same register but in two higher registers. An alto voice proceeds from F♭ to E♭ in m. 1, through D♮ at the end of m. 2, to D♭ at the end of m. 3. From this point on, the voice leading is questionable. In a lower register in m. 4, D♭ appears to merge into the upper tenor line, moving via C♭ to B♭. At the same time D♭ seems to be embellished in an upper voice by a lower auxiliary C♭ before rising to the tonic—in defiance of the tendency of these sixth and seventh degrees of the descending melodic minor scale.[3]

We are now prepared to deal with the melody itself. The basic melodic line moves from B♭♭ to G before leaping to E♭ (m. 1), an overlapping note from the alto voice. The melody then descends through G♭ and F, reaching E♭ at the same time that C from a tenor line overlaps (m. 2). The next melodic note is G♭, which recalls the G♭ heard earlier in the measure, emphasizing that the quick descent from G♭ to E♭ is actually a motion from the true melody to the alto, and not a genuine melodic motion (sketch 16b). The G♭, thus still in force melodically at

Example 16 Prelude Op. 56/1

the end of m. 2, then moves to F♭ in the same register as several inner voices overlap at once. At the end of the phrase, F♭ resolves to E♭, again in the same register, though obscured by more frequent overlappings.

In spite of the seemingly erratic leaps of the melody, the chords here progress in accordance with strict tonal contrapuntal procedures. In fact, the overlapping elements here are generally just duplicated members of voices proceeding normally in lower registers. Only once do these upper parts move independently, in m. 3, where an upper voice moves from C♭ via B♭ to A♭ (sketch 16b). This line spans the interval formed between two tenor voices at this point and thus does not constitute a primary melodic motion.

In sketch 16c overlapping voices are omitted, demonstrating the basic voice leading. Again, we can easily posit initiations for each line which yield complete spans of a prolonged tonic triad. It is preferable to interpret the initial alto F♭ here (sketch 16b) as an upper auxiliary to E♭ than as a passing note from G because it is closer to E♭. The inferred initial tonic triad is incomplete, but the missing third is provided in m. 1.

Example 16 sheds light on Scriabin's practice of converting an initial tonic chord into a dissonant V^7/IV. Such a function is realized somewhat here, but the V/IV–IV progression is subsumed within the prolongation of the tonic triad. The minor seventh of the tonic chord is introduced specifically to direct motion from the tonic root to the dominant tone.

We have seen that individual harmonic or melodic elements of Scriabin's tonal progressions are always subsidiary to the prolongation of which they are a part. Because harmony and counterpoint participate almost symbiotically in creating prolongations, it is impossible to analyze one without taking into account the other. Even though the functions of Scriabin's chords are often obscured—through rhythmic displacement of harmonic elements, for example—it is nevertheless essential to analyze harmonic structure in order to interpret voice leading.

The voice leading at the opening of the Etude Op. 49/1, for example, is clear only after an underlying harmonic progression has been discerned (example 17). Sketch 17a shows how overlapping voices continue the basic lines. Sketch 17b then restricts each line to the register in which it is most strongly established. Each line reaches an element of the E♭ tonic triad by the end of the phrase. The initial bass tone is also E♭, and the bass line strongly suggests movement from the subdominant A♭ (m. 2) to the dominant B♭ (m. 3) to the tonic (m. 4). Because this passage prolongs the tonic triad, we should therefore search for elements of this prolongation which have been displaced from positions where they would receive stronger harmonic reinforcement. First, the cadence to the definitive tonic harmony is clearly stated, delayed only momentarily by the melodic C♭ suspended from the preceding chord. (This preceding harmony is a definite dominant function, though clouded for its entire duration by unresolved unessential dissonances.) Sketch 17c shows the underlying harmonies with all unessential dissonances resolved. The melodic C and C♭ should resolve to B♭ (they

Example 17 Etude Op. 49/1

are thus an overlapping linear continuation from B♭ in the main melodic register; see sketch 17a), but this resolution is delayed until the arrival of the tonic. The G♮ anticipates the resolution of A♭ in an inner voice.

The chord preceding the dominant is almost certainly the enharmonic equivalent of ♭II^{7} (spelled for convenience as E major instead of F♭ major), a characteristic dominant preparation (see chapter 1, pp. 1–3). Here the unessential dissonances are created by ♭5 (a typical alteration), which does not resolve to ♮5 but is instead retained as the root of the succeeding dominant chord, and by G♮, an anticipation of the third of the final tonic triad. The chord immediately preceding ♭II^{7} is IV^{7}, as speculated earlier. Here B♭ and F fail to resolve to chord members A♭ and E♭, and F also takes the place of E♭ in V^{7}/IV at the beginning of m. 2. The melodic C and B♮ within V^{7}/IV are also dissonant but never resolve to B♭ as expected. The opening chord is the same V^{7}/IV (with the same unresolved dissonances). There remains, then, one chord whose function is in doubt—the chord on A♮ at the end of m. 1. This chord actually stands in the same relationship to V/IV and IV as does the chord on E♮ in m. 3 (a literal transposition of the chord on A♮, with t = 7) to V and I. It is therefore heard as ♭II$^{7}_{\flat 5}$ /IV preparing V/IV.

The underlying voice leading of the passage (sketch 17c) uses prolongations which for the most part are different from the incomplete spans discussed earlier. Here most spans are complete, except for the tenor voice which begins on

D♭ (the lowered seventh of the tonic chord) and thus renders the tonic a V^7/IV. (Positing an E♭ as the understood point of initiation of this line makes the tonic prolongation complete.) In the upper voices, the basic elements are embellished by extended upper auxiliary notes, and these voices are allowed to run their courses with only implicit reinforcement from the harmonic progression. Only C♯ in the entire melodic progression in sketch 17b (with the exception of the final B♭) is consonant. All other pitches are unessential dissonances displacing chord tones. The same is true in the alto voice beginning with F. The lower voices, however, contain strictly elements of the underlying harmonies.

Scriabin allows the upper voices here virtually unprecedented independence from most of the parts, which define a regular harmonic and contrapuntal progression. Yet these lines are directed by prolongational forces as strongly as are the other voices, and each dissonant element has a particular meaning in its own harmonic context. These voices are simply drastically out of synchrony with the regular progression. For instance, the initial melodic C in sketch 17b should resolve immediately to B♭, whereupon the progression would continue as in sketch 17c. By the time C actually descends to B♭ (m. 2), however, the B♭ is dissonant against the A♭ in the bass. The overlapping high C (m. 3) then embellishes B♭, which is consonant for the first time in m. 4. In a sense, the simple resolution of a dissonant upper neighbor has become the primary melodic gesture of the entire phrase, emphasized at the end of m. 3 by the repetition of the original C–B♮ motive, now spelled C–C♭ to stress the descent to a strong B♭. In the same manner, the resolution of F to E♭ in the alto line, which should have been immediate, takes the entire phrase. (In this voice, E♮ is a chromatic passing tone to E♭, and technically should be spelled F♭. The E♮ spelling conforms with the more convenient spelling of the entire ♭II^7 harmony.)

THE V–♭II–V PROLONGATION AND THE WHOLE-TONE AGGREGATE

Example 17 features another idiosyncratic prolongation that is fundamental to Scriabin's later tonal works: the retention of pitches in the typical progression of ♭II^7 to V^7 and the resulting expansion of the dominant. An ordinary ♭II^7 progressing to a simple V^7 involves the retention of two pitches. For instance, the third and the seventh of ♭II in m. 3 (G♯ and D♮) become, respectively, the seventh and the third of V^7 (A♭ and D). However, Scriabin alters ♭II by lowering the fifth, which allows the retention of another pitch: B♭, ♭5 of the ♭II harmony, becomes the root of V^7. Moreover, a fourth retention is implicit here; the V^7 contains no actual fifth, but, as noted previously, E♮ functions melodically as F♭ moving to the E♭ tonic root in m. 4. Hence E♮ is carried over implicitly into the dominant chord, serving as ♭5. Thus ♭$II^{7}_{\flat 5}$ and $V^{7}_{\flat 5}$ contain precisely the same pitches. Dernova defines this as the basis of a dual modality in which either version of the chord may act as a dominant to its own tonic (see chapter 1, note 7). Here, as in all of Scriabin's tonal works, the pitch-retaining properties of the characteristic chord do not establish two opposing tonic functions of equal weight. In this example, there is no hint of the chord on E♮ as the dominant of A♮ (♭V). The retention of four pitches throughout m. 3 prolongs a single function, perhaps not clear right away, but definitely established as the dominant by the cadence at m. 4. The harmony $\flat II^{7}_{\flat 5}$ occurs as a separate part of this prolonged dominant to set up a strong tension in the bass by progressing by tritone directly to V. This tension is resolved when the bass of ♭II descends chromatically to the tonic root. The prolonged $V^{7}_{\flat 5}$ is a subset of the whole-tone scale, and in Scriabin's transitional music the prolonging progression $\flat II^{7}_{\flat 5}$–$V^{7}_{\flat 5}$ is often the basis for an entire whole-tone aggregate.

Often ♭II is a type of auxiliary chord, embellishing and thus prolonging a dominant sonority which both precedes and follows it. This is precisely the means of prolonging V^7/IV at the opening of Op. 49/1. As usual, complete pitch retention between the ♭II and V chords is not realized here. Both chords, however, are equally important in the whole-tone aggregate.

The prolongational procedures discussed thus far are sufficient to determine the harmonic structure of an entire piece. In particular, the V–♭II–V progression is often the progression of primary interest in a composition, secondary in structural importance only to the cadence to the tonic (although the tonic itself may receive little durational emphasis). The Prelude Op. 48/2 (example 18) has such a structure; its three phrases cadence to three separate harmonic goals: V (m. 2), ♭II (m. 5), and (V–)I (m. 7). The nebulous harmonies result from incomplete and exceptionally wayward melodic motions which prolong progressions to these goals. Sketch 18a shows the melodic events with overlapping lines reduced to single registers. Sketch 18b then indicates the ordinary voice leading which underlies the passage. The first phrase (mm. 1–3) prolongs a progression from the (implicit) tonic to the dominant via dominant seventh chords on A♭ and D in m. 1. These are the two forms of a dual dominant which may progress to either V or ♭II. (Here, of course, it progresses to V, but later [mm. 4–5] the A♭ is the effective bass tone of a chord which progresses as a secondary dominant to a stabilized ♭II.) Pitch retention between the two chords is exceedingly weak, however, and thus the chord on A♭ may just as easily be explained as ♭VI. In the ideal voice leading of sketch 18b, the typical retention of pitches between these seventh chords a tritone apart is an important feature, though it is thwarted at the foreground.

The melody itself is the most unusual voice. It begins with A midspan and ascends much too soon to its goal, B, heard as an appoggiatura over the bass D. The B then resolves not to a consonant A but rather to an A♯. The tendency of A♯ to return to B when V is reached in m. 2 is denied by a melodic leap to the dissonant E♭ of an overlapping inner voice. Both endpoints of the main melodic span are therefore shown in sketch 18b as only implicit; the final B does occur in an inner voice, but G is not present at all at the opening.

After the dominant has been reached in m. 2, it is further stabilized by the repeated cadence (mm. 2–3). The second phrase prolongs a progression around the circle of fifths from the dominant to ♭II. The phrase begins in the second

Example 18 Prelude Op. 48/2

Example 18 (cont.)

half of m. 3 as a literal transposition (with t = 7) of the original material, and the correspondence breaks down only with V/♭II in the second half of m. 4. (V/♮II or V/V/V would have resulted in repetition at T_7.) At this point the literal repetition shifts to T_6. Because of the transpositional shift midphrase, the melodic spans are different in the second phrase, and because it occurs in a slightly lower register, the linear connections between spans of the two phrases involve different parts of the melody. For instance, in sketch 18a the melodic appoggiatura B♭♭–A♭, unlike the corresponding part of the melody in the first phrase (m. 2), is not an overlapping, for it links up with the implicit B which ends the main melodic span of the first phrase.

Each of the two phrases expands a simple progression from an initial chord (at least implicitly established) to the stabilized harmony to which the entire phrase cadences. The intervening chords are subsidiary, being simply the means by which the expansion is achieved. Sketch 18c therefore reduces the music to the background harmonies which support the prolongations. Not all of these harmonies receive equal weight in the actual composition, of course. The initial tonic is barely felt, if at all. The dominant, on the other hand, is effective throughout m. 2 and half of m. 3, achieving maximum stability by the repeated cadence. The ♭II goal reached in m. 5 is a point of arrival just as was V at the beginning of m. 2 but is not stabilized by a repeated cadence. By the end of m. 5 the harmony has moved back to V/♭II, and we might expect a repeated cadence. Instead the chord is reinterpreted as ♭VI progressing to V/V (or shifting as a dual dominant to its other aspect, V/V), from which the harmony progresses to V and on to the tonic (m. 7). Only the tonic here receives an emphasis equal to that of the dominant in mm. 2–3. Thus the tonal axis is set up unequivocally, albeit incompletely, for the tonic is not strongly established before the dominant. Thus the goal of ♭II (m. 5) appears subsidiary, especially in the compositional reinforcement it receives. We must recognize, however, that this D♭ chord actually occurs within a circular progression from the strong dominant in mm. 2–3 to the dominant at the end of m. 6. This circular progression prolongs the dominant over a large span of the composition (mm. 2–6), which explains why the dominant at the end of m. 6 need not be structurally emphasized.

The harmony ♭II is obviously the single most important chord within this dominant prolongation, for it is the only point of relative stability. A basic progression of V–♭II–V therefore underlies the prolongation, with ♭II secondary to the dominants which frame it. This prolongation expands the V–♭II–V progression which is frequent at the local level in Scriabin's compositions and which serves the identical purpose of prolonging the dominant. In this expanded V–♭II–V progression no pitches are retained between the two harmonies. Pitch retention is probably the basis for prolongation on the local level, but in the higher-level prolongation each chord must occur as a stabilized harmonic goal.

One might argue, however, that the expansion of the V–♭II–V progression with ♭II established as a main harmonic goal must have been preceded by the use of this progression on more local levels; and that, because Scriabin used this progression primarily for retaining pitches (usually members of a whole-tone scale), pitch retention (and whole-tone prolongation) may be at work in this expanded version of the same progression. In fact, the dominant chord at the end of m. 6 is a whole-tone subset. Significantly, no perfect fifth is heard in this chord; rather, D♯ in the melody replaces D♮ which otherwise might have been sustained in the tenor region. Further, the low D♭ supporting ♭II in m. 5 is present (at least conceptually) until resolved to the low C in m. 8 and therefore is also an element of the whole-tone dominant chord. (The only missing whole-tone element is A♮, which is conspicuous in the tenor line in the second half of m. 6, where the dominant takes over. Therefore the whole-tone aggregate may be viewed as complete.) It is thus possible to understand this expanded V–♭II–V as an unfolding of the whole-tone sonority; crucial to that unfolding is the displacement of the perfect fifth of the dominant by the lowered fifth introduced as the bass of ♭II. Whole-tone prolongations are considered further at the end of this chapter.

REGISTER AND CONNECTIONS BETWEEN NONADJACENT ELEMENTS

Register is vital in determining the structural significance of tonal elements or gestures. Like most composers of traditional tonal music, Scriabin leads his listeners to expect the proper resolution of tensions in certain registers. In particular, nonadjacent elements related by half or whole step will, if in the same register (especially in an extreme register which is seldom exploited), tend to link together to create large-scale motions—even if they occur only intermittently. In the Prelude Op. 51/2 the voice leading is effected by elements which, though not adjacent, are nonetheless associated linearly because they occur in a single register (example 28). The piece opens with an A minor tonic triad clouded by the addition of the sixth, F. This dissonance throws the entire tonality into doubt: the sixth or the fifth would individually form a consonant harmony with the other pitches of the chord, and thus the harmony might well be an obscured F major chord instead. Although the main progressions in the piece, particularly in the bass, strongly suggest the tonality of A minor, only the final cadence to an A minor triad settles the matter beyond doubt.

At the opening the strongest indicator of tonality is the melody, which arpeggiates the tonic triad. Both F and E are constantly present in the first three measures. The only other pitches form a third, D♯–B (m. 1), which embellishes the E–C third of the tonic triad. The motion from this auxiliary third back to the E–C third seems to take place in the chord immediately following, where E and C occur in different registers; but a completely satisfying resolution arrives only with the return of these pitches in their original register. Aside from this embellishing motion, the main interest in this extension of the initial harmony is the variety of register and texture in the exchange of voice pairs—E–C and A–F—indicated in the upper sketch in example 28 by the crossed lines. As the pairs exchange positions, they are inverted and therefore assume the forms of the original intervals in each register. (The upper-register E–C third is inverted when it enters the bass region, taking the place of the bass F–A sixth—and vice versa.) Thus the voice exchange never changes the harmony; rather, as in traditional tonal works, voices are exchanged to create a sense of motion within a single harmony. Indeed, no sooner does the first exchange occur than its converse restores each voice to the original register.

The harmony in the succeeding measures is just as convoluted, but there is an underlying tonal progression, made clear primarily by the literal transpositions of the opening chord at T_5 at the end of m. 4 and at T_7 at the end of m. 8. If we take the bass notes of these chords to be their roots (as in the opening chord), then a I–IV–V progression may be surmised. One other harmony is important to this progression—V^6_5/V, which occurs unaltered on D♯ in m. 7. The lower sketch illustrates that all voice leadings prolong the progression from one harmony to the next in a I–IV–V^6_5/V–V structure. Some voice-leading elements are acutely displaced, the most obvious being F at the beginning, which anticipates its own occurrence in the subdominant (m. 4). The underlying melodic motion is a descent from E in m. 2 to B of the dominant in m. 8. This motion is embellished when E moves to its upper neighbor F (m. 4), making it appear that the descent to B occurs from F rather than E. The F is actually an incomplete neighbor because it does not return immediately to a consonantly reinforced E. Rather, it moves quickly to D (while D is sustained in the bass as well), which begins the descent from the structural E in m. 2. The incomplete upper neighbor resolves only when E returns in the proper register as an element of V (m. 8).

Other nonadjacent pitches also participate in large-scale unfoldings which are more easily perceived because they occur in a single register. The third between the melodic E in m. 1 and the G in m. 8 is filled in chromatically by F (m. 4) and F♯ (m. 7) (sketch 28b). Scriabin always takes care in this span to repeat a tone which has been interrupted before proceeding to the next. Thus F in m. 6 recalls F in m. 4 before the line moves on to F♯. In synchrony with this unfolding, an important bass motion from D (m. 4) via D♯ (m. 7) to E (m. 8) is strongly felt even though material in higher registers intervenes. (The motion actually commences with D♯ in m. 3, which at the time appears to be the lower auxiliary to the melodic E, but in another register. The bass D♯ in m. 3 would ideally proceed from an E in the same register, but the bass E is consistently displaced by F.) The D–D♯–E bass motion is confirmed in mm. 18–20 when the same progression is condensed and proceeds uninterrupted, preparing the only direct statement of the dominant in the composition. The cadence which follows is deceptive, however; Scriabin saves the only clear statement of the tonic triad for the final chord.

LINEAR INTERVALLIC PATTERNS

As mentioned in the preceding chapter, patterned voice leading frequently creates large-scale gestures in Scriabin's tonal music. These patterns often take the form of sequential repetitions of musical subject matter, but because patterns may continue even after a change in surface features, we should consider sequences within a discussion of all patterned voice-leading relationships. Generally, patterning which determines prolongations will involve the outer voices and may be measured in terms of the intervals between them. The term *linear intervallic pattern* designates any prolongational procedure dependent on patterned voice leading.[4] Linear intervallic patterns connect one structurally important harmony, the point of departure for the pattern, with another attained as the goal when the pattern is broken. They may also prolong a single harmony, when the goal is the same as the point of departure. All harmonies between the departure and goal are subsumed within the large-scale gesture and are thus subsidiary to the harmonies it prolongs.

Example 19, from the Poem Op. 32/1, shows a linear intervallic pattern (mm. 11–14) which moves from IV (stabilized in m. 9) to V by m. 15. The pattern, shown in sketch 19a, is created by the outer voices descending in parallel tenths. It begins on IV and is barely established before it is interrupted by the premature occurrence of G♯ in the bass in m. 12 (not expected until the downbeat of m. 13) and even more by the bass anticipation in m. 13 of V, which should appear only in m. 15. (See also the discussion in chapter 1, p. 20.) The parallel tenths, so evident at first between the extreme outer voices, continue with G♯ in the bass, but B♯ occurs first in the tenor and in a middle register in m. 13, never

Example 19 Poem Op. 32/1

in the expected upper voice. Thus the actual linear intervallic pattern continues after the surface pattern has changed, and it is broken only by the structural dominant at m. 15 (sketch 19b). The pattern itself is primarily responsible for determining the progression—not the individual harmonies, even though they might be considered to function with regard to the departure or goal harmonies. The connecting function of the pattern is abundantly clear, for the progression from IV in mm. 9–10 to V in m. 15 is logical and direct.

Scriabin's linear intervallic patterns seldom contain harmonically independent chords, and the pattern in mm. 7–12 of the "Poème fantasque" Op. 45/2 (ex-

Example 20 "Poème fantasque" Op. 45/2

ample 20) is no exception. The pattern involves a basic two-measure phrase on the surface and breaks down at m. 11 when the phrase is not repeated. But a much more simple harmonic and voice-leading pattern underlies the passage. Sketch 20a shows that the same type of harmony, the familiar $V^7_{\flat 5}$ chord, occurs in each measure. The progression of the $V^7_{\flat 5}$ chords is determined entirely by a bass pattern which descends four half steps and three half steps alternately but which is somewhat concealed by displacements of the bass notes from their ideal register (sketch 20a). Harmonic variety is obtained both by the addition of a ninth to alternate $V^7_{\flat 5}$ chords (mm. 8 and 10) and by the resolution of ♭5 to ♮5 where the ninth is not added (mm. 7, 9, and 11). The melodic notes through m. 10 are consistently the fifth of each chord, and direct parallel fifths are avoided both by change of register and by alternating perfect and diminished fifths.

On the basis of harmonic structure and bass progression, the pattern appears to begin in m. 7 and to continue through m. 11. The departure harmony (m. 7) shares three pitches—E♭, D♭, and G—with the chord in the preceding measure, an altered dominant sixth. (These pitches form the left-hand chord in m. 7.) Thus the bass of the linear intervallic pattern begins earlier than expected—in m. 6 (or even in m. 5). Because the dominant root, G, is in effect in m. 6, having been strongly established in m. 5, the departure harmony is the dominant (albeit in altered form), from which the progression proceeds unbroken to the chord on D♭ in m. 11. Significantly, this chord is not spelled with C♭, which would allow us to interpret it as $V^7_{\flat 5}$ /G♭ (♭V), but rather with B♮ (the enharmonic equivalent), signaling a shift from the expected chord to the $V^7_{\flat 5}$ /C form. The shift takes place with a tritone bass progression to G in m. 12, which supports a $V^{9}_{\sharp 5}$ harmony (which also contains D♭, the lowered fifth, implicitly retained from the preceding chord and reintroduced at the end of m. 12). The goal and departure harmonies are thus both dominants with lowered and raised fifths (spelled ♯4 and ♭6 in the departure chord). The sequence progresses from V (m. 6) to $\flat II^{\flat 7}_{\flat 5}$ (or its enharmonic equivalent), which is then reinterpreted as $V^{7}_{\flat 5}$, artfully expanding the V–♭II–V progression as well as building a whole-tone sonority.

The "Caresse dansée" Op. 57/2 uses complicated, highly chromatic linear intervallic patterns. The antecedent and consequent phrases of the opening sixteen-measure period cadence respectively to V and I (example 21). Each phrase begins with the same linear intervallic pattern (transposed up five half steps in the second). Because the initial chord is dissonant, the point of departure for the pattern must be surmised from later events.

Sketch 21a demonstrates the underlying linear intervallic pattern involving chromatically descending whole-tone chords. The bass tones of mm. 2 and 4 create a separate linear motion from the main voice leading. Embellished by overlappings and rhythmic displacements, the voice leading continues through the chord on A♮ in m. 6. The bass then proceeds to A♭ as expected, but other voices break the pattern and establish the chord on A♭—a major triad and the first consonant chord in the piece—as the goal of the progression. This harmony, ♭VI in C major, progresses to V^7/V (m. 7) and V^7 (with unessential dissonances) in m. 8.

The tonic (supporting E in the soprano) might seem to be the point of departure for this linear intervallic pattern (sketch 21b), but such a choice leads to contradictions. If the opening linear intervallic pattern begins with the tonic, its counterpart in mm. 9–10, five half steps higher, should begin with the subdominant. But the harmony in m. 9 continues the dominant of the preceding measure. (The B–F tritone in m. 9 occurred in the left hand of m. 8; E is suspended from the preceding measure, and the high A recalls the A left dangling in m. 6.) It seems reasonable to interpret the harmonically uncertain beginning of the first pattern in light of the more definite departure harmony of the second. We should thus consider the point of departure of the opening linear intervallic pattern as V^{4}_{2}/V and examine the repercussions of such a reading (sketch 21c). An exceptionally convincing analysis emerges, for the departure harmony is the same as the goal, resulting in a prolongation of V^7/V. Moreover, if the A♭ triad is interpreted as ♭II/V, the progression is the familiar V–♭II–V prolongation. The entire eight–measure phrase is therefore a prolonged V^7/V progressing to V, and the second phrase correspondingly prolongs V and cadences to I in m. 16. (The transpositional repetition of the first phrase breaks down at m. 16 so that a consonant tonic triad may end the period.) Finally, despite the assumption of a V^{4}_{2} chord underlying the opening harmony, we can (and should) posit a structural tonic triad at the beginning of the piece. In fact, the outer voices of the opening chord are best explained as elements of such a structural tonic.

In most music of the eighteenth and nineteenth centuries, linear intervallic

Example 21 "Caresse dansée" Op. 57/2

patterns link an established tonal function with one which may or may not have been expected otherwise; example 19 illustrates such a traditional sequence in Scriabin's music. On the other hand, examples 20 and 21 (especially the latter) deviate from this practice, for the departure harmony is not firmly established, though it may be assumed. Scriabin's linear intervallic patterns often completely reverse the function of traditional sequential maneuvers. In these *retrogressive* patterns, the initiation of the patterned voice leading is harmonically indeterminate in light of preceding events, whereas its goal is an important tonal function—frequently the dominant. For example, "Fragilité" Op. 51/1 contains a contrasting second section (marked *animando*) in mm. 17–32 which involves two statements of an eight-measure phrase, the second one at T_2 (example 22). The first statement begins indefinitely on a dominant-seventh-type chord on G♭ which serves no clear function in the overall E♭ tonality. (For an explanation of the material preceding this chord, see example 5.) The phrase then progresses to a dominant seventh on E♭ (m. 18) which cadences weakly to IV (m. 19). The harmony $IV^{\flat 7}_{\natural 5}$ is then prolonged by a tritone bass progression through m. 25. Because m. 25 also begins the transpositional repetition of the phrase in mm. 17–24, the restatement opens on the firmly established IV and proceeds to V/V (m. 26) and V (prolonged from mm. 27–32). The second statement of the

Example 22 "Fragilité" Op. 51/1

phrase is the one grounded in harmonic logic, and the first is harmonically comprehensible only in light of it; the two phrases thus form a retrogressive progression.

The opening of the Etude Op. 56/4 is likewise a retrogressive sequence (example 23a). The pattern begins on an indefinite harmony and is broken in the third measure, establishing the dual dominant $V^{7}_{\flat 5}$ as its goal. This harmony is extended through m. 6 and cadences to ♭V (C major) in m. 7. (Later the same chord is reinterpreted so as to cadence to the tonic; see examples 6a–c.) The second measure is a literal repetition of the first at T_3. In m. 3, the melody repeats again at T_3 for the first four sixteenth notes, then deviates from the pattern. The left-hand chord, however, breaks the pattern at the outset of m. 3, for it repeats the material in m. 1 at T_2 (not at T_6 as expected). It is useful to contrast the actual events of m. 3 with those of the hypothetical continuation of the sequence depicted in example 23b. Had the melody of m. 3 continued throughout (at T_6) as in m. 1, it would have duplicated the C♯–G tritone as G–D♭, which would have been repetitive. The actual melody duplicates E♭ and G instead—but their roles are very different in the two measures. The left-hand

Example 23a Etude Op. 56/4

Example 23b

chords of example 23b contain the same pitches as those in the actual m. 1. The left hand of the actual m. 3 shares only two pitches with that of m. 1, and the two parts together constitute an entire whole-tone aggregate. A whole-tone prolongation seems to underlie this passage, with the chords in m. 2 (which occur midsequence) as passing harmonies which provide maximum contrast, for they belong to the other whole-tone scale. Most important, the bass tones of mm. 1 and 3 together form the dual dominant goal. The sketches beneath example 23a demonstrate the basic voice leading of the passage. No real tonal function may be ascribed to the chords preceding V/♭V (m. 3). However, their pitches link with elements of V/♭V, and therefore they are linear auxiliary chords to V/♭V. Thus the linear intervallic pattern embellishes its goal while arpeggiating (and thus prolonging) the goal harmony in the bass.

WHOLE-TONE PROLONGATIONS

We have seen that prolongations of tonal functions or progressions often form whole-tone aggregates. These whole-tone collections never take structural precedence over the tonal gestures, but it is remarkable that the two procedures are not mutually exclusive. Usually, whole-tone aggregates are formed when whole-tone dominant functions are prolonged—and whole-tone dominants usually occur so that they may be enharmonically reinterpreted as dual dominants. Whole-tone aggregates occur with the prolongation of a whole-tone dominant in the sequential repetition from "Ironies" Op. 56/2 (example 9), which uses transpositions up even numbers of half steps so that most pitches in any chord belong to the same underlying whole-tone scale. However, example 23a shows that a single aggregate may be prolonged by a sequential repetition even if pitches from the other whole-tone scale are introduced by transposition up an odd number of half steps. Whole-tone sequential prolongations eventually repeat original material an even number of half steps away (in these examples, $t = 6$, although in the latter example this level of transposition is only weakly represented); it makes no difference whether this is managed by odd- or even-numbered transpositions, or a combination of both.

The whole-tone prolongation in the Etude Op. 49/1 uses pitches outside the underlying whole-tone scale which are important only in embellishing or connecting capacities (example 24). Here duration is a main reinforcement of structural weight, and pitch retention among transposed forms of the same chord is the primary means for extending duration. Measures 8–15 involve a linear intervallic pattern which connects III♮ (m. 8) with V, the goal attained in m. 14. Although III occurs as a consonant triad in m. 8, it is converted to a seventh chord with ♭5 which becomes the departure harmony for the sequence beginning in m. 9. The melodic note, B, of this whole-tone chord is embellished by a chromatic lower auxiliary, and the entire configuration is then repeated twice, at T_6 (second half of m. 9) and at the original pitch level (m. 10). The four pitches of the $V^{7}_{\flat 5}$ chord are retained throughout the entire progression,

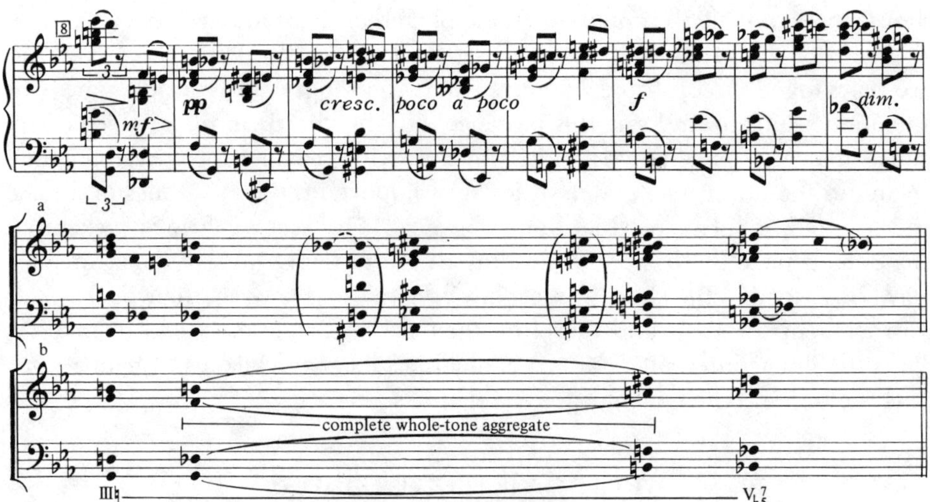

Example 24 Etude Op. 49/1

which is a slightly embellished V–♭II–V prolongation of this single chord. The unaccented embellishments have little weight relative to the retained whole-tone chord.

The chord immediately following contains four pitches of the other whole-tone scale in a relatively accented position. The voice leading conceals the fact that this configuration is another transposition, with t = 9, of the departure chord and its chromatic auxiliary note. (If E were in the bass the relation would be obvious.) This harmony is the secondary dominant (in first inversion) of the succeeding chord (mm. 11–12), which is itself an exact repetition of mm. 9–10 at T_2. In view of its status as a secondary dominant and the passing role played by its bass note, the chord in the second half of m. 9—and the corresponding chord in m. 12—is subsidiary to those both before and after, which sustain pitches from the underlying whole-tone scale.

Another sequential repetition up two half steps begins in m. 13, but the pattern is broken by V in m. 14, a function accomplished by reinterpreting the $V^{7}_{\flat 5}$ on B♮ (V/E) as $V^{7}_{\flat 5}$ on F♮, which becomes the dominant of the dominant. Note that a small change in the expected register of the chords in m. 13 allows the bass of B♮ (the enharmonic equivalent of C♭ supporting ♭II/V) to resolve to B♭ supporting V. Thus this linear intervallic pattern effects a bass progression from G to B♭, but via the chromatic upper auxiliary to B♭, an embellishment of great motivic significance (example 17). At the same time, the pattern prolongs a whole-tone aggregate, never complete in a single chord but formed instead over time by statements of the basic $V^{7}_{\flat 5}$ chord at T_0, T_2, and T_4. Only with the arrival of V (m. 14) do pitches of the other whole-tone scale take structural precedence, counterbalancing the preceding whole-tone prolongation and in a sense resolving the tension it generates.

One might suppose that the structure of whole-tone prolongations depends on the use of whole-tone chords at the surface of a composition. However, a linear intervallic pattern from the Poem Op. 32/2 (mm. 8–12) shows that such prolongations can also occur by a straightforward tonal progression of triads and seventh chords (example 27). The sketches demonstrate the patterned voice leading which begins with III♯ in D major (spelled enharmonically as ♭IV♭). The pattern continues unbroken to its goal, the French sixth on B♭ (m. 11), which resolves to V (m. 12). (The low F and other changes in the established surface pattern in m. 10 do not affect the progress of the linear intervallic pattern.) Each chord in the pattern is either a root-position dominant seventh chord or a first-inversion triad; other pitches in this passage are auxiliary. Yet the fundamental outer voices of the pattern, which move in parallel tenths, outline segments of a single whole-tone scale: G♭–A♭–B♭ in the bass and B♭–C–D in the upper voice. An E♮ is the only element missing from the aggregate, and it occurs in the melody in m. 11 while B♭ continues in the bass, supporting the French sixth. This chord is the first whole-tone harmony in the passage, yet it culminates a whole-tone prolongation begun measures earlier. It might seem that a whole-tone configuration has little bearing on the structure of a clearly tonal work, yet whole-tone chords are important sonorities elsewhere in the piece; examples are the opening chord and the whole-tone dominant at the end of m. 3. The melody here spans the same B♭–E♮ tritone which occurs vertically in the French sixth chord. This passage is unmistakably like sequences in later compositions which consistently employ whole-tone components at the surface and thus more clearly prolong a whole-tone aggregate. Example 24 shows such a whole-tone prolongation; the progression of outer voices in this more complicated and dissonant sequence is almost identical to that in Op. 32/2. The formation of whole-tone aggregates is important in reinforcing the tonal gestures effected by prolongations, especially by linear intervallic patterns. This procedure serves in a sense to prolong a whole-tone sonority, yet it never interferes with the prolongations of tonal elements or progressions, which take precedence as structural determinants. Scriabin's mastery is never more strongly in evidence than in passages such as our present examples. He actually strengthens tonal gestures by using procedures from outside the tonal system. In other hands such a practice might have destroyed tonal unity, but Scriabin's talent for melding ostensibly conflicting techniques was fully developed even in such unequivocally tonal works as Op. 32/2.

THREE
TONALITY IN THE TRANSITIONAL WORKS III
Fundamental Structure

The prolongational procedures discussed in the preceding chapter expand a single harmony or a progression from one harmony to another into a tonal gesture which can extend far beyond a local relation. At the surface or *foreground* of a tonal composition, harmony and melody typically determine prolongations so that a single harmonic-contrapuntal event is continuously effective on a deeper level of structure, known as the *middleground*. Actually, there are many levels which occupy middleground territory, each determined by prolongational procedures at the next level nearer the foreground, and the progression of harmony and melody is governed at any level by the same logic which controls events at the foreground. There is of course a deepest level of structure, the *background*, which is a projection of the tonic triad through time, accomplished by a fundamental structure, or *Ursatz*. The Ursatz horizontalizes the triad in two voices. The bass arpeggiates the triad by moving from the root to the fifth and back to the root, while the melody, or *Urlinie*, descends stepwise through an interval of the triad: the third, the fifth, or occasionally the octave. The counterpoint of bass and melody generates the tonal axis of the piece—the I–V–I progression which provides the essential structural support for the entire composition.[1]

COMPLETE URSATZ FORMS

We have come to expect Scriabin's late tonal compositions to deviate significantly from traditional tonal practice in their foreground and middleground procedures; the deeper middleground and background usually depart even farther from structural norms. Nevertheless it is useful to begin a discussion of tonal coherence in Scriabin's music (as determined by Ursatz formations) with an example of how closely he could adhere to conventional structures: the simple and beautiful "Feuillet d'album" Op. 45/1 (example 25).

Because the middleground of the first eight-measure phrase has already been analyzed (example 15), only the determination of the Ursatz by middleground

Example 25 "Feuillet d'album" Op. 45/1

Example 25 (cont.)

prolongational procedures need be considered now. We saw that the passage prolongs the E♭ major tonic triad by a circular progression; we must now ask which elements of the outer voices are prolonged as components of the Ursatz. In the bass we traced a descending arpeggiation of the tonic triad from the E♭ above middle C to an implicit E♭ an octave lower at the end of the phrase. The arpeggiation is not complete because the goal is not realized, and therefore only the opening E♭ is a likely beginning of the Ursatz in the first phrase. The lower E♭ may be implied strongly enough to be the first tone of the background bass line, however. The unusually high register of the bass in the first phrase suggests that the Ursatz root is not heard immediately, especially considering the very low E♭ heard only at the final cadence of the piece (m. 24).

The upper voice offers two candidates for the initial tone of the Urlinie. The octave of the tonic triad is not likely, for it is only implicit in the main melodic register at the beginning, and when it occurs there later it is an overlapping inner voice and not part of the primary linear activity. The third, G♮, is conspicuous in the upper register (m. 3) as the beginning of a third-span descending to E♭ understood in m. 9. The same motion is concurrent in the bass line, however, and thus the high G♮ seems to be an element of an overlapping line. Thus the most likely possibility for the initial tone of the Urlinie is the fifth, B♭, which is the goal of the most significant melodic motions of both four-measure phrases (at m. 4 and m. 8) and is thus prolonged throughout the first eight measures. We cannot decide certainly the point of initiation of either line of the Ursatz until we examine the entire composition, but it is generally useful to evaluate at the outset the possible initial pitches of the Ursatz. We can then trace the background lines which would continue from each, ascribing the Ursatz to the two lines which are structurally most coherent.

In the measures following the opening phrase, the original bass descent arpeggiating the tonic triad is elaborately restated. The most important departure from the original bass motion is the leap to C supporting V/II (m. 13), from which the harmony progresses around the circle of fifths until it cadences to I in m. 16. The cadence in the bass is certainly more complete than that in mm. 8–9, where the expected bass support was suppressed. However, other events prevent our hearing the tonic at m. 16 as the effective close of another eight-measure period. The root-position tonic chord is displaced by the end of the measure by its first-inversion form, supported by the lowest bass tone thus far, thereby depriving the earlier I^{5}_{3} of full closure. Moreover, the other voices, in particular the melody, do not indicate m. 16 as a point of arrival. There is here no evidence whatsoever of a completed motion in the Urlinie, and the melody simply continues the large patterned gesture in mm. 13–20. It appears therefore that mm. 9–16 contain another circular progression prolonging the tonic harmony, so that no progression has taken place in the fundamental bass line (although a tonic root has been established in a lower register). It is clear, however, that the upper voices have been active throughout this passage, and it may be that part of the descent of an Urlinie is supported by the harmonies of this circular progression.

Because no strong melodic descent from $\hat{2}$ to $\hat{1}$ is evident at the cadence in mm. 15–16, we may assume that the Urlinie has descended no farther than $\hat{3}$ by this point.[2] Therefore only three possible Urlinie events could be supported by the circular progression in mm. 9–16: (1) the prolongation of $\hat{3}$ as the initial tone of the Urlinie also prolonged throughout mm. 1–8; (2) the descent from $\hat{5}$ through $\hat{4}$ to $\hat{3}$; or (3) the prolongation of $\hat{5}$ throughout. Let us examine each alternative (example 26). That $\hat{3}$ is prolonged throughout (sketch 26a) is certainly possible. The high G in m. 13 (supported by V/II) is the goal of a third-span from an implicit E♭ in m. 9. The G is thereafter prolonged by its upper auxiliary A♭ (supported by II and V) in mm. 14–15, which resolves back to G in m. 16. This prolongation occurs in the upper register and is therefore conspicuous. The strength of this interpretation is somewhat diminished, however, because G appears to be an overlapping in the opening measures and never occurs as a consonance in the upper register until m. 16.

Example 26 "Feuillet d'album" Op. 45/1: Alternative Analyses

The second possibility (sketch 26b), that the circular progression supports a descent from $\hat{5}$ to $\hat{3}$ in the Urlinie, is definitely viable. The B♭ (m. 13) is approached by the same unfolding from the implicit E♭ (m. 9) and descends via A♭ (mm. 14–15) to G (m. 16). The motion from A♭ to G parallels the resolution of the upper auxiliary A♭ to G in the upper register, discussed above. Here the motion would necessarily take place in a middle register, for no strong $\hat{5}$ is established in the highest register. The upper-register A♭–G motion might reinforce or even displace elements of an Urlinie descending in the middle register. On the other hand, it might hinder perception of the basic line, for it conceals the line's progress in a single register, which would be its strongest presentation.

It is also possible that $\hat{5}$ is prolonged throughout the passage (sketch 26c) by two unfoldings to B♭, the first from the implicit E♭ in m. 9 to the B♭ in m. 12. Thereafter B♭ is contained in V^7/II and is then prolonged by an unfolding through A♭ (mm. 14–15) to G, an element of the tonic in a middle voice (m. 16). At the end of this unfolding, B♭ is restored in the upper voice. The B♭ in m. 16 is the goal of a larger-scale unfolding from the same implicit E♭ in m. 9, proceeding via D♭ (m. 12) and C♭ (m. 14), to B♭, which is displaced from m. 15 by the suspended C♭. This latter unfolding is an overlapping of the same melodic progression in the tenor range. The advantage of this choice is that B♭ continues to be active in its original register and is conspicuous at the end of m. 16 (after the highest registers have been abandoned) and later. But a final choice among these alternatives must be withheld until the rest of the composition has been examined.

The middle period of the "Feuillet d'album" is extended to twelve measures by the material in mm. 17–20, whose harmony progresses from the tonic (m. 16) to the dominant before returning to the opening phrase in m. 21. The harmonies linking I and V are straightforward: I^6 (m. 16)—V^7/V (m. 17)—V^{6-5-}_{4-3} (mm. 18–20). The duration of the dominant is greater here than anywhere else in the composition, and the opening material returns subsequently in the tonic; thus this dominant is probably the structural dominant of the Ursatz (based on the fifth of the scale in the Ursatz bass). If so, it must support $\hat{2}$ in the Urlinie, which will progress to $\hat{1}$ as the harmony cadences to the tonic. Whether the possibilities for the Urlinie conform to the harmonic progression of mm. 17–21 is the final test in choosing the basic line of the piece.

The first alternative, that G is prolonged through m. 16 in an upper register, may now be dismissed, for this register is largely neglected in subsequent measures. A strong high F would have to be assumed (to act as $\hat{2}$) in mm. 19–20, and the implicit high E♭ in m. 21 would have to serve as $\hat{1}$. Such an implicit line could be the Urlinie only in the absence of a stronger line, explicit in a single register. The second possibility, that the structural descent from $\hat{5}$ (in a middle register) has reached $\hat{3}$ by m. 16, has more credibility. The G would progress in m. 17 to F, which would then be prolonged through m. 20, where it is a conspicuous melodic element receiving the support of V^7 and would therefore be a strong $\hat{2}$. Further, the descent to $\hat{1}$ with the cadence at m. 21 is totally convincing, the connection between $\hat{2}$ and $\hat{1}$ made even clearer by the chromatic passing tone, F♭. The only weakness of the second alternative is that neither the middle-voice G nor its descent to F is prominent in mm. 16–17. The only clearly audible elements of this middle-register line, then, are B♭ (mm. 4 and 8), F (m. 20), and E♭ (m. 21). It may be, as mentioned before, that the A♭ and G of this line are displaced up an octave in mm. 14–16, or that this upper-register motion reinforces these elements in the lower register. However, this alternative—though clearly more sound than the first—also could not receive serious consideration if the elements of an alternative line are presented with equal clarity but within a single register.

The prolongation of $\hat{5}$ through m. 16 is confined to a single register and is therefore the best choice for the Urlinie. Still present in the original register in m. 16, B♭ seems to disappear until the end of m. 18. In the interim, however, the implicit E♭ in m. 16 has unfolded through D (m. 17), C and C♭ (m. 18), to this latter B♭—the same span by which B♭ was prolonged in the opening phrases! (Both even have implicit E♭ beginnings.) The B♭ is therefore prolonged until the arrival of the structural dominant, which then supports the descent from $\hat{5}$ to $\hat{2}$, and the motion to $\hat{1}$ is completed at the cadence in m. 21.

With the completion of the Urlinie, we might expect the rest of the composition to be a coda prolonging the tonic. Yet the Ursatz motion is not completed at m. 21, for here (as at m. 9) the bass does not cadence to the tonic root in a low register. The restatement of the opening phrase adds a true cadence in the bass in mm. 23–24 (otherwise equivalent to mm. 3–4), a cadence to the lowest tonic root, encountered for the first and only time at this point. This low E♭ takes precedence over all other tonic roots as the fundamental bass note of the Ursatz. (Its presence may only be inferred at the beginning.) Technically the Ursatz root should be stated simultaneously in both bass and Urlinie, but here the expected bass support for $\hat{1}$ in m. 21 is postponed. To delay this root deviates from conventional tonal structure, but it is calculated to make the return of the opening phrase more than a simple coda. A brief melodic tag is all that remains after the completion of the Ursatz in m. 24, summarizing the melodic motion of the piece. It arpeggiates the tonic from a high B♭ (the first consonant high B♭ in the piece, embellished by the motivic chromatic upper auxiliary), down to the final B♭, the same pitch which initiated the basic melodic motion of the piece. This line thus unites the high register with the main melodic register. (The initial tone of the Urlinie is frequently restated at the conclusion of Scriabin's works as an overlapping of $\hat{1}$. This gesture does not reinstate the initial tone structurally; rather, it is a codalike reminder of the origin of the fundamental melodic progression.)[3]

The fundamental structure of the "Feuillet d'album" conforms more closely than most of Scriabin's later tonal works to conventional tonal principles, largely because of a firmly established tonic at the beginning—although even here the actual root of the Ursatz is stated only at the end. This piece is not representative of Scriabin's more devious and idiosyncratic harmonic maneuvers; especially, it does not resemble the structure of works which avoid the tonic until the end—and the majority of his later tonal compositions have this type of structure. The problem of adequate harmonic reinforcement of the Urlinie is of course greater in these works. Because the reader is now familiar with both the analytical procedures required for a study of Scriabin's music and the techniques for representing analyses graphically, all subsequent analyses in this study are presented in their entirety only as graphic sketches.

Before proceeding to more problematic Ursatz structures, we should discuss two compositions, more complex than the "Feuillet d'album" Op. 45/1, which nevertheless are based on relatively conventional fundamental structures. The first is the Poem Op. 32/2 (example 27), whose opening progression from a dissonant chord to the tonic in m. 4 was analyzed in chapter 2 (see p. 24). The passage is merely a preface to this tonic chord, which contains both the root of the Ursatz bass line and the initial tone of the Urlinie, A. As in the opening of Op. 45/1, the $\hat{5}$ of the Urlinie is the goal of an incomplete span from the implicit octave of the tonic. The absence of the D stresses A as the main melodic note, even though it occurs only briefly in m. 4, having been displaced by suspensions. The A is more prominent in m. 5, but when the harmony turns toward G♭ major (m. 7), the enharmonic equivalent of III♯, the A no longer receives harmonic support. Instead, it moves circuitously in mm. 5–7 to B♭, its chromatic upper auxiliary. Although this motion is overshadowed by an overlapping inner voice, B♭ is prominent in the melody in m. 8, where it initiates the upper voice of a linear intervallic pattern. (For a complete discussion of this pattern, see p. 43.) The B♭ is prolonged until the pattern is broken with the French sixth chord in m. 11. Ordinarily B♭ would be incorporated into this harmony (B♭ does serve as its bass), so it is implicitly prolonged through m. 11. But in the local voice leading, B♭ descends via A (m. 10) to G♯ (m. 11). Embellished by both upper and lower chromatic auxiliary notes, A again becomes prominent as the French sixth resolves to V at m. 12. Prolonged by an unfolding down to E supported by the dominant harmony, A continues to be effective throughout the repetition of the opening phrase in mm. 14–17. Thus no descent from $\hat{5}$ occurs during the first half of the composition, and A remains in effect—even through harmonic areas which cannot themselves support it—by virtue of the prolongation of the chromatic upper auxiliary.

Meanwhile, the bass progression has arpeggiated the tonic triad from the root (m. 4) through the third, spelled G♭ instead of F♯ (m. 7), to the fifth (m. 12), then back to the root (m. 17). This arpeggiation is not the bass motion of the Ursatz, for the fifth in the Ursatz bass must support $\hat{2}$ of the Urlinie (according to strict Schenkerian theory). Rather, mm. 1–17 encompass a vast prolongation of the tonic triad, and in terms of the fundamental structure of the piece, no essential motion takes place in the first half of the piece. The return of the opening material in mm. 14–17 confirms the sense that no resolution of the opening tensions has yet been achieved.

A new variation of the original material (marked *con calore*) begins in m. 18.

Example 27 Poem Op. 32/2

The harmonic progression here resembles that of the opening material; V/V progresses to V in m. 19 just as in m. 3. Though a cadence to the tonic occurs at m. 4, however, no such cadence takes place at m. 20. Instead V^7/IV is constructed on the tonic root, continuing motion around the circle of fifths. Then V^7/IV cadences to IV at m. 21, which is stabilized further by a repetition of the cadence in the next measure. The subdominant provides ideal harmonic sup-

Example 27 (cont.)

port for $\hat{4}$ of the Urlinie, although G is obscured by overlapping voices in these measures. The subdominant is prolonged further by an unfolding to IV^6 in mm. 22–23, but G continues to be concealed by other melodic activity in higher registers until the progression to the Neapolitan sixth at m. 24. At this moment G emerges victorious in the upper register, one of the few pitches in this register to be set as a consonance. A melodic arpeggiation of the Neapolitan descends

Example 27 (cont.)

from G into the middle register and unites this strong $\hat{4}$ in the upper register with its weaker occurrences in the proper register of the Urlinie; $\hat{4}$ has thus been prolonged from m. 21 through m. 24. The high G is not itself an element of the Ursatz, but it is an important, almost essential reinforcement of the true $\hat{4}$. The bass G supporting both IV and the Neapolitan sixth is an element of the Ursatz bass and connects the tonic root and fifth in the background arpeggiation. The structural dominant follows immediately in m. 25, while $\hat{4}$ continues to be prolonged as the seventh of V^7 throughout most of this measure (although only implicitly in the proper register). At the end of m. 25 the Urlinie descends quickly through $\hat{3}$ to $\hat{2}$, and the Ursatz is completed at the beginning of the next measure with the simultaneous arrival of the tonic root in both melody and bass. The rest of the composition is obviously a coda over a tonic pedal—a culminating restatement of the opening phrase, clearer and more consonant than the startling and deceptive original. It also includes the only continuous melodic exploration of the upper registers, which previously were associated with dramatic upward leaps to unprepared dissonances.

The Poem Op. 32/2 demonstrates that the same Ursatz form which underlies the delicate and unassuming "Feuillet d'album" Op. 45/1 may also be the basis for complicated and grandiose expansions. Both compositions are relatively straightforward and conventional in projecting tonality. In contrast, the Prelude Op. 51/2, with its foreground progression almost unrelieved of dissonant chords, appears to be tenuously tonal at best. Yet this prelude is an expansion of an Ursatz form similar to those we have examined (example 28). We have seen that an opening progression from the A minor tonic to the minor dominant underlies the first eight-measure phrase of Op. 51/2 (see pp. 33–34). The fifth of the scale is conspicuous in two melodic registers—at the beginning in the middle range and an octave higher in m. 2—and either statement could qualify as the initial $\hat{5}$ of the Urlinie. In the upper range, E is embellished by its upper auxiliary supported by IV (m. 4), which returns to E with the arrival of V (m. 8). A literal transposition of the opening material with $t = 7$ ensues, effectively prolonging V. In m. 12, however, when the progression from I to IV in m. 4 is repeated at T_7, the prolonged V cadences back to I. The circular progression

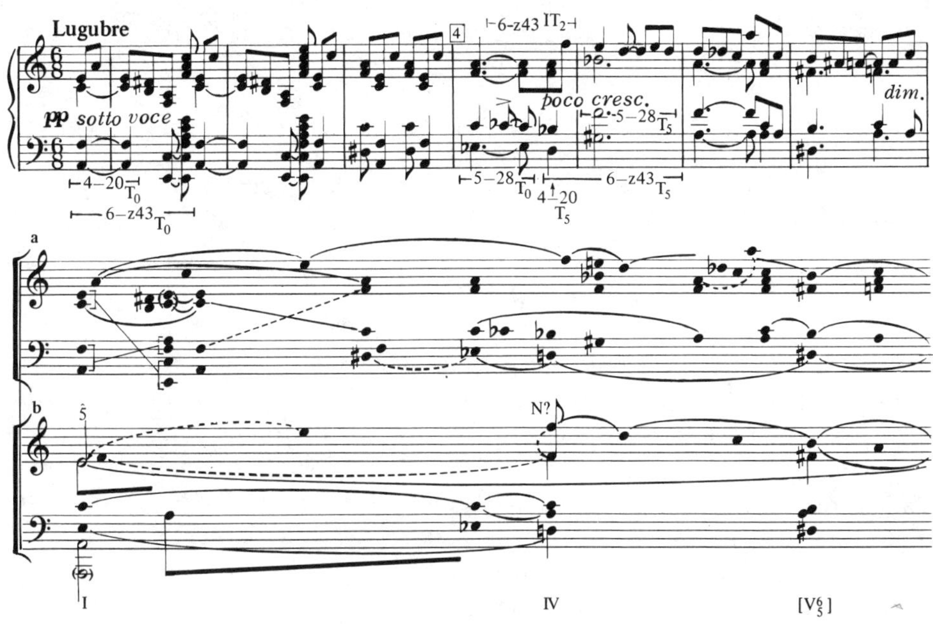

Example 28 Prelude Op. 51/2

Example 28 (cont.)

thus completed here prolongs the Ursatz tonic root in the bass and $\hat{5}$ in the Urlinie. When the tonic arrives, the middle-register E is prominent, but the higher E occurs over the prolonged tonic at m. 14. No fundamental motion has taken place up to this point in the piece, almost exactly the half-way point.[4] Rather, the first half of the piece has been devoted to the prolongation of the tonic triad which, ironically, has yet to be stated clearly at the foreground.

As if to acknowledge the completion of this vital prolongation in m. 14, Scriabin marks a pause with sixteenth rests—the first pause in the composition. (The only others occur before the repetition of the opening phrase in m. 25 and

Example 28 (cont.)

before the final cadence in m. 29.) An abrupt tonal shift follows, achieved by the literal repetition of the phrase in mm. 12–14 at T_{10}. The harmonic progression initiated by this shift is quite complex. If this passage were the same as the corresponding passages beginning in mm. 4 and 12, the low bass G would be effective throughout and the passage would prolong a ♮VII♭ harmony. However, at the end of m. 16 the low D, ostensibly part of a tenor voice (the G would presumably be effective in the bass), is transferred to the low bass. In fact D is the lowest pitch thus far, and it becomes the effective bass tone supporting IV prolonged through m. 18. In retrospect, the harmony on G is a linear chord connecting the tonic (m. 12) with the subdominant. The subdominant progresses to the dominant—the first clear function in the composition—at the end of m. 19, via a linear chord on D♯ at the beginning of m. 19, which resolves as if it were a German sixth in third inversion. As a result, the Ursatz progresses to the dominant and the Urlinie descends to $\hat{2}$. Although there are middle- and high-register alternatives for $\hat{4}$ in m. 16, the subsequent abandonment of the upper register confirms that the Urlinie occurs in the middle range. The main support for $\hat{4}$ is the IV established in m. 16, but D arrives in the course of the transpositional shift in mm. 14–16. The connecting function of this passage, however, excludes it from the fundamental progression, and thus the true $\hat{4}$ occurs only with the arrival of IV. Scale degree $\hat{3}$ is a member of the linear chord connecting IV with V, and $\hat{2}$ is supported by V.

The completion of the Ursatz motion would ideally occur at m. 20, where both the melody and the bass sound the tonic root; but instead, the fifth of the expected tonic triad is displaced by the sixth, ostensibly creating a deceptive cadence to VI^6 instead of I. The sixth does not resolve to the fifth until the final chord. The low A introduced in m. 26 (the lowest pitch in the composition) supersedes all other tonic roots and is the fundamental tone of the Ursatz. The Ursatz root has not been established in m. 20, so the Ursatz is technically incomplete. If the lowest A occurred here, the rest of the piece would be an extended suspension. Yet the effect here is certainly like the suspension of dissonant elements within a well-understood functional context. The chord at m. 20 does not behave as the typical VI^6 goal of a deceptive cadence, which would ultimately prepare the dominant. Indeed, no strong V is heard after the V in m. 19 (repeated in m. 21), which therefore must itself function as the fundamental dominant of the Ursatz. The events beginning in m. 22 are thus a delay, or perhaps a gradual realization, of the fundamental tonic, which would ideally occur immediately after the structural dominant. These measures are a coda like that in Op. 45/1, which contains the first statement of the Ursatz root. Postponing the fundamental pitch powerfully reinforces the harmonic effects at the foreground by reserving a clear statement of the tonic triad until the final cadence.

At the time of its composition in 1906, the Prelude Op. 51/2 was one of Scriabin's boldest harmonic experiments. Chords at the surface are consistently complex, and their nonfunctional (atonal) properties are exploited. (These will be discussed in the following chapter.) It may at first appear remarkable that a complete and almost conventional Ursatz form underlies the composition. Yet perhaps because of its unique powers of coherence, the Ursatz form was for Scriabin the terra firma from which his earlier experiments were launched. He achieved in Op. 51/2 what Schoenberg described as *schwebende Tonalität* (hovering tonality), although here the tonality does not drift just out of reach. On the contrary, it is the bedrock of the composition.[5]

INCOMPLETE URSATZ FORMS

The Ursatz structures of the preceding examples are relatively complete, and their fundamental lines move within single registers. These examples are not representative of Scriabin's later tonal works, in which the essential elements of conventional Ursatz structures are missing and must be assumed as implicit if one is to understand these works as tonally coherent. We have seen the need, in many of Scriabin's prolongations at middleground levels, to infer the presence of elements not actually realized in the music. Prolongations at deeper levels of structure may also occur in incomplete form.

The basic structure of the Poem Op. 32/1 is problematic: although the essential elements of the Urlinie are present, they do not occur strongly in a single register with proper harmonic support from the Ursatz bass motion (example 29). The initial tone of the Urlinie is $\hat{5}$ (C♯), which is displaced by its upper auxiliary (D♯) in m. 1 and thus is not prominent in the foreground. By m. 4, when the tonic arrives, a motion has unfolded from the melodic C♯ to A♯ in an inner voice. Yet overall the phrase prolongs the tonic and sets up C♯ as a fundamental melodic element. With a progression to IV in m. 9, the C♯ of the Urlinie moves in the same register to D♯, which is more conspicuous an octave

Example 29 Poem Op. 32/1

higher in m. 11. A linear intervallic pattern beginning in m. 11 expands the progression from IV to V, which arrives in m. 15. This pattern prolongs D♯ until C♯ returns (in the original register) supported by the dominant, which is prolonged by the pedal-point passage in mm. 15–22. The subsequent return of the opening section effects a cadence to the tonic, completing a large-scale circular progression which prolongs the tonic supporting $\hat{5}$ through m. 32. The prolongation of $\hat{5}$ by the upper auxiliary embellishment greatly expands the D♯–C♯ motive at the foreground. The upper auxiliary is again prolonged in mm. 33–36 with the repetition of the material in mm. 9–12. Here, however, the embellishment is incomplete. The V^7 harmony in m. 37 departs from both the linear

Example 29 (cont.)

intervallic pattern in progress and the repetition of material of the first section, and it supports $\hat{4}$ of the Urlinie in its original register.

The dominant seventh in m. 37 is the structural dominant of the Ursatz, for it is the last dominant before the tonic is prolonged by a tonic pedal for the rest of the piece. In order for the Urlinie to descend completely, $\hat{1}$ must arrive with the structural tonic; the tonic cannot itself provide support for $\hat{2}$, through which any Urlinie must descend. We therefore expect $\hat{4}$ to descend through $\hat{3}$ and $\hat{2}$ before the Ursatz bass progresses to the tonic root, but several events weaken

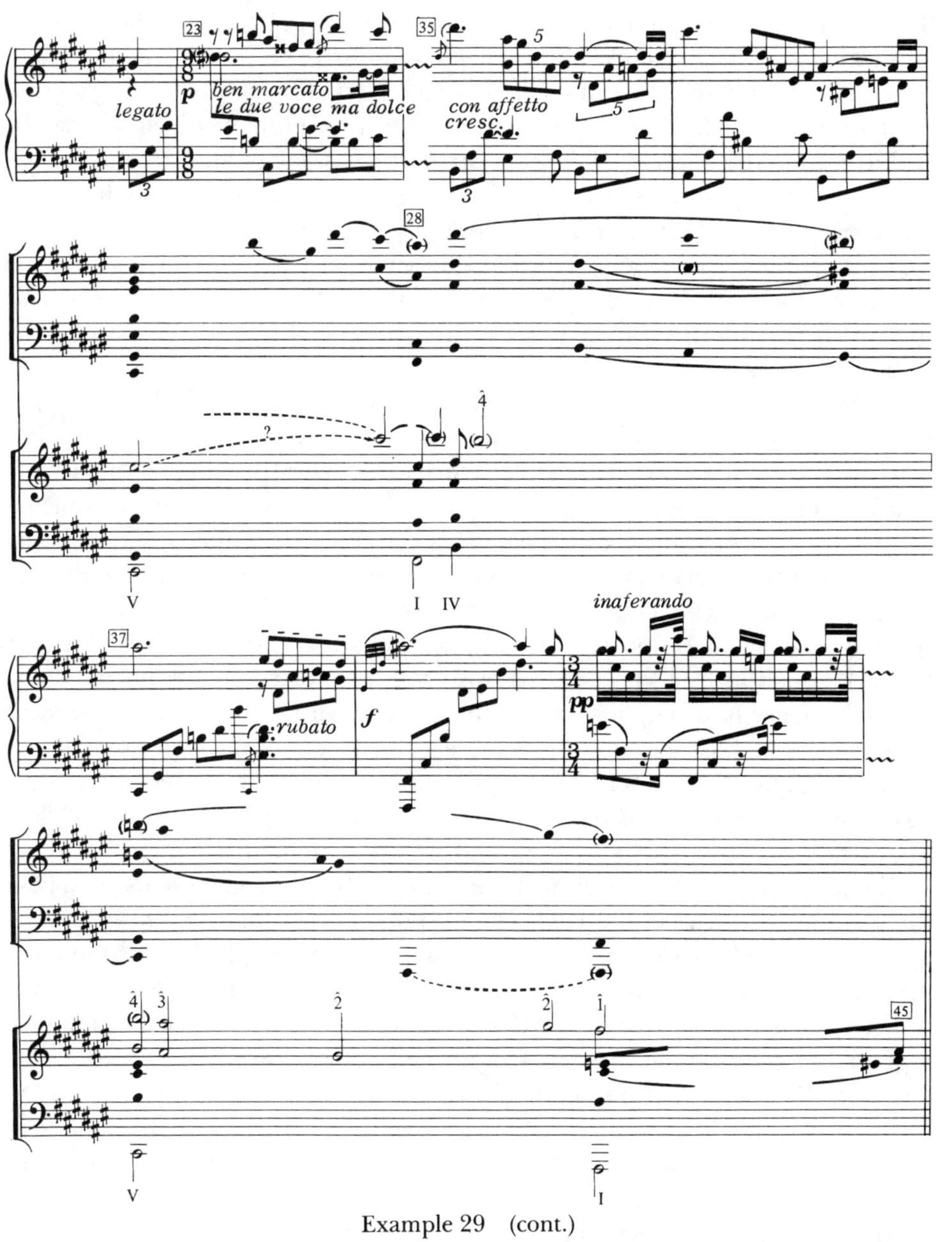

Example 29 (cont.)

that descent. First, while the structural dominant is still sounding, no strong melodic descent to $\hat{2}$ occurs. A line in m. 37—in the original register of the Urlinie—descends chromatically from A♯ to G♯, but the motion begins before B♮ ($\hat{4}$ of the Urlinie) has sounded in the main melody, and thus it appears to belong to an inner voice. The second influence weakening the Ursatz is the introduction in m. 38 of the tonic root (apparently also the root of the Ursatz). This bass tone anticipates the true Ursatz root, which should occur in m. 39.

This premature entry obscures the dominant function of the harmony of m. 38 and conflicts with the conspicuous descent from A♯ to G♯ in the upper register, which might carry the descent of the Urlinie to $\hat{2}$. (The reasons for considering the bass F♯ an anticipation, aside from the as yet uncompleted Urlinie, may be deduced from the analysis of the corresponding passage in mm. 13–15; see pp. 34–35.) This upper-register melody in m. 38 appears to be the only bearer of the motion of the Urlinie, for B♮ in the original Urlinie register is sustained throughout the measure and resolves to A♯ with the cadence to the true tonic at m. 39. Further, the F♯ prolonged prominently in the upper register over the tonic pedal for the rest of the piece is the strongest choice for the root of the Urlinie.

We have thus described an Urlinie motion divided between middle and upper melodic registers. When confronted with such an unconventional situation, it is advisable to evaluate all reasonable alternatives. One possibility would be a middle-register Urlinie which proceeds from $\hat{5}$ only as far as $\hat{3}$. The completed melodic motion of our original analysis is certainly a stronger interpretation. Another plausible analysis is that C♯ and B♮ might be strong enough in the upper register to be elements of an Urlinie moving entirely within that register. Although a high C♯ is not supported by the initial structural tonic, the high D♯ (m. 11), which in our first analysis was an upper-voice reinforcement of the upper auxiliary to $\hat{5}$, implies a C♯ in this register. In fact, it moves in the next measure to a high C♯ which, though merely an element of the continuing linear intervallic pattern, is nonetheless significant because the high register is then abandoned for many measures, leaving C♯ effectively dangling. We might then infer C♯ as an upper-voice $\hat{5}$ supported by the dominant in mm. 15–23 and anticipated in m. 12. Moreover, with the return of the opening section in m. 24, the switching of voices in invertible counterpoint effects a statement of C♯ in the upper register. This C♯ descends to B♮ in m. 26 as the prolonged dominant continues, and B♮ might reasonably serve as $\hat{4}$. This $\hat{4}$ should descend to $\hat{3}$ at the cadence to I in m. 28 but does not do so in the upper register. In m. 33 an upper-register B♮, which would serve as $\hat{4}$ supported by IV, is strongly implied by the dissonant A♯, a lower chromatic auxiliary. This implicit $\hat{4}$ would then descend to the high A♯ in m. 37 and G♯ in m. 38, both supported by the fifth of the scale in the Ursatz bass, carrying the Urlinie as far as $\hat{2}$. The Ursatz would then be completed in the next measure.

We may then choose between two imperfect statements of the basic melodic motion as the true Urlinie: either the Urlinie elements are all clearly stated, but divided between two registers, or the Urlinie is confined to the higher register with $\hat{5}$ and $\hat{4}$ only implicit. I would choose the first alternative—if indeed a choice must be made. The explicit $\hat{5}$ and $\hat{4}$ in the middle register strengthen their implied presence an octave higher, and thus the alternatives actually participate symbiotically in the Urlinie process. But an Urlinie thus formed is less coherent than single-register progressions such as those in Op. 45/1 and Op. 32/2. The Urlinie of this poem is weaker as well because of the extraordinary anticipation of the Ursatz root before the arrival of a strong $\hat{2}$. As in the other pieces, this bass root occurs in the fundamental register only after the arrival of the structural dominant, and this in itself attenuates the tonal coherence of the work.

The Poem Op. 32/1 is nevertheless a rather straightforward tonal work. Yet the implicit elements of its Urlinie and the apparent lack of foreground synchrony between the two Ursatz voices foreshadow problematic aspects of fundamental structure in many of Scriabin's later tonal works. In many pieces the Urlinie does not progress within a single register, and often elements are so conspicuously absent that we must infer a deliberate omission by the composer.

Such is the case in "Caresse dansée" Op. 57/2, where $\hat{3}$ is prolonged throughout almost the entire piece. The opening period (example 21) is a circular progression which prolongs $\hat{3}$ by a melodic unfolding from E, the third of the scale, down to C, the tonic root; the second phrase of this opening period is brought back to close the piece. In this final phrase, one would expect that the E–C unfolding would carry the Urlinie through $\hat{2}$ to $\hat{1}$. However, at the moment in the repeated version when the Urlinie should move to $\hat{2}$ (after m. 54; see example 30), Scriabin breaks the repetition, at first by a pause, then by repeating

Example 30 "Caresse dansée" Op. 57/2

the material of m. 54 an octave lower in mm. 56–57. This repeated fragment contains a D♮ in the original register of the Urlinie which might qualify as $\hat{2}$, although it implicitly resolves to D♭ (as does the D in the bass) before it can be confirmed as $\hat{2}$ by the harmonic support of V. The final cadence in mm. 58–59 does nothing to clarify matters. No descent from $\hat{2}$ to $\hat{1}$ occurs in any register; the only D here moves to D♯ in the register of a middle voice. Moreover, the leading tone is unresolved in an upper voice, where $\hat{1}$ does not occur with the arrival of the tonic. Perhaps we can infer a descent of the Urlinie in these final measures, especially in the register of middle C, for D♭ in the middle voice of mm. 56–57 is implicitly retained in the dominant chord. (The D♯ does not displace D♭ here; it is instead a brief embellishment of E which anticipates the third of the final tonic triad.) This potential ♭$\hat{2}$ resolves to middle C, which might serve as $\hat{1}$. But such inferences are pointless in light of the dramatic contrast between the simple and complete resolution of the opening period and this fragmented and unconventional variation with which Scriabin took some trouble to close the piece. "Caresse dansée" ends by virtually evaporating, an effect achieved not simply by surface features, but more by the dissolution of upper voices before the fundamental melodic motion can be completed. The analyst should not ignore the incompleteness of the Urlinie, for it affects the listener's impression. The piece is nonetheless tonally coherent because the missing elements of the Urlinie are easily inferred.

The Ursatz form of the Prelude Op. 45/3 is also incomplete, and even more vague than that of Op. 57/2 (example 31). Beneath the highly chromatic linear harmonies of the first measure lies an E♭ tonic chord, converted—as is typical of Scriabin's opening tonic harmonies—to a dominant-seventh-sounding chord by the addition of the minor seventh, D♭. The material of m. 1 is repeated in m. 3 at T_7, and thus the dominant might be understood to underlie m. 3. The whole-tone harmony in m. 2 is a linear chord which is actually a transposition of the opening chord, with $t = 7$, thus standing in the same relation to the dominant in m. 3 as does the first chord in m. 1 to the tonic. The linear progression continues through m. 3 (subsuming and thus negating any independent dominant in this measure), moving in m. 4 to a repetition of the linear chord in m. 2 at T_7. This chord, which one would expect to descend chromatically in the bass, is suddenly converted in the next measure to V/C♭ and progresses in m. 6 to a C♭ major chord, the first consonant triad in the piece. This triad is not the goal of the harmonic progression, however; it becomes ♭II/V and progresses to V/V in m. 7, which cadences to a relatively stabilized V in the next measure. Thus this entire eight-measure passage expands a I–V progression.

The most reasonable choice for the Urlinie up to this point is a motion from $\hat{3}$ (G), an element of the implicit tonic from the outset, to $\hat{2}$, clearly supported by V in m. 8. (Before descending to $\hat{2}$, G is embellished by an incomplete upper auxiliary, then moves to G♭ supported by V/♭II/V and ♭II/V in mm. 5–6; G♭ would ordinarily resolve to F of V/V.) An alternative Urlinie would begin with $\hat{5}$ (B♭) in m. 1 and descend through $\hat{4}$ (A♭ in m. 3) and ♭$\hat{3}$ (G♭ in m. 5) to $\hat{2}$. This interpretation is weak, however, because adequate harmonic support for $\hat{4}$ is

Example 31 Prelude Op. 45/3

questionable in m. 3, which is part of a linear passage involving repetition, and because ♮$\hat{3}$—so clear at the beginning—is not in this line. Moreover, there are two strong reasons for accepting the first alternative: $\hat{3}$ is melodically prominent and receives durational emphasis in m. 2, and the melodic detail resolving the suspended G to F in m. 8 summarizes the basic melodic progression up to this point.

There is one clear difficulty with the Urlinie of this composition: although the

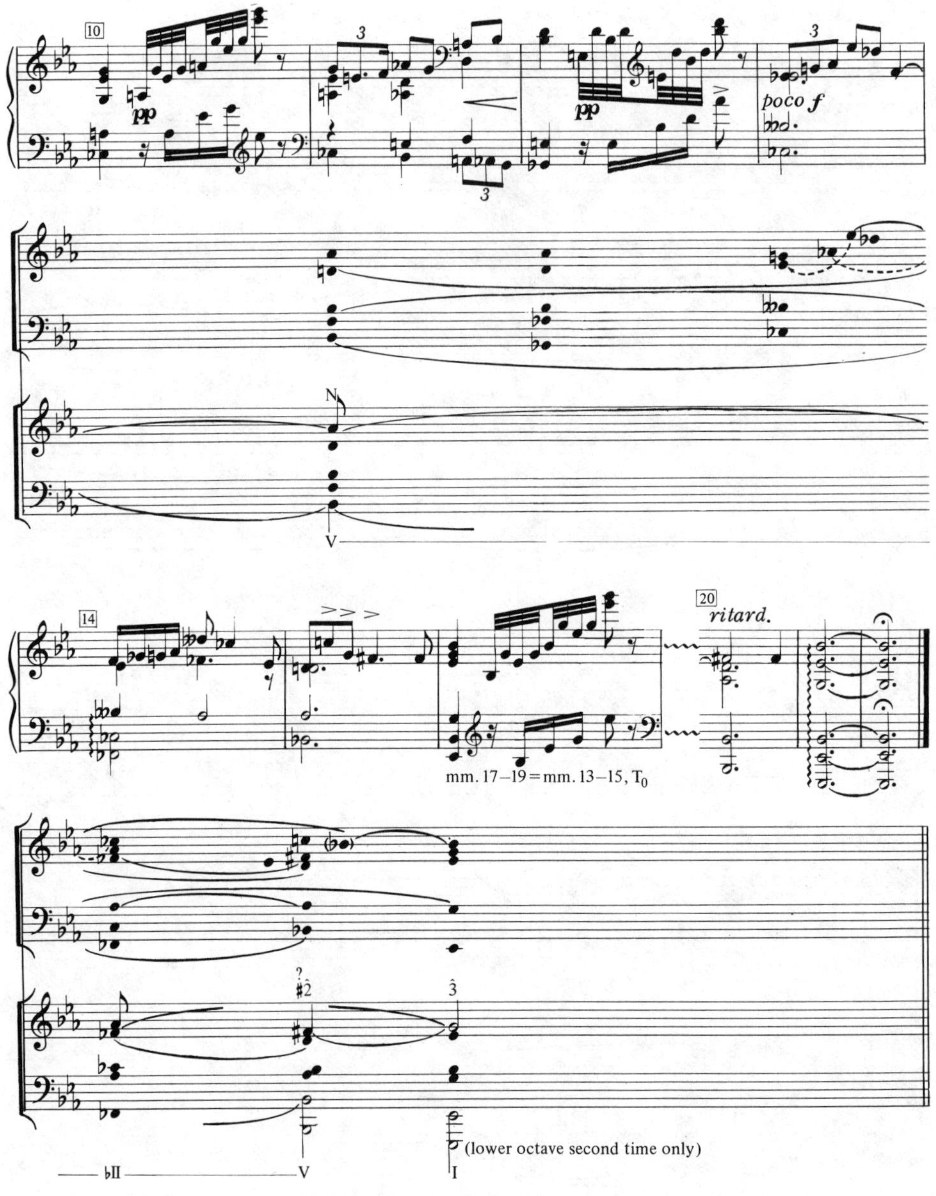

Example 31 (cont.)

tonic root is present at the beginning, a consonant tonic triad is nowhere in evidence, and thus the initial tone of the Urlinie (which must be a member of this triad) receives no consonant support. The Urlinie has almost certainly been established by m. 8; $\hat{2}$ has been attained and receives strong harmonic support from the lowest B♭ of the piece, which would appear therefore to be the structural dominant. Although $\hat{3}$ is the initial tone of the Urlinie, its consonant support must be inferred. In the many other works beginning with one or more incomplete unfoldings, consonant harmonic support for the initial tone of the Urlinie must be assumed. In most cases, however, as in this prelude, the tonic root is present in the bass and provides some reinforcement.

At the end of m. 8 the G–G♭–F motive occurs in a lower voice and connects the dominant with a repetition in mm. 9–12 of the opening phrase. The return of this material after $\hat{2}$ has been reached in the Urlinie creates the form-generating phenomenon which Schenker termed *Unterbrechung* (interruption). Because this repeated material begins with the tonic, we can interpret its return as the completion of the Ursatz—the only possible interpretation if a continuous descent of the Urlinie were mandatory. However, this analysis is unlikely for several reasons: (1) more than half of the piece remains to be heard; (2) harmonic support for $\hat{1}$ is weak in this passage (especially compared to the consonant tonic triads in mm. 16 and 21); and (3) $\hat{1}$ is not itself prominent here. Schenker found that the restatement of opening tonic material later in a composition (especially the recapitulation of thematic material in sonata form) often follows a structural dominant supporting $\hat{2}$ in the Urlinie. Such a repetition halts the Ursatz motion at this point and starts it again as if from the beginning. That the return of the opening material interrupts the Ursatz motion and reinstates $\hat{3}$ in the Urlinie is not only the most satisfactory analysis; it also demonstrates that the piece conforms to a traditional tonal procedure. The interrupted Ursatz is not, however, typical of Scriabin's later tonal structures.

After the Ursatz begins again in m. 9, the repetition of the opening phrase is unchanged until the accented A♭ at the end of m. 12. What follows is a transposition of the consequent phrase (mm. 5–8) up five half steps, which carries the progression one more step around the circle of fifths. That is, the bass progression of mm. 12–13 is the same as that of mm. 5–6 (not of the corresponding material in mm. 4–5), and thus the chord on C♭ in m. 13 is not ♭II/V (as in m. 6), but rather V/♭II in the overall tonality. The transposition ultimately prepares the cadence to the tonic in m. 16—the first consonant tonic of the piece. The entire phrase is repeated (thus stabilizing the tonic) with low bass tones added to support the final cadence in the true Ursatz register. The bass of the dominant sounds in the same register here as in m. 8, giving each note equal structural weight.

The transposition of the consequent phrase in the second half of the piece naturally affects the motion of the Urlinie. In m. 11 (as in m. 3), $\hat{3}$ is embellished by its upper auxiliary, A♭. We might then expect a descent to G♭ in m. 13 supported by the C♭ chord (as in m. 5), but G♭ is conspicuously absent in the melodic registers, and A♭ seems to be deliberately suspended through mm. 12–13 until it is adequately supported by ♭II in m. 14. The accented A♭ in the left hand at m. 12 helps to effect this suspension. It appears that A♭ is an incomplete upper neighbor to $\hat{3}$, and a descent to $\hat{2}$ should coincide with the arrival of the dominant in m. 15. Only F♯ is heard here, however, displacing F♮, the expected $\hat{2}$. The F♯ might be ♯$\hat{2}$, but it cannot carry the descending Urlinie farther. Rather, F♯ must resolve back to G when the tonic arrives, and thus the Urlinie of the second half of the piece does not successfully descend from $\hat{3}$. Ironically, $\hat{3}$ is not even present in the melodic registers of the final tonic chord but is so strongly implied that a descent from F♯ to E♭ (which seems to be the voice leading at the foreground) may not be inferred. However, the F♭ contained in ♭II (m. 14) might be an implicit ♭$\hat{2}$ retained in V (m. 15) and descending to $\hat{1}$ (m. 16).[6] This line contributes to the coherence of the final measures, yet such an implied line is structurally overshadowed by the straightforward descent to $\hat{2}$ occurring before the interruption at m. 9. We must again conclude that Scriabin deliberately chose an incomplete fundamental structure.

SYMMETRICAL URSATZ FORMS

Although Scriabin conducted his early harmonic experiments within traditional Ursatz forms, he was willing even at deep levels of structure to violate procedural norms in order to achieve particular effects. At the height of his mastery he was able to mold even the Ursatz forms according to his ideals of symmetry. For example, "Nuances" Op. 56/3, one of his most evanescent creations, has a carefully conceived symmetrical structure (example 32). The piece begins with a progression in mm. 1–2 from the tonic to the dominant, which is obscured by voices moving out of synchrony with the bass. In mm. 3–4 this material is transposed up a half step and thus might be a ♭II–V/♭II progression. After m. 4 the low bass is abandoned until the low G of m. 8, which supports the dominant. The harmonies of mm. 5–7 are difficult to decipher, but the relatively patterned voice leading here indicates movement within either a single harmonic function or a progression from one harmony to another. The intervals spanned by each voice in fact prolong the dominant seventh whose bass root arrives only in m. 8. Thus the entire second phrase (mm. 5–8) is an expanded dominant.

The dominant of m. 2 does not appear at first to be on equal structural footing with V in mm. 5–8 because it has a shorter duration and because the transpositional repetition in mm. 3–4 leads the harmonic progression away from V into the territory of ♭II. However, this brief excursion is part of an expanded V–♭II–V progression prolonging V from m. 2 through m. 8. The relation of the chord on A♭ at the end of m. 4 to subsequent harmonic events is unclear at first. Initially understood as V/♭II, it is reinterpreted as a French sixth and prepares the dominant. (Note in particular the augmented sixth between the A♭ effective in the bass and the F♯ in the melody at the end of the measure.) This harmony progresses not so much to the chord at the beginning of the next measure as to the large-scale dominant in mm. 5–8, and the connection in the low bass between mm. 4 and 8 makes the progression evident. The harmony underlying this first eight-measure phrase is a single I–V progression, to which other harmonies are subsidiary. This progression probably takes place at the Ursatz level, for it spans nearly half of the piece.

Example 32 "Nuances" Op. 56/3

Example 32 (cont.)

The fundamental melodic progression of this passage remains to be considered. Because the piece opens with voice-leading spans already in progress—one of which is the upper voice—the analyst must infer an initial melodic tone within the implicit opening tonic triad. Either C♮ or E♮ might be chosen; the latter, since it actually occurs in m. 2, is probably preferable. The decision is less important than usual, however, for the opening melodic note is not the initial tone of the Urlinie. The melody of the first four measures gradually ascends to G♮ in m. 5, which is the initial tone, $\hat{5}$, from which the Urlinie will descend. The approach to $\hat{5}$ unfolds from an inner voice to the main melodic register—a motion which Schenker termed the *Anstieg* ([initial] ascent), by which the composer may avoid an explicit foreground tonic harmonization of the main melodic note. This note is nevertheless implicit from the beginning, for the Anstieg expands a simpler statement (at a deeper level of structure) in which the main melodic tone is effective throughout. Thus the Anstieg occurs here in conjunction with a progression from the tonic to the dominant such that $\hat{5}$ is not reinforced by the tonic, nor even by a clear dominant at the foreground; rather, it arrives at the point where the unfolding of the dominant harmony begins (m. 5). However, these middleground events mean that $\hat{5}$ is supported in the background by both an initial tonic harmony and the dominant to which the tonic progresses. Underlying the obscure harmonies of the first four measures is the strict counterpoint necessary for the Anstieg to $\hat{5}$; the French sixth here provides a ♯4 (F♯) to counteract the tendency of ♮4 to descend.

One other voice deserves attention at this point. It is difficult to trace, but its main focus is the resolution of B♭, the lowered seventh prominent in the tenor range in m. 1, to B♮, its diatonic equivalent which would ideally occur in the dominant. The lowered seventh appears at first to effect a typical conversion of I into V^7/IV, yet this potential is unrealized as the harmony progresses instead to V in m. 2. Here, rather than resolving immediately back to B♮, B♭ moves to A, and we expect an unfolding toward G. This melodic tendency is also thwarted, however; sustained by an alto voice from the beginning, A moves back to B♭ in m. 3. This B♭ is then sustained in the alto through the beginning of m. 5. In mm. 5–7 an unfolding from B♭ to G coincides with other voice leadings to prolong V. The B♭ is prolonged until this unfolding is complete in m. 8, when B♭ resolves to the chord tone B♮. (Comments here relate to the middleground structure, not to the foreground.) Two analyses of this voice are possible: the seventh degree, either lowered or diatonic, is sustained throughout the passage and thus anticipates its eventual incorporation into the dominant; or an unfolding from the implicit G at the beginning (through A and B♭) to B♮ takes place in conjunction with the progression of I to V. The latter interpretation is preferable because it is based on conventional voice leading and because later developments are reciprocal to this G–B unfolding.

The second half of the piece begins in m. 9 with a repetition of m. 5. Thus, in terms of overall structure, the basic melodic line has progressed no farther in

m. 9 than the $\hat{5}$ established in m. 5. The phrase in mm. 5–8 prolongs V; beginning in m. 9 the voice leading moves instead to V/G♭ in m. 11, which then cadences to G♭ (possibly functioning as ♭V) in mm. 12–13. Measure 11 actually contains an exact repetition of the material of m. 3, repeated again in m. 14. As the harmony of m. 14 progresses to the dominant in m. 15, its function as ♭II in the overall tonal scheme is finally clear, and it becomes evident that the earlier statements of ♭II thwarted its natural function as a dominant preparation. In the background structure, the excursion into the area of G♭ in mm. 12–13 is no more than a brief delay of the progress of the Ursatz. By m. 15 the progression is back on course, and the Ursatz bass motion is complete in m. 17. The progression from V in m. 8 to its recurrence in mm. 15–16 is thus another expansion of the V–♭II–V dominant prolongation like that earlier in mm. 2–8; the dominant has in fact been prolonged from m. 2 until the final cadence.

The motion of the Urlinie above this prolongation is problematic, and it appears—especially in view of the prominent ♯$\hat{2}$ supported by the dominant—that the Urlinie never descends below $\hat{3}$. The exact means of descending from $\hat{5}$ to $\hat{3}$ is made questionable by the cadence to G♭. As usual, $\hat{4}$ is supported by ♭II, but it is unclear whether this structural ♭II is located in m. 11 or m. 14. The ♭II in m. 11 is concealed as an independent function by its use as both an element of a continuing progression and a secondary dominant of G♭. If this harmony is entirely secondary, however, then the progression beginning in m. 9 must be a prolonged progression from V to ♭V, which would be extremely unconventional—especially for the deep structure of a work—for it entails parallel octaves and fifths. The only compelling feature of this analysis is the implicit upper-voice G♭ supported by ♭V, which would be a chromatic passing tone between $\hat{5}$ and $\hat{4}$. We might also consider ♭II to be prolonged throughout mm. 11–14, an interpretation which might be preferred (despite the weakened first presentation of ♭II in m. 11) because it uses more conventional voice leading in the middleground, and because the use of precisely the same material in mm. 11 and 14 encloses and defines an area of the composition. This analysis may be refined, however, to stipulate that the material in m. 11 only anticipates the ♭II function fully realized in m. 14, and does not itself support $\hat{4}$. Thus the G♭ harmony of mm. 12–13—a digression from the main structure—provides a consonant setting for a melodic G♭ which is a passing tone to $\hat{4}$ supported by ♭II in m. 14 and by V in mm. 15–16. (Neither melodic element is explicitly stated here, however.)

The symmetry of the Ursatz of "Nuances" is now apparent. The exact first half is based on a progression from I to V, and the second half closes back to I. The initial $\hat{5}$ of the Urlinie is reached by a chromatic Anstieg from E to G, and the Urlinie then descends chromatically back to E ($\hat{3}$). Each Ursatz line is thus divided symmetrically by a G (the Urlinie G three octaves above the Ursatz bass G) in mm. 8–9, and the progression to each G is mirrored by what follows it. Another symmetry occurs in the bass at a deep middleground level: on one side of the central G, A♭ (the bass of the French sixth) occurs as the upper chromatic auxiliary, and on the other side G is embellished by the lower chromatic auxiliary, G♭ (the bass of ♭V).[7] Thus the entire bass pattern is both horizontally and vertically symmetrical relative to the central G. The symmetry of the entire piece is illustrated in example 33.

For a complete analysis of "Nuances," we must consider the large-scale progressions of the inner voices. An important unfolding spans the entire piece in the tenor register and is carried primarily by the lowest voice in the passages in mm. 5–7 and mm. 9–11. The first sequence effects the motion F–E♭–D, which in the I–V background progression is part of an implicit span from G to D. The motion from F begins again in m. 9 but moves this time to D♭, adding to the span from the implicit G: G–F–E♭–D–D♭. Clearly the span would fill in the G–C fifth of the tonic triad by descending at the end to C; although C does not occur in the expected register, it may be inferred. Thus a complete descent from the fifth to the tonic root implicitly spans the entire work—but in an inner voice, not in the melody, where the descent from $\hat{5}$ is impeded.

The unfolding from G to B in the alto register in the first half of the piece has in the second half a mirror-image counterpart, which moves (in the middleground) from B (m. 8) through B♭ (m. 12) and A♭ (m. 14) to a G implied in m. 15. This unfolding prolongs B through the entire second half; B is even conspicuously unresolved in the final tonic harmony. Ideally this B would resolve to C, completing an ascent from the implicit G begun in m. 1. Thus both inner voices fill in G–C intervals (in both cases the initial G is implicit) over the course of the composition, the tenor descending a fifth while the alto ascends a fourth.

The harmonies of this work all but melt into one another (indeed, the composer marked the piece *fondu, velouté,* designations which might belong in a cu-

Example 33 "Nuances" Op. 56/3:
Symmetrical Structure

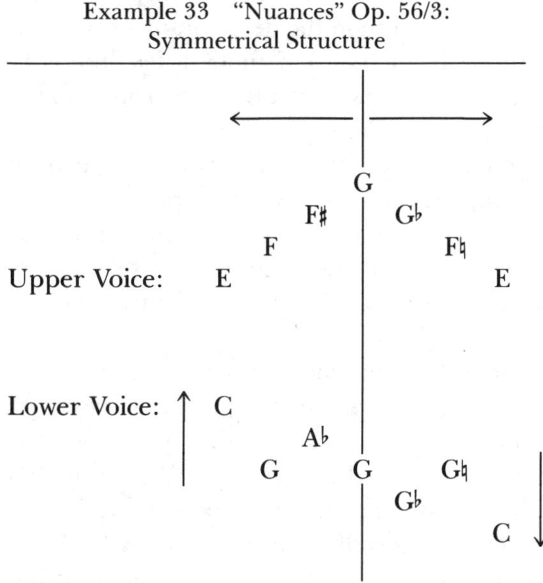

linary treatise), so at first it may seem ironic that the composition has such a logical structure. The title "Nuances" suggests the composer's desire to create subtle variations and shadings.[8] Such delicate distinctions may not be drawn in a formless vacuum, however; a musical event has meaning only in relation to structural norms, and Scriabin's formalistic symmetrical structure is thus an ideal framework for a study of tonal nuances. "Nuances" is not, however, the only instance of tonal formalism underlying an ostensibly indeterminate surface. For example, "Désir" Op. 57/1 also exploits the Anstieg to create a symmetrical progression in the fundamental melody.

The hierarchical structures of Scriabin's late tonal works are in no sense mere vestiges of the tonal system. The normal relations among elements and functions in the tonal hierarchy are preserved, but this tonality is more vague than in earlier tonal music because of such unconventional and abstruse prolongational methods as unsynchronized voice leading and incomplete unfoldings. Essential structural elements are often unstated but can always be inferred. Thus the seeming indeterminateness of Scriabin's late tonal structures is not the result of real structural ambiguity. The bewilderment we may experience on first hearing this music arises from a lack of explicitly delineated tonal gestures.

MOTIVIC COHERENCE AND ORGANIC UNITY

Scriabin depended on the tonal system for a sense of security as he proceeded with his harmonic experimentation. He also exploited the potential of that system for motivic coherence by saturating a composition with a unifying melodic or harmonic motive at various levels of structure. We have already seen such multileveled motivic statements. For instance, in the Poem Op. 32/1 (example 29) the fifth of the scale (C♯) is embellished by its upper neighbor (D♯) not only at the surface (mm. 1–5) but also in the deep middleground underlying the first half of the piece. Similarly, the G–G♭–F motion descending from $\hat{3}$ to $\hat{2}$ in the Prelude Op. 45/3 (mm. 1–8) shows up at the foreground in m. 8 (example 31).

Two more examples of motivic unity among levels of structure will demonstrate Scriabin's ingenuity in creating coherent tonal structures. The first is the Etude Op. 56/4, a complete analysis of which is presented in example 34. Commentary will be limited to deeper middleground and background structures, for the events at other levels were discussed in examples 6a–c, 8, and 23a.

The first four-measure phrase opens to (and prolongs) a $V^{7}_{\flat 5}$ chord on G, which cadences to a C major harmony in mm. 7–8. In the overall tonality, C major would function as ♭V—the most distant harmony (in terms of the circle of fifths) from the G♭ tonic. Here, however, it is a pivot chord in a modulation to B major—the enharmonic equivalent of the subdominant. The C major harmony in m. 8 becomes ♭II/IV and progresses to V/IV in m. 9, with a cadence to IV in mm. 11–12. This ♭II–V–I progression occurs locally and prolongs IV at a deeper level, where IV prepares the structural dominant; V arrives in m. 12 and is prolonged, through both a repetition in mm. 13–16 of the opening phrase

Example 34 Etude Op. 56/4

Example 34 (cont.)

and a circle-of-fifths progression in subsequent measures, until the cadence to the structural tonic at m. 20.

The varied repetition of the opening phrase in the coda (mm. 25–31) stresses an important play on the function of the whole-tone $V^{7}_{\flat 5}$ chord, heard at the beginning as V/C but reinterpreted by the end as V in the key of G♭. The conversion occurs in m. 12, immediately after the arrival of IV; there the chord occurs with the same pitch content as in mm. 4–5 but with D♭ in the bass instead of G, and thereafter D♭ is the effective bass tone. (Eventually D♭ becomes the bass of a conventional V^7 before the structural cadence.) The conversion of $V^{7}_{\flat 5}$ /C into $V^{7}_{\flat 5}$ /G♭ determines the background of the first half of the composition. Although the original chord at first appears to function merely as a secondary dominant of C—which itself plays a secondary role—it is in fact of great structural importance. In the overall tonality it progresses to V (via IV in mm. 11–12) and functions as ♭II. Therefore the ♭II–V–I progression at the surface also occurs at the deepest levels of the composition. The sketch demonstrates that the ♭II–V progression in the background supports C♭ (at first spelled B♮) as $\hat{4}$ of the Urlinie, which resolves to B♭ ($\hat{3}$) at the structural cadence. The C♭ may actually be either an upper auxiliary to $\hat{3}$, which would begin the Urlinie, or $\hat{4}$ passing to $\hat{3}$ from an implicit $\hat{5}$ (D♭). The high E♭ in the final chord—an unessential dissonance which should resolve to D♭—strongly suggests the second interpretation, which requires the inference of the tonic supporting $\hat{5}$ at the beginning of the Ursatz.

In the Prelude Op. 48/4, the harmonic and melodic progression at the background (or deep middleground) constitutes a vast expansion of foreground events in mm. 1–4. (For analytical sketches, see example 35.) The opening phrase prolongs V^7 by a bass arpeggiation in mm. 1–2 (via the lowered fifth,

Example 35 Prelude Op. 48/4

resulting in a progression by tritone), followed by a harmonic progression in m. 3 which modifies (and thus prolongs) the dominant. This progression exploits the dual dominant property in the progression from the chord on A♭ to the one on D. The functional progression of mm. 3–4 is V/♭VI–♭VI–V/V–V. The melody of the entire first phrase unfolds the octave between the high G in m. 1 and the G at the end of the phrase; the latter is the initial tone of the Urlinie. This G

Example 35 (cont.)

would ideally be supported by a tonic chord at the beginning, which is implied by the tonic root in the bass, but at first G is displaced in the melody by G♯ moving to A, the upper auxiliary, which does not resolve to a strongly supported melodic G in the register of the Urlinie until the end of the phrase. (Even there G is displaced from the downbeat of m. 4 by A, occurring now as an accented passing tone.)

The rest of the composition is determined by expansions of the harmonic and melodic events of the first phrase. The dominant is prolonged until the final cadence to the tonic in m. 23 but this does not preclude harmonic variety. At the background, V is prolonged, from m. 4 until its reappearance in m. 16, by a large-scale tritone bass progression, V–♭II–V, formed with the D♭ harmony in m. 10, which is virtually equidistant from each of these dominant chords. The bass of this ♭II harmony, the lowest pitch thus far, is attained by a bass arpeggiation from G (m. 4) through E (m. 8), which divides the G–D♭ tritone symmetrically. The E supports an E major harmony which serves no real harmonic function but is merely a consonant setting of contrapuntal events. The return from ♭II to V is managed by a sequence which expands the harmonic progression of m. 3: V/♭VI (m. 12) – ♭VI (m. 14) – V/V (m. 15) – V (m. 16). The events in the Urlinie through m. 16 are also familiar from the foreground of the first phrase. The E major chord in m. 8 supports a G♯ to which G♮ ($\hat{5}$) would normally progress. Only implicit in the main melodic register in m. 8, G♯ will appear in this register as A♭ supported by ♭II in m. 10. The A♭ is prolonged through ♭VI in m. 14 but resolves up to A♮ in m. 15. This G♯–A♭–A♮ motion is a vast expansion of the first two notes of the melody. That these two motions represent the same motive, at widely separated levels of structure, is confirmed by the fact that the same material is used at both m. 4 and m. 16 to resolve the upper auxiliary, A, back to $\hat{5}$.

The rest of the piece, aside from the final cadence, varies the first phrase. The most significant deviation is the use of the chord on A♭ in m. 19 as V/♭II (compare m. 3), which progresses precipitously to ♭II. The low D♭ supporting ♭II here is still the lowest pitch so far, and thus this statement of ♭II is linked with its occurrence in m. 10. This ♭II progresses directly to V—condensing the progression of mm. 10–16—which cadences to the first consonant tonic triad of the piece. The low C of this tonic, the lowest pitch of the piece, resolves the low D♭ of ♭II. The descent of the Urlinie also begins with ♭II in m. 19, which supports $\hat{4}$, and proceeds only to $\hat{3}$, clear from the anticipated E in the dominant in m. 22.

Before concluding this discussion of structural coherence in Scriabin's later tonal works, a final question should be considered: are the pieces collected under a single opus number unified by a single Ursatz structure? There is every indication that Scriabin conceived of his small pieces as independent of others in the same opus collection. His recitals seldom included a complete opus, and works such as "Nuances" Op. 56/3, "Fragilité" Op. 51/1, and "Désir" Op. 57/1 were often performed separately from other pieces in their collections. Each work successfully projects its own tonality and is structurally independent of other pieces. Nevertheless, motivic materials sometimes link adjacent pieces in a set. In no case do these effect large-scale prolongations between the compositions; rather, they simply facilitate transition, should a performer wish to play the complete opus. Such linkings occur in Op. 52, where "Enigme" (No. 2) is connected motivically with Nos. 1 and 3.[9]

I will discuss here the connection between "Nuances" Op. 56/3 and the Etude

Op. 56/4, both of which have been analyzed thoroughly in this chapter. Example 36 shows the final measures of "Nuances" and the opening phrase of the Etude. The final tonic chord of "Nuances" dies away without resolving the suspended leading tone; in a performance of this work alone, the listener would easily infer the resolution—while savoring the subtle effect of Scriabin's actual closing harmony. If the performance continued with Op. 56/4, however, an astute listener would hear a connection between the unresolved leading tone of the preceding piece and B♮, an element of V^7/C in m. 4 of the Etude, which occurs in the same register. In fact, there is also a link in the bass between V/C in m. 5 and the dominant in m. 16 of "Nuances." In the Etude, V^7/C cadences to C major in mm. 7–8, where the melodic B resolves to the high C expected at the end of the preceding piece. This melodic C does not complete the structure of "Nuances"; in fact, Scriabin avoids stabilizing C at this point. However, he does seem to allude satirically to the theoretical "predicament" at the close of "Nuances." Further, though it is not structurally essential, the performance of Op. 56/3 before Op. 56/4 enhances as well the irony of the cadence to C major in the latter work.

Example 36 "Nuances" Op. 56/3, end; Etude Op. 56/4, beginning

After "Nuances" the listener accepts C major as the tonic function of the Etude and through mm. 7–8 has been given little indication to the contrary. The ensuing sequence, which redirects the progression toward the true tonic—G♭ major!—comes as a tremendous jolt.[10]

Even the vaguest forms examined in this chapter possess tonal Ursatz structures. In no case has it been necessary to posit unusual background progressions, such as the contextually determined Ursatz structures involving "contrapuntal-structural" chords in many of Felix Salzer's analyses of twentieth-century compositions.[11] Scriabin's transitional music does not represent the categories of "extended" or "hovering" tonality into which so many late- and posttonal works have been placed. Rather, each work is constructed upon a conventional Ursatz—a foundation whose strength is not abated even though parts of it may exist only in concept.

FOUR
ASPECTS OF ATONALITY IN THE TRANSITIONAL MUSIC

In the preceding chapters we have seen that Scriabin's compositions from Op. 32/2 to Op. 57 (composed 1903–07) have traditional tonal structures. Elements of these structures are often not explicit but may always be inferred. In these highly experimental works Scriabin depended on prolongational procedures and especially on the Ursatz formations to unify the unconventional harmonies and progressions at the surface of his music. Indeed, most of his innovative melodic and harmonic procedures function within tonal prolongations. Yet the analyses already presented treat Scriabin's harmonic experimentation only as a deviation from traditional practice—essentially a negative viewpoint. This chapter focuses on the nature of Scriabin's innovations, particularly of the basic components of harmonic and melodic structure. Traditional classifications are clearly not sufficiently specific for such a study. If considered as pitch-class sets, however, Scriabin's unconventional components may be precisely analyzed within the framework of the set complex. Therefore the theory of the set complex will be the basis of our observations.

The theory of pitch-class set relations and complexes of relations has been comprehensively set forth by Allen Forte in his pioneering study, *The Structure of Atonal Music.*[1] Because Forte's work contains the first systematic classification of pitch-class sets (henceforth *pc sets*), I will adopt his definitions and methods of notation. (For brief definitions of set-theoretic terms, see the appendix.) Forte's book deals exclusively with music written after the abandonment of traditional tonality but before the adoption of the twelve-tone system; he makes no specific claim that his theoretical framework applies to compositions which possess tonal structures but nonetheless employ unconventional components and procedures. He states that where traditional harmonic and contrapuntal "constraints are not operative, one is obliged to seek other explanations."[2] In Scriabin's compositions of 1903–07 tonal forces determine structure at all levels but do not in themselves provide a complete explanation of his innovations. Significantly, Forte has determined that Scriabin's later works exhibit atonal structural relationships (he mentions the Sixth, Seventh, and Ninth sonatas and the Poem Op. 63/1). This suggests an added reason for examining the pc-set structure of

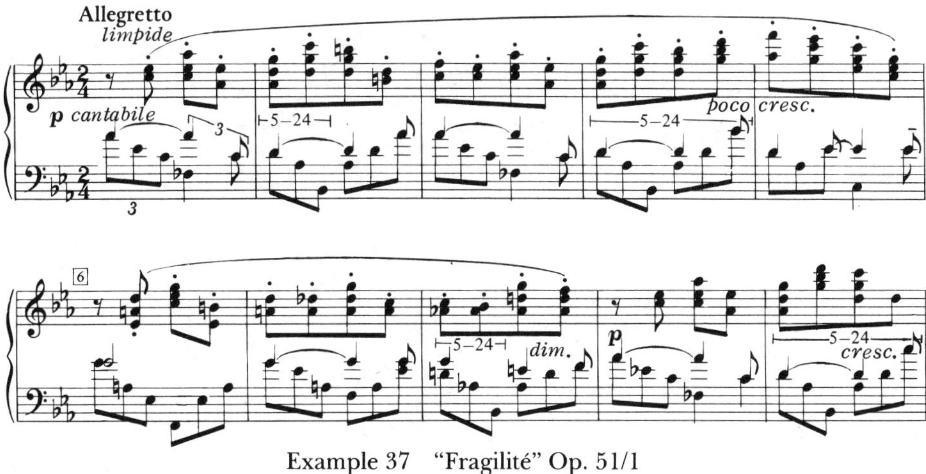

Example 37 "Fragilité" Op. 51/1

Scriabin's late tonal music: by studying both the tonal and the later works within the single framework of the set complex, we will be able to trace more precisely his evolution to atonality.

IDENTICAL AND EQUIVALENT SETS

In Scriabin's late tonal compositions, unity is achieved to a certain extent by the frequent recurrence of a limited number of unusual sonorities peculiar to each composition. The music is permeated by characteristic sonorities which retain their structural identities even in different contexts or configurations at the surface. In the simplest cases these sonorities are identical pc sets.

Example 37 illustrates four statements of the collection [7,8,10,0,2] which Forte designates as set 5–24 and which occurs in slightly varied arrangements at the opening of "Fragilité" Op. 51/1. Here each statement is associated with the dominant, and the set might be identified as a V^{13}_{9} chord. The set name is a more specific label, for different V^{13} chords can form different sets depending on either the modality of the piece or which intervals of the chord are omitted. Further, because a single set may be formed in various ways and need not be linked to a particular tonal function, functional designations often fail to identify equivalent sets. Melodic segments are especially difficult to analyze traditionally, but ascertaining the set identity of a collection—whether vertically or horizontally distributed, or both—insures maximum control of analytical data. Example 38 demonstrates the pc-set identity of two simultaneous lines at the beginning of the Poem Op. 32/1. Each contains [7,8,10,11,0,1,3] and thus forms the same set, 7–11, a fact likely to go unnoticed in a conventional analysis.

Although Scriabin usually employs characteristic sets throughout a composition, he occasionally reinforces formal divisions by limiting certain sets to particular sections. In "Ironies" Op. 56/2, pc set 6–34—most familiar as the mystic chord of *Prometheus* Op. 60—frequently appears, but only in the A section; a

Example 38 Poem Op. 32/1

new set, 6–Z26, occurs exclusively in the B section as a characteristic sonority. Sets 6–34 and 6–Z26 differ markedly in intervallic content, sharing only one corresponding interval-vector entry (for interval class 3). Example 39a shows two occurrences (mm. 8 and 33) of pc 6–34 [11,1,3,5,7,8]; example 39b illustrates two presentations (mm. 52 and 66) of 6–Z26 [11,0,2,4,6,7]. Neither pair of pc sets is linked to a single harmonic function, even though each pair involves identical pitch content.

The pc-set identity underlying these varied presentations might be discovered simply on the basis of their identical pc content, regardless of other properties of the set. However, these sets share not only pc content but also interval-class (ic) content. Collections of pitches which are not identical may still form equivalent sets, according to Forte, "if and only if they are reducible to the same prime form by transposition or by inversion followed by transposition."[3] Scriabin goes far beyond the mere repetition of identical pc collections; his late tonal music is saturated with transpositionally and inversionally equivalent sets, and applying Forte's analytical methods and nomenclature is invaluable to the analyst who wishes to grasp the unity created by Scriabin's surface sonorities.

Example 39a "Ironies" Op. 56/2

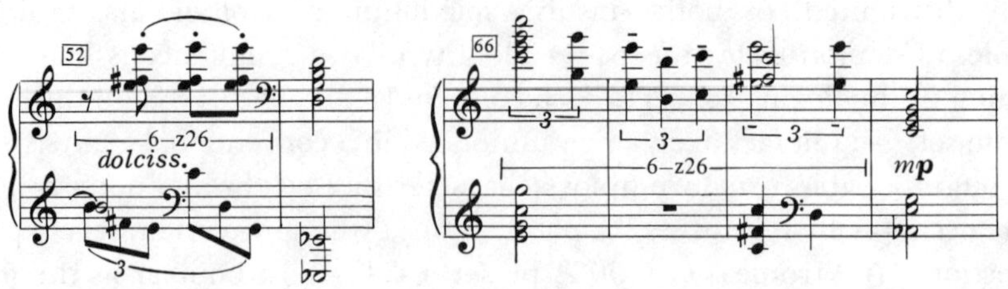

Example 39b "Ironies" Op. 56/2

Examples 40–42 illustrate occurrences of transpositionally equivalent sets which relate diverse events. The opening phrase of the Prelude Op. 48/2 is made exceptionally coherent by the recurrence of two important sets. As indicated in example 40, 5–27 occurs three times consecutively; the second and third are exact repetitions of the first at T_8 and T_2 respectively. Scriabin's remarkable control of sonority is especially evident here because the harmony appears to be secondary to the chromatic voice leading. Further, 7–Z17 is formed by the first and last chord connections within the phrase (the second at T_2), unifying the phrase as a coherent gesture.[4] Similarly, the statement of 7–35 at both the beginning and the end of the A section of the Poem Op. 32/1 delimits the section. Example 41a shows 7–35 formed in the opening phrase by the melody and the grace notes at the beginning of m. 2, which, although not in the main melodic register, are clearly notated as pertaining to the upper voice. In mm. 13–14 (example 41b), 7–35 is the composite of all voices and is equivalent to the first occurrence at T_5. One form of 7–35 is the diatonic major scale; the scale in mm. 13–14 is C♯ major—corresponding to the modulation to the dominant of F♯ major at this point. Yet the first statement of 7–35, which would be a G♯ major scale, bears no functional relation to the harmony supporting that

Example 40 Prelude Op. 48/2

Example 41a Poem Op. 32/1

Example 41b Poem Op. 32/1

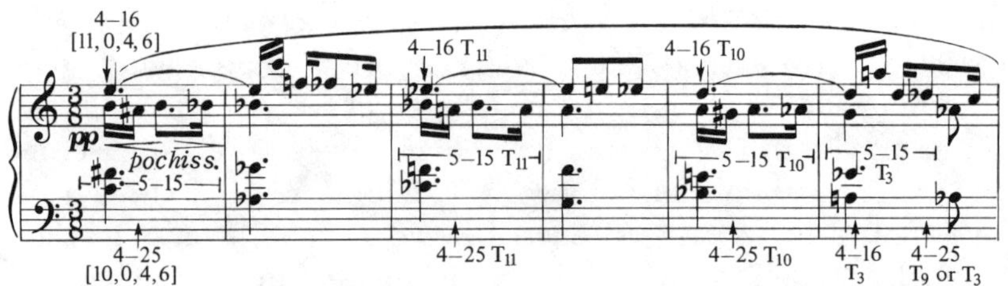

Example 42 "Caresse dansée" Op. 57/2

melodic presentation; thus diatonic sets may be involved in nontonal as well as tonal relations.

The final example of transpositional equivalence is the sequential opening phrase of "Caresse dansée" Op. 57/2 (analyzed as example 21 and also discussed on pp. 63–64). For pc-set structure, the patterned voice leading might best be traced in terms of 4–25, the second verticality in m. 1 (example 42). In m. 3, 4–25 is heard at T_{11} and continues to descend chromatically through T_{10} in m. 5 to T_9 in m. 6. This pattern continues beyond the unexpected events at the beginning of m. 6, which would seem to indicate a breakdown of the sequential motion. (Indeed, 4–25 at T_9 arrives a measure earlier than anticipated.) The entire pattern of the sequence involves other pc sets, including 4–16, the first verticality in m. 1, and 5–15, the union of 4–16 and 4–25 in m. 1. The chromatic descent of 4–16 and 5–15 accompanies that of 4–25 as far as T_{10} in m. 5; thereafter their motion is disrupted even though 4–25 descends another half step in m. 6. Instead of introducing new sets at the point of breakdown, however, a tactic which might impair the coherence of the phrase, Scriabin continues in m. 6 with the basic sets 4–16 and 5–15—but at an unexpected level of transposition, T_3, a tritone from the expected T_9. Thus Scriabin achieves a continuity of sonority even while breaking the sequential pattern, a feat possible because 4–25 replicates its entire pc content at T_6; thus the set may continue the expected pattern (at T_9) and yet belong to 5–15 a tritone away from its expected occurrence. This and similar structural characteristics of other sets are discussed when pc invariance is considered below.

Examples 43–44 demonstrate pc-set equivalences, determined by inversion followed by transposition, which might resist conventional analysis more than previous examples. Example 43 shows mm. 1–2 of "Nuances" Op. 56/3, where 5–27 prevails: three statements occur here (labeled A, B, and C respectively).

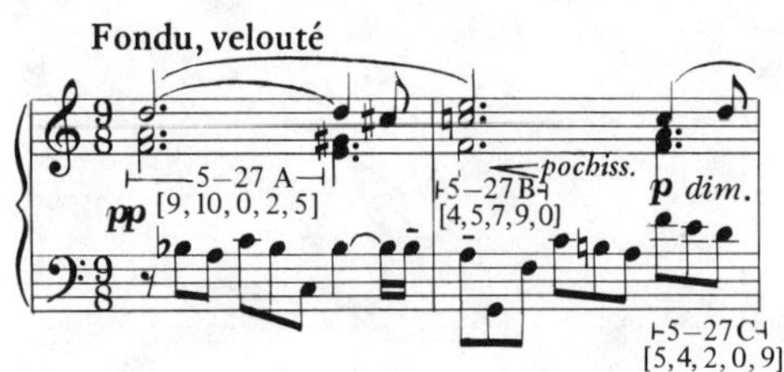

Example 43 "Nuances" Op. 56/3

Example 44 Prelude Op. 48/2

Set B is a transposition of set A with t = 7, and these two set-forms share three pcs—0, 5, and 9. (No more than three pcs can be held invariant between two forms of 5–27 equivalent under transposition.) Set C is inversionally related to A and B; it is equivalent to the inversion of A transposed with t = 2 (or, more conveniently, equivalent at IT_2) and equivalent to B at IT_9. Most remarkable about A and B and their inversionally equivalent set-form C is that C shares *four* invariant pcs with each: [0,2,5,9] (or 4–26) with A and [0,4,5,9] (or 4–20) with B. In this instance, inversional equivalence is strongly reinforced by maximum pc invariance.

Example 44 shows two inversionally related (hereafter *I-related*) statements of 8–19 which increase the coherence of the first phrase of the Prelude Op. 48/2, some aspects of which were discussed in example 40. The second 8–19 is the inversion of the first at IT_0; together they account for almost every pitch in the phrase. The E♭ at the end of the second beat of m. 1 belongs to the second 8–19 (it embellishes D here just as later). The only element foreign to both sets is C♯ at the end of m. 2. By this point the phrase is effectively over and C♯ is part of an embellished echoing of the cadence which has just occurred. Here the identity of the two eight-note sets is not strongly reinforced by shared pitches. four pcs [10,0,2,6] are retained—the minimum number for invariance under transposition for this set. Together they form 4–24, a subset of the whole-tone scale.) Nevertheless, the fact that these two collections are identical in ic content is important for the continuity and integrity of the phrase.

Although sets can technically be equivalent only on the basis of transposition or inversion, certain pairs are similar because of identical interval contents, even though they are not reducible to a single prime form. The fact that a set shares the same ic content (as listed in the interval vector) with another (nonequivalent) set is indicated by a *Z* before the ordinal number in the set name; for example, 4–Z15 and 4–Z29 have the same vector. In general for sets of any cardinal number, the Z-relation is seldom significant in Scriabin's music—at least before 1910—for only one set of a Z-related pair is usually employed in a composition. Thus 4–Z29 appears conspicuously at least a dozen times in "Ironies" Op. 56/2, but 4–Z15 never occurs. On the other hand, 4–Z15 is heard several times in the Prelude Op. 51/2, yet 4–Z29 is entirely absent. Example 45 illustrates a rare occurrence of both Z-related sets in "Fragilité" Op. 51/1. In m. 8, 4–Z15 is heard briefly, and two measures later 4–Z29 appears. Both sets are forms of the all-

Example 45 "Fragilité" Op. 51/1

interval tetrachord, containing each interval class only once, yet they are not equivalent either transpositionally or inversionally. The Z-relation is strongly reinforced by a shared three-note subset, [2,7,8], and thus the sets are as similar as possible in pc content.

COMPLEMENTATION

Example 46 illustrates that the continuity of the opening phrase of "Ironies" Op. 56/2 is guaranteed by contiguous presentations of the complements 7–13 (mm. 2–3) and 5–13 (m. 4).[5] These sets are not literal complements, for they share several pcs; they are, however, similar in the balance of their ic contents.

Complementation with regard to hexachords is complex because it is connected with the Z-relation. In twenty cases out of fifty, the complement of a six-note set is the same set. In all other cases the complement is the Z-correspondent. Although Scriabin did not generally exploit the Z-relation before 1910, he often used Z-related hexachords significantly. Few of his late tonal works stress Z-relations between sets of cardinal numbers other than six, so that the Z-relation appears to be simply concomitant with complementation between hexachords. Example 47 illustrates the unifying effect of Z-related hexachords

Example 46 "Ironies" Op. 56/2

Example 47 Prelude Op. 48/2

within the first phrase of the Prelude Op. 48/2. The melody of the entire phrase forms 6–Z44, while its Z-correspondent, 6–Z19, comprises all parts at the end of the phrase (the first three beats of m. 2).

Curiously, Scriabin frequently presents Z-related hexachords in close proximity, often as adjacent chords. For example, in Op. 48/2, 6–Z46 appears at the end of m. 5 and is immediately followed by its Z-correspondent, 6–Z24 (example 48). A favorite pairing is 6–Z10 and 6–Z39; in "Caresse dansée" Op. 57/2 they are formed at the V/V–V cadence ending the first phrase (example 49). A more complex presentation occurs in the "Feuillet d'album" Op. 45/1. In m. 2 the sum of all activity is 6–Z39 (example 50a). When repeated as the coda of the piece, this material is modified slightly so that A♮ in the bass in m. 22 descends directly to A♭ in the next measure (example 50b). As a result m. 22 contains a five-note subset (5–26) of 6–Z39 heard in m. 2. A further change is

Example 48 Prelude Op. 48/2

Example 49 "Caresse dansée" Op. 57/2

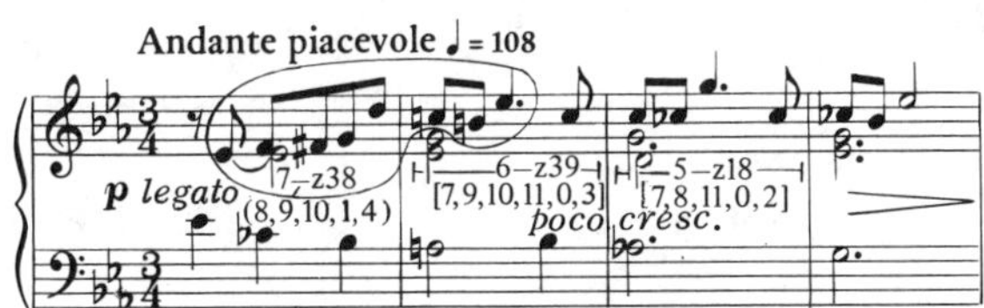

Example 50a "Feuillet d'album" Op. 45/1

Example 50b "Feuillet d'album" Op. 45/1

effected in m. 23 with the introduction of the dominant bass tone beneath the material of m. 3. The six-note set thus formed is 6–Z10, clearly paired with 6–Z39 in concept even though the sets are not stated contiguously in either mm. 2–3 or mm. 22–23. The first phrase of the "Feuillet d'album" (example 50a) also contains a rare instance of sets other than hexachords which are connected by both the Z-relation and complementation. The melody of mm. 1–2 forms 7–Z38, and 5–Z18 (the Z-correspondent of 5–Z38) comprises the material in m. 3.

Because every set of fewer than six elements (except 5–Z12) is a subset of its complement, the embedded complement is not noteworthy in the abstract; however, clear compositional presentations of this relation are extraordinary. In Scriabin's late tonal works, sets are often infixed in their complements. The cadence to V^7 at the end of the opening of the Prelude Op. 48/4 involves an interesting arrangement of related sonorities (example 51) . The entire material of m. 4, which entails the resolution of unessential dissonances to elements of V^7, forms 7–24; the dissonant chord on the downbeat of m. 4 is 5–24. Thus the complementary subset of 7–24 is conspicuous; moreover, the altered V/V at the end of m. 3 is another 5–24 (equivalent at T_7 to that in m. 4), so that the conclusion of the phrase is exceptionally unified. Example 52 illustrates a significant embedded complement in the Prelude Op. 48/2: 5–34 is formed by the altered V/V in the second beat of m. 6 and is contained in its complement, 7–34, which is an expanded statement of this same V/V function. Thus the similarity of the complement-related sets reinforces the prolongation of the secondary dominant throughout the first half of the measure. Example 53, an excerpt from "Désir" Op. 57/1, demonstrates a more complex situation, the intricate overlapping of

Example 51 Prelude Op. 48/4

Example 52 Prelude Op. 48/2

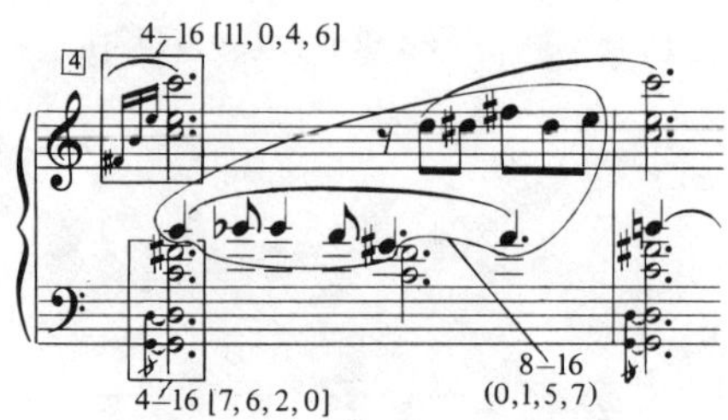

Example 53 "Désir" Op. 57/1

8–16 and two forms of 4–16. The moving parts constitute 8–16, whereas the six-note chord sustained throughout is composed of two inversionally related 4–16s (at IT_6). The upper 4–16 has the same pc content as the opening chord of the piece, here heard suspended over the dominant harmony. Scriabin's musical notation effectively conveys the segmentations most relevant to the structure of the passage.

Literal pc complementation is not usually consequential in Scriabin's late tonal music, but literal complements can sometimes be important structural determinants. The most striking literal complements occur in the last of the late tonal works (composed after 1905), as in example 54, where 5–34 and 7–34 occur at the end of the first main section of "Fragilité" Op. 51/1. These sets may in fact be considered adjacent if the chord in the first beat of m. 16 (5–24) is seen as a suspension chord created by suspending pcs 4 and 9 from 5–34 over elements of 7–34. In "Ironies" Op. 56/2 literal complements begin and end phrases, thus reinforcing them (example 55). For example, 8–24 comprises all pcs in m. 17, which begins a phrase; the 4–24 concluding the phrase (m. 20) is its literal complement. The opening phrase of the Etude Op. 56/4 (example 56), we have seen, prolongs the dual dominant harmony in mm. 3–4 (example 23a). The first two measures progress sequentially and are essentially an embellishment of the goal in m. 3. In addition to the sequencing, however, literal complementation creates continuity in the phrase: the 5–33 in the second beat of m. 1 is complemented by an adjacent 7–33, the sum of the material of m. 2. Similarly, the 4–21 in the second beat of m. 2 is followed by its literal complement, 8–21, which comprises all pcs in m. 3. Not only does literal complementation guarantee continuity by

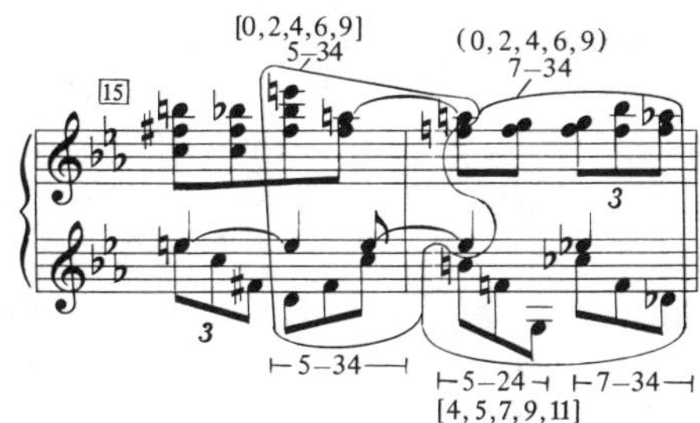

Example 54 "Fragilité" Op. 51/1

Example 55 "Ironies" Op. 56/2

Example 56 Etude Op. 56/4

successive set correspondences, but also the constant presence of all twelve tones creates harmonic instability until the basic harmony of the prolongation is reached.

A final example of intricate presentation of literal complements is the opening phrase of "Caresse dansée" Op. 57/2 (example 57). As seen in example 42, the set of all pcs in m. 1 is 5–15. This set is embedded in its complement, 7–15 (formed by all elements of mm. 1–2 except E♭, which is an anticipation of the melodic pitch of m. 3). The material of mm. 3–4, though apparently different from mm. 1–2, forms a 7–15 equivalent at T_{11} to that in mm. 1–2; the material of m. 3 is another 5–15 (embedded in the 7–15 of mm. 3–4), and m. 5 contains 5–15 as well. As we have seen, 5–15 also occurs in m. 6, despite the fact that the sequence has broken down. An even more vital connection exists between the 5–15 in m. 6 and previous material, for it is the literal complement of 7–15 in mm. 1–2, with which the sequence began.

INVARIANCE

Scriabin often exploits the properties of sets to retain certain pitches when transposed or inverted.[6] Because two forms of the same set often share pcs, we should generally regard as significant only the retention of the maximum or minimum possible number of pcs between set-forms. Remarkably, maximum or minimum invariance is common in Scriabin's late tonal compositions. Transpositional repetition as part of a larger-scale tonal progression often shifts prominent sets to a level significant for invariance. In the Poem Op. 32/2, the first phrase is immediately repeated at T_4, effecting a progression from I to III♯. Measures 3–4 of this phrase (example 58) are repeated literally at T_4, with maximum pitch retention in many of the most characteristic sets (almost all sets in m. 4). The

Example 57 "Caresse dansée" Op. 57/2

Example 58 Poem Op. 32/2

maximally invariant sets at T_4 are 4–24, 5–13, 7–28, 7–30, 6–34, and 9–3. The literal transposition of the initial phrase up four half steps is a frequent maneuver in Scriabin's compositions, and maximum pc invariance between equivalent set-forms often results. For instance, the opening phrase of "Ironies" Op. 56/2 is repeated at T_4 in mm. 5–8, yielding maximum pc invariance for many sets: 4–19, 4–24, 4–25, 5/7–13, 6–Z10, and 6–21. Given the variety of possible expansions of the I–V progression, Scriabin's frequent choice of the I–III♯–V prolongation appears to be related to—or perhaps even dictated by—the invariance properties of his characteristic sonorities. More definite conclusions must wait until the set-complex relations and the properties of the most important sets used by Scriabin from 1903 to 1910 are evaluated in chapter 5.

The progressions most basic to tonality, those by fifth, are frequently the basis for transpositional repetitions of material (with t = 5 or t = 7) in Scriabin's music. These transpositions often produce minimum invariance (maximum change in pc content) between set-forms—particularly in characteristic sonorities related to the whole-tone scale, which maximize the even-numbered interval classes. Example 59 shows the opening material of "Désir" Op. 57/1, with three whole-tone-related sets: 4–24, 4–25, and 6–21. (The two adjacent 4–25s are in fact equivalent at T_7 and share no pcs.) When this material is transposed with t = 7 (m. 6) and with t = 5 (m. 7), there is minimum invariance from the orig-

Example 59 "Désir" Op. 57/1

inal at either transpositional level. (Maximum invariance occurs, however, between the forms of 6–21 at T_7 and T_5.)

On the other hand, Scriabin often transposes other sets with t = 5 or t = 7 and achieves maximum invariance. For example, in Op. 57/1 (example 59), 6–Z6 formed by the melody at the end of m. 1 occurs in mm. 5–6 at T_7 and in mm. 6–7 at T_5, both with maximum invariance from the original. In the Prelude Op. 48/4, 6–Z26 occurs only twice, each time in a dominant context. In m. 15 (example 60a) it is an altered V/V, and in mm. 22–23 (example 60b) it comprises both dominant and tonic harmonies. Significantly, the second 6–Z26 is equivalent at T_5 to the first, reinforcing the progression around the circle of fifths (from V/V to V to I). Moreover, the two set-forms share the maximum of four pcs, which form 4–20—the same set heard conspicuously, and for the only time, in m. 15.

In his late tonal works Scriabin was thus able to fuse conventional progressions with techniques exploiting novel sonorities—techniques he was already employing with considerable expertise in 1903. His use of sets in these compositions is not merely accessory to the tonal structure. Even though Ursatz forms are primarily responsible for overall coherence, the relations among significant sets at the surface of the music are often of such consistent interest (particularly with regard to invariance) that they assume equal if not primary responsibility for foreground structure. That set relations can determine structure in the absence of tonality has been clearly established by Forte and others. In these compositions, where the tonality is deliberately vague or only implicit, other principles and methods of structure are introduced to compensate for the lack of precise functional definition at the foreground.

"Nuances" Op. 56/3 is exceptionally integrated in its set relations. Example 32 traces occurrences of 4–20, one of the most characteristic and frequent sets in the piece. Example 61 lists all set-forms and their invariance relations. The final presentation of 4–20 is taken here to be T_0 because it is identified with the tonic. In this composition every interval class is represented in the levels of transposition used, but the most frequent level is T_6, which has minimum invariance with T_0. Of eighteen pairs of adjacent sets, all but two retain either the maximum or minimum number of pitch classes. Two sequential progressions involving 4–20 are shown in example 61; the first, which is more obvious, involves successive transpositions with t = 10 (descending by whole tones) in mm. 8–11. There is

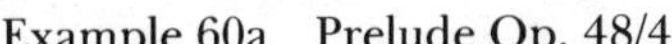

Example 60a Prelude Op. 48/4

Example 60b Prelude Op. 48/4

Example 61 Set 4–20 [101220] in "Nuances" Op. 56/3

Measure	PC Content	T	T between Adjacent Sets	
1	[9,10,2,5]	10 min.		
			t = 7 max.	
2	[4,5,9,0]	5 max.		
			t = 6 min.	
3	[10,11,3,6]	11		
			t = 7 max.	
4	[5,6,10,1]	6 min.		
			t = 9	
5a	[2,3,7,10]	3		
			t = 5 max.	
5b	[7,8,0,3]	8 max.		
			t = 5 max.	
6	[0,1,5,8]	1		
			t = 11	
7	[11,0,4,7]	0		+ 10 sequence
			t = 5 max.	
8	[4,5,9,0]	5 max.		
			t = 10 min.	
9a	[2,3,7,10]	3		
			t = 5 max.	
9b	[7,8,0,3]	8 max.		
			t = 5 max.	
10a	[0,1,5,8]	1		
			t = 5 max.	
10b	[5,6,10,1]	6 min.		
			t = 5 max.	
11	[10,11,3,6]	11		
			t = 7 max.	
12	[5,6,10,1]	6 min.		+ 5 sequence
			t = 0	
13	[5,6,10,1]	6 min.		
			t = 5 max.	
14	[10,11,3,6]	11		
			t = 6 min.	
16	[4,5,9,0]	5 max.		
			t = 7 max.	
17	[11,0,4,7]	0		

minimum invariance between each pair of adjacent 4–20s as well as between the set-forms which begin and end the pattern (T_5 in m. 8 and T_{11} in m. 11). The second sequence involves concealed statements of 4–20 which come to light when set analysis is applied consistently. This sequence is determined by the four 4–20s in mm. 9–10, transposed successively with t = 5. Here adjacent set-forms are maximally invariant.

It should now be clear that the whole-tone prolongations discussed previously may best be analyzed within the framework of the theory of pc-set relations. In general, such prolongations involve the retention of elements of a single whole-tone scale (6–35) throughout a succession of sets. Thus the term *whole-tone invariance* describes more precisely the retention of pcs which form 6–35 or a subset of 6–35. There are usually few sets involved in whole-tone invariance, but they occur in various transpositionally or inversionally equivalent forms. All of the important sets contain mostly even-numbered intervals. If this invariance entails transposition or transposed inversion, the final level of each set must be an even number of half steps from the original. (Even-numbered intervals of transposition prevail in most compositions with whole-tone invariance.) For example, each measure of the sequential progression in "Ironies" Op. 56/2 (example 62) constitutes a form of 8–24, which is transposed three times successively with t = 2; forms of 8–24 equivalent at T_2 share the six pcs of the whole-tone scale and no others. (In this instance maximum invariance is not

Example 62 "Ironies" Op. 56/2

significantly exploited; seven pcs are retained not at T_6 but at T_4.) Finally, the entire twelve-tone aggregate is formed in mm. 25–28. (Compare this description with that of the same passage in example 9.)

Another example of whole-tone invariance is the sequence in mm. 9–13 of the Etude Op. 49/1 (example 63), discussed previously as example 24. Each beat presents a transpositionally equivalent form of 5–28 (example 64). The pattern provides maximum invariance between set-forms in the first three beats of the basic material of the sequence (for example, T_0, T_6, and T_0 in mm. 9–10). Four

Example 63 Etude Op. 49/1

T of Sequential Repetition	Measure	PC Content	T	Invariance between Adjacent Sets	Comments
0	9a	[1,11,10,7,5]	0		4 pcs retained [11,1,5,7] = 4–25 T_0
				max.	
	9b	[7,5,4,1,11]	6		
				max.	
	10a	[1,11,10,7,5]	0		
	10b	[4,2,1,10,8]	3		
				min.	2 pcs retained with T_0 or T_6; 1 pc with T_2
2	11a	[3,1,0,9,7]	2		4 pcs retained [1,3,7,9] = 4–25 T_2
				max.	
	11b	[9,7,6,3,1]	8		
				max.	
	12a	[3,1,0,9,7]	2		
	12b	[6,4,3,0,10]	5		2 pcs retained with T_2 or T_8; 1 pc with T_4
4	13a	[5,3,2,11,9]	4		4 pcs retained [3,5,9,11] = 4–25 T_4
				max.	
	13b	[11,9,8,5,3]	10		
	14	[7,8,9,10,0,3]			6–Z40, which does not contain 5–28

Example 64 Set 5–28 [122212] in the Etude Op. 49/1

pcs are retained between the set-forms involved here, which are equivalent at T_6; these invariants form 4–25, a subset of 6–35. Thereafter, a form of 5–28 occurs at a level equidistant from the two sets heard previously (for example, T_3 in m. 10, three half steps from both T_0 and T_6), retaining only two pcs from either of the preceding set-forms. The entire progression is repeated twice, transposed with t = 2 each time. Minimum invariance (retaining only one pc) occurs between the closing 5–28 of a phrase (that is, in the second half of m. 10 and m. 12) and the 5–28 beginning the subsequent repetition. These 5–28s are equivalent at T_{11}. The pattern breaks down with the 6–Z40 in m. 14, which does not contain 5–28. Although all twelve pcs are represented here, the retention of a single whole-tone scale is the most important feature of the passage. The 4–25s retained during each repetition form 6–35 [1,3,5,7,9,11]. Duration is certainly a prime factor in determining the prominence of the whole-tone sonority underlying mm. 9–13: eight of the ten beats involve some four-note subset of 6–35.

According to the requirements for whole-tone invariance, a single 6–35 may underlie a passage even when elements of the complementary 6–35 might ostensibly be of equal structural importance. The opening phrase of the Prelude Op. 45/3 (example 65) involves a whole-tone "prolongation" which is not immediately apparent. The main set here is 4–24, a subset of 6–35, which forms the initial chord of the piece. In m. 2, 4–24 occurs in a form equivalent at T_7 to the original. Together these set-forms, which share no pcs, make up 8–20. In m. 3, the second form of 4–24 begins a repetition of the material in mm. 1–2 at T_7, a transposition which leads to another 4–24 in m. 4. This third form of 4–24 is equivalent at T_7 to that in m. 2 and thus shares no pcs with it. The transpositions of 4–24 with t = 7 throughout the passage, however, render the forms in mm. 1 and 4 equivalent at T_2 ($7 + 7 = 14 = 2$ [mod 12]). This equivalence does not produce maximum invariance; only two pcs are retained. But this degree of invariance allows the formation of a complete whole-tone scale from the elements of the 4–24s at T_0 and T_2. A single whole-tone scale may be said to underlie this passage because its transpositional scheme creates a complete whole-tone aggregate. In this case the passing function of the intervening 4–24 (mm. 2–3), a subset of the complementary 6–35, is reinforced by its occurrence as part of an ongoing transpositional repetition. In contrast, the component 4–24s of the basic 6–35 are conspicuous as endpoints of the pattern.

Example 65 Prelude Op. 45/3

Although whole-tone invariance resembles tonal prolongation because both differentiate an underlying sonority from surface activity, the two procedures are essentially unrelated. Tonality entails a hierarchy of functions by which multileveled structures may be generated, but whole-tone invariance produces only two levels, based not on functional relations but on simple pitch retention. Retention is effected most easily if the invariants are sustained throughout a passage, but a set of pcs may also be retained if it is both the departure and arrival of a span. (This suggests the existence of the simplest kind of auxiliary function which operates in isolation from every other aspect of the music, including the treatment of consonance and dissonance.) There are no hierarchical relationships between sets in Scriabin's late tonal music, other than those between sets associated with particular tonal functions. Significant sets are frequent at various levels of structure, but the elements which these sets comprise depend on tonal functions, which determine the stratification. Whole-tone invariance is the only systematic procedure whereby elements separated by time or intervening activity may be incorporated as elements of a single underlying set (comparable, say, to an arpeggiation in the middleground of a tonal piece). It is possible that other sets may be retained similarly, but Scriabin did not employ the technique with other sets in his later tonal music. The self-duplicating properties of the whole-tone scale and its subsets under transposition must account for its importance in his music.

SET STRUCTURE AND TONALITY

Thus far we have discussed compositions in which set-forms related under transposition, inversion, or complementation are stated in a variety of ways and are not associated with a particular tonal function or progression. Set structure may nevertheless be correlated with tonal structure at the foreground. In the Prelude Op. 51/2 tonal events are often reinforced by recurrences of particular sets. (See example 28, where sets are noted in the score.) The first half of the piece is a circular progression from I, through IV (m. 4), to V (m. 8), and back to I (m. 12). None of these harmonies occurs as a consonant triad; rather, each is marked by a statement of 4–20 at a corresponding level of transposition: T_0 (m. 1), T_5 (m. 4), T_7 (m. 8), and T_0 (m. 12). Significantly, maximum invariance occurs at T_5 and T_7. Forms of both 5–28 and 6–Z43 are subject to the same cycle of transpositions as 4–20 and thus reinforce the circular progression; however, neither set corresponds clearly to the functions of the tonal progression because both sets have varied presentations. The occurrence of 6–Z43 at T_5 in mm. 4–5 reaffirms the analysis in chapter 3 that the subdominant is effective here, even though the bass progression ostensibly proceeds farther. Set 6–Z43 occurs in several other forms which are also embellishments of the subdominant. One, at the beginning of m. 17, is equivalent at T_{10} to the original statement in m. 1. The other form is exceptionally elegant, for it overlaps the 6–Z43 at T_5 in mm. 4–5. This I-related form occurs at the end of m. 4, sharing 4–20 (corresponding to IV) with 6–Z43 at T_5.

Example 66a Etude Op. 56/4

Example 66b Etude Op. 56/4

The Etude Op. 56/4 is another example of sets used strictly to reinforce tonality. In this piece, 4–19 occurs conspicuously only three times. The first presentation (example 66a), in mm. 7–8, is formed by the C major triad plus A♭, the chromatic upper auxiliary to the fifth. The second and third statements are in mm. 20 and 24, both at T_6, with 4–19 formed by a similarly embellished G♭ major triad (example 66b). The two transpositionally equivalent forms share no pcs. In mm. 23–24, 4–19 is embedded in a presentation of its complement, 8–19, which is formed by the V–I cadence in G♭. This is the only significant occurrence of 8–19 in the piece and is the literal complement of the 4–19 associated with C major. We saw earlier that this etude exploits the potential of its dominant to cadence either to C major or to the true tonic, G♭. The powerful relations among these forms of 4–19/8–19, which are associated exclusively with these opposing goals, add to the irony inherent in their conflict.

THE MYSTIC CHORD

Before proceeding to Scriabin's vocabulary of sets in the music of 1903–10, it is appropriate to examine the properties of his most famous set, 6–34, better known as the "mystic" or "Prometheus" chord. Although this chord is generally thought to have been used as an independent harmony for the first time in *Prometheus* Op. 60, many scholars have recognized it in earlier works.[7] However, no one has perceived the extent of its use prior to Op. 60, nor has anyone examined the specific tonal contexts in which it appears. Many authors have persisted in explaining the chord as a derivation of the upper partials of the overtone series or as an arbitrary construction of superposed fourths—in spite of the evidence that the harmony originated in the context of tonality.

We must first evaluate the tonal contexts in which the mystic chord appears. Example 67 shows occurrences of 6–34 in the later tonal works. Perhaps most typical is the whole-tone dominant chord suspended over the tonic root, the

Example 67a "Désir" Op. 57/1

Example 67b Poem Op. 32/2

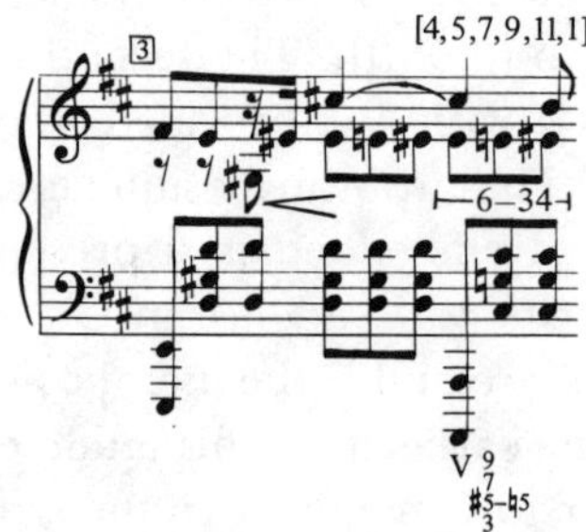

Example 67c Poem Op. 32/2

most celebrated instance of which is the final chord of "Désir" Op. 57/1 (example 67a), which is never resolved. The whole-tone dominant suspended here is actually a $V^{9}_{\sharp 5}$, and the tonic root is the only non-whole-tone element of the chord. Set 6–34 occurs in exactly the same fashion in mm. 3–4 of the Poem Op. 32/2 (example 67b), but it is resolved. Other structurally identical occurrences of 6–34 are in mm. 18 and 33 of "Ironies" Op. 56/2 and m. 7 of the Etude Op. 56/4 (not shown). Another typical occurrence of 6–34 is a complex dominant function with several unessential dissonances. Such a statement occurs in m. 3 of the Poem Op. 32/2, as $V^{10-9}_{\sharp 5-\natural 5}$ (example 67c). The only non-whole-tone element is the natural fifth of the root in the bass. This statement of 6–34 occurs near the form shown in example 67b. The two forms are inversionally related (at IT_6) and in fact share the pcs of 5–33, the five-note subset of the whole-tone scale: [5,7,9,11,1].

The presentation of the mystic chord as a dominant is not limited to the arrangement of intervals over the dominant bass tone. Other possible dominant configurations are shown in examples 67d–f. The dominant seventh in m. 1 of the Poem Op. 32/1 contains a major ninth and a raised fourth, yielding a distinctive form of 6–34 (example 67d). (This 6–34 shares 5–33 with an adjacent form of 6–34 at IT_6 [m. 2] and is thus part of a whole-tone prolongation.) In m. 7 of "Fragilité" Op. 51/1 (example 67e), 6–34 comprises the notes of a $\mathrm{V}^{9}_{\flat 6-5}$. Example 67f illustrates yet another form of 6–34, in m. 8 of Op. 51/1, associated with a $\mathrm{V}^{9}_{\substack{6\\ \sharp 4}}$ which lacks a perfect fifth and whose non-whole-tone element is the sixth.

Examples 67g–h show 6–34 in conjunction with other harmonic functions. In mm. 19–22 of the Prelude Op. 48/4, the mystic chord is formed by the chords of a tritone bass progression from ♭II to V (example 67g). (This progression is equivalent at T_5 to that in m. 3, although here the connection is less obvious because the two component chords are separated by a good deal of silence.) In this instance, the mystic chord is still closely allied with the dominant (though ♭II is also involved), especially because the ♭II–V progression prolongs V. The

Example 67d Poem Op. 32/1

Example 67e "Fragilité" Op. 51/1

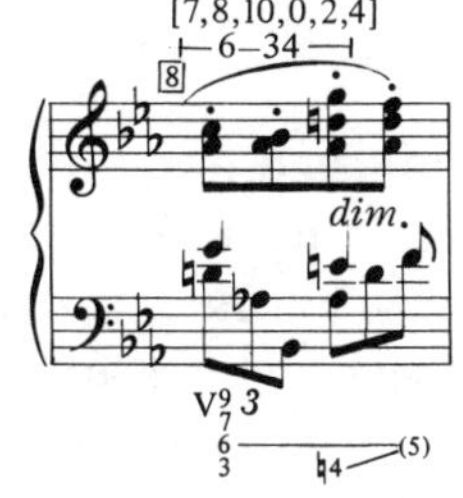

Example 67f "Fragilité" Op. 51/1

Example 67g Prelude Op. 48/4

Example 67h Poem Op. 32/1

dominant may thus be considered effective throughout this presentation of 6–34 (see also the analysis of Op. 48/4 in example 35), which might therefore be interpreted as a $V^{9}_{6\,\flat 5}$ harmony. Example 67h demonstrates a rare instance in the late tonal works of the mystic chord apart from the dominant function. In m. 44 of Op. 32/1, the subdominant in the bass supports 6–34.

These forms of the mystic chord result from the interaction of harmonic and contrapuntal factors. To describe this chord as a complex altered dominant is thus inadequate, not only because it neglects the particular voice leadings involved, but also because the context of the formation often entails more than one harmonic function. Nonetheless, the fact that the dominant is almost always a part of this sonority must influence our consideration of the origins of the mystic chord in Scriabin's late tonal works. One thing is certain: the typical description of 6–34 as a structure of superposed fourths is totally inappropriate. Scriabin may have chosen this particular distribution of the elements of the mystic chord for its use as a basic component in *Prometheus* and subsequent atonal compositions; such an arrangement never occurs in the tonal presentations of 6–34.

We have touched upon the relation of 6–34 to 6–35 (it contains five tones of a single whole-tone scale) and to Scriabin's exploitation of the properties of 6–34 to achieve whole-tone invariance. Indeed, 6–34 is often an important component in passages where an underlying whole-tone set is retained. It is by no means the only set involved in such procedures, nor is it used more frequently for whole-tone invariance than sets with similar properties, but it is clearly significant for the whole-tone structure of these late tonal compositions.

Examples 68a–c show three correspondences between paired forms of 6–34 in "Fragilité" Op. 51/1, all resulting in whole-tone invariance. In m. 47, two 6–34s are juxtaposed, the second equivalent at T_{10} to the first (example 68a), resulting in maximum invariance. The retained pcs form 4–21, the complement of which, 8–21, comprises the elements of both 6–34s. In mm. 6–7, two I-related forms of 6–34 (at IT_0) share the same non-whole-tone element (pc 0) along with pcs [3,5,7,9] (4–21); together all of the invariants form 5–34 (example 68b). Examples 68a–b each contain two forms of 6–34, which together form the entire whole-tone aggregate. Finally, in m. 18, two overlapped forms of 6–34 are inversionally equivalent at IT_{10}, sharing 5–33 (example 68c).

The importance of 6–34 in these late tonal works is not explained entirely by

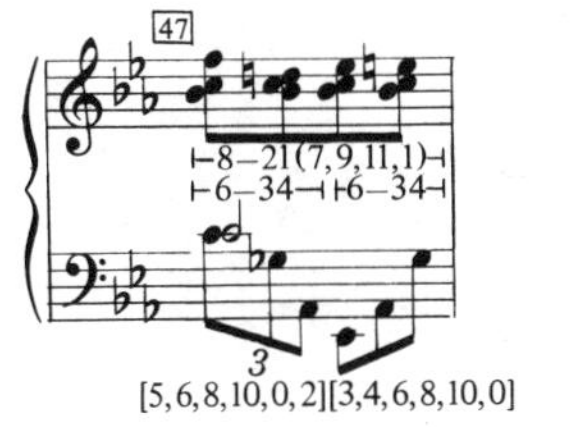

Example 68a "Fragilité" Op. 51/1

Example 68b "Fragilité" Op. 51/1

Example 68c "Fragilité" Op. 51/1

Scriabin's innovative procedure of whole-tone invariance. To achieve that end he could simply have adhered exclusively to whole-tone sets (as did Debussy throughout a large portion of "Voiles" from *Preludes*, Book I [1910]). Various authors have suggested that the mystic chord is an altered whole-tone chord which offers more possibilities than the whole-tone scale—it has twenty-four forms equivalent under inversion or transposition instead of the two forms available for 6–35.[8] However, two other hexachords, 6–21 and 6–22, are similar in structure to 6–34 in that each contains 5–33 and one non-whole-tone element. Yet 6–34 is much more widespread as a significant set in this music than either 6–21 or 6–22; this latter explanation, though persuasive, thus fails to account fully for the structural origins of the mystic chord. This chord (unlike 6–21 and 6–22) is unique because of the derivation of its non-whole-tone element; indeed, 6–34 appears to occur usually in tonal contexts distinct from those of 6–21 or 6–22. The non-whole-tone elements of the latter sets occur in many dispositions (measured intervallically from the root of the harmony concerned), but the function of the non-whole-tone element in 6–34 in this music is much more consistent. Usually the non-whole-tone element of 6–34 is determined by the fifth, the basic interval governing chord structure and harmonic progression in tonality.[9] When 6–34 occurs in a single dominant harmony, the non-whole-tone element is most often the fifth of the chord (as in example 67c). On the other hand, when 6–34 is formed at a V–I cadence (usually by the suspension of a whole-tone dominant harmony over the tonic root, as in example 67a), the bass progression by fifth introduces the non-whole-tone element. Thus the mystic chord results from the interaction of the two primary procedures determining the structure of Scriabin's late tonal compositions: tonality and whole-tone invariance.

FIVE
RELATIONS AMONG SETS IN THE TRANSITIONAL MUSIC

A survey of Scriabin's use of sets in the nineteen short pieces listed below will complete the study of the atonal aspects of the late tonal works. (Complete analytic sketches are provided in other chapters for compositions marked with an asterisk.)

Two Poems Op. 32 (1903)
  1. F major*
  2. D major*
Three Morceaux Op. 45 (1905)
  1. "Feuillet d'album"*
  2. "Poème fantasque"
  3. Prelude*
Four Preludes Op. 48 (1905)
  2. C major*
  4. C major*
Three Morceaux Op. 49 (1905)
  1. Etude
Four Morceaux Op. 51 (1906)
  1. "Fragilité"
  2. Prelude*
Three Morceaux Op. 52 (1906)
  2. "Enigme"
Four Pieces Op. 56 (1907)
  1. Prelude
  2. "Ironies"
  3. "Nuances"*
  4. Etude*
Two Morceaux Op. 57 (1907)
  1. "Désir"
  2. "Caresse dansée"
"Feuillet d'album" Op. 58 (1910, possibly 1909)*
Two Pieces Op. 59 (1910)
  2. Prelude*

In all, Scriabin wrote sixty-three short works during the period from 1903 to 1910, almost a third of which are included here. Of these sixty-three pieces, however, thirty-three were composed in 1903, if not before. (Many were probably composed earlier but not written down until Scriabin left his teaching post at the Moscow Conservatory in 1903.) Therefore the more genuinely transitional music includes only thirty short pieces dating from 1905 through 1910, seventeen (57 percent) of which have been analyzed in detail for this study. Further, at least one piece from each collection of short pieces from Op. 48 through Op. 59 has been analyzed, and the works selected cover the entire spectrum of affective moods in Scriabin's compositions. Thus this survey is based on a broad sample of Scriabin's transitional music.

Two of the small works with tonal structures more problematic than those already considered are discussed in chapter 6—the "Feuillet d'album" Op. 58 and the Prelude Op. 59/2. (In fact, the Prelude lacks an underlying tonal structure and is thus one of Scriabin's first atonal works.) These compositions are included here for the sake of completeness.

Each composition in this survey has been analyzed in terms of set content. Insofar as possible, a single method of segmentation has been applied in each analysis. Sets containing between four and eight elements have been considered structurally significant, and in each analysis the important segments comprise elements which are adjacent horizontally, vertically, or both (as opposed to elements separated by intervening events).

In the process of segmentation, I have tried to avoid selectivity; that is, all elements which might be construed as members of a segment are treated as such, and the resulting set is listed. This methodology does not always bring important set-forms to light, however. For instance, an all-inclusive segmentation might yield a set which does not appear elsewhere. In these or other circumstances (for example, when the elements of a segment are obviously of differing structural weights with regard to duration or dynamics), the analyst must consider other segmentations, usually subsets of the original. Here musical intuition is a factor in the segmentation process, but for the sake of completeness, all set-forms thus disclosed are again included in the comprehensive listing. Related or recurrent sets are generally more important than those not involved in such correspondences.

Example 69 lists occurrences of sets for all pieces considered here.[1] A dot signifies that a set occurs more than once in a piece; an *X* indicates that a set occurs much more frequently than most and is therefore *significant*. The application of this term within a piece cannot be based on a single rule for all pieces; it has been based on an evaluation of the relative frequency of sets. On average, one fourth of the sets in a composition are significant. Pieces with more significant sets than average include the Prelude Op. 45/2, the Etude Op. 49/1, and "Ironies" Op. 56/2; those with an exceptionally low number include the "Feuillet d'album" Op. 45/1 and "Fragilité" Op. 51/1. The latter compositions are among the more conventional tonal works, whereas those with more significant sonorities are more innovative in their use of related sets. Example 70 assigns each set

Example 69 Set Usage in Opp. 32–59 (1903–10)

	1903		1905						1906	
	32/1	32/2	45/1	45/2	45/3	48/2	48/4	49/1	51/1	51/2
4–2										
4–4										
4–6										
4–7										
4–11										
4–12										
4–13										
4–14									●	
4–Z15										●
4–16		●			×			×	×	
4–17										
4–18		●			●	●				
4–19	●		●		●	●	●	×	●	●
4–20		●			●	●			●	×
4–21	●	●			●		●	●	●	
4–22	×	●							●	
4–23							●			
4–24		×	●	●	×			●	●	
4–25	●	●		×	×		×	●	●	×
4–26	●	●			●	●	●		●	●
4–27	×	×	●		●		×	×	●	×
4–28								●		
4–Z29	●	●	●		●		●		●	
5–3										
5–6						●				
5–7							●			
5–8		●						●	●	
5–11	●									
5–13		×			●	●		●	●	
5–15		●			●				●	
5–16		●	●							
5–Z17						●				
5–19							●			
5–20										
5–21			●							
5–22										
5–24	●						×	×	×	
5–25		●					●		●	
5–26	●	●	●				●	●		
5–27	●		●			×			●	
5–28		×	×	●	●			×		×
5–29	●		●		●					
5–30		●			●				●	●
5–31	●	●	●							

● = Occurrence at least twice × = Occurrence as significant set

Example 69 (cont.)

1907							1909?	1910		
52/2	56/1	56/2	56/3	56/4	57/1	57/2	58	59/2	X	Total
	●								0	1
		●							0	1
					●				0	1
	●								0	1
		●					●		0	2
								●	0	1
								●	0	1
		●							0	2
									0	1
●		×			×	×			6	8
								●	0	1
	●							×	1	5
	●	×	●	●			●	×	3	14
	×	●	×					●	3	9
		●		●	●	●			0	10
									1	3
									0	1
●		×	●	×	●	●	×		5	13
×	●	×	●	●	×	●			7	15
	●		×						1	9
●	×		×	●	●			●	7	14
●								●	0	3
	●	×		●	●	×			2	11
					●				0	1
		●		●	×				1	4
		●				●			0	3
●					●				0	5
									0	1
		×		×	●	●			3	9
					×	×			2	5
		×			●	●		●	1	6
									0	1
	●								0	2
	●					●		●	0	3
		●	●		●				0	4
	×							×	2	2
		●		●	●	●	●		3	9
	●	●	●						0	6
		●		●			●	●	0	9
●			×		●				2	7
	×		●	×	●			●	6	11
									0	3
		●	×		●		●		1	8
●					●			●	0	6

Example 69 (cont.)

	1903		1905						1906	
	32/1	32/2	45/1	45/2	45/3	48/2	48/4	49/1	51/1	51/2
5–32										
5–33	●	●	●	×	×		×	×	●	
5–34	×	●		●		×	●		●	
5–35	×	●				●	●			
5–Z36					●					●
5–Z37								●	●	●
5–Z38		●							●	×
6–Z3										
6–Z6										
6–Z10/Z39			×					●	●	
6–14										
6–15										
6–18							●			
6–Z19/Z44						●				
6–21		●		●						
6–22					×		●	×	●	
6–Z23		●							●	
6–Z24/Z46	●		●			●				
6–Z25	●									●
6–Z26							●		●	●
6–27			●							
6–Z28/Z49										
6–Z29										
6–30		●						●	●	
6–31			●							
6–32	●		●			●				
6–33		●	●	●			×			
6–34	×	×	●	×	●		×	×	×	
6–35				×			●	×	●	
6–Z40					●					
6–Z43		●								×
X	5	5	2	4	5	2	6	9	3	6
Total	20	29	19	9	20	13	21	19	29	14

to the time period which most narrowly delimits its usage, and example 71 classifies the period of each set according to its occurrence specifically as a significant set.

Scriabin selected only a limited number of sets from the range of possibilities. Example 69 shows twenty-three four-element sets (79 percent of the twenty-nine

Example 69 (cont.)

	1907						1909?	1910		
52/2	56/1	56/2	56/3	56/4	57/1	57/2	58	59/2	X	Total
	•		•					×	1	3
×		×	•	×	×	×	•	•	9	16
					•				2	7
•			•						1	6
									0	2
									0	3
	•		•						1	5
					•				0	1
					•				0	1
		×			•	•	•		2	7
								•	0	1
	•						•		0	2
				•					0	2
•		•	•					•	0	5
×		×	•	•	•				2	7
		×				•	•		3	7
	•								0	3
									0	3
	•								0	3
		•	×	•	×		•		2	8
•		×						•	1	4
								×	1	1
	•								0	1
				•				•	0	5
•								•	0	3
									0	3
									1	4
•		×		•	•	•	×	•	8	15
•				•		•			2	7
	•								0	2
	×					•			2	4
3	5	13	6	4	6	4	2	5		
16	22	27	18	18	27	17	12	23		

available), twenty-eight five-element sets (74 percent of the thirty-eight), and twenty-eight six-element sets (56 percent of the fifty, counting Z-related sets individually). The selectivity is even more striking when one considers only the significant sets. They constitute only 34 percent of the four-element sets, 37 percent of the five-element sets, and 24 percent of the sets of cardinal 6. To

Example 70 Set Distribution,
Transitional Period

1903–10		
4–18	5–16	6–Z19/Z44
4–19	5–26	6–27
4–20	5–28	6–30
4–27	5–31	6–31
4–28	5–33	6–34
1903–09		
4–24	5–24	6–Z10/Z39
	5–30	6–22
		6–Z26
1903–05		
4–23	5–11	6–Z24/Z46
	5–Z17	6–32
	5–29	6–33
1903–07		
4–16	5–8	6–21
4–21	5–13	6–Z23
4–22	5–15	6–Z25
4–25	5–25	6–Z43
4–26	5–27	
4–Z29	5–34	
	5–35	
	5–Z38	
1905–07		
4–14	5–6	6–18
4–Z15	5–7	6–35
	5–19	6–Z40
	5–21	
	5–Z36	
	5–Z37	
1907		
4–2	5–3	6–Z3
4–4		6–Z6
4–6		6–Z29
4–7		
1907–10		
4–11	5–20	6–15
	5–22	
	5–32	
1910		
4–12	—	6–14
4–13		6–Z28/Z49
4–17		

Example 71 Significant Set Distribution, Transitional Period

1903–10		
4–19	—	—
1903–09		
4–24	—	6–34
1903–05		
4–22	5–34	6–33
	5–35	6–35
1903–07		
4–27	5–13	—
	5–28	
1905–07		
4–16	5–24	6–Z10/Z39
4–20	5–27	6–21
4–25	5–33	6–22
	5–Z38	6–Z43
1907		
4–26	5–6	6–Z26
4–Z29	5–15	6–27
	5–16	
	5–30	
1907–10		
—	5–22	—
1910		
4–18	5–32	6–Z28/Z49

determine the structural properties of chosen sets (especially those properties not shared by sets outside of Scriabin's repertoire) will help us understand the structural basis of Scriabin's atonal components.

We have seen that Scriabin discovered and exploited the invariance properties of certain sets. For example, he used four sets—4–25, 4–28, 6–30, and 6–35—which at some level of transposition retain all of their pcs. Only three other sets with four to six elements share this property—4–9, 6–7, and 6–20—so although Scriabin did not exhaust all possibilities, he used most sets with this property. Only 4–25 and 6–35 are significant in this music, and both are fundamental to whole-tone invariance. Sets 4–28 and 6–35 are the only sets with four to six elements which retain no subsets under either transposition or inversion, and 4–25 and 8–28 are two of four sets (the others are 4–9 and 6–20, which do not occur in this music) which retain only one subset.[2]

A special property of twenty-six sets with five to eight elements is the capability to retain under transposition a subset containing one less element than the original set.[3] Of twenty-nine possible pairings of a set of cardinal n with an invariant subset of cardinal $n - 1$, seventeen occur in the late tonal music: 8–19 (which retains 7–21), 8–24 (7–33), 8–21 (7–33), 7–28 (6–30), 7–33 (6–35), 7–31 (6–27), 7–35 (6–32), 7–31 (6–30), 7–19 (6–30), 6–32 (5–35), 5–35 (4–23), 5–33 (4–25), 5–33 (4–24), 5–33 (4–21), 5–28 (4–25), 5–21 (4–19), and 5–15 (4–25). We have already seen the exploitation of this property with regard to 5–28 (example 63). A majority of the elements in fourteen of the twenty-three sets or subsets listed above belong to a single whole-tone scale, a relation discussed in depth at the end of this chapter.

Many of Scriabin's sets are completely invariant under inversion as well, although this property is perhaps less important because a large number of sets share it.[4] Ten of the fifteen four-element sets possessing this feature are found in this music: 4–6, 4–7, 4–17, 4–20*, 4–21, 4–23, 4–24*, 4–25*, 4–26*, and 4–28. (Significant sets are marked with asterisks.) Eight of a possible ten five-note sets also occur: 5–8, 5–15*, 5–Z17, 5–22*, 5–33*, 5–34*, 5–35*, and 5–Z37. However, only eight of the twenty sets of six notes with this property are employed: 6–Z6, 6–Z23, 6–Z26, 6–Z28/Z49*, 6–Z29, 6–32, and 6–35*. The structural uses of these sets are better explained in terms of other properties shared more exclusively among sets in Scriabin's vocabulary. Another property involving invariance should be mentioned. Fourteen of the possible twenty-nine sets which hold the complementary subset invariant under transposition, inversion, or both, occur in this music: 8–6, 8–13, 8–23, 8–28, 7–8, 7–22, 7–24, 7–26, 7–30, 7–34, 7–35, 6–30, 6–32, and 6–35.[5]

In complementation and similarity relations among sets, the extrema are of primary interest because most sets participate to some degree in these relations. Among sets of cardinals 7 and 8, three contain their complements a maximum number of times: 7–21 (six times), 7–33 (six), and 8–19 (eight).[6] All three sets occur in Scriabin's late tonal works, and the latter two are significant. Indeed, the tendency toward saturation of the texture by a single type of sonority was observed in many of the analyses in chapter 4. The minima for containing the complement in sets of cardinals 7 and 8 are 7–Z12 (none) and 8–28 (two), and neither set is particularly important in this music. With regard to similarity relations, Scriabin uses 4–28, 5–33, and 6–35, which represent the minima for the relation R_p and are thus the most conspicuous sonorities. (Set 5–33 is his most widely employed five-note set.) The maxima for R_p—4–Z15, 4–Z29, 5–Z36, 6–Z11, and 6–Z40—are much less frequent; in fact, 6–Z11 never occurs in these compositions. (For brief definitions of set-theoretic terms such as R_p, see the appendix.)

The maximum interrelation among sets of the same cardinal exists within a *transitive tuple*, which Forte defines as a collection of sets in which each member is in the same relation to every other set.[7] Significantly, only twelve of forty-seven transitive tuples are completely represented in the late tonal music (example 72). (I do not take into account the eighty transitive tuples involving hexachords in R_0.) Other aspects of set structure described by Forte are not strongly correlated with the sets in Scriabin's works of 1903–10.[8]

None of the special properties discussed above is shared exclusively and universally among the sets in the late tonal works. To prove that most or all of these

Example 72 Complete Transitive Tuples, Transitional Period

R_1
4–4, 4–11, 4–14
4–7, 4–17, 4–20
4–12, 4–13, 4–18, 4–27
5–6, 5–24, 5–32
5–13, 5–26, 5–30
5–19, 5–Z36, 5–Z38
6–21, 6–22, 6–34
R_2
5–11, 5–21, 5–Z37
5–11, 5–Z37, 5–Z38
6–14, 6–15, 6–Z19
6–14, 6–Z19, 6–31
6–14, 6–31, 6–Z44

sets are related in structural properties, we must consider other features which might be uniquely characteristic of this collection of sets. The late tonal sets should be evaluated as a group according to the number of sets in which each interval class is maximized or minimized. (Only sets of four to six elements need be examined, for sets of cardinals 7 and 8 have the same interval-vector extrema as do their complements.) The results should indicate the average interval content (and therefore the invariance properties) of the sonorities in this music. In addition, the general properties of ic extrema for sets not found in Scriabin's works of this period should be evaluated.

All sets that occur in two or more compositions dating from 1903 to 1910 are listed with their interval vectors in example 73. Frequency is given as the ratio of the number of pieces in which the set is significant to the total number of compositions in which it appears. In columns to the right of the vector column are listed those ics which are maximized and minimized in each set. The data presented in example 73 are summarized in examples 74a–b. Finally, example 75 classifies sets according to whether they maximize even- or odd-numbered ics, or both.

Of the fourteen four-element sets in example 73, five maximize even-numbered ics, six maximize odd-numbered ics, two maximize both, and one, 4–Z29, maximizes neither (example 75). When these sets are weighted according to the number of pieces in which each occurs, however, a preference for even-numbered ics becomes evident. Three of the four most widely used sets (4–25, 4–19, and 4–24) maximize only even-numbered ics. (The exception is 4–27, whose special properties are discussed below.) Of the six four-element sets which maximize only odd ics, two are never significant (4–14 and 4–28) and two are significant in only one piece—4–18 in Op. 59/2 and 4–26 in Op. 56/3, both works composed late in the transitional period. Sets 4–16 and 4–27 are the only significant sets which maximize only an odd-numbered ic. In general, the

Example 73 IC Extrema, Transitional Period

Set	Frequency	Vector	Maxima	Minima
4–11	(0/2)	121110	2	6
4–14	(0/2)	111120	5	6
4–16	(6/8)	110121	5	3
4–18	(1/5)	102111	3	2
4–19	(3/14)	101310	4	2 6
4–20	(3/9)	101220	4 5	2 6
4–21	(0/10)	030201	2	1 3 5
4–22	(1/3)	021120	2 5	1 6
4–24	(5/13)	020301	4	1 3 5
4–25	(7/15)	020202	2 4 6	1 3 5
4–26	(1/9)	012120	3 5	1 6
4–27	(7/14)	012111	3	1
4–28	(0/3)	004002	3	
4–Z29	(2/11)	111111		
5–6	(1/4)	311221	1	2 3 6
5–7	(0/3)	310132	1 5	3
5–8	(0/5)	232201	2	5
5–13	(3/9)	221311	4	3 5 6
5–15	(2/5)	220222		3
5–16	(1/6)	213211	3	2 5 6
5–19	(0/2)	212122		2 4
5–20	(0/3)	211231	5	2 3 6
5–21	(0/4)	202420	4	2 6
5–22	(2/2)	202321	4	2
5–24	(3/9)	131221	2	1 3 6
5–25	(0/6)	123121	3	1 4 6
5–26	(0/9)	122311	4	1 5 6
5–27	(2/7)	122230	5	6
5–28	(6/11)	122212		1 5
5–29	(0/3)	122131	5	1 4 6
5–30	(1/8)	121321	4	1 3 6
5–31	(0/6)	114112	3	
5–32	(1/3)	113221	3	1 2 6
5–33	(9/16)	040402	2 4	1 3 5
5–34	(2/7)	032221	2	1
5–35	(1/6)	032140	5	1 6
5–Z36	(0/2)	222121		4 6
5–Z37	(0/3)	212320	4	6
5–Z38	(1/5)	212221		2 6
6–Z10/Z39	(2/7)	333321		6
6–15	(0/2)	323421	4	6
6–18	(0/2)	322242	5	
6–Z19/Z44	(0/5)	313431	4	2 6
6–21	(2/7)	242412	2 4	5
6–22	(3/7)	241422	2 4	3

Example 73 (cont.)

Set	Frequency	Vector	Maxima						Minima					
6–Z23	(0/3)	234222			3									
6–Z24/Z46	(0/3)	233331												6
6–Z25	(0/3)	233241					5							6
6–Z26	(2/8)	232341					5							6
6–27	(1/4)	225222			3									
6–Z28/Z49	(1/1)	224322			3									
6–30	(0/5)	224223			3									
6–31	(0/3)	223431				4								6
6–32	(0/3)	143250					5							6
6–33	(1/4)	143241		2			5		1					6
6–34	(8/15)	142422		2		4			1					
6–35	(2/7)	060603		2		4			1		3		5	
6–Z40	(0/2)	333231												6
6–Z43	(2/4)	322332	1			4	5			2	3			6

Example 74a IC Maximizations, Transitional Period

	Number of Times Maximized in Sets of Cardinals			
IC	4	5	6	Total
4	4	7	8	19
5	5	5	6	16
2	4	4	5	13
3	4	4	4	12
1	0	2	1	3
(6	1	0	0	1)*

*Note that ic 6 is minimized in 16 of the 29 four-element sets and is maximized only twice. Similar extrema exist for the five- and six-element sets for ic 6. Of the 38 five-element sets, ic 6 is maximized in none and minimized in 29. Of the 50 six-element sets, ic 6 is maximized in only one and minimized in 22. Thus the lack of maximization of ic 6 is inherent in set structure. For this reason, the extrema for this ic are less significant than those for the other ics, and related figures are therefore in parentheses in all pertinent charts.

Example 74b IC Minimizations, Transitional Period

	Number of Times Minimized in Sets of Cardinals			
IC	4	5	6	Total
(6	6	16	11	33)
1	6	10	3	19
3	4	8	3	15
2	3	8	2	13
5	3	6	2	11
4	0	4	0	4

Example 75 Odd and Even IC Maximizations, Transitional Period

	Sets Maximizing Only Even ICs	
4–11 (significant in 0 pieces)	5–8 (0)	6–15 (0)
	5–13 (3)	6–Z19/Z44 (0)
4–19 (3)	5–21 (0)	6–21 (2)
4–21 (0)	5–22 (2)	6–22 (3)
4–24 (5)	5–24 (3)	6–31 (0)
4–25 (7)	5–26 (0)	6–34 (8)
	5–30 (1)	6–35 (2)
	5–33 (9)	
	5–34 (2)	
	5–Z37 (0)	
	Sets Maximizing Only Odd ICs	
4–14 (0)	5–6 (1)	6–18 (0)
4–16 (6)	5–7 (0)	6–Z23 (0)
4–18 (1)	5–16 (1)	6–Z25 (0)
4–26 (1)	5–20 (0)	6–Z26 (2)
4–27 (7)	5–25 (0)	6–27 (1)
4–28 (0)	5–27 (2)	6–Z28/Z49 (1)
	5–29 (0)	6–30 (0)
	5–31 (0)	6–32 (0)
	5–32 (1)	
	5–35 (1)	
	Sets Maximizing Odd and Even ICs	
4–20 (3)	5–15 (2)	6–Z10/Z39 (2)
4–22 (1)	5–19 (0)	6–Z24/Z46 (0)
4–Z29 (2)	5–28 (6)	6–33 (1)
	5–Z36 (0)	6–Z40 (0)
	5–Z38 (1)	6–Z43 (2)

four-element sets in this music are related to the whole-tone scale at least insofar as they attain maximum invariance at an even-numbered level of transposition. Even 4–16 and 4–27 are somewhat related to the whole-tone scale, for each contains a three-note subset which is also a subset of 6–35. The four-note sets most frequently minimize ics 1 and 6, never ic 4.

In the five-note sets in example 73, the preference for ic 4 is stronger than in the four-note sets, and ic 5 is less important. As in the four-note sets, ics 1 and 6 are maximized least and minimized most, and ic 4 is minimized least. Also as in the four-element sets, three of the four most widely used sets (5–33, 5–24, and 5–26) maximize only even-numbered ics; the fourth, 5–28, in effect maximizes no particular ic, for the maximum for most of its ics is the same. There are further indications in the five-note sets that Scriabin strongly preferred even-numbered ics. Of the ten sets which maximize only even-numbered ics, five are significant in at least two compositions, and another is significant in one (example 75). Of the ten five-note sets which maximize only odd-numbered ics, on the other hand, only one is significant in more than one composition, and four are significant in a single work. Four sets, including 5–28, in effect do not favor any ic. Of these, two maximize more even ics than odd, and only these two are significant in more than one piece.

For the six-note sets in example 73, the frequencies of maximization and minimization parallel those of the five-note sets (examples 74a–b). The preference for sonorities with even-numbered ics is again corroborated by the ic content of the most significant and widely used sets. Of the seven hexachords which maximize only even-numbered ics, four are significant in at least two pieces, whereas only one of the eight hexachords which maximize only odd-numbered ics is comparably significant—and it occurs in only two pieces (example 75). Five six-note sets maximize both odd and even ics, but three of these contain four ics the maximum number of times. Only one of these three, 6–Z10/Z39, is widely used and is especially significant in more than one piece; this set has an equal distribution of maximized even and odd ics. Set 6–Z43 is the only significant set which favors odd-numbered ics.

In the sets in the works of 1903–10, ics 4 and 2 are strongly favored, especially the former (example 74a). The prominence of these even-numbered ics is essential for whole-tone invariance, discussed in chapter 4. After ic 4, however, ic 5 is most frequently maximized, no doubt because the music of this period, with the exception of only a few pieces, is tonal, and ic 5 is the basic ic of harmonic structure and progression in tonality. The single ic (apart from ic 6) maximized least is ic 1. The ic minima in Scriabin's sets of the late tonal period corroborate his preference for sonorities featuring ic 4 and his avoidance of those which maximize ic 1.

The mystic chord, 6–34, is the only hexachord (with the exception of the whole-tone scale) which maximizes ic 4 and minimizes ic 1. This property suggests another reason for the preference for 6–34 over 6–21 and 6–22, which are similar in structure to 6–34 in that all three sets contain 5–33. The only other sets which maximize ic 4 and minimize ic 1 are 4–24, 4–25, 5–26, 5–28, 5–30, and 5–33. All are frequent in this music—in fact, all but 5–26 are significant sets.

To complete our evaluation of the harmonies of Scriabin's transitional compositions, we must consider the properties of those sets not employed. Example 76, similar in format to example 73, lists the maximizations and minimizations of ics in the excluded sets (those which occur in no more than two pieces of the transitional period). The data in example 76 are summarized in examples 77a–b and support the conclusion that Scriabin favored even-numbered ics. All but two of the excluded four-element sets maximize an odd-numbered ic. The remaining two are 4–Z15, which maximizes no ic, and 4–11, which appears (though not significantly) in Op. 56/2 and Op. 58. The properties of the five- and six-element sets in example 76 are similar to those of the four-element sets. There is a clear correlation between the structural properties of these sets and the fact that they do not occur in this music. In general, their most conspicuous property is a tendency to maximize ic 1. The extrema for other ics (except for the special case of ic 6) are not significantly differentiated. It therefore seems

Example 76 IC Extrema for Excluded Sets, Transitional Period

Set	Vector	Maxima	Minima
4–1	321000	1	4 5 6
4–2	221100	1 2	5 6
4–3	212100	1 3	5 6
4–4	211110	1	6
4–5	210111	1	3
4–6	210021	1 5	3 4
4–7	201210	1 4	2 6
4–8	200121	1 5	2 3
4–9	200022	1 5 6	2 3 4
4–10	122010	2 3	4 6
4–11	121110	2	6
4–12	112101	3	5
4–13	112011	3	4
4–14	111120	5	6
4–Z15	111111		
4–17	102210	3 4	2 6
4–23	021030	5	1 4 6
5–1	432100	1	5 6
5–2	332110	1 2	6
5–3	322210	1	6
5–4	322111	1	4 5 6
5–5	321121	1	3 4 6
5–9	231211	2	3 5 6
5–10	223111	3	4 5 6
5–11	222220		6
5–Z12	222121		4 6
5–14	221131	5	3 4 6
5–Z17	212320	4	6
5–Z18	212221		2 6
5–19	212122		2 4
5–23	132130	2 5	6
6–1	543210	1	6
6–2	443211	1 2	5 6
6–Z3/Z36	433221	1	6
6–Z4/Z37	432321	1	6
6–5	422232	1	
6–Z6/Z38	421242	1 5	3
6–7	420243	1 5	3
6–8	343230	2	6
6–9	342231	2	6
6–Z11/Z40	333231		6
6–Z12/Z41	332232	1 2 5	3 4 6
6–Z13/Z42	324222	3	
6–14	323430	4	6
6–15	323421	4	6

Example 76 (cont.)

Set	Vector	Maxima	Minima
6–16	322431	4	6
6–Z17	322332	1 4 5	2 3 6
6–18	322242	5	
6–20	303630	4	2 6
6–Z29/Z50	224232	3	
6–Z45	234222	3	
6–Z47	233241	5	6
6–Z48	232341	5	6

Example 77a IC Maximizations for Excluded Sets, Transitional Period

	Number of Times Maximized in Sets of Cardinals			
IC	4	5	6	Total
1	9	5	9	23
5	5	2	7	14
2	3	3	4	10
3	5	1	3	9
4	2	1	5	8
(6	1	0	0	1)

Example 77b IC Minimizations for Excluded Sets, Transitional Period

	Number of Times Minimized in Sets of Cardinals			
IC	4	5	6	Total
(6	10	13	15	38)
4	6	6	1	13
3	4	3	4	11
5	4	4	1	9
2	4	2	2	8
1	1	0	0	1

Example 78 IC Extrema by Phase, Transitional Period

		1903–10	1903–09	1903–05	1903–07	1905–07	1907	1907–10	1910	Totals
All Sets										
Maximizations	ic 1	0	0	0	1	2	7	0	0	10
	ic 2	2	2	1	6	1	1	1	0	14
	ic 3	7	0	0	3	0	1	1	4	16
	ic 4	7	3	1	4	3	1	2	2	23
	ic 5	1	1	4	7	3	2	1	0	19
	ic 6	0	0	0	1	0	0	0	0	1
Minimizations	ic 1	5	3	3	7	1	0	1	0	20
	ic 2	5	0	0	2	3	1	3	1	15
	ic 3	1	4	0	6	3	2	1	0	17
	ic 4	0	0	2	1	2	1	0	1	7
	ic 5	4	1	0	5	1	1	0	1	13
	ic 6	6	4	7	9	6	5	4	2	43
Significant Sets Only										
Maximizations	ic 1	0	0	0	0	1	1	0	0	2
	ic 2	0	1	4	0	5	0	0	0	10
	ic 3	0	0	0	1	0	3	0	3	7
	ic 4	1	2	1	1	6	1	1	0	13
	ic 5	0	0	3	0	4	2	0	0	9
	ic 6	0	0	0	0	1	0	0	0	1
Minimizations	ic 1	0	2	5	2	3	2	0	1	15
	ic 2	1	0	0	0	3	2	1	2	9
	ic 3	0	1	1	1	6	3	0	0	12
	ic 4	0	0	0	0	0	0	0	0	0
	ic 5	0	1	1	2	3	1	0	0	8
	ic 6	1	0	3	1	6	5	0	1	17

Example 79 Summary of IC Extrema by Phase, Transitional Period

	All Sets		Significant Sets Only	
Period of Use	Maxima	Minima	Maxima	Minima
Sets used at some time during 1903–10, regardless of period	4	1	4	1
1903–10	3, 4	1, 2	4	2
1903–09	4	3	4	1
1903–05	5	1	2	1
1903–07	5	1	3, 4	1, 5
1905–07	4, 5	2, 3	4	3
1907	1	3	3	3
1907–10	4	2	4	2
1910	3	2, 4, 5	3	2

reasonable to conclude that most of these sets were excluded because they maximize ic 1.

We have evaluated the ic extrema of sets in general use in Scriabin's transitional period, but not his changes in practice within this large span of time. Examples 70–71 assigned the sets to periods; example 78 contains the data for ic extrema in all sets in use during each period, and also for significant sets only. The ics most frequently maximized or minimized are summarized in example 79.

The maximization of ic 4 and minimization of ic 1 are equally characteristic of significant sets and sets in general use during Scriabin's transition. The predominance of ic 4 is further evinced by the ic maxima for sets used in 1903–09 and 1903–10. In several other periods ic 4 is most frequently maximized: in 1905–07 and 1907–10 in collections of all sets and of significant sets only, and in the significant sets of 1903–07.

The preference for sets which maximize ic 4 corroborates the importance of whole-tone sonorities throughout Scriabin's transitional period. This is further confirmed by the maximization of ic 2 in the significant sets of 1903–05. Perhaps the best indication of the importance of whole-tone components is provided by example 79. Here even-numbered ics are most often maximized (and seldom minimized), whereas odd-numbered ics occur mostly as minima—especially for significant sets. For this group, even-numbered ics occur as maxima seven times and as minima only three times; the situation for odd-numbered ics is precisely the reverse.

In the figures for extrema in 1903–09 and 1903–10, ic 5 is maximized much less than in Scriabin's vocabulary of sets as a whole (example 78). Because ic 5 is the basic ic of the tonal system, it would not usually be maximized in the sets Scriabin used while moving away from explicit tonal structures. The ic maxima for all sets belonging exclusively to the earlier periods indicate the importance of tonal components, however. In all three earlier periods—1903–05, 1903–07, and 1905–07—ic 5 is most often maximized. Whole-tone-related sets are also important during these phases, as indicated by the maximization of even-numbered ics in the significant sets, and in the group of all sets used in 1905–07. The maximization of ics 2, 4, and 5 in the early periods supports the conclusion that both whole-tone and tonal procedures are operative in the compositions from this time. The sets involved in later periods do not generally maximize ic 5, however, and ic 5 is never strongly favored among the significant sets—even in the early phases of the transition. Thus, as early as 1903 Scriabin's most characteristic harmonies were unconventional and whole-tone-related.

A definite change in set usage is evidenced by the extrema for sets occurring exclusively in the music of 1907. The ic most often maximized is ic 1, which in earlier periods—and indeed in the general set vocabulary of Scriabin's transition—is most frequently minimized. Among significant sets belonging to the 1907 phase, however, ic 3 is most often maximized. In the larger view, ic 3 is more characteristic of the later phases of Scriabin's transition; it is predominant in both categories of sets used exclusively in the music of 1910. Significantly, ic 3 is also favored in the sets used throughout the transitional period (1903–10). Thus, the sets which maximize ic 3 (such as 4–18, 4–27, and 5–16) are particularly important factors of continuity in Scriabin's transition to atonality.

The works of the later phases of the transition are not structured entirely of radically different sonorities. In fact, in the sets employed in either 1909 or 1910 (example 69), ic 4 continues to be most frequently maximized. In this collection, ic 3 is almost as important as ic 4, whereas ic 5, so important in earlier phases, is seldom maximized.

The use of novel sonorities which maximize ic 3 must have necessitated other changes in Scriabin's compositional procedures. Whole-tone invariance no longer operated (especially in the works of 1909–10) as it had in earlier compositions. Rather, in order to exploit the invariance properties of these new sets, different schemes of transposition had to be introduced. In chapter 6 an evaluation of the specific changes in Scriabin's method is included in conjunction with analyses of the "Feuillet d'album" Op. 58 and the Prelude Op. 59/2.

The examination of ic extrema in the sets of Scriabin's late tonal music has enabled us to generalize about the structure of sets at various stages of his transition to atonality. The ic contents of individual sets were combined and averaged to ascertain the ic content most typical of sets in a given period. Although such a study is invaluable for determining the development of a compositional process, its validity is limited to generalizations. To deal with the specific properties of particular sets and their interrelations, the framework of the set complex must be adopted.

Example 80 demonstrates the relations among sets which are significant in at least one of the compositions of 1903–10. The prime candidate for the nexus set of this complex is 6–34, the mystic chord. This set is in the relation Kh with twelve other sets—more than any other hexachord. The choice of 6–34 is especially fitting because it is the hexachord most widely used throughout this music, appearing in fifteen of nineteen pieces, significantly in eight. The

Example 80 Set-Complex Relations for Significant Sets, Opp. 32–59 (1903–10)

	4–16	4–18	4–19	4–20	4–22	4–24	4–25	4–26	4–27	4–Z29														
5–6 (1)	K	K	K	K	K	K				K														
5–13 (3)	K	K	Kh	K	K	Kh	K		K	Kh														
5–15 (2)	Kh	K	K		K	K	Kh			K														
5–16 (1)		Kh	K	K		K		K	K	Kh														
5–22 (2)	K	Kh	Kh	K			K	K	K	K														
5–24 (3)	Kh		K		Kh	K	K	K	K	Kh														
5–27 (2)	K	K	K	Kh	Kh	K		Kh	K															
5–28 (6)	K	K	K		K	K	Kh		Kh	Kh														
5–30 (1)	Kh	K	Kh	K	Kh	Kh	K	K	K	K														
5–32 (1)	K	Kh	K	K	K	K		Kh	Kh	K														
5–33 (9)	K		K		K	Kh	Kh		K	K														
5–34 (2)	K		K		Kh	K	K	K	Kh	K														
5–35 (1)	K			K	Kh			Kh	K	K														
5–Z38 (1)	K	Kh	K	Kh	K	K			Kh	K														
											5–6	5–13	5–15	5–16	5–22	5–24	5–27	5–28	5–30	5–32	5–33	5–34	5–35	5–Z38
6–Z10/																								
Z39 (2)	K	K	K		K	K		K	K	Kh		K		K		K								
6–21 (2)			Kh			Kh	Kh		Kh	Kh		Kh						Kh			Kh			
6–22 (3)	Kh		Kh		Kh	Kh	Kh			Kh		Kh	Kh			Kh			Kh		Kh			
6–Z26 (2)	Kh		K	K	Kh	K		Kh		K						K	K		K				K	
6–27 (1)		Kh						Kh	Kh	Kh				Kh						Kh				
6–Z28/																								
Z49 (1)		Kh	K			K	K	K	Kh	K				K	K			K		K				
6–33 (1)	Kh				Kh			Kh	Kh	Kh						Kh						Kh	Kh	
6–34 (8)	Kh		Kh		Kh	Kh	Kh		Kh	Kh						Kh		Kh	Kh		Kh	Kh		
6–35 (2)						Kh	Kh														Kh			
6–Z43 (2)	Kh	Kh	K	K	K	K	K		K	Kh	K	K	K		K			K	K					K

structure of the complex is not completely connected, however, for twelve other sets involved are not related in K or Kh with 6–34. No other single set which might be a secondary nexus set is related to all twelve remaining sets. This is not surprising, for the complex we are considering comprises sets from compositions spanning eight years. Because we are not concerned with establishing the unity of a single work, it is useful to examine alternatives for a secondary nexus set and, if possible, to relate the sets connected by these alternatives to particular periods of Scriabin's transition.

The first alternative is 6–Z43, which encompasses seven of the twelve remaining sets; those sets unrelated to either 6–34 or 6–Z43 are: 4–26, 5–16, 5–32, 5–35, and 5–27. The first two occur significantly only in 1907, and 5–32 is significant only in 1910. On the other hand, 5–35 is significant only before 1906. The fact that these sets are identified exclusively with late or early periods in Scriabin's transition may account for their failure to connect with the complex about 6–34 and 6–Z43. Set 5–27, which is important in the compositions of 1905–07, is the only significant set from the middle phases of the transitional period which is not related to 6–Z43. An advantage of choosing 6–Z43 as a secondary nexus is that its use is widespread.

The other viable alternative for the secondary nexus set is 6–Z28/Z49, which is related to six of the twelve sets not related to 6–34. This set occurs only in Op. 59/2 (1910) and therefore seems a less desirable alternative than 6–Z43. Yet 6–Z28/Z49 is in either K or Kh with eleven of the sets in example 80; the only hexachords related to more sets are 6–34 and 6–Z43. The sets not accounted for by either 6–34 or 6–Z28/Z49 are: 4–20, 5–6, 5–13, 5–15, 5–27, 5–35, and 5–Z38. Sets 5–27 and 5–35 are the only ones not related to either alternative for the secondary nexus set, and only 5–27 is used widely as a significant set.

Nearly every significant set in the music of 1903–10 is related to 6–34 (as primary nexus) or to 6–Z43 or 6–Z28/Z49. The changes we have observed regarding the types of set structures used at various times during the period make a neatly connected complex almost impossible. It is thus reasonable to accept both 6–Z43 and 6–Z28/Z49 as secondary nexus sets. Sets 6–34 and 6–Z43 are connected through a tertiary nexus set, 5–30, to which they are related in Kh and K respectively. Set 5–35, which is not related to either secondary nexus hexachord, is in the relation (R_0, R_p) with 5–30 and is thus attached to the complex. Both 6–Z43 and 6–Z28/Z49 are connected with 6–34 and with each other through another tertiary nexus, 5–28. Moreover, 5–27—the only set of widespread significance which is not related to either the primary nexus or the two secondary nexus sets—is in the relation R_2 with 5–28. Thus the entire collection of significant sets in Scriabin's transitional music forms a closed complex.

The nexus-set relations are represented graphically in example 81. The similarity relations among the five-element sets mentioned above (5–27, 5–28, 5–30, and 5–35) are also demonstrated. The fact that all significant sets in this music are related within a single closed complex is proof that Scriabin's transition to atonality involved no sudden break with past components or procedures.

We must now ask whether all or most of the sets in the music of 1903–10 are

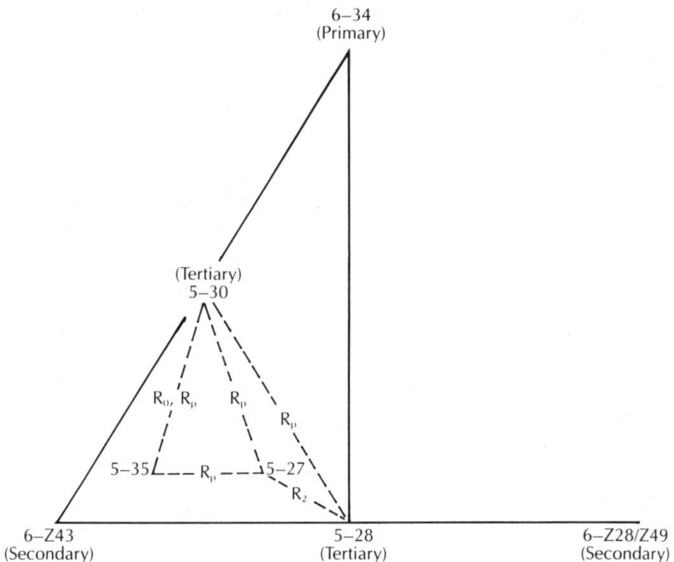

Example 81 Nexus Sets for Significant Sets, Transitional Period

derived from a single structural principle. At the end of chapter 4 we found that the structure of the mystic chord, 6–34, was based on the interaction of the two main procedures underlying the structure of the transitional music: tonality and whole-tone invariance. Set 6–34 contains five pcs of a single 6–35—the whole-tone scale—and one pc from the complementary 6–35 (which we termed the non-whole-tone element). Of course, 6–34 is not the only hexachord with this property. Both 6–21 and 6–22 are similarly structured, although they do not minimize ic 1. Set 6–34 is further differentiated from 6–21 and 6–22 in that its non-whole-tone element usually results from tonal forces (in particular, the fifth), whereas the corresponding elements of 6–21 and 6–22 originate in less consistent ways.

The fact that both 6–21 and 6–22 occur significantly in Scriabin's late tonal music suggests that more sets from this music might be derived on the basis of similar structural principles. We shall therefore list all four- and five-note sets in which all elements but one form a subset of 6–35. Further, because no other six-element set and only one seven-element set (7–33) has a structure which fits this description, we shall extend the description to include sets in which all but two elements belong to a single whole-tone scale. It is not useful, however, to extend this requirement to four- or five-element sets, for no such set is excluded by the broader description. For eight-note sets, even this extension yields only three sets (8–21, 8–24, and 8–25); for these sets we shall thus list those which contain all but three elements of a single whole-tone scale as well. This extension is useful only for eight-note sets, because all sets of lower cardinal numbers meet this description. Sets which meet these specifications—termed *predominantly whole-tone sets*—are listed according to cardinal number in example 82. Interestingly, the sets of cardinal 4 which contain only one non-whole-tone element have

Example 82 Predominantly Whole-Tone Sets

Sets of Cardinals 4 or 8

4/8–2
- (5)
- 11
- 12
- Z15
- 16
- 19
- 21
- 22
- 24
- 25
- 27
- Z29

(Ordinals apply to four-element sets with only one non-whole-tone element and to eight-element sets with no more than three.)

Sets of Cardinals 5 or 7

5/7–8
- (9)
- 13
- 15
- 24
- 26
- 28
- 30
- 33
- 34

(Ordinals apply to five-note sets with only one non-whole-tone element and to seven-note sets with no more than two.)

Sets of Cardinal 6

6–(2)
- (Z4/Z37)
- (9)
- Z10/Z39
- (Z12/Z41)
- 15
- (16)
- (Z17)/Z43
- 21*
- 22*
- Z23/(Z45)
- Z24/Z46
- Z26/(Z48)
- Z28/Z49
- 30
- 31
- 33
- 34*
- 35

(Most contain two non-whole-tone elements; those with only one are marked with asterisks.)

ordinal numbers which correspond exactly to those of the eight-note sets which contain no more than three non-whole-tone elements. A similar correspondence exists for the ordinals of sets with cardinals 5 and 7.

Most of the predominantly whole-tone sets occur in Scriabin's transitional works; those sets not used by Scriabin are enclosed in parentheses in example 82. Twelve of the thirteen sets of cardinal 4 are employed in this music, as are nine of the ten five-note sets and seventeen of the twenty-seven hexachords. Of the twelve predominantly whole-tone sets not used by Scriabin, seven maximize ic 1: 4–5, 6–2, 6–Z4/Z37, 6–Z12/Z41, and 6–Z17. No other predominantly whole-tone sets maximize ic 1 except 6–Z43, the Z-correspondent of 6–Z17, which maximizes three ics. The fact that Scriabin avoided sets which maximize ic 1 may have been the basis for his rejection of these seven. It is unclear why the remaining five fail to appear in this music. Two, 6–Z45 and 6–Z48, are the complements of hexachords which Scriabin did employ in the transitional music. Three other predominantly whole-tone sets—5–9, 6–9, and 6–16—are inexplicably absent. Nevertheless, Scriabin's nearly exhaustive exploitation of sets which meet the specifications for predominantly whole-tone structure strongly suggests the validity of the structural principle of whole-tone predominance.

To complete an evaluation of the importance of this principle, however, we must take into account the proportion of Scriabin's predominantly whole-tone sets relative to those which are not. Example 83 lists those of Scriabin's sets which are not predominantly whole-tone. (All significant sets are marked with aster-

Example 83 Sets Other Than Predominantly Whole-Tone Sets, Transitional Period

4–4	5–3	6–Z3
4–6	5–6* (1907)	6–Z6
4–7	5–7	6–14
4–13	5–11	6–18
4–14	5–16* (1907)	6–Z19/Z44
4–17	5–Z17	6–Z25
4–18* (1910)	5–19	6–27
4–20* (1905–07)	5–20	6–Z29
4–23	5–21	6–32
4–26* (1907)	5–22* (1907–10)	6–Z40
4–28	5–25	
	5–27* (1905–07)	
	5–29	
	5–31	
	5–32* (1910)	
	5–35* (1903–05)	
	5–Z36	
	5–Z37	
	5–Z38* (1905–07)	

*Significant during the period in parentheses

isks.) Eleven of the eighteen four-element sets are excluded, but only three of these occur with significance. Nineteen of twenty-eight five-element sets are excluded, but only seven of these are significant. Only eleven of Scriabin's hexachords are not predominantly whole-tone, and not one is significant. Seven of the ten significant sets which are not predominantly whole-tone occur significantly only once. The remaining three—4–20, 5–22, and 5–27—occur at most three times as significant sets, always within relatively narrow time spans. Thus a single principle—whole-tone predominance—underlies the structure of the most widespread significant sets in Scriabin's transition to atonality. Other sets with different structures are sometimes significant, but they occur infrequently and within limited phases of the transition. Predominantly whole-tone sets occur significantly in every composition of 1903–10 and almost always outnumber those which are not predominantly whole-tone. (An important exception is the Prelude Op. 59/2, one of Scriabin's first true atonal works.)

From the point of view of whole-tone predominance, the mystic chord (6–34) is one of many sets of similar structure and is thus of no special importance. However, 6–34 assumes a primary role in the late tonal works. It is among the most widespread sets in this music, and it not only meets the structural specifications for whole-tone predominance but it also possesses the extrema for ic content most strongly favored on average in Scriabin's music of 1903–10. Moreover, 6–34 originates almost always in the interaction of whole-tone and tonal procedures. Indeed, the mystic chord epitomizes the structural premises underlying Scriabin's transition to atonality.

SIX
ON THE BORDER OF ATONALITY
The "Feuillet d'album" Op. 58 and the Prelude Op. 59/2

In the preceding chapters we analyzed music dating from Scriabin's period of transition to atonality (1903–10) and found that procedures normally associated with either tonality or atonality are not mutually exclusive. Rather, both operate simultaneously and consistently throughout most of the compositions discussed. Tonal procedures generally govern structure at every level, whereas significant pc-set relations determine another type of organization at the surface. Any composition with a tonal Ursatz is at least implicitly tonal, because tonality, as a closed system of operations, is a much more powerful organizing force than set relations, which ostensibly entail no hierarchy of functions. In chapter 5, three works not previously analyzed were included in the survey of set usage in the music of 1903–10. These works—"Enigme" Op. 52/2, the "Feuillet d'album" Op. 58, and the Prelude Op. 59/2—are more problematic than most pieces of the transitional period. In this chapter we shall analyze the latter two works, discussing the interaction of tonal and atonal procedures in the determination of structure.[1]

"FEUILLET D'ALBUM" OP. 58

The "Feuillet d'album" was written while Scriabin was composing *Prometheus*, probably in late 1909. It is short because it was intended as an autograph for a music book.[2] (For a complete graphic analysis of both tonal and atonal structure, see example 84.) The composition employs just twelve sets, and only two are significant—4–24 and 6–34 (the Prometheus chord); in a sense the piece is a study of the properties of 6–34, with which Scriabin was then preoccupied.

This composition has a fairly balanced phrase structure. The first phrase, four measures in length, is transposed with t = 2 in mm. 5–8. A second phrase is introduced in mm. 9–12, and the conclusion of this phrase is repeated in mm. 12–14. At the end of m. 14 new material links the second phrase to a repetition at T_0 of the original phrase, beginning in m. 16. This repetition is literal until

Example 84 "Feuillet d'album" Op. 58

Example 84 (cont.)

m. 18, when a B♮ is introduced conspicuously as the lowest bass note of the piece (compare m. 3). The second half of this phrase is repeated in mm. 20–21 and again in mm. 21–23, with modifications—most significantly in the melody. (The notes G♯ and B♯ are introduced, in mm. 20 and 22 respectively, as overlappings of the melodic E♮.) The piece thus comprises an eight-measure first phrase, a seven-measure second phrase, and an eight-measure repetition of the first phrase; the second may also be considered an eight-measure phrase overlapping the return of the first phrase in m. 16.

Despite the differentiation of phrases, the "Feuillet d'album" is probably a through-composed structure, primarily because a single whole-tone scale is held invariant throughout. The pc content of the entire first phrase (mm. 1–4) forms 8–24 if we exclude pcs 1 and 5 at the end of m. 4. (Their exclusion is clear from Scriabin's own pedal indication; pc 1 is a chromatic passing tone to pc 0, important in mm. 5–8, and pc 5, another important element in m. 5, is anticipated at the end of m. 4.) Set 8–24 comprises all elements of the even-numbered whole-tone scale and two non-whole-tone elements—pcs 3 and 7, which are powerful inflections but are nonetheless subsidiary to the whole-tone elements. (In a sense, they behave like nonharmonic tones in tonality.) Pitch-class 7 occurs briefly in m. 3 as a lower chromatic auxiliary to pc 8. The role of pc 3 is less clear; it is the essential non-whole-tone element of 6–34 in mm. 1–2, and in the first three measures it shows no tendency to move elsewhere. In the lower part in m. 4, however, pc 3 moves to pc 2, and, after some oscillation between the two pcs, this motion continues chromatically downward, arriving at pc 0 at the beginning of m. 5, where the transposed repetition of mm. 1–4 begins. Measures 5–8 contain an 8–24 equivalent at T_2 to the original, with six pcs invariant—those of the even-numbered whole-tone scale. Pitch-class 2, the only whole-tone element missing from the first phrase until m. 4, is the prominent bass tone in mm. 5–6, reinforcing the impression that pc 3 resolves to pc 2 in m. 4 to complete the whole-tone aggregate.

In the first phrase the bass progresses by tritone, from C (mm. 1–2) to low F♯ (m. 3), with implications—especially in light of the whole-tone invariance here—of the ♭II–V progression in Scriabin's more clearly tonal works. Because of its register, F♯ is clearly effective in the bass for the entire phrase. (No harmonic change occurs at m. 3 when F♯ is introduced, for all pcs from mm. 1–2 are contained in m. 3, along with the new, subsidiary pc 7. Whether the predominantly whole-tone chord on F♯ functions as a dominant remains to be seen, but the low B♮ effective at the end of the piece suggests this possibility.)

When the first phrase is transposed with $t = 2$ in mm. 5–8, a motion from F♯ to A♭ is effected in the bass. Significantly, this motion is also carried by the highest melodic voice, from F♯ in m. 1 to A♭ in m. 5. The activity in the register of the bass F♯ resumes in m. 11 (with the low F♮) and continues in m. 17. Thus the F♯–A♭ motion in the bass is not fundamental but rather duplicates a melodic motion. The melody itself begins with the unfolding of a descending third from F♯ to D♯ (mm. 1–2), balanced by a chromatic ascent to G♭ in m. 7. In m. 9, G♭ is respelled F♯, and there is no doubt a link between the melodic F♯s in mm. 1 and 9, but the activity above F♯ must also be explained.

The same whole-tone scale underlies all of mm. 1–8, but two new non-whole-tone elements are introduced in mm. 5–8 by the transposition of the opening phrase: pcs 5 and 9, which function like pcs 3 and 7 in mm. 1–4. The resolution of pc 5 to pc 4 in m. 8 is reinforced by pc 4 as the bass tone in m. 9, even though this measure is not a sequential repetition of previous material, as might be expected. The material of mm. 9–10 is not totally new, however, for the pc content here forms another 8–24, equivalent to the original at T_6 (not at T_4 as expected). This 8–24 retains the whole-tone scale of previous 8–24s. The two non-whole-tone elements here—pcs 1 and 9—are both important. Pitch-class 1 is a lower auxiliary to pc 2, as is pc 9 to pc 10 in the melody in m. 11—the highest melodic note except the high B♯ at the end. This upper-register motion continues the F♯–A♭ motion in mm. 1–8. The A♮ not only revives interest in the upper register, it also connects chromatically two elements of a large-scale whole-tone line, A♭ and B♭.

The arrival of the high B♭ in the melody in m. 11 coincides with the first non-whole-tone bass note, F♮. This bass F♮ is part of the first potentially cadential bass progression, for it is the goal of the descending-fifth motion from C in the bass in m. 10. In spite of these significant events at the exact midpoint of the composition, continuity is ensured because the pc content of mm. 11–12 (excluding pc 1 at the end of m. 12) forms the same 8–24 which occurs in mm. 5–8. This set shares seven pcs with the 8–24 immediately preceding (mm. 9–10)—the even-numbered whole-tone scale plus pc 9—which form 7–33, and thus 7–33 underlies mm. 5–12. This continuity extends even farther, for the material of mm. 11–12 is repeated in mm. 13–14. By the end of the second phrase (mm. 14–15), F♮ is no longer the effective bass tone; rather, interest is again focused on C♮ in the bass, as at the beginning.

The repetition of the opening phrase in mm. 16–19 entails the crucial addition of the low B♮ in m. 18 below the original material of mm. 1–3. This is the first appearance of pc 11, and it completes the twelve-tone aggregate formed among all pcs in the piece. The entire pc content of mm. 16–18 forms the first occurrence of 8–19 in the composition. However, its complement, 4–19, has been prominent throughout; it is the set formed by the melodic E and preceding grace notes in mm. 3 and 18 and by similar configurations in mm. 7, 11, etc. Because B♮ is virtually a pedal tone for the rest of the piece, a pure whole-tone aggregate is not possible except as the composite of pitches above this pedal tone. In fact, the concluding section, at least through m. 21, suspends the material of the first phrase (which forms an entire whole-tone aggregate) over the B♮ pedal tone. The final two measures, which form the same 8–19 heard in mm. 16–18 and in m. 20, contain only five whole-tone elements, for pc 2 is missing here.

The other new event of the concluding phrase, introduced with the repetitions of melodic fragments typical of Scriabin's codas (see, for example, the coda of the Etude Op. 49/1), is the arpeggiation in the upper voice of an augmented triad ascending from E♮ (mm. 18–19) through G♯ (m. 20) to B♯ (m. 22); this triad is a subset of the underlying whole-tone scale. The goal of this gesture, the high B♯, is linked registrally with the large-scale whole-tone ascent—F♯–A♭–B♭—which we traced through the first half of the piece. The B♯ is the next element in this ascending whole-tone line.

The overall bass progression from F♯ (mm. 1–4 and 16–17) to B♮ (the lowest bass tone, which arrives in m. 18) strongly implies a tonal progression from dominant to tonic in B major. Several other aspects of structure confirm the impression that F♯ supports a dominant function. The tritone bass progression from C in mm. 1–2 to F♯ in m. 3 is associated with the ♭II–V progression, which produces whole-tone invariants and prolongs the dominant. Significantly, C recurs in the bass in mm. 10, 12, and 14 before the return of F♯ in m. 17. The bass progression of descending fifth in mm. 10–11 (repeated in mm. 12–13) implies that the chord on C is an applied dominant, not a ♭II dominant preparation. However, the temporary harmony on ♭2 as a V/♭V is familiar in Scriabin's more conventionally tonal works. For instance, in "Nuances" Op. 56/3 (example 32), ♭II in m. 14 typically prepares the dominant. In mm. 11–12, however, the same chord is a dominant cadencing to ♭V. The harmonic events implied by the bass progression in mm. 10–17 of the "Feuillet d'album" are virtually identical to the more explicit progression in mm. 11–15 of "Nuances." Thus the harmonies on F♮ in mm. 11 and 13 of Op. 58 may be regarded as a brief departure from the main progression. Essentially, the harmony on C—not that on F—is prolonged throughout mm. 9–16, but at the largest level this harmony is ♭II in a V–♭II–V progression prolonging a whole-tone dominant on F♯ throughout the first seventeen measures.

The retention of a single whole-tone scale throughout this portion of the piece certainly supports this interpretation, as does the repetition in the second phrase, at T_6, of several important sets from the beginning: 8–24 in mm. 9–10; 4–19 in m. 11, equivalent at T_6 to 4–19 in m. 3; and 7–26, first presented in mm. 1–3, in m. 12. Both 8–24 and 7–26 hold invariant only pcs of the underlying whole-tone scale, whereas the two forms of 4–19 share no pcs. The melodic unfolding of F♯–A♭–B♭ in the first half of the composition also supports the analysis of a prolonged dominant, for the F♯–B♭ interval is the enharmonic equivalent of the F♯–A♯ third of the dominant harmony.

The suspension chord sustained from m. 18 to the end is similar to the closing harmony of "Désir" Op. 57/1, where 6–34, the mystic chord, is formed by the suspension of the whole-tone dominant (5–33) over the tonic note. The arpeggiation of the augmented triad in these closing measures supplies the highest note of the piece, B♯, which in a suspension chord would normally occur as C♮ (♭$\hat{2}$) in B major and would—if allowed—resolve back to B♮ ($\hat{1}$). This B♮ would complete the unfolding of an ascending fourth from F♯ at the beginning, which would thus span the entire work.

Although this progression is the most strongly projected line in the piece, it does not descend, as a tonal Urlinie should. No descending Urlinie is obvious. The most likely initial tone of an Urlinie is F♯ ($\hat{5}$); conspicuous at the beginning, it is the point of departure for the important ascending fourth-span. The $\hat{5}$ is still effective when the original phrase returns in m. 16, and although a motion to E ($\hat{4}$) is evident in m. 17, there is no further descent by the end of the piece, though an ultimate descent to D♯ is strongly implied.

In the final analytical sketches for this piece, harmonies indicated at both the beginning and the end would render the tonal structure more conventional. Most important, the crucial non-whole-tone element in the opening phrase, D♯, is the third of the understood tonic harmony. The G♯ in the actual opening chord seems to originate in the subdominant.

The "Feuillet d'album" has the most subtle and tenuous tonal structure of any work we have examined. The tonality is determined principally by the bass progression, but in this work it is doubtful whether the bass progression would determine the structure without the strong reinforcement of whole-tone invariance and other set correspondences. There are other tonal phenomena, such as the ascending unfolding which spans the entire piece in the upper register, but they could not be unequivocally tonal in the absence of the primary structural determinants.

PRELUDE OP. 59/2

This is the only composition which Scriabin marked *sauvage*, and its structure is startlingly different from the others analyzed in this book. In the previous chapter we discovered that 4–12, 4–13, 4–17, 6–14, and 6–Z28/Z49 appear for the first time in Op. 59/2, and two others—4–18 and 5–32—are used as significant sets for the first time in this work. This prelude dates from approximately the same time as *Prometheus* and the "Feuillet d'album" Op. 58 (both composed in 1909). The abrupt structural changes in this piece suggest that it was composed after Op. 58, especially because the structure of the "Feuillet d'album" is determined by procedures which operate throughout the transitional music.

The Prelude Op. 59/2 is a through-composed work in that its segments of material are all part of the same basic subject matter. (For analytical sketches and a complete score of this work, see example 85.) The main formal division is delineated at m. 28, where a virtually literal repetition at T_6 of the first twenty-five measures begins. Within the sections thus defined, there are a limited number of ideas or gestures, which are repeated literally or slightly modified, at various levels of transposition. The form of the first section is outlined in example 86. There are three basic gestures here—(a), (c), and (e)—for (b) is an expansion of (a), and (d) employs the melody of (c) (albeit with different rhythm and dynamics). After the repetition at T_6 of the entire first section, new material occurs beginning in m. 54. Measures 54–57 closely resemble mm. 26–27, and another statement of (d) concludes the piece (mm. 58–61).

Various sections are determined by transpositional repetition—either the

Example 85 Prelude Op. 59/2

Example 85 (cont.)

Example 85 (cont.)

Example 86 Prelude Op. 59/2 (mm. 1–27): Form

Section	Level
(1) (mm. 1–5)	
(a) (m. 1) basic idea = 7–32	T_0
(b) (mm. 1–2) embellishment of (a)	
(c) (mm. 2–3) melody = 5–32	
(b) (mm. 3–4)	
(c) (mm. 4–5)	
(2) (mm. 5–7)	
(b) (mm. 5–6)	T_3
(c) (mm. 6–7)	
(3) (mm. 7–10)	
(a) (mm. 7–8)	T_6
(b) (mm. 8–10) repeated twice, followed by a repetition of the latter half of (b)	
(4) (mm. 11–25)	
(d) (mm. 11–14) melody from (c) *avec défi* (defiant)	T_6
(e) (mm. 14–15) arpeggiation	
(d) (mm. 16–18)	
(e) (mm. 18–19)	
(d) (mm. 20–22)	T_7
(e) (mm. 22–25) compare mm. 14–15, 18–19	
(a) (mm. 26–27) material of m. 1 at T_6 repeated three times	T_6

literal repetition of entire segments (as in section 2, a literal transposition with t = 3 of (b) and (c) from section 1) or the transposition of sets apart from any particular compositional context (as in section 4, where 5–22, 7–32, and 8–18 differ from the forms in section 1 but are equivalent to them at T_6). Successive transpositions with t = 3 differentiate sections 1, 2, and 3, and thus the shared materials in sections 1 and 3 are equivalent at T_6. Section 4 flows smoothly from section 3 despite different subject matter because important sets shared by the sections occur at the same level of transposition. Moreover, because the repetition of this material begins in m. 28 at T_6, the transition to the second section occurs easily. During the interim (mm. 20–26) the (d) and (e) segments are transposed up seven half steps from their levels in mm. 11–15, so that T_6 is not maintained throughout section 4. However, the transitional mm. 26–27 reintroduce part of the (a) segment at T_6. Because mm. 1–25 are repeated at T_6, two more successive transpositions with t = 3 occur in mm. 33 and 35, returning to the original level at m. 35 (3 + 3 + 3 + 3 = 0 mod 12). The original level of transposition is then the basis for events through m. 47, giving substantial weight to material which completes this cycle of transposition. Beginning in m. 54, however, new sets are introduced to close the piece, and therefore completion of this cycle is not the sole determinant of closure, although it certainly signals the end of the piece.

Transposition of large segments of material or of particular sets with t = 3 is not typical of Scriabin's late tonal works; the composer usually exploited those sets which have been classified as predominantly whole-tone. For maximum invariance among equivalent forms of sets of this type, an even-numbered level of transposition is required. (On rare occasions in the transitional works, Scriabin employs two successive transpositions with t = 3, but only to attain T_6. See, for example, mm. 4–10 of the Prelude Op. 48/4, where a bass progression from V to ♭II is expanded by the mediant as a connecting harmony—V–III♯–♭II—thus dividing the tritone progression symmetrically.) In fact, transpositions with t = 3 produce maximum invariance for the sets which Scriabin introduces or uses significantly for the first time in this piece, as well as for such sets as 4–28 and 6–27. (Notable exceptions are 5–22 and 5–26.)

The fact that Op. 59/2 is based on successive transpositions with t = 3 suggests that 4–28 (which appears in the tonal system as the diminished seventh chord) should be an important sonority in the piece. Actually, 4–28 rarely appears on the surface of the music. However, its complement, 8–28, is formed by the lower voices of the entire piece (excluding mm. 20–25 and the corresponding mm. 48–53, which involve transposition with t = 7). In fact, 4–28 and 8–28 may well be the main matrix of the composition, in that the structure originates in the exploitation of these sets. Many important sets on the surface of the music are subsets of 8–28, including 4–12, 4–13, 4–18, 5–16, 5–28, 5–31, 5–32, 6–27, and 6–Z49; other highly characteristic sets in the piece are not contained in 8–28: 4–19, 5–26, 6–Z28 (although its complement, 6–Z49, is), and, most conspicuously, 5–22 and 7–32.

Example 87 Prelude Op. 59/2

Example 87a demonstrates the progression of 6–27, the first hexachord of the piece, throughout the composition. (This progression is governed by successive transpositions with t = 3.) In example 87b the elements are organized to demonstrate invariance among forms of 6–27. Over the course of the progression an entire 8–28 is produced, but in a special way: one form of 4–28, [0,3,6,9], is a subset of each chord of the progression, and two elements of a second 4–28, [7,10,1,4], supply the fifth and sixth elements of each 6–27. The complement of this 8–28, [2,5,8,11], is delineated as the sum of the high, accented melodic notes connected with forms of 6–27 (example 87c). The elements of the complementary 4–28 are thus highly differentiated from those of the basic 8–28, which comprises the elements of the lower voices and serves as a significant superset containing sets found at various important points in the structure. During the course of the composition as defined by the progressions in example 87, the entire twelve-tone aggregate is completed.[3]

Example 88a illustrates the relation of one significant component, 7–32, to the 4–28/8–28 matrix. This set is the sum of all pcs in the initial gesture, the (a) material. It also comprises all pcs in mm. 12–15, the first phrase of section 4. This second form of 7–32 is equivalent at T_6 to the first. In fact, 7–32 is generally subject to the same cycle of transposition as 5–31 and 6–27, though it is not itself a subset of 8–28. In example 88, 7–32 is the combination of a form of 6–27 (a subset of the basic 8–28) and one element from the complement of 8–28. The invariance properties of 7–32 as exploited by the transpositional scheme of this prelude determine its relation to the 8–28 matrix. Presentations of 7–32 equivalent at T_3 are overlapped to insure continuity. Invariance under transposition is maximum for 7–32 with t = 3, and the invariant pcs form 5–31, the same set which occurs at the point of overlap (m. 5). The 5–31s here are also equivalent at T_3, and they share 4–28 ([0,3,6,9]). The invariance is emphasized by an exchange of tritone-related pairs of voices (example 88b) which form the invariant 4–28. (The compositional exploitation of invariance properties of

Example 88 Prelude Op. 59/2

6–27 coincides exactly with that of 7–32, for 6–27 contains all pcs of 7–32 except the high melodic pc, which is not part of the basic 8–28.) Although 7–32 is not contained in 8–28, its complement, 5–32, is a subset. The presentation of 7–32 in mm. 12–15 features the complement, 5–32, embedded midphrase (mm. 13–14); this 5–32 is a subset of the basic 8–28.

Although the cyclical transpositions of 5–31, 6–27, and 7–32 determine the basic structure of the composition, not all events of the piece can be explained simply by this transpositional scheme. (If they could, the composition would be a series of unrelieved sequential repetitions.) After m. 7, the basic sequence is broken in the bass. (The expected 6–27 at T_6 occurs in mm. 7–8, despite the change.) Example 89 shows the voice leading in the low bass throughout the piece. The basic pattern entails four pcs; [7,9,0,3] (4–27) are the pcs in the original statement. This set is divided into two-note groupings separated by rests, the first forming ic 6 and the second ic 5. In example 89 these patterns are distinguished by stems in opposite directions. For convenience, the progress of the sequential repetitions may be traced with respect to the first (lower) interval, which forms ic 6. These repetitions are labeled according to transpositional equivalence, with the original interval as T_0.

After the repetition at T_3 (mm. 5–7), the first interval is transposed up another three half steps, as if for another literal repetition at T_6. The expected second interval of the pattern (a descending fourth from F♯ to C♯) does not occur in m. 8, however. Instead, another ic 6 is heard on the downbeat (where previously only ic 5 has occurred)—in fact, the same ic 6 associated with T_3. Thus the progression from T_3 to T_6 which begins in m. 7 is thwarted by returning at the last moment to T_3 in m. 8. (The interruption of the patterned voice leading does not prevent the important sets of the basic pattern from occurring at T_6 as expected.) Only in m. 26 does the pattern return, and here T_6 is successfully established. The voice leading in the bass in mm. 8–25 is connected both linearly and registrally. Most important, the ic 6 (at T_3) in mm. 8–10 recurs

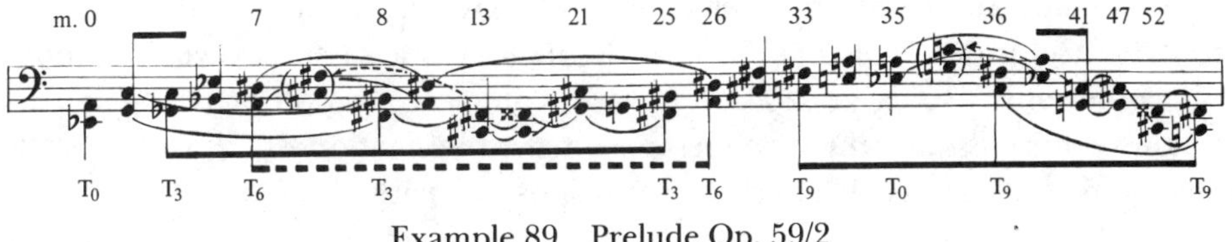

Example 89 Prelude Op. 59/2

in m. 25 in the same register—but on an upbeat, conforming to the original pattern. Thus the material of mm. 8–25 is a section unto itself. In mm. 8–9, ic 6 at T_6 continues, but the ic 6 at T_3 prevails in m. 10. More surprising, the F♯–C♯ interval expected at the beginning of m. 8 (in parentheses in example 89) is stated an octave lower in mm. 13 and 17 as the lowest pair of pitches thus far. The pcs of this interval are connected linearly (and, in some cases, by octave transfers) with the elements of the ic 6 at T_3 framing the section. The bass progression in mm. 8–25 (example 89) implies a tonal prolongation. The two most important bass pcs in terms of register and temporal placement are F♯ and C♯, which are related by ic 5, the basic ic of tonality.

The most striking feature of mm. 8–25, aside from this bass progression, is the literal repetition of the material of mm. 12–14 at T_7 in mm. 20–22. This level of transposition is characteristic of neither this piece nor any of the transitional music. Virtually none of the sets at the surface in this material attains either maximum or minimum invariance at T_7 (though T_7 produces minimum invariance for the 4–28 contained in many). Thus another explanation must be sought. Because transposition with t = 7 is a basic maneuver in traditional tonality, the structure here may prolong some sonority as a tonic. The 4–19 in m. 12 supported by A in the bass is the most likely candidate for a tonic function because it is triadic. Presumably it would be an A minor triad with a raised seventh (G♯) which would ideally resolve to the octave. When transposed up a fifth in m. 20, the chord would be $V^{7}_{\natural 3}$ of the A minor tonic. Finally, when a similar A minor chord (lacking the third) occurs in m. 29, a circular progression prolonging A minor in mm. 12–29 might be understood to take place (example 85). The impression of a progression from dominant in m. 20 to tonic in m. 26 is reinforced by the repetition of the 8–27 formed by all pcs in mm. 20–24 transposed up five half steps in mm. 26–27.

Even if a prolongation of some sonority is assumed in mm. 12–28, the function of this quasi-tonic sonority in the overall structure remains a question. Because mm. 12–25 are almost literally repeated in mm. 40–53, we might expect the prolongation of another quasi tonic, equivalent at T_6 to the first. The two quasi tonics would be of equal structural importance, for their presentations would be essentially the same. In the repetition, however, Scriabin avoids completion of the circular progression which would occur if all the material of mm. 54–55 were equivalent at T_6 to that of mm. 26–27. Instead, an unexpected set is introduced in m. 54: 6–34, the mystic chord. The thwarted prolongation of a quasi tonic in mm. 40–56 might suggest that the quasi tonic in mm. 12–28 is the true tonic of the entire structure. There is no indication, however, that any such function takes structural precedence over other sonorities at any other point in the structure. Indeed, the basic transpositional scheme of successive repetitions at T_3 inherently avoids gravitation toward a single collection of pcs. The bass motion of mm. 8–25, which suggests a tonal prolongation of F♯, overlaps the prolongation of A possibly effected by transposition with t = 7 and t = 5 in mm.

12–28. The conflict between these two procedures negates the effectiveness of either as a more fundamental determinant of tonal structure.

Because mm. 28–53 duplicate at T_6 mm. 1–25, only the closing measures of the second half need be examined in detail. Beginning in m. 33 the entire pattern (equivalent to section 2) is stated at T_9. Just as the pattern was broken in m. 8 before all of the original material could be stated at T_6, so the pattern is interrupted in m. 36 before the original level (T_0) is attained. (An exact repetition of the opening measures an octave higher is thus avoided.) Instead, ic 6 at T_9 (F♯–C♮) becomes effective at m. 36 and is prolonged through m. 52 (as it was at T_3 in mm. 8–25). In m. 54 (unlike m. 26) this same ic 6 continues in the low bass, and the piece closes with its lowest pitch, the low C. The low bass notes of m. 52 are the same as those of m. 19, implicitly connecting the two halves of the piece. An equally important unifying connection is made between the bass notes (C–G) at the beginning of mm. 1 and 41, where the transpositional cycle is complete for the ic 5s (noted with stems upward in example 89). Finally, the main melodic notes at the beginning and end of the piece are connected. In m. 53, the melodic D occurs in the same register and melodic role as the D in the opening measures. In fact, the melody beginning in m. 58 is exactly the same as in mm. 4–5. The original D is prolonged through an ascending arpeggiation of 4–28 which reaches the D an octave higher in m. 36—the highest pitch of the piece. An arpeggiation down to D in the original melodic register (m. 53) is effected via A in m. 48.

There seems to be no tonal basis for the closing measures of the composition. The low bass C seems no stronger in structural weight than the bass notes supporting the pattern at other levels of transposition (or at least no stronger than the F♯ effective in the bass in mm. 8–25). With respect to pc-set content, the closing section (mm. 53–60) is set off from the rest of the piece. The entire section forms 7–26, the only occurrence of this set on the surface; however, 7–26 is the complement of 5–26, which is significant in mm. 8, 14, and corresponding places. This 7–26 is similar to the opening 7–32 in m. 1, for the two sets are in R_p, though weakly represented here. However, the two sets share five pcs—[2,0,10,9,6]—which form 5–26. More significant is the occurrence of 6–34 in mm. 54–59; the set has appeared only once previously, in m. 24, and these two forms of 6–34 are literal complements! The form of 5–28 in m. 54 is the same as that in m. 5. In fact, mm. 58–61 closely resemble mm. 4–5; the main difference is that in the closing section pc 4 replaces pc 3.

The final chord is 6–Z49, the only occurrence of this set in the piece; however, 6–Z49 is the Z-correspondent of 6–Z28, which occurs frequently. Set 6–Z49 shares four pcs (the maximum possible) with 6–Z28 in mm. 4–5: [0,10,9,6] which form 4–12. This set is significantly embedded in its complement, 8–12, in mm. 4–6. Scriabin probably chose 6–Z49 rather than 6–Z28 as the final sonority because only the former is a subset of the basic matrix, 8–28. Thus the final chord has the interval content of 6–Z28 (formed throughout the piece as a combination of elements from the basic 8–28 and its complement, 4–28) but resolves into the 8–28 matrix.

The most important sets in Op. 59/2 are related to 4–28 and 8–28. We thus see a change in Scriabin's vocabulary of sets coincident with his abandonment of tonality as a determinant of structure (although the unity of certain sections may result in part from implicit tonal relations). Scriabin may have relinquished tonality at this time because of the properties of his newly chosen sonorities, which contain the diminished seventh chord, a harmony often dissociated from specific tonal function in late romantic music. By adopting 4–28/8–28 as a basic matrix, Scriabin virtually eliminated whole-tone invariance, for even- and odd-numbered pcs occur in equal distribution in these sets. (He seems, however, to have discovered the invariance properties of 8–28 much earlier in the transitional period. For example, in mm. 18–22 of "Enigme" Op. 52/2, 8–28 is a transitional set between the two complementary whole-tone planes which underlie the A and B sections of the piece.) In his least explicitly tonal structures, tonality is defined almost entirely by the bass progression supporting a whole-tone sonority. Without the whole-tone sonorities and their tonal associations, Scriabin might not have achieved tonal coherence without returning to a more conventional system. Such a reversion would have contradicted both his aesthetic aims and the tremendous achievement of the late tonal works, where tonal structure is largely implicit.

Despite the drastic changes in Scriabin's vocabulary of sets and method of composition in the Prelude Op. 59/2, the structural procedures in this piece are related to those of the late tonal music. The basic sets of Op. 59/2—4–28 and 8–28—share an important property with 6–35, the basis for whole-tone invariance in earlier works: all three can be duplicated completely at certain levels of transposition. Set 6–35 retains all pcs when transposed any even number of half steps, and 4–28 and 8–28 do so at T_3, T_6, and T_9. In addition, 4–28 and 6–35 are the only sets which hold no subsets invariant under transposition. Elements of the 4–28/8–28 matrix are retained by cyclic transposition of sets—the same procedure used to retain elements of an underlying whole-tone scale in the late tonal works. Only the intervals of transposition are changed to exploit the properties of particular sets. Maximum invariance is produced for both 6–35 and 4–28/8–28 at T_6, and thus this level is significant in Op. 59/2 as well as in the late tonal works.

This work reflects Scriabin's expansion of techniques of invariance beyond the whole-tone scale. It was natural that the first new sets he adopted had properties similar to those of 6–35. The Prelude Op. 59/2 is thus part of a transition which began in conventional tonality. It represents a significant development in the transition to atonality, for in this work functional relations are totally suspended, at least for the overall structure. The relations among sets—especially those based on pitch-class invariance—are the primary determinants of structure.

SEVEN
RELATIONS AMONG SETS IN THE ATONAL MUSIC

In the preceding chapters, the structure of Scriabin's music composed during his transition to atonality (1903–10) was examined in terms of both conventional tonal elements and novel extratonal aspects. In order to comprehend fully the significance of the changes in Scriabin's method of composition during the transitional period, we must evaluate the structure of the music written after 1910 as well. For this purpose, we shall survey Scriabin's use of sets in seventeen short pieces taken from Op. 61 (1911) through Op. 74 (his final completed work, written in 1914). The method of preparing and presenting this study parallels that of chapter 5; the similar layouts of the surveys should facilitate comparisons of structural factors in the music of either period.

We shall continue to call the years from 1903 to 1910 the *transitional period*; the remaining years of Scriabin's career (1911–14) are termed the *atonal period*, a designation which implies that none of the compositions from this time possess tonal Ursatz structures. There is not, to my knowledge, a means of demonstrating unequivocally the presence (explicit or implicit) of an Ursatz underlying any of the compositions written after 1910. For this reason, it appears that Scriabin's transition was complete by 1910, with the abandonment of the tonal Ursatz in such works as the Prelude Op. 59/2. Thus the atonal period actually includes at least part of 1910 (and probably part of 1909), but because the earliest work in this survey was composed in 1911, any reference in this chapter to Scriabin's atonal period denotes the span of 1911–14. In all works in the survey, the relations among sets are assumed to be the primary determinants of structure.

Seventeen (85 percent) of the twenty short works of 1911–14 are analyzed in this survey:

Poème-Nocturne Op. 61 (1911)
Two Poems Op. 63 (1911)
  2. "Etrangeté"
Three Etudes Op. 65 (1912)
  1. Ninths
  2. Sevenths
  3. Fifths

Two Preludes Op. 67 (1913?)
 1. Andante
Two Poems Op. 69 (1913)
 1. Allegretto
 2. Allegretto
Two Poems Op. 71 (1914?)
 2. En rêvant, avec une grande douceur
"Vers la flamme" Op. 72 (1914)
Two *Danses* Op. 73 (1914)
 1. "Guirlandes"
 2. "Flammes sombres"
Five Preludes Op. 74 (1914)
 1. Douloureux, déchirant
 2. Très lent, contemplatif
 3. Allegro drammatico
 4. Lent, vague, indécis
 5. Fier, belliqueux

Aside from the twenty short pieces, the only compositions Scriabin completed after 1910 were the last five piano sonatas. The same methodology used in chapters 4–6 to examine atonal aspects of the transitional works has been applied to the atonal works to obtain the data for this survey. In all, thirty-six (43 percent) of the eighty-three short pieces composed from 1903 through 1914 have been treated in chapters 5 and 7. This sample is sufficiently broad to provide a firm foundation for determining the structural principles underlying Scriabin's transition to atonality.

Example 90 lists the set content of each composition under discussion. As in the transitional works, on average approximately 25 percent of all sets in a piece are significant. The ratio of significant sets to total sets varies more widely in the atonal works, however. Only 5.6 percent of the sets in the Prelude Op. 74/1 are significant, compared to 53.8 percent in "Etrangeté" Op. 63/2. Two of the works considered in this survey, Op. 61 and Op. 72, are considerably longer and more varied than any covered in chapter 5, and it is not surprising that each of these contains more sets than any of the transitional compositions. Yet on average the transitional works contain 19.6 different sets (of cardinals 4 through 8), whereas the atonal works contain an average of only 15.5, despite the larger number of sets in Opp. 61 and 72. The average in the atonal works considered here, excluding these two, is 13.2. Thus Scriabin's use of sets in the atonal pieces is more economical than in the transitional works, probably because tonal contrapuntal progressions necessarily generate sets which are not related to those involved in extratonal procedures. Where set relations alone determine structure—as in the later, atonal pieces—fewer superfluous sets need be generated.

As in chapter 5, it is possible to list sets according to the time span of their use. However, Scriabin's compositional practice with regard to set usage was in greater flux in the atonal period than in earlier years. Certain sets may be found in only one work, even though that work is one of several written in a short span of time. "Vers la flamme" Op. 72 is especially conspicuous in this regard; in spite of the fact that all pieces from Op. 72 (and probably from Op. 71) through Op. 74 were written in the first half of 1914, eleven sets are employed exclusively in "Vers la flamme." For this reason, the listing of sets according to phase in the atonal period includes eleven spans—some involving a single opus. Example 91 assigns each set used at all in the atonal period to the span which best defines the limits of its occurrence. Example 92 lists only the significant sets of the atonal period, each assigned to the span in which it is significant.

In the atonal period Scriabin expanded his overall vocabulary of sets (even though on average fewer sets are used in each work than were used in the transitional period). Twenty-five (86 percent) of the twenty-nine four-element sets are used in this period, whereas only twenty-three (79 percent) occur in the music of 1903–10. Similarly, twenty-nine (76 percent) of the thirty-eight five-element sets are found in the atonal works, compared to twenty-eight (74 percent) in the transitional music. Thirty-one hexachords (62 percent of the fifty) are represented in the atonal works, but only twenty-eight (56 percent) are used in the transitional works. In spite of the enrichment of Scriabin's repertoire of sets after 1910, however, the number of significant sets in the atonal works is smaller than that in the transitional period. Only seven sets of four elements (24 percent) are significant, compared to ten (34 percent) in the earlier period. Eleven five-note sets (29 percent) are significant after 1910, fourteen (37 percent) in the transitional period. Twelve hexachords are used significantly in each period.

In chapter 5 we saw that Scriabin's use of sets for the transitional period included four of the seven with cardinals 4 through 6 which retain all pcs at some level of transposition—4–28, 4–25, 6–30, and 6–35—all of which are predominantly whole-tone except 4–28, which is not significant in the transitional works. In the atonal period, Scriabin continues to use these sets but also introduces the remaining three: 4–9, 6–7, and 6–20. Because none of these is predominantly whole-tone, it appears that Scriabin discovered complete invariance in connection with whole-tone invariance. In his posttonal works he continued to exploit this property, discovering it also in sets not related to the whole-tone scale. Even in the atonal period, only the three predominantly whole-tone sets are significant in the short pieces. Set 6–20, however, is a focal sonority in the Tenth Sonata Op. 70 (example 120).

Because a greater percentage of all possible sets occurs in the atonal than in the transitional music, it is likely that categories of sets with special properties will be more nearly exhausted in the later period. Since the only category from which every set is used is complete invariance under transposition, this property is probably an especially important determinant of structure in the atonal music, as it was in the Prelude Op. 59/2. It seems likely that Scriabin's choice of new sets in the atonal period was not arbitrary but rather was based on structural

Example 90 Set Usage in Opp. 61–74 (1911–14)

	1911		1912			1913?			1914?
	61	63/2	65/1	65/2	65/3	67/1	69/1	69/2	71/2
4–3						×			
4–4						●			
4–6									
4–7						●			
4–8	●								
4–9						●			
4–11	●				●				
4–12	●			●		●			●
4–13						●			
4–14									
4–Z15		●				●			
4–16	●						●		
4–17	●								
4–18	×					●			
4–19									
4–20									
4–21	●		●				●	●	
4–22									
4–23					●				
4–24	●				●		●		●
4–25	×		●		×	●	●	●	●
4–26									
4–27	×	×				●	●		●
4–28		●	●			●			
4–Z29		●		●	●				
5–1						●			
5–3						●			
5–6									
5–8	●								
5–9			×						
5–10									
5–15							●		
5–16		×		×	●	●			
5–Z17									
5–Z18	●								
5–19						×			
5–20									
5–21							●		
5–22									

● = Occurrence at least twice   × = Occurrence as significant set

Example 90 (cont.)

1914

72	73/1	73/2	74/1	74/2	74/3	74/4	74/5	X	Total
								1	1
								0	1
			●					0	1
						●		0	2
								0	1
								0	1
			●					0	3
	●	●			×			1	7
				●				0	2
●								0	1
●	●	●		●		●		0	7
●								0	3
	×			●		×	●	2	5
●		●		●		×		2	6
×						×		2	2
						●		0	1
								0	4
●								0	1
●								0	2
		●						0	5
●		●			●			2	10
●								0	1
×	●	×		●				4	9
	●	●			●	●	●	0	8
●		●		●		●		0	7
								0	1
			●					0	2
			●					0	1
								0	1
								1	1
					●			0	1
								0	1
	●	●	●				●	2	8
●						●		0	2
●						●		0	3
				×	●			2	3
			●					0	1
●			●			●		0	4
						●		0	1

Example 90 (cont.)

	1911	1912			1913?				1914?
	61	63/2	65/1	65/2	65/3	67/1	69/1	69/2	71/2
5–23									
5–24					●		●		
5–25				●					
5–26	×	●		×	●	●	●		×
5–27	●			●					
5–28	●	×		×		●			●
5–29									
5–30	●	●			●		×	×	
5–31	●	×	●			×		●	
5–32	×	×		×				×	
5–33	×		×			●	×	×	
5–34	●				●				
5–35									
5–Z36									
5–Z38									●
6–Z3									
6–5									
6–7					●				
6–Z10/Z39	●					●	●		
6–Z13						●			
6–15	●						●		
6–16									
6–Z17/Z43									
6–Z19/Z44	●					●			
6–20									
6–21	×						●		
6–22			●				●		
6–Z23/Z45									
6–Z24/Z46	●				×				
6–Z25/Z47									
6–27	●	×							
6–Z28/Z49	×	×		×				●	
6–Z29/Z50	×	●				×			
6–30						×			
6–31	●			●					
6–33	●				●				
6–34	×		●		×	●	×	●	×
6–35			×				●	●	
X	10	7	3	5	3	5	3	3	2
Total	31	13	9	10	14	25	17	9	8

Example 90 (cont.)

1914

72	73/1	73/2	74/1	74/2	74/3	74/4	74/5	X	Total
●								0	1
●								0	3
●								0	2
●	×	×	●					5	11
●								0	3
●	●	●	●				●	2	10
×								1	1
×								3	6
●	●	●	●	×	×		●	4	12
●	●		●	●				4	8
●		●						4	7
×							●	1	4
●								0	1
●								0	1
								0	1
					●			0	1
					●			0	1
								0	1
								0	3
			●					0	2
	●	●						0	4
			●					0	1
●			●					0	2
●			●					0	4
						●		0	1
								1	2
		●						0	3
●								0	1
								1	2
●								0	1
			●	●			●	1	5
	×	×	×		●		●	6	9
				●	●			2	5
		●		×				2	3
	●							0	3
×								1	3
×		×	●				×	7	11
								1	3
7	3	4	1	3	2	3	1		
34	13	18	18	12	10	13	9		

Example 91 Set Distribution and IC Extrema, Atonal Period

Set	Vector	Maxima	Minima
Throughout (1911–14)			
4–11	121110	2	6
4–12	112101	3	5
4–Z15	111111		
4–16	110121	5	3
4–17	102210	3 4	2 6
4–18*	102111	3	2
4–23	021030	5	1 4 6
4–24	020301	4	1 3 5
4–25	020202	2 4 6	1 3 5
4–27*	012111	3	1
4–28*	004002	3	
4–Z29	111111		
5–16*	213211	3	2 5 6
5–Z18	212221		2 6
5–24	131221	2	1 3 6
5–25	123121	3	1 4 6
5–26*	122311	4	1 5 6
5–27	122230	5	6
5–28*	122212		1 5
5–30	121321	4	1 3 6
5–31*	114112	3	
5–32	113221	3	1 2 6
5–33*	040402	2 4	1 3 5
5–34	032221	2	1
6–15	323421	4	6
6–Z19/Z44*	313431	4	2 6
6–22	241422	2 4	3
6–27*	225222	3	
6–Z28/Z49	224322	3	
6–Z29/Z50	224232	3	
6–31*	223431	4	6
6–33	143241	2 5	1 6
6–34*	142422	2 4	1
Opp. 61–63 (1911)			
4–8	200121	1 5	2 3
5–8	232201	1 3 4	5
Op. 65 (1912)			
5–9	231211	2	3 5 6
6–7	420243	1 5	3
Opp. 61–65 (1911–12)			
6–Z24/Z46	233331		6
Op. 67 (1913?)			
4–3	212100	1 3	5 6
4–4	211110	1	6

*Found throughout the music of 1903–10 also

Example 91 (cont.)

Set	Vector	Maxima						Minima					
4–9	200022	1				5	6		2	3	4		
5–1	432100	1										5	6
Opp. 61–69 (1911–13)													
4–21	030201		2					1		3		5	
6–Z10/Z39	333321												6
6–21	242412		2		4							5	
6–35	060603		2		4			1		3		5	
Opp. 69–71 (1913–14)													
5–15	220222									3			
5–Z38	212221								2				6
Op. 72 (1914)													
4–14	111120					5							6
4–22	021120		2			5		1					6
4–26	012120			3		5		1					6
5–23	132130		2			5							6
5–29	122131					5		1			4		6
5–35	032140					5		1					6
5–Z36	222121										4		6
6–Z23/Z45	234222			3									
6–Z25/Z47	233241					5							6
Opp. 67–74 (1913?–14)													
4–7	201210	1			4				2				6
4–13	112011			3							4		
5–3	322210	1											6
5–19	212122								2		4		
5–21	202420				4				2				6
6–Z13	324222			3									
6–30	224223			3									
Opp. 71–74 (1914)													
4–19	101310				4				2				6
5–Z17	212320				4								6
6–Z17/Z43	322332	1			4	5			2	3			6
Op. 74 (1914)													
4–6	210021	1				5				3	4		
4–20	101220				4	5			2				6
5–6	311221	1							2	3			6
5–10	223111			3							4	5	6
5–20	211231					5			2	3			6
5–22	202321				4				2				
6–Z3	433221	1											6
6–5	422232	1											
6–16	322431				4								6
6–20	303630				4				2				6

Example 92 Significant Set Distribution, Atonal Period

Throughout (1911–14)		
4–18	5–26	6–Z28/Z49
4–27	5–31	6–34
Opp. 61–63 (1911)		
—	—	6–21
		6–27
Op. 65 (1912)		
—	5–9	6–Z24/Z46
		6–35
Opp. 61–65 (1911–12)		
4–25	5–16	—
	5–28	
Op. 67 (1913?)		
4–3	—	—
Opp. 61–69 (1911–13)		
—	5–32	6–Z29/Z50
	5–33	
Op. 72 (1914)		
—	5–29	6–33
	5–34	
Opp. 67–74 (1913?–14)		
—	5–19	6–30
	5–30	
Opp. 71–74 (1914)		
4–17	—	—
4–19		
Op. 74 (1914)		
4–12	—	—

properties of the new sets that corresponded to properties of sonorities already in use. The addition in the atonal period of sets belonging to certain categories of structural properties therefore seems to indicate the importance of those properties as determinants of structure.

Only twenty-six sets of cardinals 5 through 8 retain under transposition a subset with one less element. Of the twenty-nine possible pairings of a set of cardinal n with an invariant subset of cardinal $n - 1$, seventeen occur in the transitional period (see p. 111). All of these are also represented in the atonal period, along with five other pairs: 5–1 (which holds 4–1 invariant), 5–19 (4–9), 7–21 (6–20), 6–27 (5–31), and 7–15 (6–7). Of these sets only 7–15 is predominantly whole-tone, compared to fourteen of the twenty-three sets involved in this relation in the transitional period. Again Scriabin seems to have expanded his vocabulary to include non-whole-tone sets with invariance properties similar to those of predominantly whole-tone sets.

The repertoire of sets in Scriabin's atonal music also includes many sets not found in the transitional music which are completely invariant under inversion. (See p. 112 for a listing of the sets with this property in the transitional music.) Ten of the fifteen four-element sets with this property are used in the transitional period; three more are added in atonal works—4–3, 4–8, and 4–9—but only 4–3 is significant. Eight of the ten five-element sets in this category are used in the music of 1903–10; after 1910, 5–1 also occurs. Whereas only eight hexachords in the transitional works have this feature, ten such sets occur in the later works: 6–7, 6–Z13, 6–20, 6–Z23/Z45, 6–Z28/Z49*, 6–Z29/Z50*, and 6–35*. (Those marked with asterisks are significant.) Not all of the hexachords found in transitional works occur in the atonal music; 6–Z26 and 6–32 are used in the earlier period but not in the posttonal music.

Only fourteen of the twenty-nine sets which hold the complementary subset invariant under transposition, inversion, or both, occur in the transitional works (see p. 112); four more occur in the atonal period: 7–23, 7–29, 6–7, and 6–20. (The two hexachords are completely invariant under both transposition and inversion. Their invariant subsets are improper.)

A major contrast between the use of sets in the transitional and atonal periods occurs in the number of transitive tuples completely represented: of a possible forty-seven (not including the eighty tuples for hexachords in R_0) twelve are represented in the transitional music, sixteen in the atonal music (example 93). Only six complete tuples are shared by the transitional and atonal repertoires of sets. The greater number of complete transitive tuples in the atonal music may indicate that Scriabin achieved greater interrelatedness among sonorities in this music.

The final difference worth noting is that 8–28 plays a much more important role in the atonal than in the transitional period. Thus the dramatically new sets and transpositional schemes associated with the 4–28/8–28 matrix underlying the Prelude Op. 59/2 (see chapter 6) seem to be conventional components of Scriabin's later music.

As in the survey of sets used in Scriabin's transition (see chapter 5), the special properties discussed above are not themselves an adequate basis for a complete system of composition in the atonal works, for many sets in his atonal repertoire do not exhibit any of these properties. Only in the case of complete invariance under transposition are all possible sets used after 1910. This property is fundamental in Scriabin's atonal works, yet it accounts for few of the sets in this music. Actually it is a special case of invariance in general. An efficient means of evaluating invariance properties among sets in the music of 1911–14 is to measure the extrema for containment of particular interval classes. Example 94 contains the data for ic extrema in all sets, and in significant sets only, in use during each phase defined in examples 91–92. The ics most frequently maximized or minimized in each collection are summarized in example 95.

In the sets used throughout the atonal period (1911–14), the prevalence of ic 3 provides a striking contrast to the ic extrema of the transitional period (example 94, first column). In the early music even-numbered ics (especially ic 4)

Example 93 Complete Transitive Tuples, Atonal Period

R_1
4–4, 4–11, 4–14*
4–7, 4–17, 4–20*
4–12, 4–13, 4–18, 4–27*

R_0
5–6, 5–23, 5–33
5–16, 5–23, 5–33

R_1
5–6, 5–24, 5–32*
5–9, 5–16, 5–20
5–Z18, 5–19, 5–Z36
5–19, 5–Z36, 5–Z38*

R_2
5–23, 5–27, 5–29

R_1
6–15, 6–16, 6–31
6–21, 6–22, 6–34*
6–Z13, 6–Z23, 6–Z28, 6–Z29, 6–30
6–Z13, 6–Z28, 6–Z29, 6–30, 6–Z45
6–Z13, 6–Z29, 6–30, 6–Z45, 6–Z49
6–Z13, 6–30, 6–Z45, 6–Z49, 6–Z50

*Found also in the sets of the transitional period

are favored overall, and ic 3 is characteristic mainly of the late phases of the transition. (For a summary of ic extrema in the transitional period, see example 79.) In sets employed throughout the atonal period, ic 1 is never maximized and is most frequently minimized. In both the transitional and the atonal period ic 4 is least often minimized. The ic extrema for all sets used throughout the music of 1911–14 are roughly the same as those for the significant sets of this phase. One notable difference is the clear predominance of ic 3 over ic 4 among the significant sets. More important, the significant sets used throughout the transitional period differ greatly from those of the atonal music: ic 4 is strongly favored in the former group, ic 3 in the latter.

Many sets appearing throughout the atonal works also occur throughout the transitional music. It is instructive to examine the ic extrema of these sets used in 1903–14 (indicated by asterisks in example 91), which are summarized in example 96. Because they occur throughout both the late tonal and the atonal music, their structure is essential to the continuity of Scriabin's compositional transition. In these sets ic 4 is certainly favored, but ic 3 is maximized even more frequently. Significantly, ics 1 and 5 are never maximized. The frequency for ic

Example 94 IC Extrema by Phase, Atonal Period

		1911–14	Opp. 61–63	Op. 65	Opp. 61–65	Op. 67	Opp. 61–69	Opp. 69–71	Op. 72	Opp. 67–74	Opp. 71–74	Op. 74	Totals
All Sets													
Maximizations	ic 1	0	2	1	0	4	0	0	0	2	1	4	14
	ic 2	8	0	1	0	0	3	0	2	0	0	0	14
	ic 3	12	1	0	0	1	0	0	2	3	0	1	20
	ic 4	11	1	0	0	0	2	0	0	2	3	4	23
	ic 5	4	1	1	0	1	0	0	7	0	1	3	18
	ic 6	1	0	0	0	1	0	0	0	0	0	0	2
Minimizations	ic 1	14	0	0	0	0	2	0	4	0	0	0	20
	ic 2	6	1	0	0	1	0	1	0	3	2	5	19
	ic 3	7	1	2	0	1	2	1	0	0	1	3	18
	ic 4	2	0	0	0	1	0	0	2	2	0	2	9
	ic 5	7	1	1	0	2	3	0	0	0	0	1	15
	ic 6	15	0	1	1	3	1	1	8	3	3	7	43
Significant Sets Only													
Maximizations	ic 1	0	0	0	0	1	0	—	0	0	0	0	1
	ic 2	1	1	2	1	0	1	—	2	0	0	0	8
	ic 3	4	1	0	1	1	2	—	0	1	1	1	12
	ic 4	2	1	1	1	0	1	—	0	1	2	0	9
	ic 5	0	0	0	0	0	0	—	2	0	0	0	2
	ic 6	0	0	0	1	0	0	—	0	0	0	0	1
Minimizations	ic 1	3	0	1	2	0	2	—	3	1	0	0	12
	ic 2	1	0	0	1	0	1	—	0	1	2	0	6
	ic 3	0	0	2	1	0	1	—	0	1	0	0	5
	ic 4	0	0	0	0	0	0	—	1	1	0	0	2
	ic 5	1	1	2	3	1	1	—	0	0	0	1	10
	ic 6	1	0	2	1	1	1	—	2	1	2	0	11

Example 95 Summary of IC Extrema by Phase, Atonal Period

	All Sets		Significant Sets Only	
	Maxima	Minima	Maxima	Minima
1911–14 (some works)	4	1	3	1
1911–14 (throughout)	3, 4	1	3	1
Opp. 61–65 (some works)	1	3	2	5
Opp. 61–69 (some works)	1	5	2, 3	5
Opp. 67–74 (throughout)	3	2	3, 4	—
Opp. 71–74 (throughout)	4	2	4	2
Op. 72	5	1	2, 5	1
Op. 74	1, 4	2	3	5
Opp. 71–74 (some works)	5	2	—	1

Example 96 IC Extrema, Transitional and Atonal Periods

IC	Maxima	IC	Minima
1	0	1	5
2	2	2	3
3	6	3	1
4	5	4	0
5	0	5	4
(6	0)	(6	4)

minimization in 1903–14 is the same as that for all sets found throughout the atonal period.

An evaluation of the sets used during 1911–14 but not during 1903–10 should provide a clue to the structural basis for Scriabin's choice of novel sonorities in the atonal music (example 97). The maximization of even-numbered ics in this collection equals that of ic 3. The pattern of ic minimizations is roughly the same as that for all sets used throughout this phase, with ic 1 most conspicuously avoided.

To evaluate the changes Scriabin made after his abandonment of tonality in 1910, we should examine ic extrema in sets used in the remaining phases of the atonal period. The second, third, and fourth columns of example 94 contain

Example 97 IC Extrema, Atonal Period Only

IC	Maxima	IC	Minima
1	0	1	9
2	6	2	3
3	6	3	6
4	6	4	2
5	4	5	3
(6	1)	(6	11)

data for collections of sets occurring only in the early atonal compositions. These sets bear little structural resemblance to those found throughout the transitional or atonal period. In these phases ic 1 is most frequently maximized and least often minimized, and ic 3 is most frequently minimized. Scriabin seems deliberately to have dramatized the arrival of a new musical era by injecting unusual sonorities into his early atonal works. However, the extrema for significant sets used only in these early phases conform with the structure of significant sets in both the transitional and atonal periods. Even-numbered ics are favored in these sets, and ic 5 is most often minimized.

The extrema for sets used in Opp. 61–69 are listed in the sixth column of example 94. Significantly, in these sets, which are more widespread than those in the second through fifth columns, the even-numbered ics are greatly preferred. In fact, all of these sets are predominantly whole-tone, which reaffirms that whole-tone predominance is a major factor of continuity in Scriabin's transition to atonality.

To gain a broader view of the structure of sets used in any composition from Op. 61 to Op. 69, the data for sets listed in the second through sixth columns are brought together in example 98a. For all sets occurring somewhere in these works (but not in later works) ic 1 is favored strongly. Interval classes 2 and 4 are maximized about as much as ics 3 and 5, but ics 3 and 5 are much more frequently minimized than ics 2 and 4. For significant sets used in any phase through Op. 69, the ic extrema are summarized in example 98b. The significant sets stand in sharp contrast to the collection of all sets used in these phases: ic 1 predominates in the overall collection, but ics 2, 3, and 4 are most important (and almost equally so) in the significant sets.

The extrema for sets used in the Opp. 67–74 phase indicate that a modification of Scriabin's repertoire of sets occurred in 1913 (when Op. 67 was composed) or thereafter. This group is distinctly different from collections already examined. Both ics 1 and 3 are most frequently maximized, whereas previously one was emphasized to the exclusion of the other. Further, ic 4 is favored but ic 2 is not. (Both previously received similar treatment.) Finally, the minimizations for these sets reverse the usual pattern; the even-numbered ics are most frequently minimized, the odd-numbered ics not at all.

Example 98a IC Extrema, Early Atonal Period Only

IC	Maxima	IC	Minima
1	7	1	2
2	4	2	2
3	2	3	6
4	3	4	1
5	3	5	7
(6	1)	(6	6)

Example 98b IC Extrema for Significant Sets, Early Atonal Period Only

IC	Maxima	IC	Minima
1	1	1	5
2	5	2	2
3	5	3	4
4	4	4	0
5	0	5	8
(6	1)	(6	5)

Sets used only in Opp. 71–74 conform to those found throughout the atonal music in that they emphasize ic 4; however, ics 2 and 3 are unusually scarce. An even more striking change in Scriabin's vocabulary occurs in the sets used only in Op. 72, where ic 5 appears more prominently than it has since the early years of the transitional period. Further, ic 4 is never maximized among these sets and is quite often minimized. As in the sets used throughout the atonal period, ic 1 is most frequently avoided. The changes in Scriabin's repertoire of sets in Op. 72 have an especially strong impact because new sonorities are employed as both secondary sets and significant sets. In the significant sets occurring only in Op. 72, ics 2 and 5 are equally prominent. The emphasis on ic 5 is peculiar to Op. 72, however, for the only significant set occurring exclusively in Op. 74 minimizes ic 5. The sets found only in Op. 74 are also unique, favoring ics 1 and 4 but also emphasizing ic 5 and avoiding ic 2. The single significant set used only in Op. 74 minimizes ic 3.

Example 99 summarizes the data for sets used in the last part of the atonal period. This count of the ic extrema for sets occurring only in Op. 71 or later works reaffirms that Scriabin's use of sets in the atonal period was in continual flux. In the last compositions he reintroduced sonorities which had fallen into disuse even before he had abandoned the tonal system. In particular, Op. 72 (1914) includes three sets not used since 1907: 4–22, 5–Z36, and 5–29—the latter as a significant set. Other sets used in Op. 71 and later works occurred previously only in works before 1909: 5–6, 5–25, 5–35, and 6–Z25. (Of these reintroduced sets, 4–22, 5–29, and 6–Z25 maximize ic 5.)

The ic extrema for all sets used at some time during the atonal period are shown in the last column of example 94. These data correspond in several ways to the extrema for the entire collection of transitional sets. In both cases ic 4 is most prevalent, and the frequencies of minimization correspond almost exactly. There are significant differences between the sets of the two periods, however. In the transitional period ic 2 is somewhat favored and ic 1 is seldom maximized; in the atonal music ic 2 continues to receive some emphasis, but ic 1 has equal weight. More important, in the atonal music ic 3 is second in prevalence only to ic 4, whereas it ranks third—behind ic 5—in the late tonal works.

A final consideration in evaluating the ic extrema of all sets in the atonal music is the structure of sets not employed in these compositions. These sets are listed

Example 99 IC Extrema, Op. 71 or Later

IC	Maxima	IC	Minima
1	5	1	4
2	2	2	7
3	3	3	4
4	7	4	4
5	11	5	1
(6	0)	(6	18)

in example 100 and their extrema are summarized in example 101. The ic extrema for these sets closely resemble those for the sets not used in the transitional period (examples 76–77). In both cases, ic 1 is most frequently maximized and least minimized. Therefore, despite the fact that Scriabin introduced some sets maximizing ic 1 in the atonal period, in general he continued to avoid such sets, as he had in the transitional period. Indeed, in no phase of either the atonal

Example 100 IC Extrema for Excluded Sets, Atonal Period

Set	Vector	Maxima	Minima
4–1	321000	1	4 5 6
4–2	221100	1 2	5 6
4–5	210111	1	3
4–10	122010	2 3	4 6
5–2	332110	1 2	6
5–4	322111	1	4 5 6
5–5	321121	1	3 4 6
5–7	310132	1 5	3
5–11	222220		6
5–Z12	222121		4 6
5–13	221311	4	3 5 6
5–14	221131	5	3 4 6
5–Z37	212320	4	6
6–1	543210	1	6
6–2	443211	1 2	5 6
6–Z4/Z37	432321	1	6
6–Z6/Z38	421242	1 5	3
6–8	343230	2	6
6–9	342231	2	6
6–Z11/Z40	333231		6
6–Z12/Z41	332232	1 2 5	3 4 6
6–14	323430	4	6
6–18	322242	5	
6–Z26/Z48	232341	5	6
6–32	143250	5	6
6–Z36	433221	1	6
6–Z42	324222	3	

Example 101 Summary of IC Extrema for Excluded Sets, Atonal Period

IC	Maxima	IC	Minima
1	13	1	0
2	7	2	0
3	2	3	7
4	3	4	7
5	7	5	5
(6	0)	(6	22)

or the transitional period is ic 1 most frequently maximized among the significant sets.

As a final step in this survey, we should consider the extrema for significant sets occurring in any phase of the atonal period, which are listed in the last column of example 94. These figures correspond closely to the frequencies of ic extrema for all sets used from 1903 through 1914. Most strongly favored is ic 3, but ics 2 and 4 receive almost as much weight. On the other hand, ics 5 and 1 are weakly represented.

A number of sets significant in the atonal works also occur significantly in the music of 1903–10 (example 102). An examination of their ic extrema (example 103) should reveal a structural basis for continuity in Scriabin's transition to atonality. These figures corroborate the data for all sets found throughout the music of 1903–14 (indicated by asterisks in Example 91). In the significant sets, however, ics 2, 3, and 4 are almost equally prominent and ics 1 and 5 are deemphasized. Predominantly whole-tone sets are thus certainly significant in both

Example 102 IC Extrema for Sets Significant in Both Periods

Set	Maxima	Minima
4–18	3	2
4–19	4	2 6
4–25	2 4 6	1 3 5
4–27	3	1
5–16	3	2 5 6
5–28		1 5
5–30	4	1 3 6
5–32	3	1 2 6
5–33	2 4	1 3 5
5–34	2	1
6–21	2 4	5
6–27	3	
6–Z28/Z49	3	
6–33	2 5	1 6
6–34	2 4	1
6–35	2 4	1 3 5

Example 103 Summary of IC Extrema for Sets Significant in Both Periods

IC	Maxima	IC	Minima
1	0	1	10
2	7	2	4
3	6	3	4
4	7	4	0
5	1	5	6
(6	1)	(6	5)

tonal and atonal works, but ic 3 (which was favored over other ics for the first time in the late transitional works) is just as important a link. Sets maximizing ic 1 or ic 5 do not usually connect tonal and atonal methods of composition, although each type is important in individual phases of both periods.

An evaluation of the ic extrema of significant sets in the atonal music that are not significant in the transitional music (examples 104–05) should show a structural basis for Scriabin's innovations after 1910. In these sets ic 3 is clearly prevalent, but the even-numbered ics are emphasized much less than in sets used significantly in both periods. In both collections ics 1 and 5 are least frequent, and in sets significant only in the atonal period ic 2 is also weakly represented. The significant sets introduced after 1910 are thus similar in sonority only to those significant sets used in the transitional music of 1907 or later—for only these maximize ic 3.

The findings of our survey are summarized in example 95. In the collection of all sets used at some time during this period, ic 4 is most frequently maximized and ic 1 most often minimized. These same extrema are also characteristic of the collection of all sets used in 1903–10 (example 79). A basis for continuity in Scriabin's transition to atonality thus exists in the structural similarity of repertoires of sets for each period. In the transitional period, the significant

Example 104 IC Extrema for Significant Sets, Atonal Period Only

Set	Maxima	Minima
4–3	1 3	5 6
4–12	3	5
4–17	3 4	2 6
5–9	2	3 5 6
5–19		2 4
5–26	4	1 5 6
5–29	5	1 4 6
5–31	3	
6–Z24/Z46		6
6–Z29/Z50	3	
6–30	3	

Example 105 Summary of IC Extrema for Significant Sets, Atonal Period Only

IC	Maxima	IC	Minima
1	1	1	2
2	1	2	2
3	6	3	1
4	2	4	2
5	1	5	4
(6	0)	(6	6)

sets have generally the same ic extrema as the collection of all sets. There is, however, a discrepancy between the extrema for all sets used during the atonal period and those for the significant sets only. In the significant sets, ic 3 is maximized, as opposed to ic 4 in the collection of all sets. (Interval class 1 is minimized in both collections.) This difference results from the small ratio of significant to nonsignificant sets, which are often structurally dissimilar to the significant sets. The collection of significant sets used throughout the atonal period resembles those of significant sets used in 1907 only and 1910 only; these collections all maximize ic 3, which is another basis for continuity in Scriabin's transition. The ic extrema for sets significant throughout the atonal period are identical to those for the significant sets occurring at some time during the period. Among all sets used throughout 1911–14, however, ics 3 and 4 are equally favored.

In the early phases of the atonal period Scriabin deliberately injected novel sonorities which contrast highly with the sets generally encountered in this music—a contrast evident in the structure of the collections of all sets used in Opp. 61–65 and in Opp. 61–69. In both phases ic 1 is maximized, whereas it is typically minimized in Scriabin's atonal sets. Further, ic 3—generally the prominent ic in his significant atonal sets—is minimized in the Opp. 61–65 phase. In Opp. 61–69, ic 5 is minimized, as it is in the significant sets of Opp. 61–65 and Opp. 61–69. This practice marks a further break with transitional sets, for ic 5 is maximized in earlier phases of the transition. In the significant sets found only early in the atonal period (Opp. 61–65 and Opp. 61–69), ic 2 is maximized, along with ic 3 in the more inclusive phase. This trend is a reversal of sorts, for ic 2 is similarly predominant only in the earliest phase of the transition (1903–05).

The structure of sets occurring only in Opp. 67–74 conforms more with that of the most widely encountered atonal sets; ic 3 is maximized in the collections of all sets and of significant sets only. In addition, ic 4 is maximized in the significant sets. Among all sets found in Opp. 67–74, ic 2 is minimized, as it is in several other collections in the late phases of the atonal period. The sets employed only in Opp. 71–74 do not deviate dramatically from the norms for ic extrema in sets of the atonal period. In all sets and in significant sets only, ic 4 is maximized and ic 2 minimized.

The most drastic change in Scriabin's use of sets in the atonal period occurs with "Vers la flamme" Op. 72 (1914); ic 5 is maximized in the collections of all sets and of significant sets used only in this work. Interval class 5, the basic ic of the tonal system, was previously maximized only in the early phases of the transitional period, and even there never in the collections of significant sets only. In the atonal period ic 5 appears in the extrema of the early phases only as a minimized ic. In Op. 72 Scriabin introduces novel sonorities as significant sets—a deviation from his previous practice in the atonal works, in which new sets were generally secondary.

The structure of sets found only in Op. 74 evidences a return to the more conventional sonorities of the atonal period, for the extrema for sets in this opus are similar to those of several other phases. On the other hand, the extrema for all sets of the Opp. 71–74 phase reflect the changes effected in Op. 72, for ic 5 is most often maximized. In the significant sets of this phase, however, no ic is predominant.

From the extrema listed in example 95, it is evident that whole-tone invariance is not the main compositional procedure of the atonal music; in most phases, odd-numbered ics are most frequently maximized. Especially important are the extrema for sets used throughout 1911–14. In this category ic 3 is most often maximized among all sets and among significant sets. The possibility of whole-tone invariance in the atonal works may not be ruled out entirely, for even-numbered ics are maximized in some phases, including that of Opp. 71–74. But in this category ic 4 is maximized and ic 2 minimized, suggesting that many of the sets involved are not predominantly whole-tone—and this is in fact the case. Most important, ic 4 is maximized in the collection of all sets occurring at some time during the atonal period. Whole-tone invariance may influence sections of works not dominated by the most characteristic significant sets. The exploitation of invariance properties of significant sets (whether predominantly whole-tone or not) remains an important procedure throughout Scriabin's music.

Example 106 lists all sets in the music of 1911–14 which are not predomi-

Example 106 Sets Other Than Predominantly Whole-Tone Sets, Atonal Period

4–3* (Op. 67)	5–1	6–Z3
4–4	5–3	6–5
4–6	5–6	6–7
4–7	5–10	6–Z13
4–8	5–16* (Opp. 61–65)	6–Z19/Z44
4–9	5–Z17	6–20
4–13	5–Z18	6–Z25/Z47
4–14	5–19* (Opp. 67–74)	6–27* (Opp. 61–63)
4–17* (Opp. 71–74)	5–20	6–Z29/Z50* (Opp. 61–69)
4–18* (throughout)	5–21	
4–20	5–22	
4–23	5–23	
4–26	5–25	
4–28	5–27	
	5–29* (Op. 72)	
	5–31* (throughout)	
	5–32* (Opp. 61–69)	
	5–35	
	5–Z36	
	5–Z38	

*Significant during the period in parentheses

nantly whole-tone. (For a complete listing of predominantly whole-tone sets, see example 82.) Many of Scriabin's sets are not related to the whole-tone scale, including eleven significant sets (marked with asterisks in example 106). Further, many of these eleven are used widely in the atonal music. (The limits of their use as significant sets are indicated in parentheses.) Nearly all of these significant sets maximize ic 3. The only exceptions are 5–19, which maximizes no ic, and 5–29, which maximizes ic 5 and occurs significantly only in Op. 72. In the atonal music, then, nearly all significant sets are predominantly whole-tone or maximize ic 3.

In the Prelude Op. 59/2 invariance properties of sets maximizing ic 3 are the primary determinants of structure (see chapter 6). The transpositional scheme of Op. 59/2 operates within a basic matrix of 4–28/8–28. These sets share with 6–35 (the whole-tone scale) the property of complete self-duplication at some levels of transposition. In Op. 59/2 the pitch-retention procedures are comparable to those associated with whole-tone invariance in the late tonal works. Only the intervals of transposition used to achieve complete invariance are different. Every significant atonal set which is not predominantly whole-tone is contained in 8–28, with the exception of 5–29 and 6–Z29. (As mentioned previously, 5–29 is a special set used only in Op. 72. Set 6–Z29, whose Z-correspondent is contained in 8–28, itself contains 4–28.) Two of these sets—5–31 and 6–27—are in Kh with 4–28. The 4–28/8–28 matrix identified in the Prelude Op. 59/2 is thus as important as 6–35 in Scriabin's atonal works; together 6–35 and 4–28/8–28 are the main structural referents to which almost all significant sonorities in this music are related.

Example 107 demonstrates the interrelations among the significant sets of 1911–14. The most likely candidate for a primary nexus set for a complex of all these sets is 6–34, the mystic chord, which is also the primary nexus for the transitional period. Set 6–34 is related in Kh to nine other sets (more than any other hexachord) and is also the hexachord most widely used throughout the atonal period; it occurs in eleven of seventeen works, significantly in seven. Further, 6–34 is used throughout 1903–14. It is related in K or Kh to all sets except 4–3, 4–17, 4–18, 5–9, 5–16, 5–19, 5–29, 5–31, and 5–32. The set best equipped to be a secondary nexus is 6–Z28/Z49, which is used more widely than all sets except 6–34 and occurs significantly in six of the nine pieces in Opp. 61–74 in which it occurs. Further, 6–Z28/Z49 is the only significant hexachord besides 6–34 found throughout the music of 1911–14. Remarkably, it is also a secondary nexus in Scriabin's transitional works. Together 6–34 and 6–Z28/Z49 are related in K or Kh to all significant sets except 5–9, 5–19, and 5–29. Set 5–19 occurs significantly in two compositions, the others in only one each.

The primary and secondary nexus sets are connected by two possible tertiary nexus sets, 5–26 and 5–28, each contained in both hexachords. Because the three sets which are not related to 6–34 or 6–Z28/Z49 are all related in R_p to 5–28 (and not all are related to 5–26), 5–28 is the more effective tertiary nexus. Example 108 illustrates the nexus sets for the significant sets in Scriabin's atonal

Example 107 Set-Complex Relations for Significant Sets, Opp. 61–74 (1911–14)

	4–3	4–12	4–17	4–18	4–19	4–25	4–27
5–9	K	K			K	K	K
5–16	Kh	Kh	Kh	Kh	K		K
5–19		K		Kh		K	K
5–26	K	Kh	K	K	Kh	K	Kh
5–28		Kh		K	K	Kh	Kh
5–29			K	K			Kh
5–30		K	K	K	Kh	K	K
5–31	K	Kh	K	Kh		K	Kh
5–32	K	K	Kh	Kh	K		Kh
5–33		K			K	Kh	K
5–34	K	K			K	K	Kh

	4–3	4–12	4–17	4–18	4–19	4–25	4–27	5–9	5–16	5–19	5–26	5–28	5–29	5–30	5–31	5–32	5–33	5–34
6–21		Kh			Kh	Kh	Kh	Kh			Kh	Kh					Kh	
6–Z24/ Z46	K	K	K	K	K		Kh	K			K		K	K		K		K
6–27	Kh	Kh	Kh	Kh			Kh		Kh						Kh	Kh		
6–Z28/ Z49	K	Kh	K	Kh	K	K	Kh		K		K	K			K	K		
6–Z29/ Z50		K	K	Kh			Kh			K			K		K	K		
6–30		Kh		Kh		Kh	Kh			Kh		Kh			Kh			
6–33							Kh						Kh					Kh
6–34		Kh			Kh	Kh	Kh				Kh	Kh		Kh			Kh	Kh
6–35						Kh											Kh	

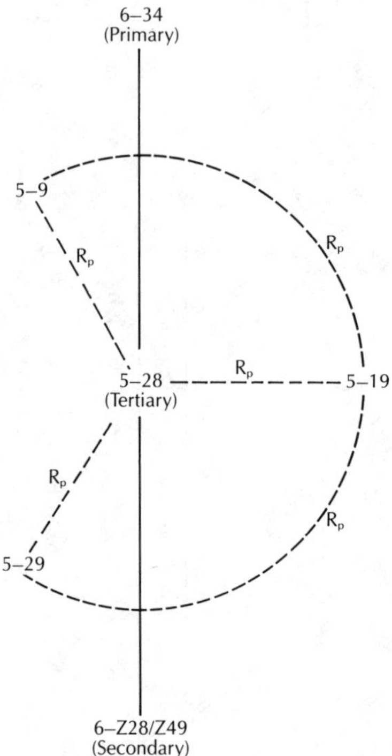

Example 108 Nexus Sets for Significant Sets, Atonal Period

music, along with the similarity relations connecting otherwise unrelated sets to the complex. Set 5–28 is also a tertiary nexus in the significant sets of the transitional period.

The structure of the complex of sets in the atonal music is strikingly similar to that in the transitional music (compare examples 108 and 81). In both cases 6–34 is the primary nexus, 6–Z28/Z49 is a secondary nexus, and 5–28 is a tertiary nexus connecting the two hexachords. In the transitional period, there is another secondary nexus (6–Z43) and another tertiary nexus (5–30), but in the atonal music one secondary and one tertiary nexus suffice. All predominantly whole-tone sets are related to 6–34, and 6–Z28/Z49 is the nexus for sets related to the 4–28/8–28 matrix in atonal works such as the Prelude Op. 59/2. (Set 6–Z49 is contained in 8–28 and 6–Z28 contains 4–28.)

It is curious that 6–Z28/Z49 should serve so well as a secondary nexus for Scriabin's transitional sets, for it occurs for the first time in Op. 59/2 (1910)—an atonal work. Its appearance here, however, culminates a trend toward the use of sets maximizing ic 3 which began around 1907. The 4–28/8–28 matrix is evident for the first time in 1910, but it becomes more and more prevalent in the music of 1911–14. The secondary nexus set 6–Z28/Z49 is therefore the focal component for the innovations through which Scriabin abandoned tonality, whereas the mystic chord, employed throughout both the tonal and the atonal music, is the basis for continuity in his evolution.

EIGHT
TONALITY AND ATONALITY IN THE EXTENDED FORMS I
The Sonatas

Having traced Scriabin's creative evolution through a close study of many of his short compositions, we can now examine the impact of his novel procedures on his extended forms. The focus of this chapter shall be the Fifth Sonata Op. 53, Scriabin's most splendid conception and his last large composition clearly based in tonality. This work was written in December 1907, immediately after—and perhaps even as a sequel to—the *Poem of Ecstasy* Op. 54 (although the order of their opus numbers is reversed).[1] The first of Scriabin's sonatas to consist unmistakably of a single movement, the Fifth Sonata established the basic formal scheme to which all five of his later sonatas conformed.

In order to evaluate how Scriabin's treatment of extended forms changed in the course of his transition to atonality, we shall compare the Fifth Sonata with the Fourth and Tenth sonatas. The Fourth Sonata Op. 30, written in 1903, was the first work completed in the creative surge which followed an unusual yearlong hiatus in Scriabin's compositional activity. This sonata is generally regarded as initiating a new period in the composer's development, a period of self-confident, individualistic expression and conscious innovation; it marks, in effect, the beginning of his transition to atonality. The Tenth Sonata Op. 70, written in the summer of 1913 along with the Eighth and Ninth sonatas, is one of Scriabin's last complete extended compositions. Although entirely atonal in structure, it is related to the Fourth and Fifth sonatas in its chief aesthetic aim—the creation through music of effects of light. Thus in several respects the Tenth Sonata culminates the development examined in this chapter.

THE FIFTH SONATA: THE OUTER LIMITS OF IMPLICIT TONALITY

Example 109 outlines the form of the Fifth Sonata, with special attention to motivic and thematic subject matter and the overall modulatory-transpositional scheme. The thematic treatment in this work adheres to the traditional tripartite division of exposition, development, and recapitulation, even though its tonal

Example 109 Fifth Sonata Op. 53: Form

		Measures	Derivation	T	Comments
Exposition (mm. 1–156)					
1–12 Intro	1a (1)	1–2			trill over tremolo bass
	(2)	3			abrupt ascending interjection
	b	3–5	1a	0	
	c	5–7	1a	0	
	2a (1)	7	1a(2)	0	
	(2)	7	2a(1) (r.h.)	5	
	b	8–11	2a	12	repeated in several octaves
13–46	A1a	13–14			G♯–D♯ motive from Intro 2; motive a_1
	b	15–16	A1a	0	
	2a	17–18			contains G♯–D♯ motive; motive a_2
	b	19–20			
	3a	21–22	A1a	0	but with D♮ instead of D♯
	2c	23–24	2b	0	
	3b	25–28			begins with A3a, t = 0
	2d–e	29–33	A2a–b	0	
	1c	34–35	A1a	0	
	2f	36–37	A2e	0	
	1d	38–41			begins with A1c, t = 0
	4a	42–43			5–35 = 5–35 in m. 40, t = 0
	b	44–46	A4a	6	6–32s in mm. 43 and 45 are literal complements
47–95	B1a	47–52	A4b	0	motive b_1
	b	53–58	B1a	5	over C♯ pedal
	2	59–60	B1		motive b_2
	3a (1)	61			
	(2)	62	B3a(1)	0	octave lower
	b	63–64	B2	10	
	c (1)	65			begins as B3b, t = 0
	(2)	66–67	B3c(1)	0	
	4	68–79	B1 (r.h.)	0	but over different harmony (B1, t = 5?); 6–32s in mm. 47 and 68 are identical
	5a (1)	80–81	B2	0	but over different harmony
	(2)	82–83	B5a(1) (r.h.)	0	but bass = B5a(1), t = 5
	b	84–87	B5a	2	
	6a	87–89			5–27 = 5–27 in m. 80, t = 10 (compare B3b); motive b_3
	b	89–91	B6a	0	
	7a	92			6–32 = 6–32 in B6, t = 0; motive b_4
	b	93	B7a (r.h.)	1	
			B7a (l.h.)	8	
	c	94–95			
96–119	C1a	96–97			motive c_1

Example 109 (cont.)

		Measures	Derivation	T	Comments
	b	98–99	C1a (harmony)	6	motive c_2
	2a	100–01	C1a (l.h.)	0	
			C1a (r.h.)	5	
	b	102–03	C1b (l.h.)	2, 10	successive transpositions
			C1b (r.h.)	0, 8	
	3a	104–05	C2a	1	begins as C1b, t = 7
	b(1)(a)	106–07	C2b	11	motive c_3
	(b)	107	C3b(1)(a) (l.h.)	6	
			C3b(1)(a) (r.h.)	8	
	(2)	108–09	C3b(1)	0	
	(3)	110–11	C3b(1)	2	
	(4)	112–13			
	4a	114–16	C3b(4) (l.h.)	0	l.h. figuration from C1a; r.h. has rhythm of C1a, related to B1; motive c_4
	b	116–19			
120–39	D1a	120–22			accompaniment derived from C1b; first chord like downbeat of m. 104, t = 8; motive d
	b(1)	122			
	(2)	123	D1b(1)	0	
	2a	124–26	D1a	0	last note of melody is different and helps form complete 6–35 in m. 126
	b	126–27	D1b	0	but with different melodic element
	3	128–30	D2a	5	but with different harmony on downbeat of m. 130
	4	130–33			
	5	134–37	D2	0	but with B♭ in bass (not C♭)
	6	138–39	D3 (melody)	0	
			D5 (harmony)	0	
140–56	E1	140–41	C4a	0	4–20 = 4–20 in m. 112, t = 0; 4–20 = 4–20 in m. 61, t = 0
	2a(1)	143–45	B2 (m. 59)	9	melodic phrase in m. 143 occurs in m. 144 at T_7 and m. 145 at T_{10}
	b(1)	146	C4a	7	
	2a(2)	147–48	E2a(1)	0	
	3a	149–50	B6a	9	6–Z25 = 6–Z25 in m. 145, t = 0
	2b(2)	151–52	E2b(1)	0	
	3b	153–54	E3a	0	
	2b(3)	155–56	E2b(1)	0	
Development (mm. 157–328)					
	Intro 3–4	157–65	Intro 1–2	2	
	A5–7b	166–82	A1–3b	2	

Example 109 (cont.)

	Measures	Derivation	T	Comments
7c	183–84	A6b	0	extension; root-position harmony
B8	185–90	B1 (melody)	3	harmony in mm. 187–90 comparable to mm. 74–77, t = 10
C5	191–92	C2	8	
B9	193–94	B8	0	
C6a	195–96	C5	0	
b	197–98	C6a	6	
A8	199–206	A2 (melody)	0	but E^7 harmony instead of F♯
B10–C8	207–18	B8–C6	9	mm. 207–08 are slightly different in the accompaniment
A9a	219–25	A8	9	
b	225–27			extension
B12a	227–28	B2	5	
b	229–34	A2 (melody)	5	
		E2a, E3	1?	derived from B
B13	235–42	B12	5	
B14	243–46	B6 (r.h.)	3	
Intro 5	247–50	Intro 2 (r.h.)	3	l.h. continues harmony of mm. 243–46
A10–11	251–62	A1–2	3	harmony in root position instead of third inversion
A12a(1)	263–64	A1a	3	plus countermelody
(2)	265–66	C2	1	modulatory progression corresponds
b(1)	267–68	A12a(1)	1	
(2)	269–70			
D7–8	271–78	D1–2	1	but with added B♮ pedal
9	279–80	D3 (melody)	1	but with same harmony as D7–8
E4	281–82	E1	1	
D10	283–84	D1	1	
E5	285–86	E4	3	
D11	287–88	D9	0	
E6a (1)	289–90	E4	3	
(2)	291–92	E4	7	
(3)	293–96			
b(4–6)	297–304	E6a(1–3)	2	except for m. 304
C9	305–08	C4a	3	motives c_2 and c_4
10	309–12	C4	3	includes anticipation of next bass note (compare m. 118)
D12	313–16	D1	3	half-step motive inverted in mm. 315–16
13	317–20	D2	3	
14	321–24	D13	5	compare D3
15	325–28	D14	5	or D2, t = 1

Example 109 (cont.)

	Measures	Derivation	T	Comments
Recapitulation (mm. 329–456)				
B15–18	329–56	B4–7	5	
C11–14	357–80	C1–4	5	
D16–21	381–400	D1–6	5	
E7a (1)	401–02	E1	5	
(2)	403–04	E7a(1)	0	
b(1)	405–06	E7a(1)	3	compare E4–5
(2)	407–08	E7b(1)	0	
8	409–16	E7	0	expanded registers
C15	417–21	C4	5	begins with 5–Z38 = 5–Z38 in m. 401, t = 0; E♭ pedal; r.h. derived from B1
16	425–32	C15	5	over E♭ pedal
A13	433–36	A1	4	continuing over E♭ pedal
14	437–40	A2 (melody)	4	
E9a (1)	441–43	E2a(1)	5	expected immediately following E7a(1)
b(1)	444	E2b(1)	5	motive c_4 now at T_0
a (2)	445–46	E2a(2)	5	
10a–b	447–50	E3a–b	5	
Intro 6	451–56	Intro 2	0	

plan departs radically from the norm. In fact, throughout his career Scriabin consistently based his sonatas and symphonies on the tripartite division.

In the outline, basic thematic groupings are identified by capital letters, major subdivisions by arabic numerals, further subdivisions by small letters, then by arabic numbers in parentheses, and so on. If a section is derived from previous material, the original is identified in the column headed "derivation," with the level of transposition, if applicable, in the next column.

The main motivic subject matter of the Fifth Sonata is shown in example 110. Each motive is labeled with a small letter (followed in most cases by a numerical subscript) which corresponds to the capital-letter label of the thematic grouping with which it is associated. Motive a is divided into two phrases: a_1 begins with the G♯–D♯ interval heard in the introduction (mm. 1–12), and a_2 begins with 4–19, the set occurring later as the *imperioso* motive (c_1). Sets 4–20 and 5–27 are also important in conjunction with motive a. The melodic contour formed by E♮–B♯–C♯ in a_2 is a significant gesture linking a_2 with many other motives.

Motive b involves a melodic unfolding of a succession of thirds. Underlying the opening phrase (mm. 47–52) are the three notes of the a_1 motive—D♯, F♯, and G♯. This phrase is then repeated at T_5, allowing the chain to continue its descent to E♮. The basic 5–27 thus formed is identical with that in motive a. Set 4–20 is also an important link between b_1 and a_1. Further, the a_2 contour occurs at T_{11} in b_1: D♯–A♯–B♮. The most important characteristic of b_2 is the wildly oscillating leap of the seventh, which occurs, though not repeated in the same way, in b_1. Motive b_3 appears to be derived from b_1. It also forms 5–27, related at IT_{10} to the 5–27 in a_1 (the sets share pcs 4, 6, and 11). Motive b_4 is related to

Example 110 Fifth Sonata Op. 53: Basic Motives

the descending chain of thirds in b_1, but may also bear some relation to a_1, as indicated. The pitches E♮ and A♮, so alien to the F♯ tonality, were significant in the introduction.

Section C contains four motivic ideas. Motive c_1 forms 4–19, heard earlier in a_2, and the a_2 contour is certainly evident here. Motive c_2 repeats the lower auxiliary idea of a_2 in a pulsating rhythm. Motive c_3 then incorporates c_2 in a larger gesture of successive ascending intervals of eight, nine, and (continuing into c_4) ten half steps. Motive c_4 seems to be a response to c_3, for both use set 5–34, as shown; c_4 also contains 4–22, as in b_4. However, instead of a stepwise descent, D♮–C♮–B♭, as would occur in b_4, the *quasi trombe* (as if a trumpet) motive substitutes an ascending seventh from C♮ to B♭, thus alluding to a_1, b_1, and b_2 as well.

The d motive is related to a and c. The first four notes are a contracted version of c_1, and the final three notes form the basic a_1 trichord. When this phrase is repeated immediately, the final melodic interval is an ascending fourth (in place of the ascending third). At the level of transposition at which d occurs in m. 275 (shown in the example), the connection with the G♯–D♯ fourth of a_1 is clear. Motive e, the most chromatic, is an intensification—both rhythmic and chromatic—of c_2.

Having described the basic subject matter of the Fifth Sonata, we should now consider its tonal structure. As a basis for this discussion, analytical sketches are provided in example 111. In the analyses in preceding chapters, attention was focused on voice leadings and prolongations near the foreground. Our commentary here shall concentrate on procedures at middleground and background levels.

The Fifth Sonata: Commentary on the Sketches

Exposition (mm. 1–156): Example 111a

Introduction (mm. 1–12). Despite the key signature of F♯ major, the scale here is E major, with E♮ and A♮ falling outside the F♯ tonality. These measures surely depict the "mysterious forces" which Scriabin summons from "obscure depths" in his epigram, a citation from his literary work, the "Poem of Ecstasy." Although the musical gestures here do not lend themselves to definite analysis, what seems implicit is a V^6_5–I progression in E major (or [V^6_5]–V–I in A major), with the trilled E♮ as a kind of pedal tone. (This E♮ continues in the bass of the following section.) The head tones of the thrusting gestures in mm. 7–11—D♯ and G♯—are the main melodic elements. Two half-step relations stand out: D♯–E♮ and G♯–A♮.

A Languido (mm. 13–46). In m. 13, when A♮ resolves to A♯, the harmony for the first time bears a semblance of relation to F♯ major. However, E♮ continues in the bass, forming a harmony resembling V^4_2/IV. In fact, such a conversion of the tonic into an applied dominant is typical of Scriabin's openings. Significantly, the D♯–G♯ melodic motive has been held over from the introduction. In mm. 13–39

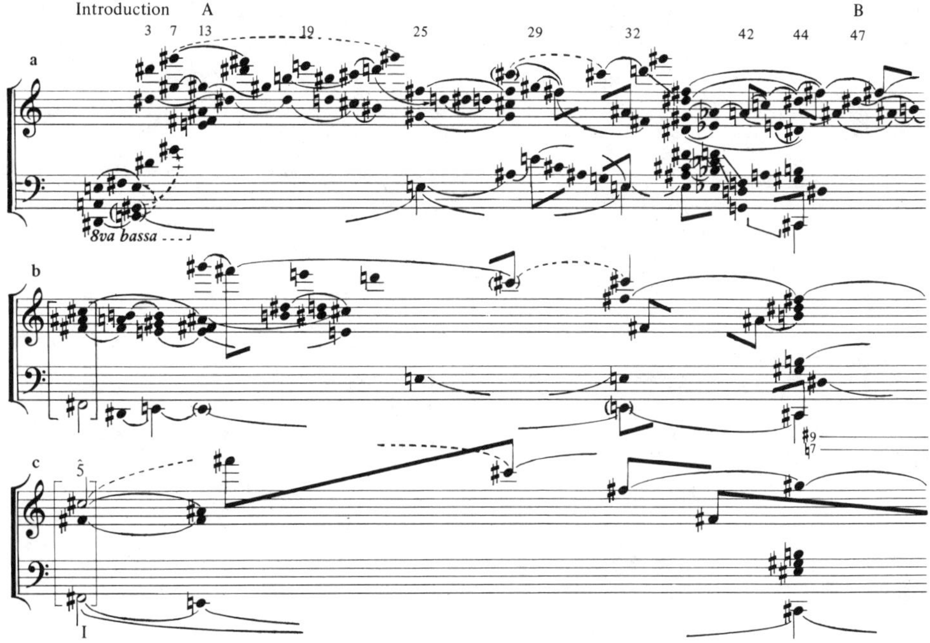

Example 111a Fifth Sonata Op. 53: Exposition

Example 111a (cont.)

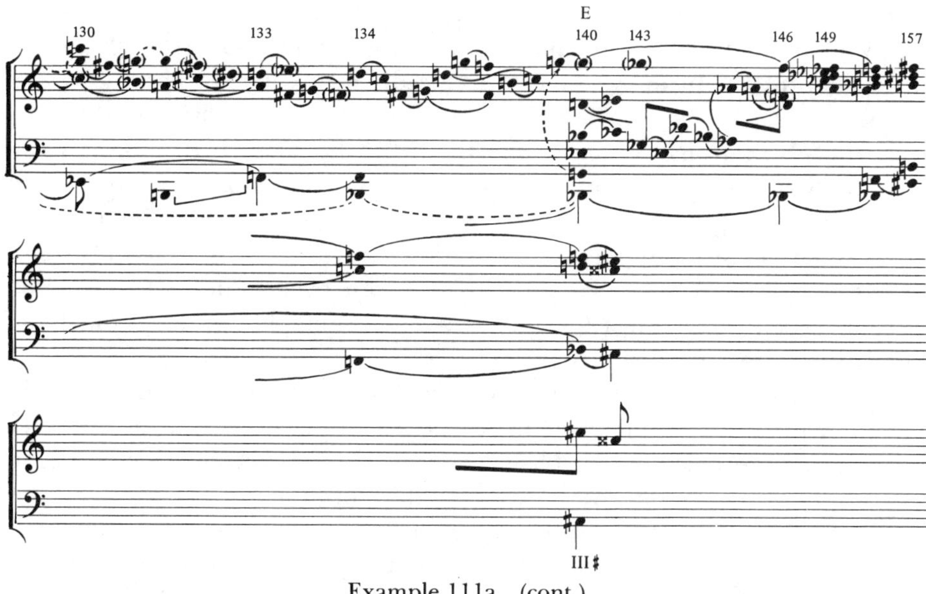

Example 111a (cont.)

E♮ is prolonged in the bass, and intervals of the F♯ tonic are unfolded in the upper voices. Of particular interest are the octave transfer by a tritone bass progression (mm. 25–29) and the subsequent bass arpeggiation of the diminished seventh chord (mm. 29–32).

At m. 40 the bass begins a chromatic descent from E♮ to C♯, the latter supporting the first dominant harmony. This unfolding underlies a transition to section B. The first forty-six measures are a typical progression for the opening of a work by Scriabin, implying a bass arpeggiation from I to V (compare mm. 1–3 of the Poem Op. 32/2; see example 27). At the beginning we may hypothesize an unfolding from I$^5_3$ to "V$^4_2$/IV" which incorporates the elements of the introduction as shown in the middleground sketch. Within the larger context, the $^4_2$ harmony is not a secondary dominant but rather a linear chord expanding the progression from I to V. Beginning in m. 42, the melody unfolds an ascending arpeggiation of the diminished seventh chord, answering the descending arpeggiation of that harmony in mm. 29–32 in the bass.

B Presto con allegrezza (mm. 47–95). This section contains the main theme of the work, or at least what corresponds to a main theme according to traditional notions of sonata form. Everything preceding this section seems to be an introduction, including the *languido* section, which, as we shall see, is the formal equivalent of the entire first movement in the Fourth Sonata. The music in mm. 47–67 is grounded in the dominant, not the tonic as might be expected. The melody, which contains the a_1 motive, moves essentially by descending third at the surface (compare the bass motion in mm. 38–46). Underlying this progression is a stepwise ascent from F♯ to C♯ in the middleground, the F♯ receiving harmonic support from the tonic implicit at the beginning of the piece.

Measures 53–58 contain a sequential repetition of the melody of mm. 47–52 at T_5 while the C♯ pedal is retained. This transposition leads naturally to the introduction of E♮. In m. 59 A♮ is introduced, and A♮ and E♭ harmonies are juxtaposed in mm. 59–62. Together these events refer to the introduction, where the A♮–D♯ tremolo clashes with the trilled E♮. Most interesting in mm. 59–67 is the nesting of identical progressions, as shown in the foreground sketch. The basic progression occurs over C♯, which is implicitly retained as a pedal throughout, with upper voices resolving lowered sixth to perfect fifth and minor to major third. A similar progression occurs over G♮ in the bass in mm. 61–63, a section which interrupts the basic voice leading but prolongs the dominant harmony by a tritone bass progression.

Measures 63–64 repeat at T_{10} the material of mm. 59–60, resulting in a middleground melodic descent from an A♮–C♯ third to G♮–B♮. This succession is condensed and reversed in mm. 65–66, and thus the underlying melodic ascent to C♯ occurs, albeit through A♮, the lowered third of F♯ major.

At m. 68 the dominant cadences to the tonic, completing an arpeggiation of the tonic in the bass. This cadence is the only strong progression from dominant to tonic at deep levels of structure in the entire piece. In fact, the dominant in mm. 44–67, which is subsumed in a tonic prolongation not far beneath the surface, is the strongest dominant in the work. The repercussions of this extraordinary situation with regard to the tonal coherence of the work are discussed later. A tonic pedal is sustained through m. 81, while the right-hand part in these measures is precisely the same as in mm. 47–60. The melody unfolds another ascent from F♯ to C♯, again through A♮ and B♮ as in mm. 32–67, even though the material beginning in m. 82 is new and the accompanying harmony different, entailing an unfolding from F♯ to A♮ in the bass. The progression in mm. 80–87 is sequential, involving T_5 in the bass progression within the pattern and T_2 for the repetition of the entire pattern. Beginning in m. 92 the bass progression leads by a motivic succession of descending thirds from A♮ to D♮, which progresses by tritone to G♯, the next main harmonic goal (m. 96). In the middleground the bass A♮ (m. 87) is a chromatic upper auxiliary to G♯.

C Imperioso (mm. 96–119). Harmony in this section is continually in flux. Melodies and chords are involved in transpositional shifts, but right- and left-hand parts seldom shift at the same time or to the same level. At first a G♯ harmony is prolonged by a tritone bass progression. Then in mm. 102–04 G♯ moves to A♮ by a descending major seventh unfolded in a chain of thirds. A patterned progression leads from A♮ through B♮ to C♮ (m. 116), which supports an applied dominant of F♮. The F♮ in the bass in mm. 118–19 anticipates its proper arrival at the beginning of the following section.

An alternative reading of the bass motion in mm. 68–116 entails a tritone progression from F♯ to C♮ which would prolong the tonic throughout. (This interpretation is demonstrated beneath the regular middleground graph for these measures.) This analysis does not conflict with the reading of the essential motion from I to III♯ as the underpinning of the entire exposition. Further, it places less emphasis on the first statement of the *imperioso* motive (c_1), instead indicating c_4 (*quasi trombe*) as the main goal after the establishment of the tonic in m. 68. This analysis is thus a more cogent explanation of the directedness of the C episode, and it discloses a grand expansion of Scriabin's most favored progression.

D Meno vivo—accarezzevole (mm. 120–39). This section takes place over an F♮ pedal, which supports the dominant of B♭. Although B♭ is anticipated in the bass in mm. 134–39 and even earlier in mm. 128–29, it is not effectively tonicized until the arrival of section E. (When B♭ supports a harmony in m. 128, it is an applied dominant seventh chord.) The structure of the melody is especially interesting here. The first phrase ends with the harmonic tone F♮ in mm. 122–23. This phrase is repeated, but with G♮ substituted for F♮ as the final tone. We expect G♮ to resolve to F♮ over C♭ in the bass, but it does not. The next phrase is a literal transposition at T_5 of the preceding one, which results in the G♮ being suspended further and then resolved to F♮ as expected, but over a different harmony.

E Allegro fantastico—Presto tumultuoso esaltato (mm. 140–56). In this section the basic harmonic underpinning is B♭, which in the overall F♯ tonality is the enharmonic equivalent of A♯ (supporting III♯). The passage in mm. 143–46, a development of the B theme, entails a middleground chromatic descent from G♭ to F♮—and G♭ is itself a chromatic connector in the resolution of the G♮ left unresolved at the end of section D.

Development (mm. 157–328): Example 111b

The subject matter of the sonata has been set forth in a rather straightforward fashion in what may be regarded as a conventional sonata-form exposition. The material is itself traditional: a tentative, languid introductory section (which includes section A), an exuberant main theme (B) connected through an episode (C) to a tender contrasting idea (D), with the entire exposition wrapped up by a vigorous closing section (E) bearing strong motivic ties to preceding events. Although the underlying harmonic progression of the exposition—a motion from the tonic to the major mediant—is unusual, it is by no means problematic in its assertion of the tonality. Scriabin's plan is a logical extension of earlier romantic sonata forms, such as Beethoven's Op. 53 (the "Waldstein"), where the same progression occurs in the exposition of main and contrasting themes in the first movement.

At the deepest level, the development section of the Fifth Sonata moves from mediant (A♯) to subdominant (B♮) in the bass, with $\hat{4}$ in the Urlinie supported by the subdominant. This motion spans the entire development and is not complete until the recapitulation begins in m. 329. The conventionality of the formal layout belies the uniqueness of Scriabin's harmonic scheme.

The development section begins with a startling chord (m. 157) which culminates the dynamic buildup at the close of the exposition; this chord is followed by the unexpected return of the material of the introduction, transposed to T_2.

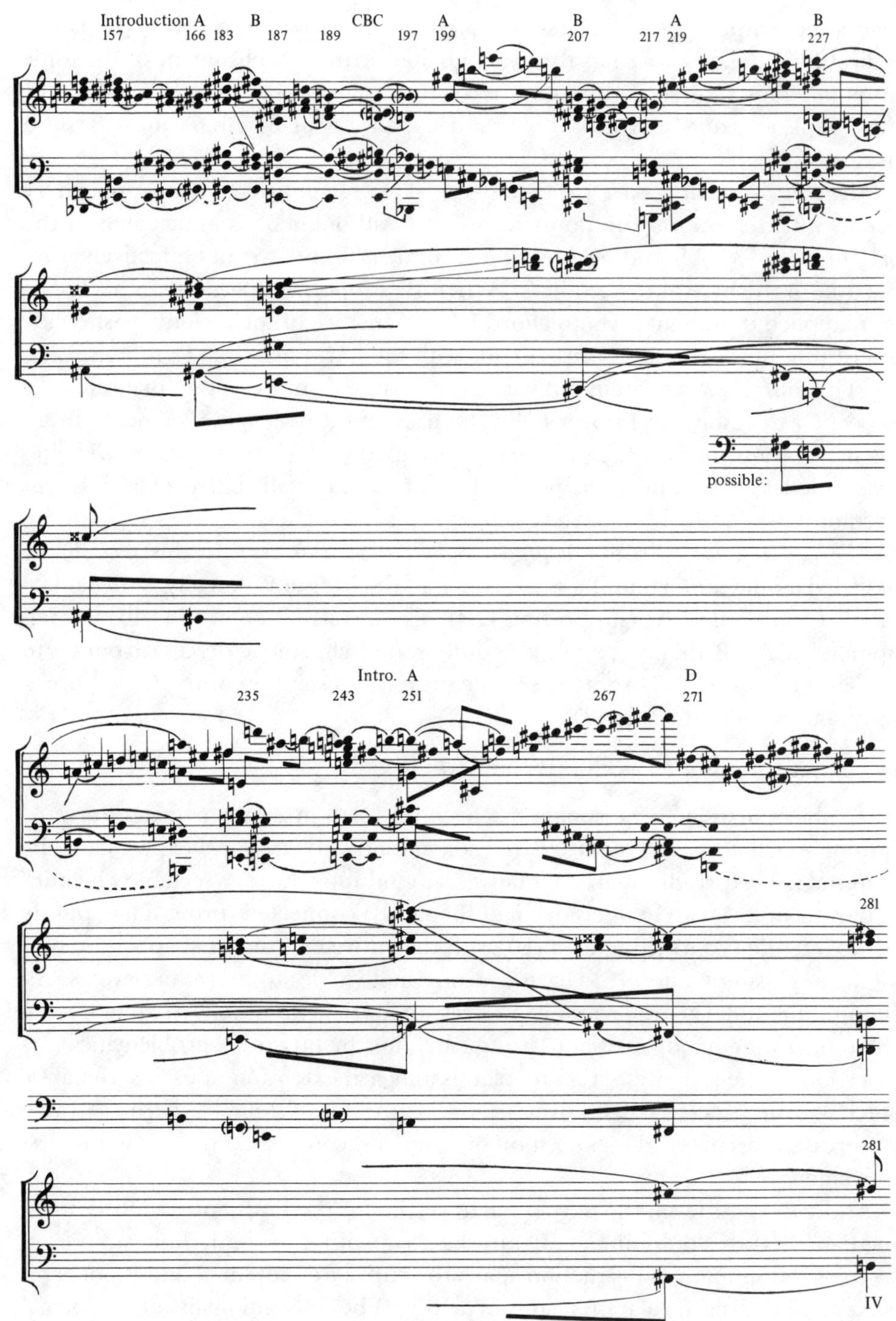

Example 111b Fifth Sonata Op. 53: Development

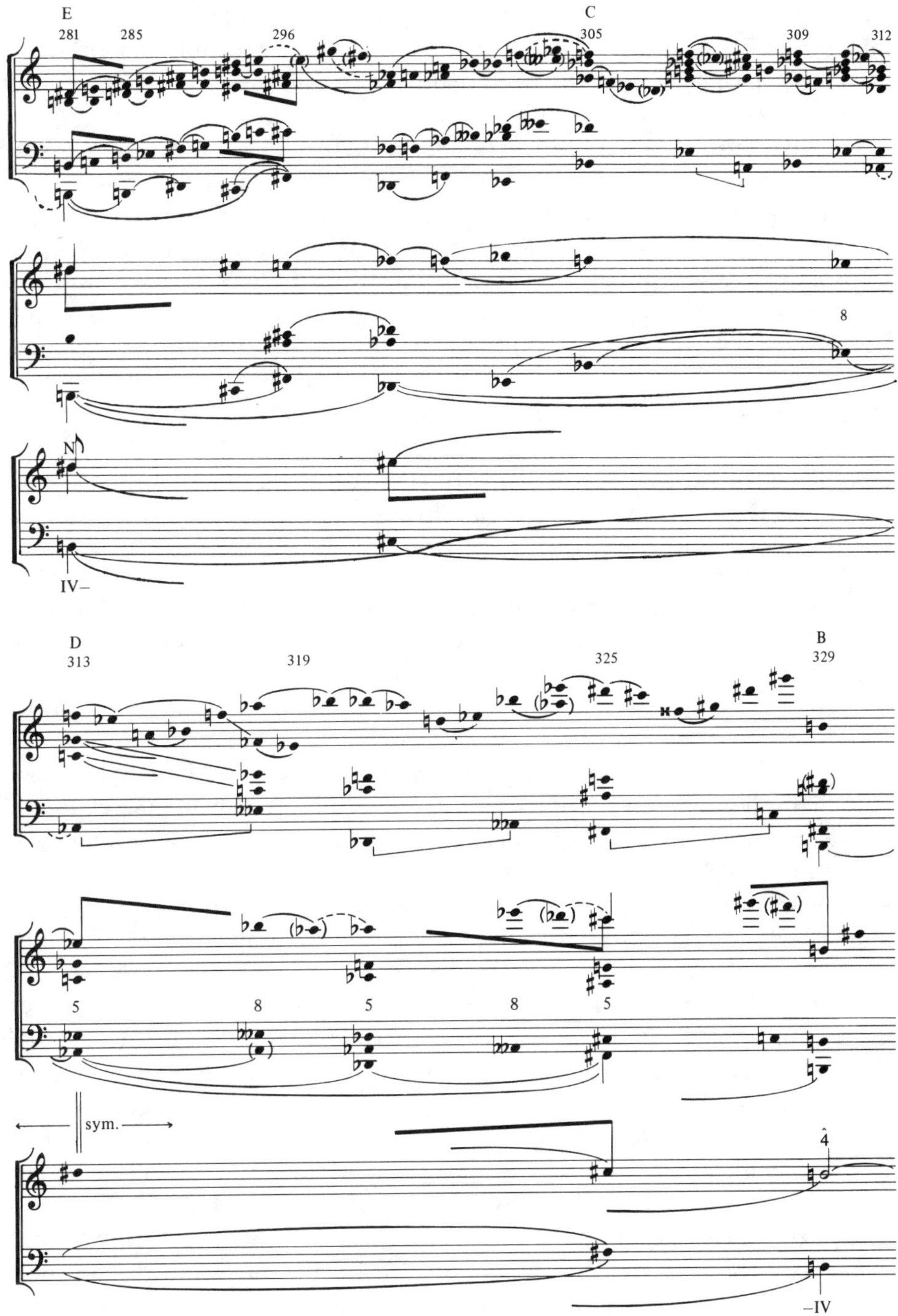

Example 111b (cont.)

The A material follows, an exact repetition at T_2 until m. 183. The purpose of this transpositional level is one of the great puzzles in this work. The solution lies in the voice leading of the deep middleground, but we should first discuss events nearer the surface.

The fifth-relation between the bass notes B♭ (A♯) and E♯ in mm. 156–57 is the clearest connection between exposition and development at the foreground. (The E♯ spelling corroborates the interpretation of B♭ as A♯ in the overall tonal scheme.) It is ironic that here, and not in the corresponding passage at the opening of the piece, the F♯ major scale is the aggregate set. In accordance with our reading of the opening, however, the underlying harmonic reference is a dominant seventh chord on G♯, heard first in third inversion in m. 166. This interpretation is confirmed in m. 183, where the G♯ root occurs in the low bass. (There was no such confirmation for F♯ as the fundamental at the beginning of the piece, but the G♯ in m. 183 validates our readings of both passages.) The G♯, then, is set up strongly as the main referent at the beginning of the development, and the Ursatz bass, which has already ascended as far as A♯, seems to backtrack for no clear reason.

After a static beginning, the harmonic progression of the development reaches the fastest pace in the entire piece. This pacing, and the extensive fragmentation and recombination of themes and motives in this section, conform to expected sonata development. Also typical are the frequent sequential passages here. In m. 187 the bass descends a third abruptly from G♯ to E♮, and E♮ is the focus through m. 206. An E^7 harmony is prolonged by both a tritone bass progression in m. 197 and an octave coupling accomplished by the bass arpeggiation of a diminished seventh chord in mm. 199–206. The melody in mm. 200–06 is the same as that in mm. 29–33 (at T_0), and the bass progression in mm. 187–206 is essentially the same as that in section A (mm. 25–33). Because E♮ was prolonged as the bass of a $\frac{4}{2}$ chord in the introduction, it appears that the same diminished seventh chord is used in mm. 199–206 to prolong an entirely different harmonic function.

Measures 187–205 are repeated almost exactly at T_9 in mm. 207–25, effectively prolonging a C♯ harmony throughout. Thus the development section through m. 225 is based on a fifth descending in the bass from G♯ through E♮ to C♯. (Transposed repetition makes it easy to perceive the prolonged harmony on E♮ as connective.) At m. 225 harmony and melody are altered to extend the development to a climactic deceptive cadence in m. 227. At this point a harmony on B♮ is expected. However, the F♯ bass note of the applied dominant seventh in m. 226 is held over while A♯ resolves irregularly to A♮, thus forming the D major sixth chord on the downbeat of m. 227. During the next eight measures, a dominant seventh harmony on B♮ is unfolded (as shown in the foreground sketch). Therefore a B♮ is implicitly present throughout the passage. When this passage is transposed to T_5 in mm. 235–42, the middleground bass progression moves one step around the circle of fifths to E♮, which is retained in the bass while material from the introduction is set over a C major sixth chord (mm. 247–

50). This harmony is a transitory linear chord within the progression a step further around the circle of fifths—to A♮, the bass in mm. 251–62. Here melody and harmony are essentially those of A1–2 (mm. 13–20) at T_3, but the harmony is in root position, whereas it was in third inversion earlier.

Measures 263–69 are a transitional episode which departs from the circle-of-fifths progression. The harmony and melody at the beginning of the passage continue the A1 material at T_3. However, a chromatic shift is quickly effected from A♮ to A♯ (spelled first as B♭ in mm. 267–69) in the bass. The progression in this shift was heard earlier in conjunction with completely different subject matter—the C material in mm. 96–104. Thus the recurrence of this progression entails a subtle developmental relation. Once A♯ has been stabilized, it is assimilated into a dominant seventh chord on F♯ in m. 270.

At a larger level, the underlying bass progression of this section is a descending third from A♮ to F♯. Counterpointed against this motion is a middleground ascent from A♮ to F♯ in mm. 251–70. Thus these measures are unified by simultaneous unfoldings of this interval in contrary motion.

Whereas the first part of the development has concentrated on subject matter from sections A and B, the rest is devoted primarily to the D material, specifically to its gradual transformation from a tender, caressing melody to an impassioned and fiery theme whose rapturous climax culminates the entire development. The underlying harmony of the D material in mm. 271–80 continues to be a dominant seventh on F♯ (V/B♮), despite the B♮ pedal point which anticipates the true harmony on B♮ in m. 281. (See the analysis of the comparable passage in mm. 120–39.) In mm. 281–88, D material is alternated with E material, and the latter is the basis for a complicated sequential passage (uninterrupted by D material) in mm. 289–304. The harmony of the E material in mm. 281–82 is based on B♮ (compare mm. 140–41), and B♮ is held over in mm. 285–86, where the material is essentially equivalent at T_3 to that in mm. 281–82. Measures 289–90, a literal repetition of mm. 285–86, also have B♮ in the bass. Thus the cadence to the subdominant occurs with the arrival of the E material as early as m. 281.

Before we proceed with an analysis of the remainder of the development, it will be useful to survey the progress of the section thus far. Beneath the middleground sketch for mm. 226–271 is an alternative reading of the bass progression as an unfolding of the F♯ octave through descending thirds. This reading draws attention to a possible link between the F♯ dominant seventh chords in m. 226 and mm. 270–80. According to this interpretation, the strong cadence to B♮ expected at m. 227 is denied; only after the cycle of thirds is complete with the F♯ in m. 270 does such a cadence take place. However, certain links in the chain of thirds are weak: the harmonies on D♮, G♮, and C♮ are actually sixth chords. In the more persuasive analysis these chords are interpreted as the result of rhythmic displacement, linear progression, or both, with the bass moving by descending fifth (ascending fourth). The underlying connection effected by this succession, however, is that of a descending third from C♯ in m. 207 to A♮

in m. 251. On a larger level, this interval is part of a succession of descending thirds, beginning with G♯ in the bass at m. 166, which is completed with the descent from A♮ (or its chromatic equivalent, A♯) to F♯ in m. 270. Thus the pattern which unfolds in mm. 166–280 effects a stepwise descent from G♯ to F♯. Further, this descent is part of a larger descending-third bass motion in the deep middleground, from A♯ at m. 140 to F♯ in m. 270, with G♯ as a connecting note. As we have seen, F♯ in m. 270 supports an applied dominant, cadencing to B♮ in m. 281. Therefore, underlying the entire development thus far is the stepwise ascent in the bass from A♯ (m. 140), the fundamental note concluding the exposition, to B♮; the motion to V/B♮ is an elaboration of this basic progression.

The level of transposition at which Scriabin chose to repeat the introduction and A material at the beginning of the development is not arbitrary, but rather begins a directed motion toward B♮ which spans much of the composition. The basic motion from A♯ to B♮ is emphasized by the recurrence of the original D and E materials (mm. 120–42) at T_1 in mm. 271–82.

After the return of the E material in m. 281, the D material twice interrupts a patterned progression which originates nevertheless with the E material in mm. 281–82. The first phrase effects an opening progression from I to V in B major (mm. 289–96). Within this phrase, the transposition of the material of mm. 285–86 to T_4 in mm. 291–92 extends the B major harmony in first inversion. In the following measure, V/V in B♮ is introduced, and the phrase is capped by V/B♮ in m. 296. The phrase in mm. 297–304 is a near replica of that in mm. 289–96, transposed to T_2. Although it begins with a D♭ major harmony, however, it fails to progress from V/V to V in D♭ at the end of the phrase. Instead, the harmony moves to the relative minor, B♭, with the beginning of an eight-measure transitional phrase in m. 305. As tension mounts, the progression oscillates between VI and V/V in D♭, progressing finally to V/D♭ in mm. 313–14 with the climactic return of the D theme. (Motives from section C are particularly appropriate in this transition, for the C material originally led directly to D.) The arrival of this A♭ harmony completes the opening progression from D♭ which was expected by the end of m. 304. Yet this arrival is also the point of departure for a succession of fifths descending toward B major, the harmony with which the recapitulation begins in m. 329. (Each harmony in this progression is expanded by a tritone bass progression.) Significantly, A♭ in m. 313 is an axis of symmetry, for the fifths descending from A♭ to B♮ are the retrograde of the progression underlying mm. 281–313.

The background sketch shows that the latter part of the development is based on a progression opening from tonic to dominant in B major (the subdominant in the overall F♯ tonality). Within this progression, V/V is most significant because it initiates a transposed repetition in m. 297. (The proper spelling for this harmony is clearly a chord on C♯, although Scriabin shifts to the more convenient spelling in flats in mm. 299–324.) Both the B♮ and C♯ harmonies are extended by progressions to their dominants, and V of C♯ (m. 313) proceeds sequentially to the next important function, the dominant in m. 325. Thus the E material in mm. 289–96 contains in microcosm the progression upon which the rest of the development is structured.

At the largest level, the B major subdominant is prolonged in mm. 281–329 by a circular progression completed with the arrival of the recapitulation. Within this prolonged subdominant the melodic progression in the deep middleground is essentially an unfolding from D♯, the upper auxiliary to the C♯ Kopfton, to B♮, $\hat{4}$ of the Urlinie. The arrival of B♮ coincides with the return to the subdominant in m. 329. At more local levels, several unfoldings are noteworthy. The progression from I to V in B in mm. 281–96 supports an unfolding of a minor ninth from D♯ to E♮. The E♮ is actually a chromatic passing tone, connecting D♯ with E♯ (F♮), an element of V/V in mm. 297–328. The melody in mm. 313–25 unfolds from D♯ (E♭) to C♯ in conjunction with the harmonic progression to V. The D♯ here is a passing element in an unfolding from E♯ (m. 296) to C♯ (m. 325) supported by the underlying progression from V/V to V. In the deep middleground, C♯ is itself a passing note connecting D♯ with B♮.

Recapitulation (mm. 329–456): Example 111c

The events beginning in m. 329 are a recapitulation, but only in a limited sense. This section is a repetition (albeit transposed) of an extensive span of the exposition. In fact, mm. 329–402 repeat almost note-for-note the music in mm. 68–141—an excerpt encompassing the latter half of section B, all of sections C and D, and the beginning of section E—but at T_5. Therefore, Scriabin's sonata does not conform to the traditional harmonic scheme in either the recapitulation or its preparation in the development. The tonic, though an implicit long-range goal, is not attained in either the recapitulation or the coda. Harmonically, the recapitulation begins in the familiar area of B major (IV), which was reached midway through the development. Only the arrival of $\hat{4}$ in the Urlinie makes the moment of recapitulation important in deep structure. Significantly, Scriabin includes in the recapitulation only that portion of the B material which occurred after the cadence to I in m. 68. The preceding B material, grounded on a dominant pedal, was part of an implicit circular progression. The wonderfully tentative effect of this dominant pedal in the exposition arises because the tonic has not yet been stated explicitly. The transpositional level T_5 in the recapitulation insures an adequate completion of the prolongation of IV. This might not have been possible had Scriabin stated more of the B material than that firmly grounded in the tonic.

The most important effect of the transposition to T_5 in the recapitulation is that the stepwise ascent of the bass, the underlying progression of the piece thus far, is continued without interruption. In the exposition the essential bass line ascended from F♯ through G♯ to A♯, and A♯ moved to B♮ in the development. In the recapitulation, the bass line begins with B♮ and moves through C♯ to D♯ (E♭). The arrival of the dominant in m. 357 is not pivotal in the deep structure. Both in concept and in traditional formal schemes, a large-scale stepwise ascent from I to V should create a primary musical gesture, with the arrival of V as a

Example 111c Fifth Sonata Op. 53: Recapitulation

crucial event. In Scriabin's sonata, the dominant harmony occurs in conjunction with episodic rather than thematic material, which is less stable harmonically than the materials supported by the subdominant or submediant harmonies before and after; C♯ seems no more important than the other elements of the middleground bass ascent—perhaps even less important than B♮ or D♯. The way in which the dominant occurs attenuates the tonality at the deepest levels. This usage differs markedly from occurrences of the dominant in almost every other tonal work by Scriabin, where the dominant is the most strongly defined harmonic component.

The concluding section of the piece draws together almost every motive of the sonata. Beginning with the E material in m. 401, it grows frenetically, climaxing with the apotheosis of the A material in an ecstatic explosion of light meant to shake the very firmament. (Indeed, this finale is to the piano sonata what the Immolation Scene is to opera!) The E material in mm. 401–02 is equivalent at T_5 to that in the exposition (mm. 140–41) and is thus based harmonically on E♭. This E♭ is retained as a pedal point for the rest of the piece, occurring as D♯ in the final passage. The E material in mm. 405–06 is a transposed repetition (over the E♭ pedal) of mm. 401–02, with $t = 3$. (Each phrase is actually stated twice in succession.) This process relates directly to the E material in the development, where the phrases in mm. 281–82 and 285–86 (which are separated by the return of D material) were equivalent at T_3. A variation of the material of mm. 401–08 occurs in expanded registers in mm. 409–16. The passage beginning in m. 417, with a right-hand part based on B material, starts with the same harmony contained in m. 401. The c_4 motive is now trumpeted forth, at T_5 from the original (m. 114), but at the same level at which it was heard earlier in the recapitulation (m. 375). In mm. 425–32, still over an E♭ pedal, the preceding eight measures are repeated at T_5. The basic harmonic progression effected by these occurrences of c_4 is V/V–V in E♭, all over the E♭ pedal. The climactic statement of the A theme occurs at T_4 from the original; thus it is also based on V/E♭, which is unfolded (over the E♭ pedal) in mm. 433–40.

A cadence to E♭ occurs in m. 444 with the return of E material, corresponding to that in mm. 143–50, which has not yet been repeated. Had the recapitulation of E material at T_5 continued regularly in m. 403, the material of the final presto would have occurred immediately after the phrase in mm. 401–02. To a certain extent, then, the restatement of this material completes the recapitulation, for all other primary materials have been restated. Because it is linked naturally with the material which begins the concluding section in m. 401, the final presto ties together this section and insures the prolongation of E♭. (In terms of the recapitulation, it is significant, too, that the c_4 motive in m. 444 occurs at the same level of transposition as the original in m. 114.) Most important, however, this material also closed the exposition and was followed by the abrupt return of the introduction. Here, at the end of the work, the material is again followed by the introductory passage, which intrudes even more unexpectedly than before. The E material is cut off before it can cadence again to E♭ as expected. The foreground sketch demonstrates, however, that the introduction links strongly with the linear chord in mm. 447–50 (also found in m. 443). Most clearly, the E♭ pedal carries over to become the bass D♯ in mm. 451–55. Perhaps, too, there is a connection between the melodic A♭ left dangling in m. 439 and G♯, one of two accented motivic elements in the final measures.

The return of the chaotic opening progression at the end of the sonata creates an obvious cycle with a direct bearing on the program of the work. Out of the "obscure depths" the composer has created from mere "outlines of life" a universe which has expanded to the very limits of its potential. In a tremendous burst of energy, it collapses in on itself, and only the smallest particles of musical matter remain, scattered chaotically as at the beginning. The cyclicity of the sonata has a much deeper basis than the mere return of the opening material, however—it is related directly to the tonal coherence of the work as a whole. Because the piece reaches no firm conclusion but rather could (and perhaps should) continue, it is helpful in understanding the tonal implications of the actual conclusion to consider the voice-leading events which would naturally follow. If another cycle began, the bass D♯ (E♭) which has been prolonged from m. 401 would progress to E♮, implicit in the opening measures and explicit at m. 13. Most interesting is the essential melodic progression which would take place over E♮ in the bass. The prominent G♯ of the introductory material resolves to F♯ (supported by the $\frac{4}{2}$ chord) in m. 14—precisely the progression required for the completion of the Urlinie (see the background sketch for mm. 401–56).

The completion of the Urlinie may thus be implicit, but the progression of the bass is more problematic. Example 111d shows a condensed sketch of the essential Ursatz of the sonata, in which the bass line ascends stepwise through a seventh, from F♯ to E♮. The effect of a possible arpeggiation from tonic to dominant is minimized in this work; instead the subdominant seems to be the focal element in the bass progression, for the recapitulation begins in m. 329 with the subdominant and thereafter is a transposition of the exposition at T_5, the level of the subdominant. The ultimate reduction of the voice-leading structure is shown in example 111e. The ascending seventh in the bass is essentially a stepwise descent from the F♯ tonic to E♮, the minor seventh and a note outside the tonic scale. Taking into account the melodic descent from C♯ ($\hat{5}$) to A♯ ($\hat{3}$), the basic progression is a familiar one at the foreground of Scriabin's works and one which was inferred at the beginning of this sonata at a local level—that is, the conversion of the tonic into a dominant seventh of the subdominant by adding the lowered seventh (see the background sketch for mm. 1–13). This procedure is typical of Scriabin's opening progressions—for example, those of the Poem Op. 32/2, the Prelude Op. 45/3, and the Prelude Op. 48/4. Because the I–V$\frac{4}{2}$/IV progression is thus the fundamental structure of the Fifth Sonata, the forces of tonality are strained here considerably more than in the other late tonal works examined in this book. This is especially true because this work is relatively large and because there is no strong bass arpeggiation from I to V at the background of the work.[2] At the deepest levels of structure the Fifth Sonata is fraught with

Examples 111d–e Fifth Sonata Op. 53

unprecedented ambiguity, for the subdominant, which controls almost all of the development, threatens to pull the tonic within its own gravitational field.

In spite of its adventurous harmonic scheme, the Fifth Sonata is fundamentally tonal. A question of the utmost importance for such an expansive and complex work is whether atonal correspondences also govern its structure at larger levels, as they do in many of Scriabin's shorter works. In terms of three of the most important sets in the sonata—5–27, 6–32, and 6–34—there are relatively few recurrences of identical sets or of literal complementation with strong structural repercussions. The most powerful correspondence involves the background of the sonata, for the hexachord formed by the Ursatz bass—F♯, G♯, A♯, B♮, C♯, D♯—is a form of 6–32 identical to its presentation in the main theme (B) in the tonic beginning in m. 68 (example 113b). Because 6–32 is a diatonic collection, however, it is impossible to consider this correspondence a nontonal relation.

Example 112 shows recurrences of identical set-forms which create references across large spans. In example 112a, three appearances of the same form of 5–27 relate subjects at the beginning, middle, and end of the piece. The occurrence in m. 447 is an important link with the introductory material, which re-

Example 112a Fifth Sonata Op. 53

turns immediately following in m. 451. The 5–27 in m. 59, the goal of a patterned progression around the circle of fifths which began in m. 47 (all over a dominant pedal), is linked motivically with the introduction. This link is strengthened by the surprising juxtaposition of this 5–27 against the equivalent set at T_6 in the following measure—a dramatic contrast, for forms of 5–27 at T_6 share no pcs. The roots of the two harmonies, A♮ and E♭, form the same tritone as the low bass rumblings at the beginning of the sonata.

Example 112b shows two occurrences of the same form of 5–27 at significant points in the formal scheme. The first occurs at the beginning of the main body of the exposition (m. 47), the second at m. 441, the beginning of what could be called the codetta—the passage which closes the work. Example 112c traces a recurrence of the 5–27 based on E♭ in m. 61, discussed in conjunction with example 112a. In mm. 114–15 the identical 5–27 is associated with the triumphant c_4 motive, while in the codetta (m. 444) c_4 is trumpeted forth at the same level of transposition (example 112b). Example 112d demonstrates that the 6–34 in m. 397 (in the recapitulation of D material) anticipates its own climactic statement in m. 440.

All of these recurrences of identical set-forms are important in unifying the sonata. In particular, the conclusion corresponds motivically with significant

Example 112b Fifth Sonata Op. 53

Example 112c Fifth Sonata Op. 53

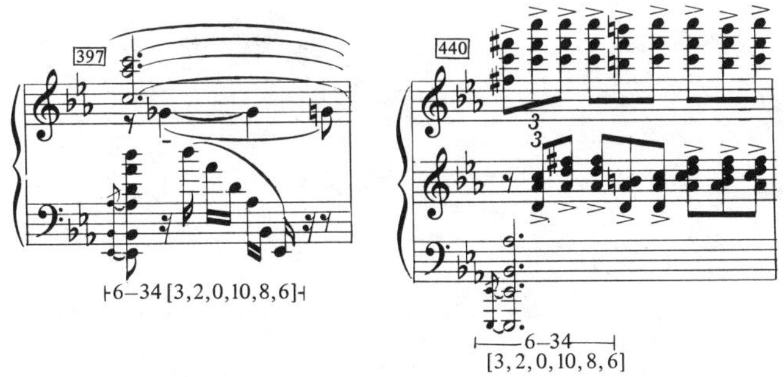

Example 112d Fifth Sonata Op. 53

Example 112e Fifth Sonata Op. 53

events at many points in the composition. In general, the most widespread sets in the sonata—such as 5–27 and 6–32—are almost always connected with the same or closely related subject matter. A significant exception is 6–34, which occurs in a variety of contexts, two of which were shown in example 112d. Example 112e shows three more appearances of 6–34 (at different levels of transposition), each formed differently. Such recurrences lend an underlying unity to a work which, to the casual listener, may seem episodic and sprawling.

We have described large-scale correspondences spanning large portions of the sonata, relations created by recurrences of the same set-form or, more weakly, by the same set in different motivic-thematic guises. It is difficult to establish whether relations of maximum or minimum invariance are of similar structural importance. It is clear, however, that such atonal relations are exploited locally; several are illustrated in example 113. Example 113a shows a passage from the development in which two statements of c_1 are juxtaposed. The two forms of 6–34 here are equivalent at T_6 and share four pcs, [2,4,8,10], the maximum possible. Example 113b, a reduction of an extended passage of B material from the exposition, shows that the progression around the circle of fifths effects

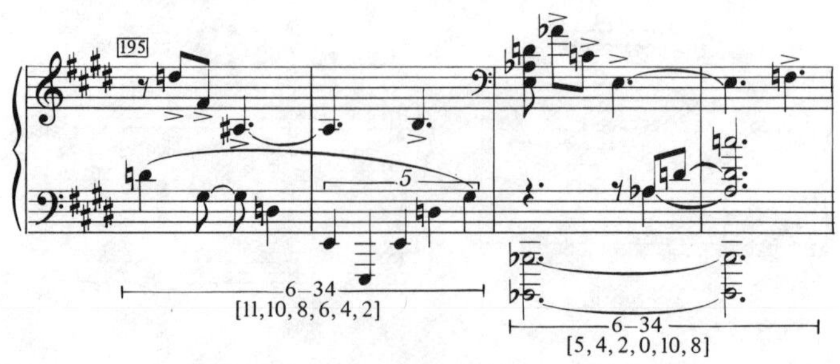

Example 113a Fifth Sonata Op. 53

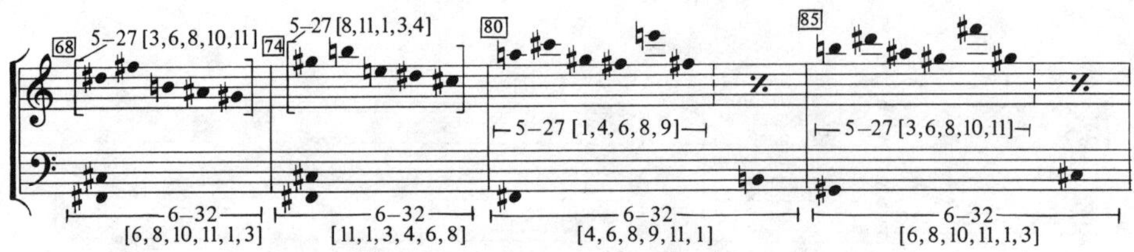

Example 113b Fifth Sonata Op. 53

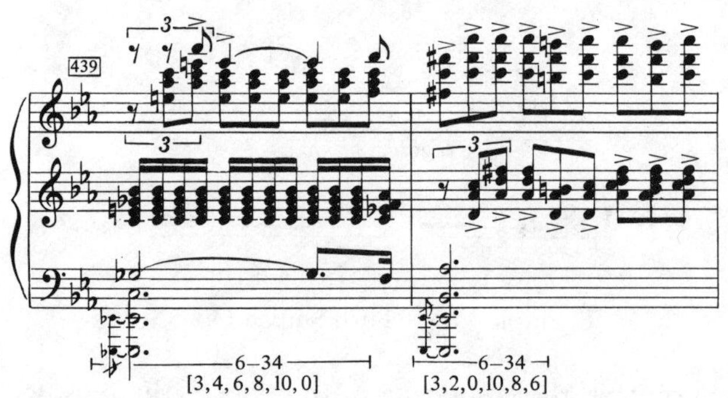

Example 113c Fifth Sonata Op. 53

maximum invariance for forms of the diatonic hexachord 6–32 and its subset 5–27. After two transpositions with t = 5, these sets are transposed up two half steps, yielding forms identical to those at the start of the passage (5 + 5 + 2 = 12 = 0). Example 113c shows an extraordinary occurrence of maximum invariance at the climax of the sonata. Here adjacent forms of 6–34 are inversion-related and share five pcs, more than is possible under transposition alone.

Minimum invariance often occurs with a shift of tonal planes. Example 113d shows the modulatory passage leading to the first occurrence of D material in the development. The forms of 6–34 in mm. 264 and 268 are equivalent at T_1 and share only one pc, the minimum possible under transposition. Example 113e is an excerpt from the transition from A to B in the exposition, in which adjacent forms of 6–32 are equivalent at T_6 and share no pcs. Minimum invariance here reinforces the strangeness of the tritone bass progression and heightens expectation before the exposition of the main theme.

Example 113d Fifth Sonata Op. 53

Example 113e Fifth Sonata Op. 53

Example 113f Fifth Sonata Op. 53

Example 113f shows the E2 material, a four-measure phrase which culminates with the c_4 motive. As shown, E2 is composed of four subphrases, each a form of 5–27. The successive transpositions here are T_7, T_3, and T_6. Maximum invariance occurs between the forms equivalent at T_7, whereas T_6 produces minimum invariance. The 5–27s in mm. 145–46 share no pcs, which helps to create a cadential effect at the moment the *imperioso* motive arrives.

We might wonder whether maximum and minimum invariance involving 5–27 and 6–32 are in fact atonal procedures, for these are diatonic subsets, and invariance was achieved here by tonal procedures. These examples illustrate the remarkable pitch-retention properties of the diatonic collection, which is just one among many sets with potential for pc invariance. Set 6–34 is entirely different (it is predominantly whole-tone) and, not surprisingly, is involved in significant invariance relations in the sonata. The whole-tone scale is especially evident in the exposition of the languid and dreamy A material. Example 113g shows the unfolding of the whole-tone aggregate in mm. 19–20 in association with the a_2 motive. The only non-whole-tone element here is C♯, which appears to be a passing tone within a voice exchange. This C♯ is actually an element of the underlying $\frac{4}{2}$ harmony, though on the surface it is almost swallowed up by

Example 113g Fifth Sonata Op. 53

Example 113h Fifth Sonata Op. 53

the whole-tone sonority. Example 113h shows the varied presentation of this material in mm. 29–33. Here the basic harmony is further obscured by nondiatonic sets, including the chromatic scale and augmented, diminished, and whole-tone chords, which saturate the texture. Of special interest are the whole-tone tetrachords (forms of 4–24) labeled a, b, and c. Together a and c form the full whole-tone aggregate, and b, the harmonization of a passing tone (in terms of whole-tone prolongation), shares no pcs with a or c.

THE FOURTH SONATA: NEW MATERIALS IN SEARCH OF A FORM

Scriabin composed his Fifth Sonata in a burst of inspiration during six days in December 1907. He considered this work a miraculous revelation, for he had just completed the *Poem of Ecstasy* and was seemingly at the point of physical exhaustion.[3] This sonata marks a major advance in Scriabin's creative evolution, and the full measure of its innovation is evident only in comparison with earlier compositions. The Fourth Sonata Op. 30—also in F♯ major—is itself a pivotal work in Scriabin's career and bears a special relation to the Fifth Sonata.

Example 114 outlines the form of the Fourth Sonata. Example 115 shows some of the most characteristic sets associated with A, B, and C materials in this piece; in particular, it demonstrates close ties between the A theme and the B and C themes. The opening eight-measure phrase is unified by strong set correspondences in mm. 2 and 8 (example 115a). Each measure comprises 5–28, the two forms equivalent at T_6, producing maximum invariance. Moreover, each 5–28 is formed by the same two vertical harmonies—4–25 and 4–27—and the forms of 4–25 are identical. Anoth characteristic sonority, 4–19, appears in m. 3 and recurs in m. 5 at T_5. The transition connecting the first and second movements (mm. 59–66) contains 4–19 at T_5, which occurs twice in mm. 61–62 in a type of voice exchange (example 115b). In mm. 61–63, the aggregate set is 5–Z37, formed by 4–19 and the succeeding 4–26; 5–Z37 was formed similarly at the end of m. 3. An even tauter connection exists between this transition and the beginning of the first movement, for both open with identical forms of 4–20.

Set 4–20 is also the main link between themes A and B. As shown in example 115c, the form of 4–20 which opens the first movement also underlies the initial phrase of theme B and is subsequently heard as the first verticality in m. 2 (second movement). Also derived from the A material, theme C opens with the same progression found in the latter half of m. 3 and m. 4 in the first movement, with voice-leading elements shifted only slightly (compare examples 115a and d). The forms of 4–19 and 7–3 in the two passages are identical.

In light of the Fifth Sonata, the Fourth seems to have been based on an incipient single-movement principle. Its exposition is straightforward, presenting A, B, C, and D materials in direct succession. The A material is languid and rambling, with a main idea (A1) and two subsidiary ideas, each involving sequential motion. The first section (mm. 1–66) is clearly an introduction to the main body of the work. Themes B and C, the primary themes of the main allegro, are both derived from A and are not strongly contrasted. The D material is a conventional closing derived from B.

The exposition of the Fifth Sonata is considerably more complex. There is nothing comparable to its introduction (mm. 1–12) in the Fourth. The A materials of the two sonatas coincide closely, however, not only in their languid mood but also in motivic substance: the G♯–D♯ motive of the Fifth Sonata is integral to the A theme of the Fourth (see m. 2, first movement). Moreover, passages in the A section of the Fifth contain many sets which appear in similar relations in the A section of the Fourth: compare mm. 7–8 of the first movement of the Fourth with mm. 19–20 and 34–37 of the Fifth (examples 115 and 116). Even closer are the two B themes; in fact, that of the Fifth is essentially a variation of the Fourth's. Both are themes which "take flight"—a characteristic type for Scriabin—beginning quietly and growing gradually louder and more confident, and both use the same sets at the same levels of transposition. (The passage in the Fifth Sonata beginning in m. 68 is especially comparable to theme B in the Fourth.) The B theme opens tentatively in the Fifth, over a dominant pedal; in comparison, the same idea in the Fourth is overly terse and summary. Both presentations involve transposition of the melodic material while a pedal tone is retained (compare mm. 1–4, second movement, in the Fourth and mm. 68–79 in the Fifth). Curiously, both touch on the harmony of A major (m. 18, second movement, in the Fourth and mm. 57 and 88—the latter at least implicitly—in the Fifth), an unusual function in the F♯ tonality. In both, A♮ is an upper auxiliary to G♯ in the bass.

Although the two sonatas are similar in the exposition of A and B materials, their forms later in the exposition diverge almost entirely. Nothing in the Fourth

Example 114 Fourth Sonata Op. 30: Form

		Measures	Derivation	T	Harmony	Comments
Exposition						
(First movement)						
1–66	A1a (1)	1–7			I (implicit)→V	
	(2)	7–8				
	b	9–17			→ III♯	mm. 9–13 = mm. 1–5, t = 0
	2a (1)	18–19	A1a(2)	9		
	(2)	20–21				
	b	22–25	A2a	2		A1a(2), t = 11
	c (1)	26–27	A2a(1)	11		A1a(2), t = 8
	(2)	28–29				
	d(1)	30–31	A2a(1)	10		A1a(2), t = 7
	(2)	32–34			V/V→ V	
	1c–d	35–50	A1a–b	0		but over I pedal
	3a	51–54			→ V/V	
	b	55–58	A3a	10	→ V/IV	
	c	59–66			IV→ V	
(Second movement)						
1–47	B1a (1)	1–2			I—	
	(2)	3–4	B1a(1)	5		but over I pedal
	b	5–8				compare A3a
	2a	9–12	B1a	0		
	b(1)	13–14				bridge; begins like B1b, t = 0
	(2)	15–16	B2b(1)	2		
	c	17–21			→V/V	progression equivalent to mm. 26–35, first movement, at T_5
	C1a	21–25			V—	compare mm. 3–4, first movement

	b	25–30			V→I	
	D1	30–47			I→V	closing material; derived from B1b and B2b–c
Development						
48–81	B3a	48–51			→A (V/♭VI?)	compare mm. 26–28, first movement
	b	52–55	B3a	5	→D (♭VI)	
	D2	56–66				chromatic ascent in bass
	A4a	66–69			D^6	
	b	70–73	A4a (melody)	5	D^7 (+6)	
	C2a (1)	74–75			V—	
	(2)	76–77	C2a(1)	2		
	b	78–81				
Recapitulation						
82–169	B5a	82–85	B1a	0	I	
	b	86–89			→V	
	6	90–101			→V	bridge
	C3	102–11	C1	5	I→ IV	
	D3	111–28	D1	5	IV→V→I	
episode {	C4	129–35			D (♭VI)→V/V	begins like C1, t = 1; C and D material alternated; use of D major alludes to development (mm. 66–69)
	B7	136–39	B1a	0	V—	but over V pedal
	D4	140–43				
	A 5–6c	144–57	A1c–3c (mm. 35–64)	0	I→V/V	
	6d	158–59			V—	
	A7a	160–61	A5 (mm. 144–45)	0	I—	codetta; I pedal
	b	162–69	D1 (mm. 46–47)	5		

Example 115a Fourth Sonata Op. 30, first movement

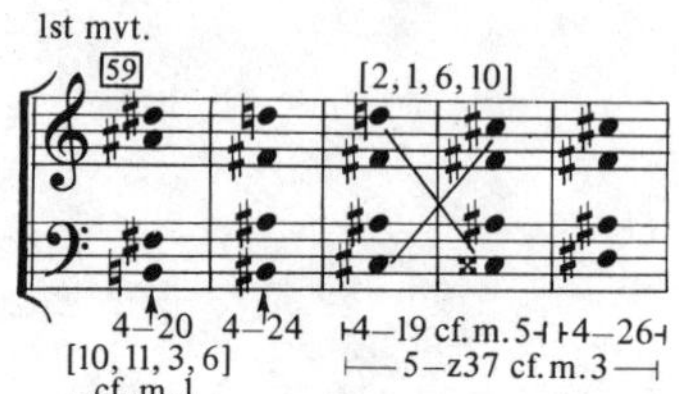

Example 115b Fourth Sonata Op. 30, first movement

Example 115c Fourth Sonata Op. 30, second movement

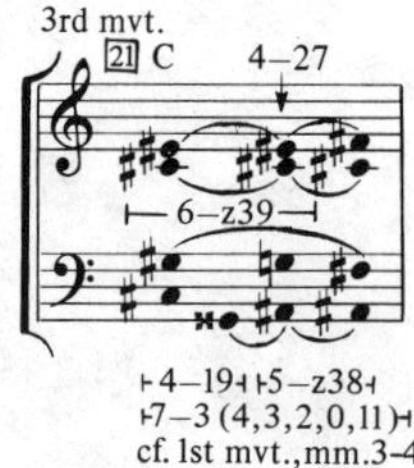

Example 115d Fourth Sonata Op. 30, second movement

Example 116 Fifth Sonata Op. 53

Sonata is comparable to section C of the Fifth, which leads to what in conventional terms would be the contrasting theme, theme D, in m. 120. The contrast is much greater between B and D in the Fifth than between the corresponding themes B and C in the Fourth. The mood of D is tender and caressing, the pacing languid, the harmonic underpinning (V/III♯) obscure. The squarely phrased, assertive theme C of the Fourth Sonata, set clearly in the dominant, is in comparison a model of straightforwardness and clarity. Both expositions close with material referring back to B, but in the Fifth this material also depends heavily on the C episode. Thus, in the interaction of B and C materials, the close of the Fifth Sonata is more complex and dramatic.

The development sections of the two sonatas are entirely different. The thirty-three-measure development of the Fourth is less than a sixth of the length of the entire piece, whereas the development of the Fifth is slightly longer than either the exposition or the recapitulation. The development of the Fourth begins by sequencing B material through the distant harmonic areas of A major and D major (alluding to the exposition in mm. 26–29, first movement). A passage based on D material involves a chromatic ascent in the bass with a gradual crescendo, culminating in the return of the A theme, now trumpeted fortissimo and repeated sequentially. At the arrival of the dominant in m. 74, the C theme, the last of the four to appear, is played in octaves in the bass while the development winds down with a diminuendo.

Everything about the development of the Fifth Sonata is more original than the Fourth. The startling reappearance of the introductory material in m. 157 produces an effect altogether different from the standard use of distant harmonies at the beginning of the development of the Fourth. The unusual return of such a large portion of A (at T_2) in the development of the Fifth Sonata creates confusion as to whether the exposition is being repeated or the development has begun. In m. 185, however, B and C materials interact (as they did at the close of the exposition) in a clearly developmental passage which culminates in the reappearance of a reharmonized and more assertive a_2. (The idea for this transformation was perhaps borrowed from the development of the Fourth Sonata.) This interaction is more complex than anything in the earlier sonata. When the passage is repeated at T_9 in mm. 207–25, tension increases, especially with the reappearance of the A material. An extension of this passage culminates with a deceptive cadence and the arrival of the next section in m. 227. The new passage (mm. 227–42) involves interaction of A and E materials (the latter derived from B) as well as sequential motion, but in a compact, eight-measure phrase and its repetition at T_5—a considerable condensation compared to the preceding sequence. More A material and the introduction are brought back in mm. 247–70.

The arrival of D material in m. 271 begins the last main section of the development, which concentrates on D and E materials. The E material is much expanded from its occurrence in the exposition and undergoes extensive transpositional repetition. The climax of the entire development is the apotheosis of theme D, beginning in m. 313, which contrasts sharply with the development of the Fourth Sonata. There the contrasting theme C also concludes the development, but its occurrence is almost cursory. The dominant, the goal of the large-scale progression of the development, has been reached by the beginning of C, and the tension in the latter part of this statement subsides. In the Fifth Sonata, the contrasting D material is expansive, moving with a continual crescendo toward the expected dominant (V/IV), which arrives climactically only at the end of the passage.

In the development of the Fourth Sonata, the transpositional and harmonic schemes are perfunctory, whereas those in the Fifth involve complex, large-scale directed motions. Both recapitulations begin with B material, continue with the materials from the exposition in their original sequence, and culminate with the apotheosis of the original A material. The Fourth Sonata closes abruptly with a transformed restatement of the final progression of the exposition. The harmonic frame for the recapitulation is conventional, almost Mozartean. The only real elaboration is in the episode in mm. 129–43, which uses B, C, and D materials and alludes harmonically to the development.

The strategy of the recapitulation of the Fifth Sonata is more sophisticated. The restatements of B, C, and D are actually simpler than those of B and C in the Fourth, for in the Fifth they are almost literal, note-for-note repetitions, all at T_5. The recapitulation of the E material begins as expected at T_5 but does not continue immediately to its conclusion as did the closing material in the Fourth Sonata. Rather, in mm. 403–32, an episode constructed first from E materials and then from B and C materials combined leads to the climactic statement of A beginning in m. 433. Only after this recapitulation of A does the restatement of E continue; it is never completed, however, for a link with the introductory material is made. The handling of the closing material here is much more effective than in the concluding section of the Fourth Sonata, where most of the closing material precedes the apotheosis of A.

While the harmonic plan of the Fifth Sonata deviates almost entirely from the norm, there are important correspondences in transpositional strategies, particularly in the recapitulation, where most materials occur at T_5, as does the contrasting theme in a conventional sonata movement. Only A is heard at another level, for the sake of continuity in large-scale voice leadings.

Clearly, the Fifth Sonata is a reworking of the Fourth—a recomposition of considerable depth and magnitude. It is no coincidence that the two sonatas—and only these two—are in the same key. The main (B) themes of both are structured on identical forms of 6–32 and its subsets 4–20, 4–22, and 5–27, and these themes are related through 4–20 to their respective A themes (examples 110, 112b, and 115c). Another noteworthy set in both works is 4–19. In the Fourth Sonata it is a characteristic chord (mm. 3–5, first movement, and the beginning of theme C, m. 21, second movement; see example 115), whereas it is most often a melodic motive in the Fifth. The most conspicuous 4–19 is in the *imperioso* motive (c_1), but it is also found within a_2 (example 110). Set 5–24, the characteristic sonority at the beginning of the A material of the Fifth Sonata (mm. 13–14), occurs in the identical form in the Fourth (m. 5 of the second movement; see example 117). In the earlier work the bass E♮ is part of a straightforward local unfolding from tonic to dominant (mm. 5–8). As we have seen, the bass E♮ prolonged through most of the A section of the Fifth Sonata also participates in the unfolding from the tonic, implicit at the beginning, to the dominant in m. 44. The expansion of the conventional gesture of the Fourth Sonata in the Fifth exemplifies the sophistication and complexity of the transformations of materials from the Fourth Sonata throughout the Fifth.

Although the surface sonorities of the Fourth and Fifth Sonatas are often identical, the underlying tonal foundations differ drastically. The tonal scheme of the earlier work is simple and clear and conforms surprisingly in nearly every respect (save the cyclic return of theme A) to the sonata forms of the late eighteenth century, especially those of Mozart. Though elegant, the austere tonal foundation is at odds with the lush, deliberately vague foreground harmonies. Thus despite its brilliant pianistic writing and wondrous themes, the Fourth Sonata is deeply flawed; because Scriabin returned to the materials of this piece and recomposed them in the Fifth Sonata, it seems that he himself came to feel dissatisfied with the Fourth Sonata.[4]

A central thesis of this book is that Scriabin conducted his first experiments with unusual sonorities within compositions firmly grounded in tonality. Only after mastering procedures of invariance and implicit tonality at the surface was he willing to apply them at deeper levels. There is no better example of this evolutionary process than the Fifth Sonata, which reflects a gigantic conceptual leap beyond the Fourth. Here the fundamental structure accords with the basic elements at the surface. Indeed, the bass unfolding from tonic to minor seventh (E♮) which implicitly spans the piece is a magnificent expansion of the $\frac{4}{2}$ harmony

Example 117 Fifth Sonata Op. 53; Fourth Sonata Op. 30

with which the exposition begins. The extensive use of T_5 in the recapitulation of the sonata seems to be an obvious concession to traditional form, where themes heard first in the dominant are restated in the tonic. Here, however, T_5 has more to do with the invariance potential of the main sets, many of which only coincidentally are diatonic collections. In any case, transposition with $t = 5$ accomplishes no such direct return to the tonic in the recapitulation of the Fifth Sonata; instead, it continues a motion, initiated at the beginning of the piece, which links exposition, development, and recapitulation in a structure of singular breadth and unity.

THE TENTH SONATA: SONATA FORM AS A FRAMEWORK FOR ATONALITY

The Fifth Sonata is the last of Scriabin's extended compositions with a fundamentally tonal structure. To understand fully this landmark in Scriabin's evolution, we must compare it with his later, atonal extended forms. The Tenth Sonata is the basis for the comparative study which follows. (For an outline of this work, see example 118.)

Example 119 condenses the conclusion of the first main section of the exposition of the Tenth Sonata (mm. 29–38). This passage contains all of the basic motives of the composition. Motives x, y, z_1, and z_2 (together with the left-hand part on the lower staff) are all of the essential A material. The sketch beneath mm. 29–32 shows that this material unfolds the mystic chord, 6–34. The only non-whole-tone element of durational significance is the conspicuous bass E♭, sustained for several measures. Together motives z_1 and z_2 echo this same 6–34 in a high register. Motive w_1 is derived from the interaction of the y and z_1 motives; w_1 and w_2 form 6–34 at T_6 from the original, yielding four invariants, [0,2,6,8], the maximum possible. Motive w_2 contrasts with the other motives in its intervallic content, for it contains 4–20 and 5–27, the only sets in the example (except 3–10) which are not predominantly whole-tone.

Other important sets in the A material are 3–12 (m. 29) and 3–10 (m. 30). These chords, the augmented and diminished triads, are symmetrical and thus devoid of strong tonal implications; in succession they create a striking and eloquent opening. The sum of the x, y, and z motives, with their accompaniment, is 7–28, whose complement, 5–28, is the sum of z_1 and sustained parts. The same form of 5–28 also occurs in w_1. Finally, sets familiar from the earlier sonatas appear: 4–19 with motive x, 4–20 and 5–27 with w_2.

Nearly all thematic materials in the Tenth Sonata are related to the motives discussed above. However, the relations among several important motives—including x and w_2—are best explained in terms of being contained in a common superset, 6–20, the structural underpinning of theme D, which in conventional terms would be the main theme of the composition (example 120a). Announced by the w_2 motive, this theme begins in m. 39 with 4–20 (identical to the form in w_2), formed by the main melodic element, E♮, and its accompaniment. Similarly, 4–19 occurs in the following measure. These sets sum to 6–20, which is also

Example 118 Tenth Sonata Op. 70: Form

Measures			Derivation	T	T of x	Comments
Exposition (mm. 1–115)						
1–8	A1	1–4			0	motives x, y, and z_1
	2	5–8	A1	0	0	motive z_2 added; low bass; added alto
9–28	B1a	9–10				pedal point throughout B
	b	11–12				motive y
	2	13–16	B1 (upper)	6		
			B1 (lower)	0		pedal
	3a	17–18	B1b	0		
	b	19–20	B3a	0		
	c (1)	21–22				motive y, t = 10
	(2)	23–24	B3c(1)	0		
	(3)	25–28				y, t = 10 (m. 25); t = 7 (m. 26); t = 5 (m. 27)
29–32	A3	29–32	A1	0	0	but with z_1 and z_2
32–38	w_1	32–34				
		34–36	w_1	0		octave lower
	w_2	37–38				
39–58	C1a	39–40			2	same 4–20 as w_2, t = 0; motive x implied
	b	41–42	C1a	0		
	c	43–44	C1a	8	6	motive x implied (compare m. 164)
	2a	45–46	C1a	0		
	b	47–48	C2a	0		
	c	49–50				extension
	3a (1)	51–52	C1a	0		
	(2)	53–54	w_2	11		
	b	55–58	C3a	11		w_2, t = 10 in mm. 57–58
59–70	D1a	59–60				motives y (t = 7) and w_2 (t = 10)
	b	61–62	D1a	6		
	2a	63–66	D1	0		but invertible counterpoint; m. 66 differs
	b	67–68	D2a (mm. 65–66)	0		
	c	69–70	D2a (m. 65)	0		w_2, t = 4
71–83	E1a	71–73				w_2 (T_4) + w_2 (T_8) = 6–20 (T_1)
	b	73–75	w_1, w_2	4		
	c	75–76				motives z_1 and z_2, t = 7
	2a	76–77	E1a	3		
	b	77–78	E1b	3		
	c	79–80	E1c (parts)	0		
			E1c (parts)	3		
	3a	80–81	E1a	3		
	b	81–83	E1b	3		
84–115	F1a	84–87	E1c	3		
	b	88–89				
	2a	90–91	F1a (mm. 86–87)	0	1	
	b	92–93	F1b	0		

Example 118 (cont.)

	Measures	Derivation	T	T of x	Comments
c	94	F2a (l.h.)	0		
d	95	F2c (m. 94)	3		
e	96–97	F1b	6		
3	98–100	F1a (mm. 86–87)	6	7	
E4	100–02	E1b	3		
F4a	103–06	F1a	0		
b	107–08	F1b	0		
5a	109–10	F2a	0	1	but invertible counterpoint
b(1)	111–12				begins like F2b, t = 0
(2)	113–14	F5b(1)	0		
(3)	115	F5b(2) (m. 114)	0		
Development (mm. 116–223)					
A4	116–19	A2	10	10	x, y, z_1, z_2
5	120–23	A2	10	10	octave lower; x, y
B4	124–27	B1	10		without y
D3	128–31				y, w_2
A6–D4	132–47	A4–D3	4	2	A6 has x and y only; in D4 counterpoint from D3 (mm. 130–31) is inverted
D5	148–51	D1	11		but with invertible counterpoint
6	152–53				extension; w_2, t = 0
A8	154–57	A2 (mm. 7–8)	0		same 6–34; y, z_1, z_2
C4–6	158–77	C1–3	3	9	m. 159
				5	m. 161
				1	m. 163
				9	m. 164
				9	m. 166
				5	m. 172
				4	m. 176
C7a	178–79	C6 (mm. 174–75)	11	3	
b	180–81	C7a	11		or C1a, t = 0
c	182–83	C7b	0		
A9	184–87	A2	2	2	x, y; or A6, t = 0 } reversal
10	188–91	A2	10	10	x, y; or A5, t = 0 } reversal
B5–6	192–99	B1–2	0		but with added y motive in tenor and different registers; w_2
7	200–03	B5	0		
8	204–07	B7	4		
9	208–12	B7	7		but with extended link to . . .
E5–6	212–19	E1–2	11		
7	220–21	E6c	4		or mm. 214–15, t = 7; w_2, t = 0
w_2	222–23	w_2	0		

Example 118 (cont.)

	Measures	Derivation	T	T of x	Comments
Recapitulation (mm. 224–306)					
C8–9	224–35	C1–2	0		
w_2	236–37	w_2	8		
C10	238–45	C3	8		
D7–8	246–58	D1–2	8		w_2 (m. 248), $t = 0$
E8–10	258–70	E1–3	8		w_1, $t = 0$
F6–8	271–86	F1–3	8		
E11	287–89	E4	8		
F9	290–93	F4 (mm. 103–05)	8		
B10–12	294–306	B7–9	9		but with added alto line (y), different trills
Coda (mm. 306–66)					
E12	306–09	E1b–c	8		w_1 (m. 307), $t = 0$
13	310–13	E2b–c	8		
14	314–15	E3	8		
F10–12	316–31	F1–3	8	9	m. 322
				3	m. 330
E15	332–33	E4	8		
F13–14	334–47	F4–5	8	9	m. 340
B13	348–51				codetta; chromatic descent through octave F♮–F♮; y
14	352–59	B3c	9		
A11	360–66	A1	9	9	but includes motives z_1 and z_2 (compare A3)

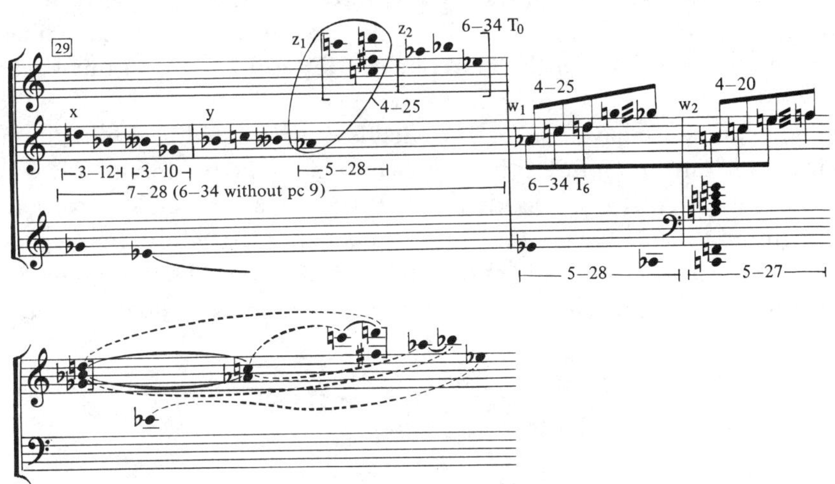

Example 119 Tenth Sonata Op. 70: Basic Motives

Example 120a Tenth Sonata Op. 70: 6–20 as a Nexus Set

Example 120b Tenth Sonata Op. 70: 6–20 as a Nexus Set

formed in the melody as the material is transposed down four half steps in mm. 43–44. Set 6–20 is symmetrical; we might think of it as composed of two augmented triads equivalent at T_1. (Note the relation to the augmented triad in the opening measure of the sonata.) This set thus has special properties of invariance. In fact, T_8 in mm. 43–44 yields complete invariance for 6–20—the only level of transposition (except its inverse, T_4) to do so. This transposition may foreshadow more extensive transpositions at T_8 later in the sonata. Example 120b shows the important motives contained in 6–20. In addition to 4–19 and 4–20, the significant three-note phrase from the E material is a subset, as well as F material based on that phrase.

The E theme (*avec une joyeuse exaltation*) is derived entirely from w_1 and w_2, as shown in example 121. (For purposes of comparison, the E theme is shown at its level of transposition in m. 260.) Although the contour of w_1 is maintained in this theme, the derivation of the final pitches—F♮ and A♮—from the w_2 chord is less obvious.

The only theme we have not yet discussed is B, first stated beginning in m. 9. The chromatic saturation in B is in strong contrast to the predominantly whole-tone sonorities of A. It is no accident that B is set against motive y in counterpoint beginning in m. 11, for the chromatic ascent effected by the serpentine movement of B responds to the chromatic descent of y. (The motion of B was foreshadowed by the alto line added in mm. 5–8 of A.) As shown in example

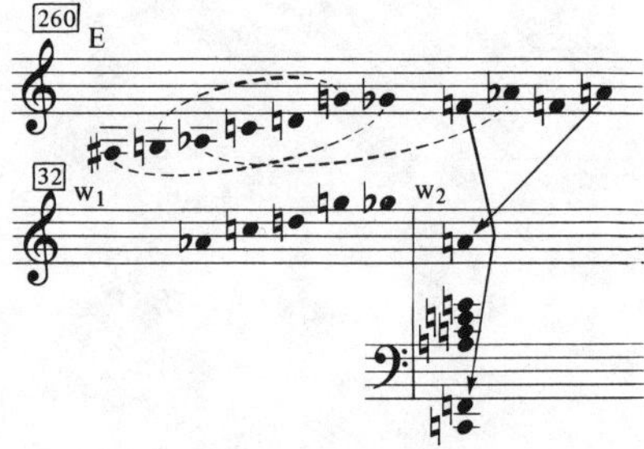

Example 121 Tenth Sonata Op. 70: Derivation of Theme E

Example 122 Tenth Sonata Op. 70: Underlying Structure of Theme B

122, however, sets which underlie the intense chromaticism relate B strongly to other motives. In mm. 9–12 the melody ascends from E♭ to G♮ while the tenor part descends from G♮ to E♭, thus participating in a voice exchange. These two pcs, with the sustained pitches E♭, A♭, and C♮, form 4–20 and, with the passing tone F♮, 5–27. Sets 4–20 and 5–27 relate the B material to motive w_2. In mm. 13–16 the melodic motion of mm. 9–12 is transposed down six half steps while the A♭–E♭ interval is retained as a pedal, resulting in a melodic third-span from B♭♭ to D♭. These pcs, with E♭ and G♮ from mm. 9–12, form 4–25, the whole-tone subset associated also with motives z_1 and w_1. If the passing tones F♮ and C♭ are also taken into account, the B theme forms a complete whole-tone scale.

The connections among these materials are numerous and extremely taut. No idea is isolated from the rest, and most are related to one of the predominant hexachords, 6–20 and 6–34. In comparison to the Fifth Sonata, the ideas here are more succinct and less susceptible to the climactic buildup so frequent in Scriabin's tonal works. In short, these ideas do not behave like typical tonal themes. Further, the Tenth Sonata creates a different sense of time because of its more concentrated motivic development.

The Tenth Sonata retains the tripartite form of the Fourth and Fifth sonatas, modified in that part of the recapitulation is repeated (though drastically varied) as a coda. As in the Fifth Sonata, the three main sections are almost equally weighted. In contrast to the straightforward succession of materials in the exposition of the Fifth Sonata, however, the exposition of the Tenth involves several thematic recurrences. The restatement of A (at T_0) in mm. 29–32 defines an introductory section preceding the exposition of the main theme, C. This introduction resembles those of the Fourth and Fifth sonatas in its languid yet expectant mood but differs in that it encompasses two themes: the pristine, epigrammatic A material frames the yearning, passionate B material.

Motives w_1 and w_2 (mm. 32–38) herald the arrival of the allegro and its primary C theme in m. 39. This theme is related motivically both to themes A and B and to motive w_2, which is alternated with phrases of C in mm. 51–58 in a chromatically descending sequence leading to D. The D material serves the same purpose in the Tenth Sonata as did C in the Fifth: it connects the main theme to a sensuous contrasting idea, in this case theme E. Whereas the connecting episode in the Fifth Sonata introduced new motives, episode D is entirely derivative, a complex dovetailing of motives y and w_2 in two parts. The identity of D is based in this motivic interaction. After the initial two-measure phrase has been transposed with t = 6, the resulting four-measure phrase is repeated, but with parts switched in invertible counterpoint. The passage eventually comes to rest with w_2 (at T_4) beginning in m. 69.

In mm. 71–72 forms of w_2 (at T_4 and T_8) sum to 6–20, the basic set of the C theme, and lead to the first statement of theme E. (Because it is intertwined with E material, this 6–20 is labeled Ela in the outline.) Theme E corresponds to the traditional contrasting theme, although it is derived from motives w_1 and w_2 (hence w_2 is appropriate in the transition from D to E). Motives z_1 and z_2 appear for the first time since A at the end of the E phrase. They occur here at T_7, which links perfectly with the next phrase, a transposed repetition of all E material, with t = 3. (Because the original E phrase began with w_2 at T_4, the transposed phrase begins with w_2 at T_7.) A portion of the E material is repeated again at T_3 in mm. 80–83.

In the exposition of the Fifth Sonata, the connection of the contrasting theme (D) with the closing material involved an abrupt change of mood: theme D faded out unresolved, and after a pause the e motive belligerently asserted itself. The corresponding link in the Tenth Sonata is entirely different. The E material trails off incomplete in m. 83, but the closing section, F, begins after a brief pause with a varied presentation of the material from mm. 75–76 at T_3, precisely what is required to complete the last phrase of E. Further, this phrase is spun forth sequentially to create a four-measure phrase (mm. 84–87). In this unique formal overlapping, the most significant change is the austere chordal texture of the F1 material. As section F continues, F1 is alternated with a brief enigmatic passage (*avec ravissement et tendresse* [rapturous, tender]) in mm. 88–89 which recalls the gestures of the D episode and, in the left-hand figuration, perhaps section B. In addition, 6–34, the basic set of the A material, underlies the passage. When part of the F1 phrase is repeated beginning in m. 90, motive x occurs in the counterpoint. As in sections B and D, the F materials are transposed to T_6 in mm. 96–100. As if to underscore the relation between themes E and F, the final phrase of the E section is repeated in mm. 100–02, followed by a literal repetition of F1. The F2 material is then repeated at T_0, but with voices switched in invertible counterpoint. In mm. 113–15 the preceding two measures are repeated (at T_0), but in an enigmatic rhythmic variation which foreshadows the coda.

As closing material for the exposition, F differs in effect from the closing (E) material of the Fifth Sonata. There, the closing referred clearly to the main theme (B) and to the *imperioso* motive of section C. It was a fiery gesture, propelled forward until the introductory material arrived in a burst of energy, signalling the beginning of the development. In the Tenth Sonata, the closing material continues the music immediately preceding. Relations to earlier materials exist, but are too subtle to be considered motivic allusions. The gestures are quiet and refined, and the section seems more a transition than a summary. In view of the use of A material to frame a subsection of the exposition, it is not clear when A returns following section F whether it begins the development or closes the exposition. Only when the passage beginning with A in m. 116 is repeated at T_4 in mm. 132–47 is it evident that the material belongs to the development. Thus the occurrence of A in mm. 116–23 is an elegant overlap arising from structural ambiguity. This overlap exemplifies a refined and subtle continuity in Scriabin's atonal music, which depends more on motivic relations for structural coherence than did his tonal compositions.

The developments of the Fifth and Tenth sonatas begin in similar ways. Material from the opening returns at an unexpected level of transposition, T_2 in the Fifth and T_{10} in the Tenth. In the Fifth, Scriabin moves directly to the main thematic material (B), which becomes the subject of an extended passage, subsequently repeated at T_9. In the Tenth the comparable sequential passage begins the development. Here he skirts the main material (C), using A, B, and D instead. The resemblance of the D3 passage (mm. 128–31) to the original D material is slight, although motives y and w_2 are present in both. The relation to D becomes clearer, however, when the entire passage in mm. 116–31 is repeated in mm. 132–47: in the repetition the parts are inverted, and invertible counterpoint is the most conspicuous attribute of the D material. The following passage (mm. 148–53) is closer to the original D material and leads to the climax of this section of the development—the only transformation of the A material in the sonata, beginning in m. 154. In this apotheosis, motives y, z_1, and z_2 occur at the original level of transposition for the underlying set, 6–34; motive x is not included. (In the sequential repetition of A material beginning in m. 132, Scriabin excluded motives z_1 and z_2, reserving them for this moment.) This resounding presentation of A materials is charged by rapid repetitions of the accompanying chord, and the impact is reinforced by an immediate repetition of the passage.

The main theme now makes its first appearance in the development, in a slightly varied transposed repetition of all of the C material from the exposition (with $t = 3$). In this variation, motive x is woven into C (as in mm. 159 and 161), and contrasting passages based on x and w_2 occur as well (mm. 172–73 and 175–76). The x motive is repeated at successive transpositions with $t = 4$, corresponding to the underlying structure of both x and 6–20, the basic set of the C material. Beginning with its statement in mm. 172–73 at T_5, each restatement of motive x occurs a half step lower. This process continues through an extension of C in mm. 178–83 until m. 184, when x is heard at T_2 with a repetition of A material at the same transpositional level. As is often the case with A, the basic four-measure phrase is repeated. Here, however, it is not restated at T_2 but rather at T_{10}. This progression within A mirrors the transpositional levels of A at the beginning of the development: T_{10} followed by T_2. Thus the A material in mm. 184–89 defines a major section of the structure.[5]

The process beginning in m. 170 dissolves the tensions momentarily and fades to the quietest moment of the piece (m. 191). This calm is short-lived. The B material, heard briefly in the sequential passage at the beginning of the development, now takes over. It is stated at T_0 and T_6 (as in B1 and B2), and the counterpoint is thickened with additional y and w_2 motives. However, with a continuing crescendo, B is restated in octaves in the melody, first at T_0, then at T_4 and T_7, building to a climactic return of the E material. As in the Fifth Sonata, the development here culminates with the apotheosis of the contrasting theme. The E theme is now brilliantly transformed (*puissant, radieux* [powerful, radiant]), accompanied by w_2 trill motives which have become electrifying tremolos. Virtually all of the E material from the exposition is repeated at T_{11}, followed by an extension leading to the climactic chord in m. 221. This chord forms 7–30, which, though not a frequent set in its own right, contains some of the most important sets in the piece, including 5–21 and 6–34. Most important, it contains the basic set of motive w_2—5–27—at the original level of transposition, and this relation is explicit when w_2 is restated in m. 222 at T_0, precisely as in the exposition, to signal the arrival of the recapitulation.

The recapitulations of the Fifth and Tenth sonatas are similar in several important respects. Both begin with main thematic material, although in the Tenth, unlike the Fifth, most of the C material recurs at T_0 as in traditional sonata forms. After w_2 is restated at T_8 in mm. 236–37, however, the remaining C material also occurs at T_8, and D, E, and F follow at T_8 as well. This process is comparable to that of the recapitulation of the Fifth Sonata, where themes B, C, D, and E are stated in original sequence at T_5. As in the Fifth Sonata, the recapitulation of the closing material in the Tenth is cut short at m. 293, so that only part of the original F4 material and none of F5 occur. In mm. 294–306 Scriabin unexpectedly recalls and varies a passage from the development (mm. 200–12) as a transition to the remarkable coda.

The bulk of the coda is a variation of the recapitulation of E and F, again at T_8, although the faster tempo and drastic rhythmic alterations make the relation barely perceptible. This coda departs completely from the procedures of the Fifth Sonata. There the closing material was cut short and a new episode built to the apotheosis of theme A. Here there is no transformation of A. (The only real transformation of a portion of A occurred in mid-development in mm. 154–57.) The transformation in the coda is a further metamorphosis of E (along with F), whose apotheosis was reached at the climax of the development. This transformation is not a traditional climax; rather, it is a type of culmination peculiar to Scriabin's late works. The motives are brought to life, and, quivering with energy (*frémissant, ailé*), they dart skittishly about until their brief cycles are complete. In a sense, this transformation is the fallout of the energy of the apotheosis. It is no coincidence that the same material is involved in both transformations.

In mm. 334–47, the final portions of the closing material (mm. 103–15), previously skirted, are repeated at T_8. (Compare this to mm. 441–50 in the Fifth Sonata, where the recapitulation of the later portions of E, postponed from m. 403, takes place.) There follows a descending passage based on B3 material, leading to the recapitulation of B3 at T_9—the only recurrence of this material in the piece. (Similarly, in the Fifth Sonata E2 and E3 recur in full only at the close.) The last chord of this passage fades to the final phrase of the sonata, a hushed restatement of A (also at T_9), with z_1 in an extremely high register and the final quasi-cadential descending fourth played slowly in octaves in the low bass.

Despite the many similarities in the disposition of subject matter in the Fifth and Tenth sonatas, their transpositional schemes are almost entirely different. Most notably, T_5, the most fundamental tonal progression and the single most important level of transposition in the Fifth Sonata, is not used in the Tenth. Conversely, the most frequent levels of transposition in the Tenth Sonata—T_8 and T_4—are uncommon and of limited significance in the Fifth. However, the use of T_6 with B, D, and F in the Tenth Sonata is similar to its usage in the Fifth in the passages beginning in mm. 42, 96, and 195. In both sonatas T_6 is associated with the exploitation of minimum or maximum invariance, although in neither piece is this level used frequently. Levels T_3 and T_9, used primarily in the development of the Fifth Sonata, occur more widely in the Tenth—with E and F in the exposition, in the development beginning in m. 158, and, on the largest scale, in the recapitulation of B and A.

In the Tenth Sonata transpositions at T_{11} are significant, tying in with the chromatically descending motions of both motive y and the C material. In particular, beginning in m. 53 a transposition of the C material with $t = 11$ effects a transition to D. In mm. 172–77, a section of the development where C material interacts with motive x, a chromatic descent occurs, most clearly connected to the x motive. This descent continues in an extension of the passage (mm. 178–79) leading to the original level of the C material in m. 180. The transformed presentation of E which culminates the development also begins at T_{11}. In the Tenth Sonata, though chromatic descent is important on several levels, transposition at T_1 seldom occurs, with the significant exception of the surface motion of theme B. The opposite is the case in the Fifth Sonata, where T_{11} is rare but T_1 is of great importance, especially on the large scale. Beginning in m. 265 of the development, a modulatory shift places D and E materials a half step higher than in the exposition. This transposition occurs with an ascent from A♯ to B♮ in the bass of the deep middleground. The climactic phrase of D material which concludes the development is also at T_1, linking with the D material in mm. 271–80.

In the Fifth Sonata, transposition with $t = 10$ or 2 is frequent, generally associated with a patterned voice leading. Even when the introduction and A material are repeated at T_2 at the beginning of the development, this progression is part of a broad middleground gesture. Levels T_2 and T_{10} are less frequent in the Tenth Sonata and occur chiefly in the development section. The development begins with A and B materials at T_{10} in mm. 116–28, restated sequentially at T_2 in mm. 132–44. Although here a prolongational purpose for the levels of transposition is not clear, their occurrence is analogous to the formal strategy at the beginning of the development of the Fifth Sonata. Here, at least, we have the same sense of a shift of tonal planes. Yet the use of T_2 and T_{10} is different, entailing a symmetry about the material at its original level of transposition. This symmetry is most striking in mm. 184–91 when the A material occurs at T_2 and then at T_{10} (the reverse ordering), followed by B material at T_0. Most significantly, the materials juxtaposed at T_{10} and T_2 are separated at T_4, the fundamental level of transposition for this sonata.

We come then to the question of overriding importance: what are the reasons for the transpositional levels in the recapitulation of the Tenth Sonata? The use of T_8 throughout the large portion of the recapitulation dealing with C, D, E, and F is surely related to the fact that the fundamental set, 6–20, is completely invariant only at that level (and at its inverse, T_4). The shift from T_0 to T_8 in the C material in mm. 236–38 is an expansion of the progression from T_0 to T_8 within the C material itself, through which the underlying arpeggiation of 6–20 is completed (mm. 39–44). Thus, because most materials in the sonata are related directly or indirectly to the basic 6–20, the use of T_8 creates a general situation of maximum invariance between exposition and recapitulation. It is also important that when certain materials are transposed to T_8 in the recapitulation, their motives are shifted to original transpositional levels. In particular, w_2 occurs at T_0 in mm. 248–59, at the end of the D material. This links directly with E (at T_8), where the melody is structured on w_1 at T_0.

But if T_8 is the general transpositional level in the recapitulation, why are A and B restated at T_9? This is similar to the recapitulation at T_4 of A in the Fifth Sonata, where the general level was T_5. There, tonal voice leading necessitated a different level of transposition. In the Tenth Sonata, the recapitulation of A and B at T_9 does not exploit properties of maximum or minimum invariance, unlike the rest of the recapitulation. A voice-leading basis is not immediately apparent; yet if one examines the connection between A material at T_0 at the opening and at T_9 at the close, one discovers a relation which occurs frequently at the surface of the sonata. Example 123 shows several instances in which the dyads A♭–E♭ and F♮–C♮ are juxtaposed horizontally or vertically. The most important such pairing accompanies w_1 and w_2 in mm. 34–38 (example 123a). Example 123b shows a retrograde of this progression at the arrival of the transformed A material at the climax of the first portion of the development. The relation is particularly obvious in mm. 352–59 (example 123c), where the dyads are alternated several times at the approach of the codetta. A similar progression occurs in the recapitulation of F material beginning in m. 271 (example

Example 123a Tenth Sonata Op. 70

Example 123b Tenth Sonata Op. 70

Example 123c Tenth Sonata Op. 70

Example 123d Tenth Sonata Op. 70

123d). Example 123e shows that the dyads together form an important harmony in the B material. The use of T_9 in the recapitulation of A and B is thus based in voice leading after all. The A sections framing the sonata are a composing-out of the progression from A♭–E♭ to F♮–C♮, a progression which unifies the composition by mirroring on the largest level an important motivic relation at the surface. This large-scale correspondence is clearly meant to create in an atonal composition an organic unity among levels of structure like that of the

Example 123e Tenth Sonata Op. 70

Fifth Sonata, which was accomplished by unconventional but essentially tonal means.

Finally, many characteristic sets of the tonal sonatas are also important in the Tenth, despite its clear abandonment of tonality. These sets include 4–19, 4–20, 5–27, and 6–34. On the other hand, such diatonic sets as 7–35, 6–32, and 5–34 are predictably absent in the Tenth, along with the levels of transposition T_5 and T_7, used to exploit their invariance properties. The most conspicuous addition to Scriabin's vocabulary in the Tenth Sonata is 6–20—a set which appears almost nowhere in the other pieces examined in this book, with the exception of the Prelude Op. 74/4. Sets 6–20 and 6–34 are highly contrasted; they are in R_0 and not in R_p, and are related primarily through 4–19 and its subset, the augmented triad. In 6–20 Scriabin has found a basis for a new degree of unity, for this set contains both 4–19 and 4–20 (associated in the Tenth Sonata with x and w_2 respectively), whereas 6–34 does not. Set 6–20 is one of seven hexachords which include both tetrachords, but it is the only one with such a potential for invariance, a crucial property for Scriabin. The Tenth Sonata, with its basis on a new hexachord, exemplifies Scriabin's evolution: he worked within older forms but sought a new, more refined and precise structural balance. At the same time he created new sonorities, modifying his treatment of form to exploit fully their special properties. The result was a unique union of traditional form and innovative content.

NINE
TONALITY AND ATONALITY IN THE EXTENDED FORMS II
The Orchestral Works

This chapter is devoted to Scriabin's two most imposing compositions, the most central works in his transition to atonality—the *Poem of Ecstasy* Op. 54 and *Prometheus: The Poem of Fire* Op. 60. Both are single movements for huge orchestra, each almost half an hour long. Scriabin expands sonata form to its utmost limits in these works; they culminate his strivings for timbral and textural variety and for rich thematic content which is nevertheless tautly controlled through processes of derivation. In the *Poem of Ecstasy* every aspect of Scriabin's craft is touched by the spirit of innovation. By the time of *Prometheus*, Scriabin's method has evolved to such an extent that harmony, melody, and form are almost entirely original and personal.

The *Poem of Ecstasy* occupied more of Scriabin's time than any other composition, and it is the only completed work which originated as both a literary and a musical project. As early as 1904, Scriabin was making notes for a literary work entitled "Poème orgiasque," which was completed and privately published in Russian as "The Poem of Ecstasy" in May 1906. By early 1905 Scriabin was also at work on a fourth symphony which would illustrate musically the mystic doctrines of the poem. Although there is certainly a programmatic connection between the literary and musical poems, Scriabin did not regard one as essential for comprehending the other. He decided not to include the poem in the orchestral score of the *Poem of Ecstasy*, saying: "In general, I would prefer for [conductors] to approach it first as pure music."[1] By the end of December 1906 the composition was fully sketched in draft. In the following months Scriabin refined the score but did not finish copying parts until December 1907.

It is clear that Scriabin regarded the *Poem of Ecstasy* as revolutionary, not simply in musical substance, but especially in its embodiment of a new social, political, and spiritual ethos.[2] In attempting to convey his grandiose aspirations, Scriabin confronted significant problems in composing the *Poem of Ecstasy*; he wrote: "A colossal structure such as the one I now erect needs total harmony within all its parts on a solid foundation."[3] The composer's concern for structural coherence is certainly evident in the piece.

Shortly after completing the *Poem of Ecstasy* and its companion piece, the Fifth Sonata, Scriabin began to draft the text of a gigantic work to be called the *Mysterium.* All forms of artistic expression would be fused in this piece, creating music which Scriabin believed would elevate and unite the human race. In 1908 his publisher, Koussevitzky, bought the rights to this work, which was expected to take five years to complete. When Scriabin began composing the *Poem of Fire,* he fully believed he was beginning work on the *Mysterium.* He later limited his task to a project more immediately within grasp, an orchestral poem based on the myth of Prometheus. He first mentioned the piece by name in November 1909. Remarkably, the work progressed much more smoothly than the *Poem of Ecstasy* and was first performed on 2 March 1911.

Prometheus is an apt subject for a work concentrating on the synesthetic fusion of color and music. Prometheus was the Titan who, in defiance of the gods, presented man with the divine gift of fire. For Scriabin, fire symbolized not only light and color which dazzle the senses, but even more the inner spark of creativity. Just as Prometheus elevated man's knowledge with the gift of fire, Scriabin set out in the *Poem of Fire* to bring his listeners to new heights of spiritual awareness. In forging an entirely personal compositional method, Scriabin may well have identified with his hero as archrebel. *Prometheus* has traditionally been regarded as the work in which Scriabin broke the bonds of tonality once and for all. If this is true, the *Poem of Fire* is one of the first atonal works by any composer, an especially remarkable feat because of the huge dimensions of the work (compared with the relatively short early atonal works by the Viennese composers and others).

THE *POEM OF ECSTASY*

Motivic Materials

The essential motivic content of the *Poem of Ecstasy* is shown in example 124. The diversity and expansiveness of this work contrast it with its companion piece, the Fifth Sonata. Many of the nineteen motives listed in the example are related, but all are used differently in the composition. In comparison, the Fifth Sonata is limited to twelve such motives (example 110). In both works there are five essential thematic groupings with which the motives are associated. (For a formal outline of the *Poem of Ecstasy* see example 125.)

The initial section of the piece (mm. 1–38) is typical of Scriabin, harmonically vague and filled with luxuriant, yearning chromaticism. The piece opens with a_1, a motive used throughout the piece in counterpoint with motives from other thematic groups. This motive is a form of 4–19, one of Scriabin's favorite sets, which appeared in two of the most important motives of the Fifth Sonata, a_2 and c_1. Here a_1 is transposed several times in a sequence which culminates in the imperious motive a_2 in the trumpet in mm. 13–19. (Motive a_2 is associated consistently with the trumpet throughout the piece.) In the second half of the introduction, the main motive is a_3, played expressively by the clarinet (m. 19) and

Example 124 *Poem of Ecstasy* Op. 54: Basic Motives

Example 125 *Poem of Ectasy* Op. 54: Form

Measures			Derivation	T	Motives	Comments
Exposition (mm. 1–180)						
1–38	A1a(1)	1–6			a_1	flute
	(2)	6–10				violin
	(3)	11–13				piccolo
	b	13–19			a_2	trumpet
	2a	19–27			a_3 (mm. 19–23)	clarinet I
					a_1 (mm. 22–27)	clarinet II
					a_4 (mm. 22–27)	oboe
					a_5 (mm. 23–27)	flute
	b	27–38	A2a	5		but extended
					a_3 (mm. 27–30)	flute
					a_1 (mm. 30–38)	clarinet I
					a_4 (mm. 30–38)	oboe
					a_5 (mm. 31–38)	flute
39–70	B1a(1)(a)	39–40			b_1, a_3	
	(b)	41–42			b_2, a_1	
	(2)(a)	43–44				compare B1a(1)(a)
	(b)	45–46				compare B1a(1)(b)
	b	47–54	B1a	2		
	2a(1)(a)	55			b_1, a_1	
	(b)	56			b_2, a_1	
	(c)	57–58			b_3	
	(2)	59–62	B2a(1)	0		but m. 62 differs from m. 58
	(3)	63–66	B2a(1)	11		
	b	67–70	B2a(1)	10		extension
71–95	C1a(1)	71–75			c_1, c_2	
	(2)	75–78				begins like C1a(1), T_{11}
	b(1)	79–83	C1a(1)	4	c_1, c_3	
	(2)(a)	83–85	C1a(1)	0	c_1, c_3	extension
	(b)	85–87			c_1, c_3	extension, continued
	c	87–95	C1	5	c_{1a}, c_{1b}, c_3	m. 87
			C1	10		m. 91, c_3 comes to fore; c_{1a} and c_{1b} in counterpoint
95–110	D1	95–102			d_1, a_2 (T_7)	
	2a	102–06			d_{1-4}	
	b	106–10	D2a	5		melody only
110–80	E1a(1)	110–13			e_1, a_1	
	(2)	114–17				
	b	118–26	E1a	0		parts inverted
	2a	127–36			e_2, e_3	e_3 canonic treatment
	b	137–40			e_3	
	1c	140–47	E1b	2		

Example 125 (cont.)

Measures			Derivation	T	Motives	Comments
	1d(1)	148–51	E1a	2		
	(2)	152–55			e_4	
	1e(1)	156–59	E1a(1)	4		or E1d(1), T_2
	(2)(a)	160–63	E1d(2)	2		
	(b)	164–68	E1e(2)(a)	2		
	1f(1)	168–71	E1a(1)	4		but different bass
	(2)	172–75	E1f(1)	0		m. 172 differs
	(3)	176–80	E1f(2)	0		extended
Development (mm. 181–313)						
181–213	D3a	181–84			d_{2-3}, b_{1-2}, e_1, d_1	
	b(1)(a)	185–86				
	(b)	187–88				violin derived from C1b (compare violin II, m. 87)
	(2)(a)	189–90	D3b(1)(a)	0		
	(b)(1)	191–92	D3b(1)(b)	0		
	(2)	193–94	D3b(2)(b)(1)	0		octave lower
	(3)	195–96				extension
	c(1)	196–200			d_{2-3}, c_{1b}, d_1	
	(2)(a)	200–04				
	(b)	205–06				
	(3)(a)	207–09			d_{1-2}	
	(b)	209–11				octave lower
	(c)	211–13				two octaves lower
213–24	4a(1)	213–14			$a_2 + d_2$	
	(2)	215–16			a_2, b_1	
	b	217–20	D4a	0		
	c	221–24	D4a	0		
225–60	5a(1)(a)	225–29			d_1, a_2	compare mm. 95–96
	(2)(a)	229–32				mm. 228–29, T_0; C1b in woodwinds, mm. 231–32; extension
	(b)	232–36	D5a(2)(a)	4		
	(c)	237–38				= mm. 235–36, T_4
	b(1)(a)	239–43			d_1, a_2, c_1 (violin)	begins as D5a, T_6
	(b)	243–44			b_1 (cello)	echo of a_2, T_6
	(2)(a)	245–47				mm. 240–43, T_0; a_2 in high woodwinds (diminution), including echo effect
	(b)(1)	247–49				pacing of imitation in trumpets doubled
	(2)	249–51	D5b(2)(b)(1)	2		sequence
	(3)	251–52	D5b(2)(b)(2)	2		
	(4)	252–53	D5b(2)(b)(3)	2		
	(c)(1)(a)	253–54			d_1, a_2	
	(b)	254–55	D5b(2)(c)(1)(a)	0		
	(2)	256–59				

Example 125 (cont.)

Measures			Derivation	T	Motives	Comments
	(3)	259–60				mm. 100–01, T_1
260–96	6a(1)	260–64			d_{1-4}, b_2	= mm. 102–06, T_1, transformed
	(2)	264–68			d_2	= mm. 106–10, T_1
	b(1)(a)	269–72			d_3, d_4	consequent phrase begins with d_3
	(b)(1)	273–74				= mm. 269–70, T_5
	(2)	275–76				echo of mm. 273–74, T_6
	(c)	277–80				mm. 277–78, compare mm. 257–58; trumpet mm. 279–80 anticipates mm. 305–13, compare mm. 13–14
	(d)	280–85			d_3	begins like D6b(1)(a), T_4
	c	285–88			d_1, d_2	compare mm. 257–58
	b(2)(a)	289–92	D6b(1)(b)	1		
	(b)	293–96				= D6b(2)(a), T_{11}, or D4b(1)(b), T_0
297–313	7a(1)(a)(1)	297			a_1, a_2, d_3	mm. 297–313 = recapitulation of mm. 1–19
	(2)	298	D7a(1)(a)(1)	6		
	(b)	299–300	D7a(1)(a)	0		
	(2)(a)	301–02	D7a(1)(a)	0		
	(b)	303–04				
	b	305–13			a_2	= mm. 13–19, T_0 (transformed)
Recapitulation (mm. 313–605)						
313–40	A3a(1)	313–17			a_3	mm. 19–23, T_0
	(2)	317–20			a_1	no a_4 or a_5 (compare mm. 22–27); chord in m. 320 different from exposition
	b	321–29	A2a	1		a_{3-5} complete
	c	329–40	A2b	1		
341–76	B3a	341–48	B1a	1	b_{1-2}, a_1	
	b(1)	349–52				mm. 51–54, T_1 (truncated recapitulation)
	(2)(a)	353				m. 349, T_6
	(b)	354				m. 349, T_8
	(c)	355				m. 349, T_{10}
	(d)	356				m. 349, T_0 (or m. 51, T_1)
	4a	357–68				mm. 55–66, T_5 (mm. 367–68 varied)
	b	369–76				extension, chromatic ascent
377–84	C2a	377–84				mm. 71–78, T_5; reorchestrated, c_2 changed, different counterpoint

Example 125 (cont.)

Measures			Derivation	T	Motives	Comments
	b	385–96				mm. 79–90, T_5; c_1 and c_3 often inverted from original register
	c (1)(a)	397–98				mm. 91–92, T_5; transition
	(b)	399–400	C2c(1)(a)	6		
	(2)(a)	401–02	C2c(1)	0		diminution
	(b)	403–04	C2c(1)	0		
405–34	D8a (1)	405			d_1 + c_1	melody = m. 403, T_8
	(2)	406–08			a_2, d_1	mm. 96–98, T_{11}
	b(1)	409–12				mm. 97–100, T_5
	(2)	413–14				melody = mm. 101–02, T_9; mm. 413–15 substitute tritone bass progression for V–I in mm. 101–03
	9a	415–18			d_2, a_3, c_{1b}, c_2	not a recapitulation; melody mm. 414–16 = mm. 102–04, T_{10}; counterpoint in low strings derived from a_3, c_2; violin m. 418, compare m. 188
	b(1)	419–22				d_2 melody begins as in D2a, T_3, but changes to T_4; a_3 in low strings as in D2a, T_0
	(2)(a)	423–24				mm. 421–22, T_0
	(b)(1)	425				m. 424, octave lower
	(2)	426				m. 425, T_0
	c (1)	427–30			d_1	transition
	(2)	431–34				chromatic descent in bass
435–47	A4a	435–38			a_3, a_2, a_5, d_{1-2}	apotheosis; cello I derived from e_1; trombone derived from a_2 + d_2 (compare m. 213)
	b	439–42				begins as A4a, T_1; ends at T_{11}
	c	443–47				begins as A4b, T_7
447–76	D10	447–68	D5b–c	4		
	11	468–76	D2	5		true recapitulation; based on V pedal
477–86	E3a (1)	477–78				recapitulation of E (?); freely derived, possibly from a_1, a_5, b_2, or e_3; V pedal throughout
	(2)	479–80	E3a(1)	5		
	(1)	481–82	E3a(1)	0		
	b	483–86				condensation of E3a, repeated

Example 125 (cont.)

Measures			Derivation	T	Motives	Comments
487–506	D12	487–90			d_1	no a_2, V pedal continued
	13a	490–94	D2a	10	d_{2-4}	I pedal through m. 506; anticipation of true recapitulation beginning in m. 553
	b	494–98			d_{2-3}	
	a	499–502			b_{1-2} added	
	c	502–06			b_{1-2}	= D2b, T_{10}
507–30	E4a (1)	507–08			a_3	compare mm. 477–86
	(2)(a)	509–10			a_1	
	(b)	511–12				
	b(1)	513–14				= mm. 507–08, T_1
	(2)(a)	515–16				= mm. 511–12, T_1; a_1 motive rises chromatically
	(b)	517–18				= mm. 515–16, T_2
	5	519–30	E4	2		mm. 529–30 = mm. 527–28, T_2 = mm. 515–16, T_6
531–605	D14a (1)(a)	531–32			d_1, b_2	transition
	(b)	533–34			d_1, b_2, b_1, a_1, a_3, d_3	
	(2)(a)	535–36				
	(b)	537–38	D14a(1)(b)	8		
	(3)	539–40	D14a(2)(a)	6		
	b(1)	541–46			a_2	m. 15, T_0, or m. 97, T_5
	(2)	547–53				bass in mm. 550–53 = mm. 16–19, T_0
	D15	553–605			d_{2-4}	apotheosis of theme D; begins as in m. 102, T_{10} (therefore grounded in I), but continues freely; no significant contrapuntal combinations

then at T_5 by the flute (m. 27). Both statements involve a rich counterpoint with two subsidiary motives: a_4 in the oboe, related to a_2 and a_3, and a_5, played by the flute and derived from a_1. Motive a_1 is also used here in counterpoint with a_3 and is played by the clarinet.

The main body of the *Poem of Ecstasy* begins with section B (*allegro volando*) in m. 39. The theme of this section, which can be considered the traditional main theme, comprises a main motive, b_1, and two ancillary ideas, b_2 and b_3. As shown in the analysis of b_1, this theme is not entirely new, but rather is related through 4–7 to a_5 and in its melodic contours to a_2, a_4, and a_5. As a main theme, it is more forward-looking than the corresponding idea (b_1) of the Fifth Sonata. The theme of the sonata is more certain in its tonal direction and is akin to several of Scriabin's more conventional themes, such as that of "Fragilité" Op. 51/1. The b_1 motive of the *Poem of Ecstasy* anticipates the nervous flightiness of the codas of *Prometheus* and the Tenth Sonata and is related directly to the theme of the experimental Etude Op. 56/4.

Motive b_2 (mm. 41–42) is alternated in clipped phrases with b_1 and depends on the texture of high string trills coupled with detached, lightly articulated chords in steady rhythm. (The a_1 motive works in counterpoint against b_2.) Motive b_3 enters later in the section (m. 57); played legato in the high register of the violins, it is derived from a_3 and a_4.

In the Fifth Sonata, the activity of the B section increased as section C was introduced, climaxing in the *quasi trombe* (c_4) motive at the end of the episode. In the *Poem of Ecstasy* a similar motive (a_2) is introduced by the trumpet in m. 13 but does not return immediately after section B. Instead, the increasingly frenzied statements of b_1 break off abruptly in m. 70, and after a grand pause a new section (C) changes the mood completely. The primary subject of section C, c_1, marked *carezzando* (caressingly), resembles the chief contrasting idea of the Fifth Sonata (motive d), not only in its tender, languid character, but also in the initial contour of a descending minor sixth followed by an ascending half step. The c_1 idea is a direct response to b_1, for several of its contours are retrograde forms of contours in b_1. Much of c_1 is related to a_5 by inversion. Motive c_1 is set in counterpoint with c_2 (*serioso*), then with c_3. The predominance of the tritone in c_2 makes it a distinct idea, although one of its contours is an almost exact retrograde of a_2. On the other hand, c_3 is almost totally derivative, composed of an inversion form of b_1 followed by the initial contour of c_1. In a subsequent form in the violins beginning in m. 86, c_3 leads to a fragment of a_5. (This passage is enriched by the juxtaposition of the two halves of motive c_1 [c_{1a} and c_{1b}] in counterpoint.)

The counterpoint of c_1 and c_2 arches to a climax at m. 91 but quickly subsides, linking with a new section, D, beginning in m. 95. Here the restive syncopated fanfare in the horns (d_1) introduces a new tempo and mood. The a_2 *imperioso* motive returns in the trumpet, announcing the arrival in m. 102 of a new theme, also in the trumpet, accompanied by the triplet rhythms of the d_1 fanfare. This new theme, D, comprises successive (or perhaps overlapping) motives d_2 and d_3 and is intimately associated with A materials and with b_1 as well. Through 4–19 it is related to a_1, through 5–Z17 to a_3, and through 6–Z19 to the main theme, b_1. The contours of d_2 are those of a_2 and a_3, whereas the descending chromatic line of d_3 occurs in b_1. Most occurrences of theme D in the piece are paired with d_4 in counterpoint. This motive consists of a literal transposition of a_2 followed by a chromatic ascent in contrary motion to d_3. The exposition leads us to expect D to be a dramatic culmination; yet that expectation, heightened by the literal transposition of the initial phrase to T_5 in mm. 107–10, is thwarted when this repeated phrase subsides, fading to a new section, E, without further development of the D idea.

Section E (*moderato avec délice* [with delight]), which begins in m. 110, concludes the exposition. The mood is similar to that of section C, although here the main line, e_1—which like c_1 begins with a descending minor sixth—develops over a broader span and pushes toward a much larger climax (*presque en délire* [almost delirious], m. 169). Motive e_1 is related in set structure to materials from section A, in particular to a_3 through sets 6–Z37 and 5–Z37 (the Z-correspondent of 5–Z17 in a_3). The most conspicuous contours in e_1 are slightly compacted versions of a_2, and 4–19 from a_2 is outlined in e_1 as well. A further connection with section A is the use of a_1 in counterpoint with e_1 throughout section E. Motives e_2 and e_3 result from the free development of e_1 in mm. 127–40. Both are characterized by a compound melodic structure and involve chromatically ascending lines. Motive e_3 is closely related to a_5; in fact its first seven pitches are a literal transposition at T_6 of the earlier motive. As e_3 continues, part of its compound structure unfolds a progression—G♮–B♭–A♭–B♮–A♮—which underlies a_5 (at T_0) as well (mm. 132–33). Beginning in m. 152, the solo violin introduces e_4, a combination of the original e_1 melody and the chromatic ascent of e_2 and e_3.

Like all sections except B, section E closes in mm. 177–80 by dying away. In the more tempestuous Fifth Sonata, only sections A and D conclude in this manner; thus the exposition of the *Poem of Ecstasy* lacks the drive of its companion piece. Rather, the succession of thematic groups in the exposition involves a series of climaxes increasing in intensity, each followed by a relaxation of tension. This process, clearly connected with the erotic program of the work, reflects on a large level the undulating shapes of many of Scriabin's motives, including a_3, a_5, c_1, and particularly e_4.

Tonal Plan

The harmonic motion of the exposition is sketched in terms of bass progression in example 126a. The upper staff shows most of the pitches of the actual bass line, and the lower is a reduction demonstrating the underlying tonal motion. Thematic groups and motivic content are indicated above each system. Unlike the Fifth Sonata, the *Poem of Ecstasy* opens with harmonies closely related to the C major tonic; the opening chord on E♭ is an auxiliary chord resolving to I^6 in m. 5. (The E♭–E♮ bass motion is motivic in the piece, returning at the end in the violin melody to build to a triumphant cadence in C major; see mm. 586–605.) The progression moves quickly to the dominant in m. 13, which supports the introduction of a_2. The bass then moves to the tonic in m. 19 when a_3 enters in the clarinet. The feeling of a full cadence is diminished, however, by the suspension of elements of the dominant over the tonic bass and by the diminuendo in mm. 16–19. The tonic is prolonged in mm. 19–27 by a I–V–I progression modified by progressions of tritones and descending fifths. Beginning in m. 27 the tonic bass tone supports a_3 at T_5 from its appearance in m. 19. The harmony no longer involves a suspended dominant, but is rather the C major tonic with a minor seventh added—the harmony with which section A concludes in m. 38. The bass progression in mm. 27–39 expands that in mm. 19–27.

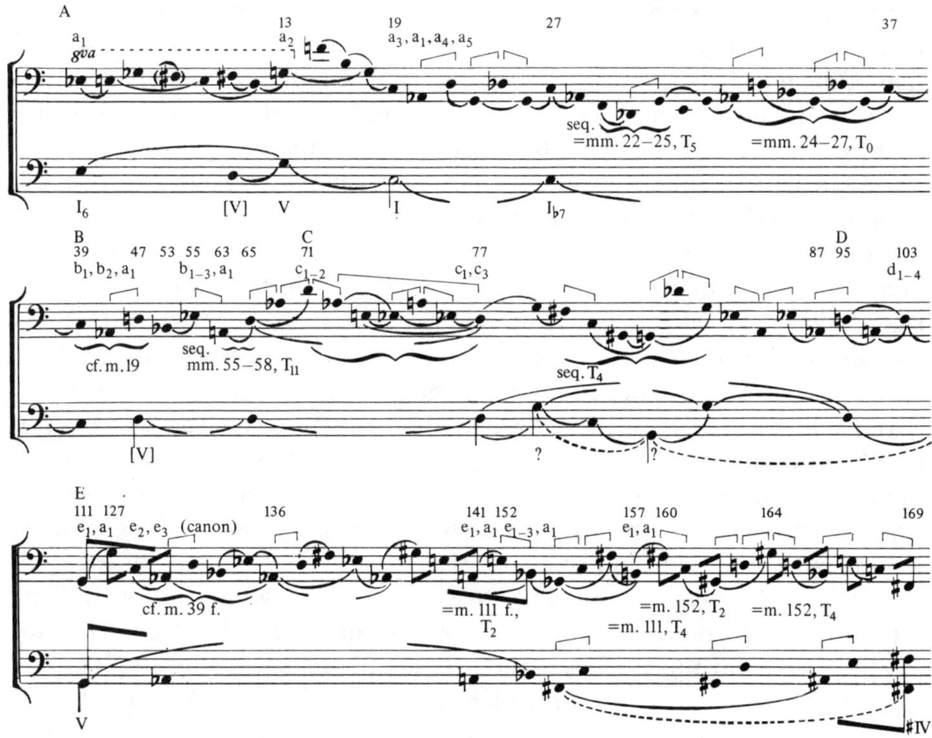

Example 126a *Poem of Ecstasy* Op. 54: Exposition

Section B, the beginning of the main body of the work, opens with the continuation of I♭7. (Compare this foundation with the Fifth Sonata, where the dominant first arrives only with the B material, and the tonic occurs for the only time halfway through the B section.) A transpositional shift to T_2 in m. 47 moves the fundamental bass note from C♮ to D♮, and the new pitch remains the focal element until the arrival of section C in m. 71. Ultimately D major proves to be V/V in C major, but within section C, V/V never progresses definitively to V. Thus D major continues into section D, which is announced by a fanfare at m. 95, and is prolonged by its dominant, introduced in mm. 101–02. At m. 103 A♮ cadences to D♮ in the bass while elements of V/D♮ remain suspended in upper parts. In m. 107, the resolution of the suspension chord over the sustained bass D♮ coincides with the addition of the lowered seventh. Thus the treatment of D major in mm. 103–10 parallels that of the tonic chord in mm. 19–27.

Only with the arrival of section E does the D major harmony progress (as a secondary dominant) to the dominant, thus completing a I–V progression spanning the entire exposition through m. 111. The dominant is then retained in the bass through m. 126. We might expect the dominant to be prolonged for the rest of the exposition, but here the harmonic progression deviates from the norm. Beginning in m. 127, the bass progresses quickly in a pattern which parallels (at T_0) that at the beginning of section B. The bass thus moves away from the dominant, ultimately progressing through A♭ to A♮, which supports a repetition of the initial E material at T_2 beginning in m. 141. This motion continues as level T_4 is reached in m. 157. In a sense, this level of transposition is prolonged for the rest of the exposition, for e_1 is repeated at T_4 at the climax of section E beginning in m. 169 and remains at this level thereafter. However, the bass in these measures deviates from the pattern of transposition, sustaining F♯ instead of the expected B♮.

The bass unfolding from G♮ to B♮ in mm. 111–57 might be consistent with a prolongation of the dominant. However, the bass later departs more radically from the dominant, moving in a pattern which seems to be an expansion of the motivic bass progression in mm. 128–32. Beginning in m. 160, the bass moves entirely within the even-numbered whole-tone scale, progressing finally to F♯ in m. 169. There are two distinct underlying progressions here: an ascending fourth (descending fifth) from B♮ (m. 157) to F♯ (m. 169), and a compound line involving whole-tone ascents from C♮ to F♯ and from F♯ to A♯. In the end, however, the most important connection is between G♮ at the beginning of section E (m. 111) and F♯ at the end (m. 169). What has taken place in section E is the replacement of the dominant note in the bass by the raised scale-degree $\hat{4}$. Thus a progression from I to ♯IV spans the exposition—yet another example of the tritone as a governing interval of prolongation. This tritone is particularly dramatic because it literally displaces the normal opening progression from tonic to dominant. The first half of the exposition of the Fifth Sonata (through m. 116) entails a strikingly similar tonic prolongation effected by a tritone bass progression.

The motivic content and underlying harmonic progression of the development are shown in the sketch in example 126b. The development of the *Poem of Ecstasy*, unlike that of the Fifth Sonata, is dominated by a single theme, D. The formal divisions of the development are thus all considered subsections of thematic group D. The focus on theme D in the development is appropriate because in the exposition its potential was intimated but never exploited. However, the development is also marked from the outset (m. 181) by the unexpected contrapuntal combinations of motives which hitherto have been independent. First, B materials are set against those of D, played by the same instruments as in the exposition—the woodwinds and brass respectively. In addition, the trilled appoggiaturas in the violins continue into the development from section E of the exposition.

In mm. 187–88 the violins take up motive c_{1b} with tremolo bowing, recalling the climax of the exposition of theme C (mm. 87–94). This idea leads to the turbulent *allegro drammatico* (mm. 191–212), where it is the main countersubject in a development of theme D in the minor. Throughout most of the first subsection of the development (mm. 181–212), section D3 in the formal outline, the harmonic focus is on E♭, which cadences to A♭ at the climax of this section (m. 207). As we enter the next main section, *tragico* (D4), the bass progresses by tritone to D♮. The bass progression thus connecting D3 and D4—E♭–A♭–D♮—is

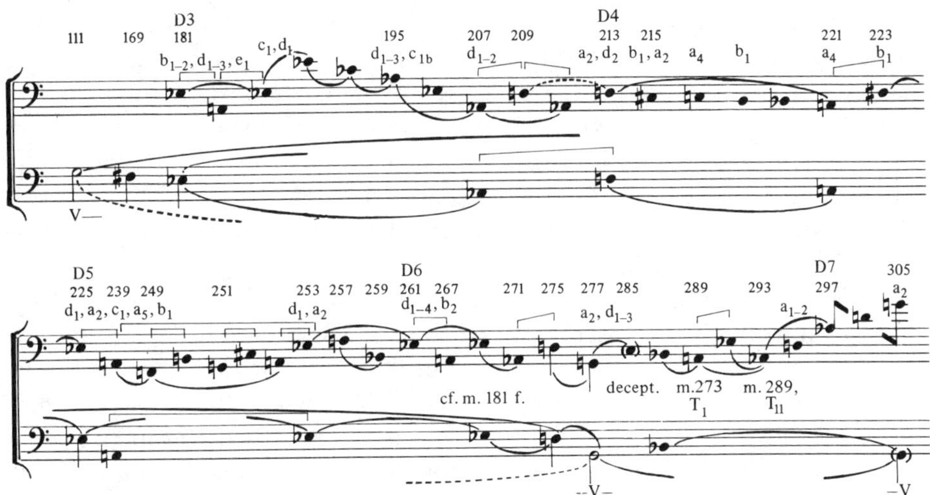

Example 126b *Poem of Ecstasy* Op. 54: Development

the same as that moving from the climax of section C to section D in the exposition (mm. 86–95). This is a motivic association, for these sections provide the materials for this portion of the development.

The powerful trombone theme in the *tragico* section is derived from different motives. Its rhythms are essentially those of d_2 augmented, but the contour of the descending minor seventh is associated mainly with a_2. The setting of this heavy theme conforms to conventional orchestration depicting a storm at sea; the cellos have surging chromatic runs in sixteenth notes supported by tremolo chords in the low woodwinds and strings, and b_1 lashes out intermittently in canon between the higher strings and woodwinds. (One is reminded in particular of the final movement of Rimsky-Korsakov's *Scheherazade*.) Here the bass descends chromatically from D♮ to A♮, which then progresses by tritone to E♭ (spelled first as D♯) as the music proceeds to a new section marked *tempestuoso* (D5).

Section D5 is a gigantic upbeat to the arrival of theme D in the following section. Appropriately, Scriabin now develops materials associated with section D1 in the exposition (mm. 95–102): d_1 and especially a_2. In mm. 225–38 (D5a) he uses successive transpositions at increasingly close time intervals to heighten tension. (Even at the outset, tension is greater than at the point where this material occurred in the exposition, for it begins here a half step higher.) As the *tempestuoso* material continues past m. 238, Scriabin dispenses with the chromatic interjections in the high woodwinds, which linked this section with the preceding material. A new subsection, D5b (mm. 239–53), begins at T_6 from the point at which D5a began. A counterpoint based on c_1 is now introduced by the violins in an extremely high register, while a_2 is repeated in imitation between trumpets and horns. At m. 246 this imitative treatment is taken up in the woodwinds in diminution by half. Successive transpositions at T_2 of mm. 247–49 lead to a climax at m. 253, supported again by E♭ in the bass. The sequential whole-tone progression from A♮ in m. 239 to E♭ in m. 253 has effected a tritone bass progression prolonging E♭ from the beginning of D5 (m. 225). The climactic section D5c (mm. 253–60) is marked by the powerful statement of d_1 in augmentation in the brass, set against the continuing frenetic imitations of a_2 in the woodwinds. In mm. 257–61, a progression by descending fifth leads to a cadence to E♭ coinciding with the arrival of theme D in section D6.

The reappearance of theme D here might be understood as a recapitulation of sorts. Indeed, through m. 266 it is a modified repetition of the original D material at T_1. However, because theme D was introduced in the exposition only in incipient form, the fact that it now expands suggests that this recurrence is a development of the theme. The addition of d_1 in the woodwinds and b_2 in the strings also indicates a developmental process. The first sign of the growth of theme D occurs in m. 267, where the sustained high F♮ replaces the expected d_3. However, d_3 is the basis for a new consequent idea in mm. 269–72, an idea which becomes the subject for a sequence, enriched by imitation between the trumpets and culminating at m. 277. During this statement of theme D, the bass progresses from E♭ to the dominant by the same alternation of descending fifths and tritones (E♭–A♭–D♮–G♮) which approached the dominant in the exposition in mm. 86–111. Here, however, the dominant is not stabilized; rather, the material it supports in this passage (D6c) manifests an increasingly strong cadential tendency, beginning with a statement of d_1 in augmentation in the horns comparable to that in mm. 257–58, continuing with a trumpet call on high A♮ like that in mm. 13–14 of the introduction (at T_0), and culminating with a d_3 consequent phrase which will almost certainly lead to a cadence in C major.

It is here that Scriabin creates his most Wagnerian gesture. In a deceptive progression, the tonic expected at m. 285 is replaced by a $\frac{4}{2}$ chord, the third inversion of a C major chord with lowered seventh added. While the horns blare out d_1 in augmentation (compare mm. 257–58 and 277–80), the trumpet responds with d_2, initiating another sequence of d_3 phrases in imitation, comparable at T_1 to those in mm. 273–76, but extended to progress to D♮ by the end of the section.

The final section of the development, D7, has overlapping functions in the formal scheme. It is the seemingly inevitable goal of the directed motion through the development since the deceptive cadence in m. 285. The essential bass progression here is a descending fifth from D♮ to G♮, continuing the pattern initiated in m. 289. But D7 is also a frenetic transformation of the opening of the composition (mm. 1–19), the climax of which is the apotheosis (at T_0) of the a_2 trumpet call in mm. 13–19—a true recapitulation. The dominant which supports this material cadences to the tonic in m. 313, coinciding with the recapitulation of a_3.

Scriabin adheres strictly to conventional sonata procedures in approaching the recapitulation of the *Poem of Ecstasy*, and in this regard this work contrasts starkly with the Fifth Sonata. The harmonic strategy earlier in the development is not so clear, however. Throughout much of the development, harmony centers on E♭, a foreign element in C major. Only shortly before the arrival of the dominant in m. 277 is the voice-leading tendency of E♭ realized when it resolves to D♮ in the compound bass line. In the larger view, E♭ continues a descending motion which was initiated near the end of the exposition in the descent from G♮ (m. 111) to F♯ (m. 169). Thus the motion from G♮ to F♯, so peculiar within the context of a sonata exposition, belongs to a conventional unfolding which is unusual only because it crosses ordinary formal boundaries. However, even the unfolding of the fourth from G♮ to D♮ (m. 275) is part of a larger motion arpeggiating the dominant in mm. 111–277 (middleground sketch, example 126b). The deceptive cadence in m. 285 is an elaboration prolonging the dominant further (mm. 277–312). A descending third from B♭ to G♮ is part of the compound bass line in mm. 285–305.

The harmonic and motivic features of the recapitulation are sketched in example 126c. Given the conventional return to the tonic at the beginning of the recapitulation, we might expect the rest of the piece to conform to normal sonata procedures. As soon as a_3 has been stated at T_0 in mm. 313–18, however, it trails off before a_4 and a_5 can participate with it in counterpoint. After a pause on an unexpected chord in m. 320, the violin restates a_3 at T_1, leading to a full recapitulation of A2 (somewhat reorchestrated) at T_1 (mm. 321–40). The reca-

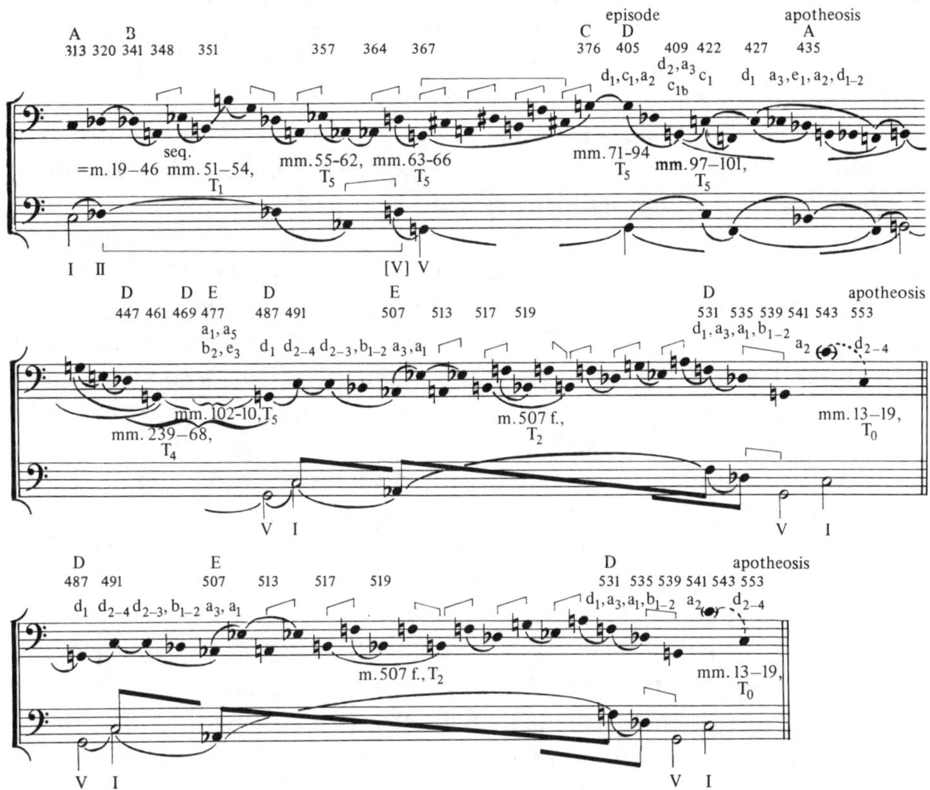

Example 126c *Poem of Ecstasy* Op. 54: Recapitulation

pitulation of B follows, beginning in m. 341 with a literal though slightly truncated repetition of B1 (mm. 39–54), also at T_1. After a sequence in mm. 353–56, the recapitulation continues with a literal repetition of B2, but at a new level of transposition, T_5. The transpositional strategy in the recapitulation thus far is straightforward. In setting A and B materials at T_1, Scriabin bases the harmony on ♭II instead of on the expected tonic. He chooses T_5 when the original harmony (m. 65) of the exposition was V/V, thus producing V in m. 367. The successive transpositions at T_1 and T_5 create a tritone bass progression preparing and prolonging the dominant. This prolongation continues through the recapitulation of C material in mm. 377–404, also at T_5. The repetition is again fairly literal, modified only by reorchestration and a slightly more active texture. The most conspicuous change is that c_1 and c_3, which are combined in counterpoint, are often inverted in register.

Beginning in m. 401 Scriabin constructs a bridge based on a diminution by half of the material of the four preceding measures. This overlaps in m. 405 with the return of material roughly equivalent to D1. We expect a full recapitulation of D, but this section is less a recapitulation than a developmental episode. Levels of transposition are freely selected and do not correspond to those in previous statements of D material. The d_2 motive in the trumpet in mm. 415–17 is accompanied by a new line in the low strings, related through sets 5–13 and 6–Z37 to a_3 and in its contour (by inversion) to c_2. Further, d_2 is not answered by d_3 as expected, but rather by the horns, which in mm. 417–18 play 4–19, a set found within d_2 itself. (Could the descending G♮–E♭ third allude here to Beethoven's Fifth?) The consequent d_3 phrase in mm. 419–21 is a free alteration rather than a literal transposition as in the exposition. The bass line is repeated here at T_0, however. This episode continues in mm. 424–26 with an allusion to the beginning of the development (m. 188), leading to an augmented statement of d_1 in the horns in mm. 427–30 (compare mm. 257–59 in the development). This phrase is immediately repeated as the bass line descends chromatically, serving as a transition to a new section in m. 435. In terms of harmonic support, this episode is in the dominant until the transitional section beginning in m. 427. Then the harmony progresses by sequential and linear means to the B♭ at the beginning of the next section.

The section beginning in m. 435 is a grand apotheosis, similar to the culmination of the development in the Fifth Sonata. Whereas the climax there was based on the transformation of the main contrasting idea (D), here mostly A material is transformed. By contrast, the apotheosis of A material in the Fifth Sonata was reserved for the grand climax near the end of the recapitulation (mm. 433–40). The transformation of A in the *Poem of Ecstasy* is similar to this culminating passage in the Fifth Sonata because it entails both the transformation of a_3 and the dramatic recombination of several important motives in the composition. Here the bassoons and trombones play the line combining a_2 and d_2 from the *tragico* section of the development (mm. 213–24). A line in the first cello in mm. 435–36 is derived from e_1, and the simultaneous English horn line is related to a_5. Each statement of a_3 is answered by d_1 augmented in the horns. Unlike the transformation of d in the Fifth Sonata, the apotheosis of a_3 does not involve literal transposition. Rather, the bass returns in m. 437 to G♮, which remains the focal element until it progresses by tritone to D♭ as the next section begins.

Scriabin now returns to D material, with an almost literal repetition of D5b–c (mm. 239–60), the immense preparation for the return of theme D in the development. The level of transposition here is T_4; because the original passage was part of a prolongation of E♭ in the bass, the harmonic effect here is a prolongation of the dominant. This passage culminates with a statement of D roughly equivalent to D6a (mm. 260–68) at T_4. On closer examination, however, this statement is a literal (though transformed) repetition at T_5 of the original theme D in the exposition (mm. 102–10), thus now supported by a dominant pedal. This recurrence of D is therefore a strict recapitulation although, as in the beginning, it is peculiarly tentative, especially in light of its expansive treatment as a full-fledged theme in the development.

As the D theme fades, it is replaced by a brief, enigmatic passage (*charmé*) supported by the continuing dominant pedal. The relation of this material to the previous music is obscure. The underlying chromatic descent of the melody suggests an association with d_3 or possibly with e_1, whereas the trills relate it to b_2. In addition, some of the contours are similar to those of a_1. In the course of the entire piece, Scriabin never returns specifically to thematic group E from the end of the exposition. In view of his predilection for systematic and exhaustive treatment of thematic materials, it is important to recognize a certain correspondence between thematic group E and the *charmé* materials. This may be more evident in the return of these materials in mm. 507–53, now increasingly voluptuous, approaching ecstasy (*avec une volupté de plus en plus extatique*); for here the a_1 motive is used consistently in counterpoint against motive e_1. In any case, the two passages based on *charmé* materials are the only possible recapitulations of thematic group E.

As a transition to another transformation of theme D in m. 491, d_1 is stated in the horns in mm. 487–88, followed by the ascending chromatic gesture of m. 102. This D material arrives with little preparation; unlike the other appearances of the theme, it is not announced by an a_2 trumpet fanfare. However, another crucial event occurs with the arrival of this statement: the dominant, effectively prolonged since m. 367, progresses to the tonic. This transformation of theme D, though twice as long as the previous statement in mm. 468–76, does not build to a climax. In contrast to the tremendous expansiveness of this theme at the end of the development, here the phrases are so squarely balanced that there is little increase in tension. This passage is essentially an expansion of the original statement of theme D in the exposition, transposed to T_{10} so as to be grounded in the tonic. The present passage consists of four phrases instead of the original two; the first and third are equivalent to the original antecedent phrase, the second is a free variant, and the final phrase is equivalent to the original consequent. One developmental procedure makes this transformation of theme D more than just a longer version of the original. In the latter two phrases (mm. 499–506), marked scherzando, b_1 and b_2 are added to the texture, recalling the counterpoint at the beginning of the development.

As in section D11 (mm. 468–76), the present statement of theme D fades into a recurrence of E material in m. 507. A transitional factor here is the trilled appoggiatura motive in the scherzando treatment of D (mm. 499–506), as at the beginning of the development. There this motive continued from the preceding E material. That it recurs in a strikingly similar context and continues into mm. 507–53 (*avec une volupté de plus en plus extatique*) reinforces the interpretation of this section as a recapitulation of E material. The transition from D to E in the recapitulation also introduces symmetry at a large level, for this process reverses that in the transition from exposition to development.

Although the basis for this section is the *charmé* episode (mm. 477–86), other motives, notably a_1 and a_3, are combined with it to elicit a feeling of tender nostalgia often associated with a coda. (The closing section of Debussy's *Prelude to "The Afternoon of a Faun,"* for instance, creates a comparable effect.) Whereas the preceding E material in the *charmé* section was supported throughout by a dominant pedal, the harmonic motion here is chromatic, sequential, and relatively rapid. The sketch in example 126c shows that the underlying motion in this passage is an ascending sixth from A♭ to F♮, the latter pitch attained in m. 531 when a transition to the final section begins. Both A♭ and F♮ are auxiliary to the dominant, which arrives in m. 539 immediately before the a_2 trumpet fanfare.

Section D14 beginning in m. 531 is analogous to D5 (especially D5b–c) in the development in that it prepares the grandiose transformation of theme D. To that end, both passages use the d_1 and a_2 motives, transformed in brilliant orchestral settings. The emphasis in D14 is on the effect of flight, and motive b_2 is especially important. The texture in mm. 531–40 is that of section B, but with the driving rhythms of d_1 superimposed, alternated between the trumpets and woodwinds. In mm. 550–53, at the arrival of theme D, the final cadence to the tonic splendidly transforms the initial approach to the tonic in mm. 16–19. The final maestoso (D15), the culmination of the entire work, is the apotheosis of theme D, often hinted at throughout the piece but denied until the end. As in the statement in D13, the beginning of the theme is equivalent at T_{10} to its original statement and is thus grounded in the tonic, which is sustained for the rest of the piece as a pedal tone. The phrases of D in the final section correspond at T_4 to the first two phrases of the theme at the beginning of the development. The final statement of theme D is most like that in D6 at the climax of the development, especially in its first two phrases (mm. 260–68).

It is interesting that D15 and not D6 is the true apotheosis of theme D, particularly because D6 entails more contrapuntal interaction among independent motives—a treatment certainly appropriate for the dramatic high point of the development. Specifically, great tension is generated by the continual presence of the d_1 and b_2 ideas. The syncopated rhythms of d_1 are absent at the close of the piece. Further, D6 is charged by the imitative treatment of the theme itself and by the sequential progression of melody and harmony. By contrast, D15 employs no imitation and is harmonically stable. At the moment of apotheosis, concentration is on the theme itself, backed by sonorous, richly orchestrated chords. The organ is added only at this point to strengthen these harmonies, which are also enhanced by trills and tremolos, and bells are unique to the finale. The accompaniment consists mostly of arpeggiations with little motivic identity, although the arpeggiated triplets in the second and third trumpets recall the a_2 fanfare motive. Perhaps the greatest contrast between D6 and D15 is in tempo. The great weight of the finale results largely from the augmentation of the theme to twice its original length. The resulting ponderous allargando is sustained by a gradual increase of dynamics and tension until m. 585. The mood then changes abruptly as soft, sustained chords and harp arpeggiations support a caressing treatment of the germinal descending half-step motive in the violins. The pitches are those of the bass progression at the opening of the work. After several repetitions with continual crescendo, this motive becomes the basis for a melodic line ascending to a high E, supported by a thundering tonic harmony which closes the piece. This melodic line forms 6–Z19 (example 127) and is thus the ultimate transformation of theme D.

Thematic Transformation and Form

Although the *Poem of Ecstasy* conforms to the tripartite division of sonata form, its procedures and form are dramatically different from those of the piano sonatas analyzed in chapter 8. Compared with the Fifth Sonata, the *Poem of Ecstasy* is conventional in overall harmonic scheme. Its treatment of thematic material, however, depends much more on thematic transformation, especially with regard to theme D. The successive transformations of this theme throughout the piece are at least as strong a factor in determining its form as are the development and recapitulation of other themes. (Example 128 summarizes the occurrences of theme D throughout the *Poem of Ecstasy*.) As stated earlier, there is nothing comparable to theme D or to its treatment in the Fifth Sonata. In that work the materials which undergo the most important transformations are the A materials and the contrasting theme (D). In the *Poem of Ecstasy* neither c_1 nor e_1, which come closest to conventional contrasting themes, is the subject for grandiose transformation. However, a_3 is strikingly similar to the contrasting theme in the Fifth Sonata, and its apotheosis in the recapitulation of the *Poem of*

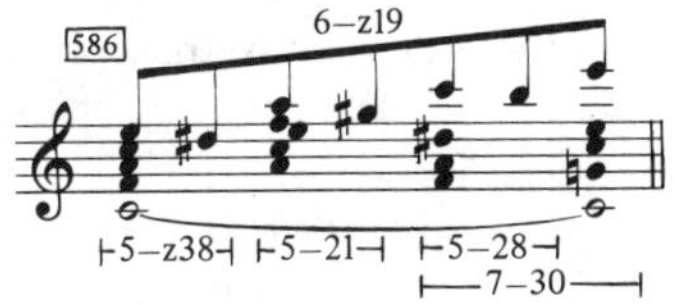

Example 127 *Poem of Ecstasy* Op. 54

Ecstasy (mm. 435–47) parallels the transformation of A in the recapitulation of the Fifth Sonata. In its treatment of the theme, this transformation resembles even more the climax at the end of the development in the sonata. The apotheosis of a_3 in the *Poem of Ecstasy* is not a grand culmination; in fact, its arrival in m. 435 is unexpected. Moreover, a_3 does not unfold here to a full climax; after three statements it moves prematurely into the next section. (In the apotheosis of D in the Fifth Sonata, mm. 313–28, on the other hand, the motive reaches a full climax at the end of four phrases.)

In the *Poem of Ecstasy*, Scriabin's most extended tonal composition, the originality of the form lies primarily in the treatment of a special theme, D. Example 128 gives an overview of the transformation of this theme throughout the piece. This material occurs in the exposition only in section D2, in a tentative statement which suggests little of its potential for expansion. Consisting of two transpositionally equivalent phrases, this statement quickly loses momentum, fading to a quieter section. It is based on V/V. When theme D returns in D3 at the beginning of the development, it is more energetic. Here the second phrase does not parallel the first but instead opens to new material. The harmonic support for this statement is E♭, rather distant from the C major tonic.

The expansiveness of theme D is fully realized in D6, at the height of the development. Its freely derived phrases are spun forth in sequence and in imitation. The harmony progresses continually and fairly rapidly, beginning with E♭ (a link with D3) and moving through a deceptive cadence. This section is not harmonically closed; it ultimately progresses to V/V, leading to V in the remaining section of the development.

The first statement of theme D in the recapitulation (D9) thwarts our expec-

Example 128 *Poem of Ecstasy*: Treatment of Theme D (d_{2-3})

Section	Measures	Harmony	Comments
D2	102–10	D (V/V)	two transpositionally equivalent phrases; fades away
D3	181–91	E♭	set in counterpoint against b_{1-2}; opening, slightly expansive; no conclusion
D6	260–96	E♭–V–I (thwarted)–V/V	sequential progression from E♭ to V (m. 277); deceptive cadence (m. 285); further sequence leads to V/V (m. 295); expansive climax of development; imitative writing; d_1 and b_2 in counterpoint; not conclusive
D9	415–22	V	developmental episode (compare D3), not the expected recapitulation
D11	468–76	V	literal recapitulation of D2 at T_5
D13	490–506	I	like D2, though constructed to be twice as long; fades away
D15	553–605	I	apotheosis; true recapitulation; theme in augmentation; first two phrases are the same as corresponding phrases of D3 (at T_4); closure

tations: it is not a genuine restatement but is instead part of a freely composed developmental episode recalling section D3. Like D9, D11 is based on V, but this section contains a literal, though somewhat transformed, repetition of D2 (at T_5). Like D2, however, D11 is inconclusive. Section D13 entails the first statement of theme D in the tonic, yet this is only a slight expansion of D11 with the same weaknesses in dramatic impact. Only at the end of the *Poem of Ecstasy* does Scriabin provide a satisfying recapitulation of theme D. A unique feature of section D15 is the aspect of closure, both harmonic and melodic. Based on a tonic pedal, it is the only statement of D which provides consequent melodic material to resolve the tensions inherent in the theme.

In view of the importance of the transformation of theme D in the *Poem of Ecstasy*, it is clear why Scriabin called the work a poem. Had the piece conformed more strictly to the single-movement sonata form which he had developed in his piano sonatas, he might have called it the Fourth Symphony. However, the work is not simply a sonata for orchestra. On the contrary, its form is determined largely by its development of special thematic content with strong extramusical connotations. In this respect, the *Poem of Ecstasy* is a symphonic poem in the Lisztian tradition, its unique form truly poetic in its sense of freedom and fantasy.

PROMETHEUS: THE POEM OF FIRE

Scriabin's last completed orchestral work is seldom performed and little understood, even though it is probably the one for which the composer is best known. Reputed to be his first atonal composition, *Prometheus* calls for a huge orchestra with the unusual additions of piano, organ, and mixed chorus. The piece is most famous, however, as one of the first attempts to combine effects of light and music. The scoring includes a type of continuo for color organ, a device not even invented when the work was being composed. *Prometheus* is without doubt the most extended, ambitious, and imaginative of Scriabin's completed works.

Motivic Materials

The motivic subject matter of *Prometheus* is shown in example 129. There are eighteen discernible motives, about as many as in the *Poem of Ecstasy*. Here, however, the motives are so closely interrelated that their labels are somewhat arbitrary. The exposition of most of the basic subject matter occurs in an incredibly condensed introductory passage, making *Prometheus* very different in form from the works examined previously. There are fewer associations between motives and particular formal divisions in the piece than in the earlier sonata forms, and in this analysis there are no correspondences between lowercase and capital-letter labels. (For example, motive b_1 is not necessarily associated with thematic group B.)

The beginning of example 129 shows the opening chord of *Prometheus*, which forms 6–34, the basic harmonic component of the work, the mystic chord.

Example 129 *Prometheus* Op. 60: Basic Motives

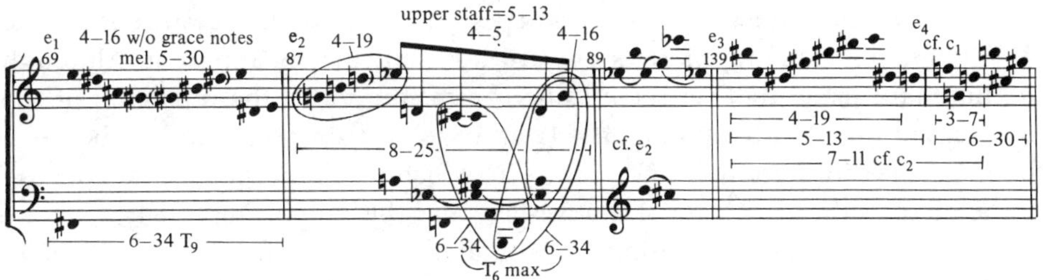

Example 129 (cont.)

Contrary to a widely held impression, 6–34 almost never appears as a melodic motive in *Prometheus*. Whether we consider them as ordered or unordered sets, the motives are quite diverse and in many cases involve sets not closely related to 6–34. The mystic chord is essentially a harmonic component although the harmony usually consists of subsets of 6–34, with the complete set formed only in the combination of melody and harmony.

The initial melody stated in the low register of the horns over the opening chord in mm. 5–12 is the main theme of the composition, comprising three motives, a_{1-3}. Motive a_1 forms 3–3, and a_2 restates this set, capping it with an ascending fourth from F♯ to B♮. This fanfarelike gesture forms 4–19. Motive a_3 contains two overlapping statements of 3–3 (at T_0 and T_4) and forms 5–21, which is also the aggregate of a_{1-3}. Sequential repetition of a_2 in the woodwinds leads to a statement of new motives in the brass. In m. 21, motive b_1 involves two chords, forms of 3–9 equivalent at T_6. The structural basis for this motive, however, is the invariance potential of 6–34. Each 3–9 in b_1 forms 6–34 in combination with its supporting harmony. These two forms of 6–34 are equivalent at T_6, with four invariant pcs (the maximum possible)—those of the sustained harmony.

In mm. 23 and 24, b_1 is repeated, followed each time by b_2, a chromatically ascending phrase in the woodwinds. The underlying melodic set in b_{1-2} is 4–Z29, on which relations with several other motives are based. The statements of b_{1-2} are followed in m. 26 by a new section (*contemplatif*) with a new motive, c_1, played by the flute. This motive forms a strikingly different set, 5–11, which is not closely related to many other motives and thus appears to be the "contrasting theme." This motive is followed by c_2, asserted by the piano in its flamboyant first entrance. (Motive c_2 is anticipated by the solo trumpet in m. 22.) The piano concludes with a cadenzalike flourish arpeggiating 5–30; this gesture is motive c_3. The relations among motives c_{1-3} are not immediately apparent. Although the flute and piano motives seem to be contrasting ideas, the repetition of the materials of mm. 26–34 in mm. 34–42 at T_9 reinforces the connection between them. The set formed by c_1 and c_2 is 7–26, which was important at the opening of the piece as the aggregate of motives a_{1-3} and the supporting 6–34.

The piano passage comprising c_{2-3} contains many significant sets. Motive c_2 itself forms 5–30. As a single gesture, c_{2-3} is structured of overlapping forms of 5–30 (equivalent at T_3) sharing only pc 0, which occurs at the overlap. Sets 4–19 and 5–21 are formed as indicated, suggesting a derivation from a_{1-3}. The final c motive, c_4, first occurs in the piano accompaniment in mm. 155–56. Stated in even eighth notes, c_4 is actually an ordered presentation of c_2, with elements alternating between two registers, so that the original intervallic sequence +2 +3 +1 +4 becomes −10 +15 −11 +16. Motive c_4 is particularly important in the orchestration of the main theme's apotheosis, beginning in m. 467, where it is assigned to the chimes and flutes.

The next new motivic material enters in the piano in m. 53. This motive, d_1, recurs in slightly expanded form in mm. 61 and 63, followed by the poignant d_2 motive (*délicat, cristallin*), the last four notes of which allude to a_1. The upper voice of d_1 is an ordered repetition at T_7 of the second through sixth elements of c_{2-3}. The combination of upper and lower voices in d_1 yields 5–30, the set formed by c_2. (Together d_1 and d_2 form 7–30, the complement of 5–30.) Motive d_2 forms 4–Z15—also contained in c_2—which with the 4–19 in the upper voice of d_1 forms 5–30. With the grace notes, d_2 forms 6–34.[4]

Two other ideas stated in conjunction with motive d_2 may properly be considered motives. In mm. 151–56, in a solo piano passage marked *étrange, charmé*, the d_2 motive returns for the first time after its initial presentation in m. 65. Here it is an antecedent phrase. The consequent phrase, d_3, is derived from d_2, for it consists of two consecutive statements of 3–5, the set formed by the first three notes of d_2. Motive d_3 forms set 4–9, which will occur (at T_0) in an entirely different manner as d_4. Whether d_3 and d_4 are independent motives is questionable. Because these materials are transformed at the end of the piece, however, they are included as motives. On the other hand, the waltzlike material beginning in m. 163, clearly derived from d_{3-4}, is not considered motivic because it occurs nowhere else in the piece.

Another motivic grouping is based on e_1, the subject introduced by the piano in scherzando fashion in m. 69. This idea, which is strikingly similar to b_1 in the *Poem of Ecstasy*, is another 5–30 and thus might be a derivative of c_2. The poignant phrase (*voluptueux, presque avec douleur* [voluptuous, almost sad]) introduced abruptly in m. 87 is related to e_1 in its contours—particularly the ascending grace-note arpeggiations and the dramatic descending leap of thirteen half steps—and is thus labeled e_2. In set content, however, this motive is distinctive: it forms 5–13, a set not previously found. Significant subsets are 4–19 and 3–5, which relate the idea to a_2 and d_2 respectively. The material which follows in m.

89 is actually a development of e_2, as the reduction in example 129 shows. Because this treatment does not recur, it is not considered an independent motive. A third idea related to the e material is the climactic arching phrase (*avec enthousiasme*) introduced by the violins in m. 138. This motive, e_3, is closely associated with e_2 in both set content and contour. It is paired with a highly contrasting idea, e_4, which forms 3–7, recalling the latter part of c_1. Moreover, e_3 and e_4 together form 7–11, reinforcing the association with c_1, which forms 5–11, the complement of 7–11.

The final motive in this analysis is the cadenzalike fanfare in the piano (mm. 192–97) which signals the beginning of the development. This motive, f_1, is actually a huge expansion of b_1 and is considered an independent idea chiefly because a similar fanfare occurs as the triumphant gesture concluding the piece (mm. 591–606). As indicated in example 129, f_1 contains two forms of 3–9 equivalent at T_6. As in b_1, each 3–9 combined with its accompanying chord yields 6–34, the two forms of which are also equivalent at T_6. The f_1 motive is associated with c_2 through set 5–30 and because its presentation closely resembles the first c_2 in mm. 30–33.

Form

The overall form of *Prometheus* is outlined in example 130. This work is strikingly different in form from Scriabin's earlier extended compositions in that it depends to an unprecedented degree on the transformational development of materials—a process that begins almost immediately and continues throughout the piece. Nevertheless, even this highly innovative form evinces the traditional tripartite division of sonata form. In this regard the piano is particularly important, announcing each main section with a flamboyant fanfare. The opening of the main body of the exposition coincides with the first entrance of the piano, the development begins with the f_1 passage discussed above, and the arrival of the recapitulation in m. 370 is marked by the literal restatement of c_{1-3} (mm. 26–34) at T_8.

The exposition of *Prometheus* opens with a twenty-six-measure introduction (section A), in which a_{1-3}, b_{1-2}, and c_2 appear. The concentration of significant subject matter differentiates this introduction from the opening passages of the Fifth Sonata and the *Poem of Ecstasy*, although in mood and compositional procedures the introductions to the latter work and *Prometheus* have much in common. The main theme, comprising motives a_{1-3}, rises out of the murky opening sonority, and a_2 spins forth sequentially, culminating in two trumpet calls, b_1 and c_2. (The latter anticipates a more forceful presentation in the next section.) The chromatic ascent of b_2 is a response to b_1 and is repeated twice, effecting a transition to a new section.

Section B begins by juxtaposing the contemplative statement of c_1 by the flutes (mm. 26–30) and the quasi cadenza for piano introducing c_{2-3}. The rest of B develops these materials. The opening passage of this section (mm. 26–34) is extended by literal repetition, first of the entire passage at T_9 in mm. 34–42,

Example 130 *Prometheus* Op. 60: Form

		Measures	Derivation	T	Motives	Comments
Exposition (mm. 1–192)						
Intro						
1–26	A1a	1–4			6–34	
	b	5–8			a_1	
	c	9–12			a_{2-3}	
	2a (1)	13–14	a_2	6		
	(2)	15–16	a_2	3		
	(3)	16–17	a_2	0		
	b (1)	17–18	a_2	0		A2b = A2a, T_6
	(2)	19–20	a_2	9		
	(3)	20–21	a_2	6		
	3a (1)	21			b_1	
	(2)	22–23			c_2	foreshadows mm. 30–34
	b (1)	23–24			b_{1-2}	
	(2)	24–26				
26–69	B1a (1)	26–30			c_1	
	(2)	30–34			c_{2-3}	compare accompaniment, mm. 14–15
	b	34–42	B1a	9	c_{1-3}	
	c (1)	42–45	c_2	6		
	(2)	45–46	c_2	0		
	(3)	46–47	c_2	6		
	2a (1)(a)	47–48	c_1	0		transitional; foreshadows C1
	(b)	49–50	B2a(1)(a)	8		
	(2)(a)	50–53	c_1	7		
	(b)	53	b_2			
	(3)	53–54			d_1	
	B2b (1)	55–58			c_1	B2b(1–3) = B2a, T_{12}
	(2)	58–61			c_1	
	(3)	61–65			d_1	repeated to extend
	(4)	65–66			d_2	anticipates mm. 151–56
	(5)	67–69			b_2	transitional
69–114	C1a (1)	69–73			e_1	
	(2)(a)	74–76				
	(b)	76–78				= mm. 74–76 an octave lower
	b (1)	79–81			b_2, d_1	compare mm. 53–54
	(2)	81–83			b_2	= mm. 67–69, T_0
	a (3)	83–86			e_1	= mm. 69–71, T_0
	(4)	86			b_2	
	2a (1)(a)	87–88			e_2	C2 is a developmental episode
	(b)	89–91				development of e_2
	(2)(a)	91–92			e_2	mm. 91–93 = C2a(1), mm. 87–89, T_0
	(b)	93–94			e_2	m. 94 = m. 93, T_1 for melody
	(3)(a)	95–96	e_2	8, 2	e_2	

Example 130 (cont.)

		Measures	Derivation	T	Motives	Comments
	(b)	97–99			e_2	compare C2a(2)(b), m. 97 = m. 93, T_2; successive Ts with t = 1
	b	99–106	a_1 (m. 99)	6	a_1, e_3	e_3 represented in chromatic appoggiatura figure
			(m. 103)	6		
			(m. 105)	2		
	a (4)	107–11			e_2	
	c	111–14			c_2	transition
115–30	D1a	115–18			a_3, c_2, b_2	
	b	119–22	D1a	1		
	2a (1)(a)	123				= m. 115, T_7
	(b)	124	D2a(1)(a)	6		
	(2)	125–26	D2a(1)			one octave lower
	b(1)(a)	127			a_3, e_2	
	(b)	128				= m. 127, T_0
	(2)	129–30			b_2	
130–51	E1a	130–34			a_{1-2}, b_2	transformed
	b	134–38	E1a	5	add c_2	
	2a	138–43			e_3	climactic phrase
	b(1)(a)	143–44			e_4	
	(2)(a)	145				
	(b)	146			f_1	derived from a_2
	(1)(b)	147–49	E2b(1)	6		
	(3)	149–51				transition
151–72	F1a (1)	151–52			d_2, a_3	
	(2)	153–54			d_3, a_3	
	(3)	154–56			d_4, c_4	
	b	157–62	F1a	0		
	2a	163–66			d_3	compare mm. 146 and 166
	b(1)	167–70	F2a	0		
	(2)	171–72				extension
Close						
172–92	G1	172–80	B		c_1, d_1, d_2	= mm. 58–66, T_{10}
	2	181–86	E		e_4, f_1	mm. 181–84 = mm. 143–46, T_0; mm. 185–86 = mm. 183–84, T_0
	3	187–92			a_1 (T_3)	ascending fourth derived from a_2 (compare m. 146)
Development (mm. 192–370)						
	(B?) 1a (1)	192–97			f_1	derived from a_2, b_1
	(2)	197–200			b_1	
	(3)	200–02			c_2, b_1	
	b(1–3)	202–12	Devel. 1a	8		
	(4)	213–14			c_2	= mm. 111–14, T_0
	(D) 2a	215–18			a_3, c_2, b_2	= mm. 115–18, T_4
	b(1)	219–21				= mm. 119–21, T_4 (or 215–17, T_1)
	(2)	222				= m. 221, T_3

Example 130 (cont.)

	Measures	Derivation	T	Motives	Comments
(A + B) 3a (1)	223–25			c_2, c_4	c_2 in augmentation and diminution
b	225–26			a_1 (T_9)	accompaniment from m. 31
a (2)	227–29	Devel. 3a(1)	0	c_2	
c (1)	229–31			d_1, c_2	
d(1)	231–33			a_1, b_1, c_2	a_1 at T_8; anticipation of mm. 236–41
c (2)	233–35	Devel. 3c(1)		d_1, b_1, c_2	an octave higher
e	235–36			b_1, c_2	
(A + B) 4a (1)	236–41			a_{1-2}, c_2, f_1	a_{1-2} at T_8; transformation
b(1)	241–42			c_2	
c	243–44			e_1	= mm. 69–71, T_4
b(2)	245–47			c_2	
(A + B) 3c (3)	247–49	Devel. 3c(1)	5	b_1, d_1	
d(2)	249–51	Devel. 3d(1)	5	a_1, b_1, c_2	
f	251–52			e_1, c_2	compare mm. 243–44; accompaniment = mm. 235–36, T_5
g	253–54			a_3, c_2	compare mm. 115–16; accompaniment = mm. 235–36, T_5
(A + B) 4a (2)	254–59			b_1	mm. 254–60 = mm. 236–42, T_5
b(2)	259–60				
(B + D) 5a	261–64			c_2, a_3	bass = 5–13 (derived from e_2); m. 264 compare section D
b(1)	265–68	Devel. 5a	1		mm. 261–70 compare mm. 115–22
(2)(a)	269–70				= mm. 267–68, T_1
(b)	271–72				= mm. 269–70, T_1
c	273–76			a_3, c_2, c_4	transition
(B + F) 6a (1)	277–81			c_2, c_4	
b(1)	281–83			c_2	
c (1)	283–85			c_4	
a (2)	285–89	Devel. 6a(1)	9	c_2, c_4, d_2	
d(1)	289–93			c_4, d_2	cello derived from a_1, a_2 = 6–Z19, compare mm. 131–34
e (1)	293–98	Devel. 6a(2)	5		transformation; strings (mm. 281–86) combined with trumpet (mm. 285–89)
(2)	299–301				transitional; a_1 in cello
f (1)	301–04			c_4	compare mm. 127–30
(2)	305–08			c_4, f_1	
(D) 7	309–24			a_3, c_2, b_2	= mm. 115–30, T_4
(E) 8a (1)	325–28			a_{1-3}	= mm. 131–34, T_4, transformed; setting from Devel. 7

Example 130 (cont.)

	Measures	Derivation	T	Motives	Comments
(2)(a)	329–30			a_3, b_1, c_{2-3}	
(b)	331–32			c_{1-2}, d_2	
b	333–40	Devel. 8a(1)	5	c_4	c_4 added in mm. 339–40 as transition to . . .
(E) 9a (1)(a)	341–42			a_1, c_2, c_4, a_3	a_1 begins at T_5 from m. 333
(b)	343–44	Devel. 9a(1)(a)	2		
(2)(a)	345–47			a_{1-3}, e_3, f_1	
(b)	348–50	Devel. 9a(2)(a)	2		
b	351–60	Devel. 9a	2		
c (1)(a)	361–63			a_{1-3}	= melody in mm. 355–57 at T_3
(b)	363–64			b_2	apotheosis
(2)(a)	365–67				9c(2) = 9c(1), T_0
(b)(1)	367–68				
(2)	369–70				= mm. 367–68 two octaves lower
Recapitulation (mm. 370–606)					
B3	370–90				= mm. 26–46, T_8
C3a	391–408				= mm. 67–84, T_8
4a (1)	407–08			e_1, b_1	= mm. 393–94, T_0
(2)	409–10			c_{2-3}	
b	411–14	C4a	2		
5a	415–16				
b	417–18	C5a	4		
4c – d	419–26	C4	7		
5c – d	427–30	C5	7		
e (1)	431–32				= mm. 429–30, T_4
(2)	433				= m. 432, T_3
f	433–35				
6a (1)	435–36				
(2)	437–38	C6a(1)			one octave lower
D3	451–58	D1	8		
D4a (1)	459–61			a_3, c_2	transition
(2)	461–62			add c_4	
b	463–66			a_3, c_4	
E3a	467–78			a_{1-3}, c_4	apotheosis; = mm. 130–34, T_8; a_3 subjected to successive Ts with t = 1
b	479–90			a_{1-2}	= mm. 135–38, T_8
4a	491–503			e_3	= mm. 138–43, T_8; a_3 in m. 492 = a_3 in m. 459, T_0; violins reach high C in m. 498, an octave higher than in m. 468
b(1)	504–06			e_4	= mm. 143–45, T_8 (or mm. 147–49, T_2)

Example 130 (cont.)

		Measures	Derivation	T	Motives	Comments
	(2)	506–07			c_2, d_1	= mm. 149–50, T_2
	c	508–09			e_3	
	b(2)	510–11			c_2, d_1	= mm. 506–07, T_0
	(3)	512–13				= m. 507, T_2
Coda (?)						
	F3a(1)	514–17			d_{2-3}	= mm. 151–54, T_2
	(2)	518–19				extension
	(3)	520–21			d_4	= mm. 155–56, T_2
	b(1)	522–29			a_1, c_2	mm. 522–41 compare mm. 407–38; mm. 526–29 compare mm. 415–18
	(2)	530–37	F3b(1)	0		
	(3)	538–41				extension
	4	542–57				= mm. 514–29, T_0
	E5a	558–61				mm. 558–73 = mm. 131–44, T_8
	b	562–65				
	6a(1)	566–69			e_3(?)	
	(2)	570–73			e_4	
	5c	574–75				= mm. 558–65 condensed
	d(1)	576–77	E5c	5		
	(2)	578				= m. 577, T_3
	(3)	579				= m. 577, T_6
	(4)	580				= m. 577, T_9
	6b(1)	581–84	E6a	0		condensed
	(2)	585–88	E6b(1)	0		
	(3)	589–90				= mm. 587–88, T_0
Codetta		591–606			f_1, c_4	compare mm. 192–97, T_8

then of c_2 alone at T_6 in mm. 42–45 (echoed in the brass at T_0 and T_6 in mm. 45–47). A jocular transformation of c_1 occurs in the piano in mm. 47–50, foreshadowing the scherzando mood of section C and effecting a transition to a lush setting of c_1 in which the previously opposed winds and piano are entwined. Motive d_1 is interjected in the piano in mm. 53–54, and then the passage in mm. 47–54 is varied in mm. 55–65. This repetition is extended by an enigmatic statement of d_2 by the piano (mm. 65–66), immediately following d_1. The meaning of d_2 will not be clear until its return in m. 149, where it occurs in expanded form as the theme of section F. In m. 67, the tempo quickens after a brief pause as a chromatic ascent in tremolo strings leads to section C. This gesture, derived from b_2, corresponds closely to the upbeat gesture which usually preceded theme D in the *Poem of Ecstasy*—a gesture which had strong tonal connotations in the earlier work.

The e_1 motive with which section C begins in m. 69 is itself reminiscent of the

Poem of Ecstasy, in this case of b_1, the main theme of that work. Indeed, the arrival of motive e_1 in *Prometheus* is much like the arrival of the main theme after a slow introduction in a conventional sonata. The piano spins forth this scherzolike theme, its phrases intermittently echoed by various woodwinds until m. 79, when b_2 and d_1 interrupt the regular meter. Motive e_1 is reintroduced in m. 83, but the mood is broken shortly thereafter by the unexpected seriousness of motive e_2. As explained above, the contrasting phrase which follows e_2 in mm. 89–90 is a development of that motive. In subsequent measures, the original e_2 alternates with this developmental phrase, progressing sequentially. This leads to a new section (*avec délice*) beginning in m. 99 in which a_1 is played successively by tremolo violins, solo violin, and solo horn. In m. 107 the development of e_2 resumes with a rapid crescendo, culminating in a statement of c_2 in mm. 111–14. The episode connecting the sequential treatment of e_2 in m. 91 and the climactic statement of c_2 in the trumpet in mm. 111–14 is a single gesture developing the e_2 subject. (If e_2 is considered a derivative of e_1, then the entire section C2 would constitute a development of e_1.) Significantly, no portion of mm. 87–114 recurs in the composition, reinforcing the analysis of this material as developmental. Certainly the statements of a_1 in mm. 99–106 are best understood as part of a developmental process.

Section D (mm. 115–30) is based on the development of a_3 in a new transformation (*avec émotion et ravissement* [emotional, rapturous]). Here the oboe and English horn play a version of a_3, set against a motive in the harp and viola which is derived from the first four pitches of a_3. This gesture is answered by b_2, and the texture is further enriched by c_2 played almost as a glissando by the clarinets. This material, stated within two measures, is extended over the next fourteen measures, effecting a transition to section E.

In sections C and D, a_1 and a_3 were reintroduced, developed, and, in the case of the latter, considerably transformed—a process which distinguishes this work altogether from Scriabin's earlier extended forms. The transformation of these materials culminates at the beginning of section E (mm. 130–51), when the piano presents a_{1-2} as a *thème large majestueux*. The four-measure phrase is repeated at T_5 with a crescendo, climaxing with the arching phrase of e_3 (*avec enthousiasme*), which enters here for the first time. Played in the high register of the violins, this phrase quickly dies away, and the piano replies with e_4. The passage continues with further abrupt shifts in mood. The moment of repose provided by the limpid material of m. 145 is disturbed in the following measure by an ominous trumpet call. As quickly as it came, this gesture is replaced by the transposed repetition of e_4 played tenderly by solo violin.

In section F (mm. 151–72), the unaccompanied piano presents the d_2 material extended by d_3 and d_4. The setting of d_{2-3} is enriched by statements of a_3 in counterpoint, and the introduction of d_4 coincides with the first appearance of c_4. This material is then repeated, somewhat transformed, at T_0. Motive d_3 is freely developed in the undulating, waltzlike material which extends section F to m. 172.

Section G closes the exposition. No real development of motives occurs here;

rather, the tensions of the exposition diminish as quieter motives are repeated literally. Measures 172–80 are a variation of the presentation of c_1, d_1, and d_2 in mm. 58–66 of section B, transposed to T_{10}. This leads directly to a literal repetition (at T_0) of the enigmatic conclusion of section E (specifically mm. 143–46). The portentous trumpet call sounds again at the end of the exposition (mm. 184 and 186), followed by a_1 in its original setting (but at T_3). Fading in the distance, the trumpet call sounds twice more.

Given the extent to which motives are developed and transformed thus far, we might well doubt that the exposition extends as far as m. 192. There is strong evidence that it does, however. The parallelism of the cadenzalike piano fanfares beginning each section is a conspicuous and significant feature in the overall form. The function of section G as a codetta cannot be ignored. This is the only section thus far in which subsections of other formal divisions are literally repeated; in fact, the entire codetta is formed by literal repetitions from sections A, B, and E. These materials all help to reduce tension. The exposition as presently defined is framed by the restatement of the opening a_1 motive (mm. 5–8) in mm. 187–92 and, at a larger level, by sections A and G, which introduce and close the main body of material. As evidence for this view, sections B–F—and only these sections—recur in the recapitulation. The correspondence between recapitulation and exposition indicates that each of these sections is a traditional thematic group; even in the case of D, where content is entirely derivative, each section is distinct because of the special character of its material. Therefore thematic identity depends in some cases on factors other than motivic content.

In the development (mm. 192–370), the combination of various thematic groups is so complex that it would be misleading in the outline (example 130) to label each section with a single letter. Accordingly, the nine sections have been numbered instead, with thematic correspondences in parentheses. An interesting feature of the opening piano fanfare is that the ascending f_1 motive, whose derivation from b_1 is not obvious, is the antecedent phrase of the descending phrase extending the original b_1 motive. A counterpoint, beginning in m. 194 in the horns, gradually spells out the c_2 motive. This counterpoint begins with the first two elements of c_2, followed by a restatement of these to which the third element is added. This process continues until the full motive occurs in mm. 201–02 as a transition to the repetition at T_8 of mm. 192–202.

In mm. 213–14, c_2 is repeated as a transition to the second section of the development, which is a literal repetition of section D (mm. 115–21) at T_4. The sweeping, quasi-glissandi statements of c_2 associated hereafter with this material are integral throughout the development to the increasingly contrapuntal texture. Section 3 presents a highly charged situation in which c_2, stated in augmentation in the trumpets, is an antecedent phrase answered fortissimo in the horns by the first statement of a_1 at a loud dynamic level. Repeated in mm. 227–29, c_2 is answered the second time by d_1 in the piano. In an episode marked *avec un effroi contenu* (with fear held in check), a_1 is stated softly by the oboe and is answered by d_1 an octave higher. Motive b_1 is prevalent throughout this passage.

Motive a_1 returns in section 4, a stormy passage with repeated surges of c_2 in the strings and bellicose horn calls in driving rhythms. This is the backdrop to a mezzo piano statement of a_1 by two trombones; at this level the idea may well be engulfed by the counterpoint, particularly when three horns enter in m. 239 with motive f_1 played forte. Such a dynamic marking is clearly significant in this depiction of a superhuman struggle. In this passage, a_1 is followed directly by a_2. In m. 241, the climax of the passage, the solo trumpet plays a confident statement of c_2, which is cut off before the final tone, displaced by oddly contrasting e_1 material in a condensed version of mm. 69–71 at T_4. The trumpet repeats c_2 to an increasingly agitated accompaniment, completing the motive in m. 247. Material from section 3 (mm. 229–33) now recurs at T_5, with a_1 played piano by two horns. In mm. 251–54, the accompaniment corresponds at T_5 to that in mm. 233–36, but instead of returning to d_1 as expected, Scriabin alludes to sections C and D. The tempestuous material of mm. 236–42 is restated at T_5 in mm. 254–60, modified by the addition of a_3 played glissando in the woodwinds and by the abbreviated version of f_1 in the horns. As before, c_2 is cut off at the penultimate note, and a new section follows.

Section 5 (mm. 261–76) alternates two highly contrasting passages: in one, c_2 wails in tremolo strings and woodwinds, with a syncopated bass transformation of e_2; the other is a brief, veiled statement of the sensuous material of section D. Section 5 is transitional, with successive repetitions of the juxtaposed materials (first literal, then truncated) with $t = 1$. At the end the bells and flutes introduce the sparkling c_4 motive in anticipation of the scintillating orchestral effects of the following section.

Section 6 is essentially a transformation of c_2, stated broadly in augmentation by the horns in mm. 277–81. When this statement is repeated fortissimo at T_9 by the trumpets in mm. 285–89, Scriabin increases the drama by adding in counterpoint a glorious transformation of d_2, played in the high register of the violins, with trills and tremolos. The transformation climaxes in m. 293 when mm. 281–89 are restated at T_5. Tension is heightened in the counterpoint by a shift in the alignment of parts: horns play c_2 as in mm. 285–89 while the strings repeat mm. 281–86. The moment of joy subsides during the transition in mm. 301–08.

Absent since m. 250, the piano enters in m. 305 with a passage unique in its mechanical repetitions and its emphasis on the unadorned augmented triad. As shown in example 131, however, the passage is actually a fanciful development of b_1 and c_2 through sets 3–9 and 5–30 respectively. The forms of 5–30 are equivalent at T_8, yielding maximum invariance. Three pcs are retained in all forms—[3,7,11]—the augmented triad formed by all elements on the middle staff, conspicuous in the right-hand part as well.

Having restated part of the original D material at T_4 early in the development (mm. 215–22), Scriabin now returns to this material at the same level. In fact, section 7 is an almost literal restatement at T_4 of the entire original D episode. As in the exposition, this episode leads to E material, also at T_4, as the subject of section 8. Here, however, E is presented in a new light. In the original, a_{1-2} were the *thème large majestueux*, but here they are stated tenderly by solo violin

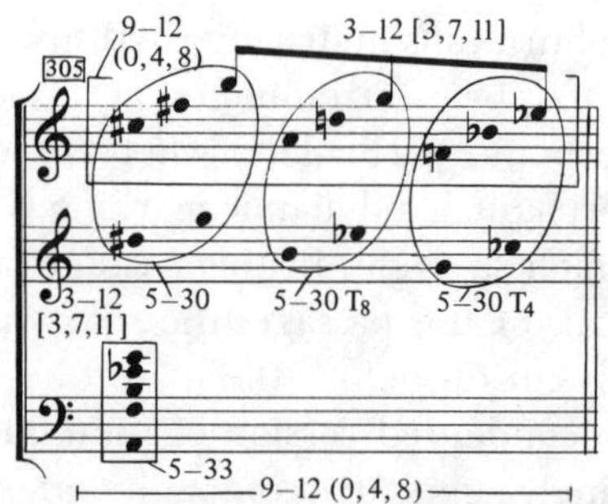

Example 131 *Prometheus* Op. 60

in a setting which continues from the preceding section. As in the original E section, the first four measures in section 8 are subsequently transposed to T_5. Here, however, each basic four-measure phrase is extended by a phrase of equal length, thus doubling the size of this section. The first extension is based on a rich assortment of motives: a_1, b_1, c_1, c_2, c_3, and d_2. The motivic content of the phrase in mm. 325–32 mirrors the first two sections of the exposition (mm. 1–69); in fact, the order of these ideas here is almost their original sequence. In the second extending phrase (mm. 337–40), c_4 replaces d_2 in the bells and flutes, anticipating the sparkling orchestration of section 9.

This section begins with a_1 stated at T_5 from its presentation in m. 333 of section 8, thus continuing the pattern of transposition. Here, however, a_1 is not followed by a_2; rather, the initial two-measure phrase is repeated at T_2. Thus the pace of the sequence increases drastically with the instruction *de plus en plus animé*. Tension is also heightened by the complex counterpoint of this setting. The sparkling motive c_4 is now played in sixteenth notes in the flutes, bells, and—for the first time—celesta, while the piano plays rapidly descending arpeggiations of c_2 in alternation with descending glissandi in the harps. The clarinet part is a thirty-second-note diminution of c_2, fragmented as in the horn part at the beginning of the development (mm. 194–202). Most conspicuous here is the addition of an expressive countermelody, based on a_3, in the cellos and English horn.

The phrase in mm. 341–44 is the antecedent of a powerfully arching consequent phrase in mm. 345–46, in counterpoint with f_1 in the horns and trumpets. (Motive c_4 and associated orchestral effects drop out in this consequent phrase.) The antecedent, played with great intensity in multiple octaves by both the piano and the strings—a unique coupling—is based on e_3. Indeed, the basic sequence of events at this point in the development continues to follow the exposition, where e_3 was a broader phrase (mm. 138–43) culminating the sequential treatment of the transformed a_{1-2} idea. However, the consequent phrase has another, equally important source of derivation: motives a_{1-3}, the main theme of the work. As shown in example 132, the first five notes of this melody form 5–21, the aggregate set of a_{1-3}. To balance the antecedent phrase in mm. 341–44, the material in mm. 345–47 is repeated at T_0.

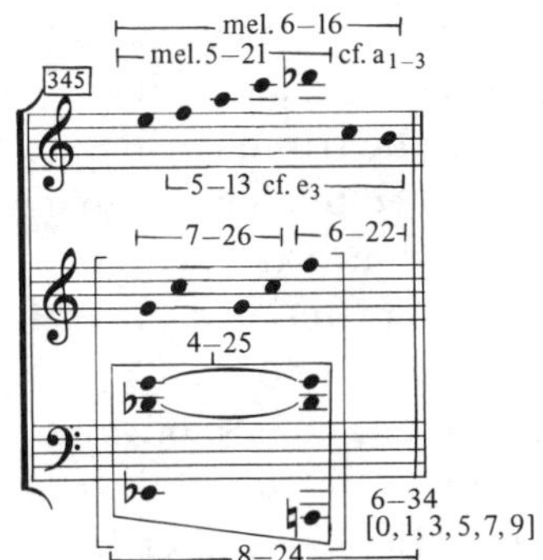

Example 132 *Prometheus* Op. 60

Tension mounts as the arching phrase in mm. 341–50 is transposed up two half steps. The repetition is almost literal; the main change involves even more active parts in mm. 351–54 for the oboes and clarinets, which now resemble the surging figures in the strings in section 4 of the development. The victorious apotheosis of a_{1-3} occurs in mm. 361–63, the phrase now answered by the assertive chromatic ascent of b_2 replacing the ebbing descent of previous statements. As before, the climactic phrase is repeated at T_0, followed by a repetition of b_2 two octaves lower in mm. 369–70. The sublime transformation of c_1, now presented sonorously by the strings, horns, and bassoons, culminates the development and begins the recapitulation.

The recapitulation opens with a literal restatement in mm. 370–90 of the B material, without the extending B2 episode, at T_8, the general level of transposition throughout the recapitulation. Proceeding directly to the C material, Scriabin repeats (at T_8) mm. 67–84 of the exposition with only minor changes. Hereafter, however, he departs from exact repetition. In mm. 407–38 a tension-building episode alternates material directly derived from C (C4 in the outline) with a passage of dazzling arpeggios in the piano (*flot lumineux* [flooded with light]) accompanying the sequential development of a_1 (C5). The latter passage crescendos to the climactic C6 material (*aigu, fulgurant* [sharp, flashing]) after which tension subsides as the original C material returns in m. 439. In a jocular way Scriabin now eliminates altogether the second measure of this material, thereby obtaining an unexpectedly square and conventional two-measure phrase. To this antecedent he replies with c_3 material, set in counterpoint against material from the D episode. An extension of these materials climaxes with the huge crescendo and ponderous hemiola rhythm in mm. 449–50.

With an abrupt change to pianissimo, a portion of the D episode (mm. 115–22) is now recapitulated at T_8, transformed by the addition of the chorus. Only the altos and basses sing here; in fact, only half of the altos sing a moving line, while the other singers hum sustained chords. In m. 459 the chorus drops out and a transition combining a_3, c_2, and c_4 builds to the grand climax of the composition, the apotheosis of E material.

At this point Scriabin pulls out all the stops. The full chorus (singing vowel sounds) and the organ perform a glorified version of the original section E, again at T_8. Almost all of E is restated, including motives e_3 and e_4. The former reaches a tremendous climax in the trumpets in mm. 498–99, and after a complete diminuendo the latter is stated tenderly by solo violin in mm. 504–06. The original transition from E to F (mm. 149–51) is expanded in mm. 506–13, accelerating to a recapitulation of F material, completely transformed.

Originally an enigmatic single motive (mm. 65–66), later expanded into a full yet still mysterious theme (mm. 151–62), motives d_{2-4} are now played prestissimo and take on the scherzando character of the C material. In fact, mm. 522–41 are not derived from F material, but rather from the developmental extension of C material in the recapitulation (mm. 407–38). Following the pattern of section F in the exposition, the piano introduces the theme (mm. 514–21), which is subsequently repeated (at T_0) by the oboe and doubled by the flute.

Although the restatement of F in mm. 514–57 is technically part of the recapitulation, the character of its transformation is associated in Scriabin's later music with the coda. In this delirious dance the theme is dematerialized, as in the coda of the Tenth Sonata (mm. 306–66), where the E and F materials are similarly transformed. The function of the restatement of F is clarified when it is linked in m. 558 with the ultimate transformation of the E material (at T_8). Having reached its apotheosis at the culmination of the recapitulation, the E material is now caught up in the swirling activity. Already incredibly condensed when it returns in m. 558, the theme is further compressed in mm. 574–75 and 581–84, disappearing altogether in m. 588. As a concluding gesture, the full orchestral forces are summoned for a victorious statement of the f_1 fanfare, equivalent at T_8 to the original presentation. The fanfare reaches its climax with the final chord, an astonishing F♯ major triad, the only simple consonance in the piece. As shown in example 133, the final gesture resolves the Prometheus chord to the F♯ chord over an F♯ pedal (spelled initially as G♭). The entire progression forms 7–30, the complement of c_2 and other motives, and an important set in its own right.

Novel Aspects of Style and Structure

During the three years between composition of the *Poem of Ecstasy* and *Prometheus*, Scriabin's craft had evolved to such an extent that no aspect of his method was unchanged. Nevertheless, the *Poem of Fire* shares many features with the earlier work; even in his most expansive piece, Scriabin adhered to the basic

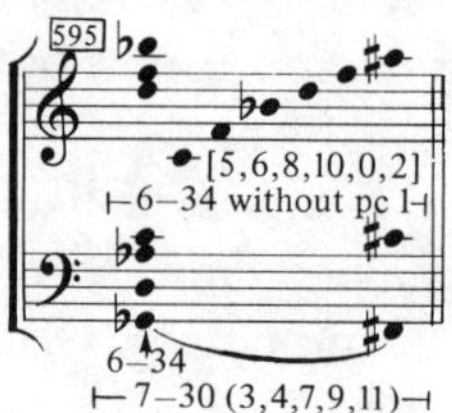

Example 133 *Prometheus* Op. 60

sonata principle. The overall strategy of thematic transformation in *Prometheus* generally parallels that in the *Poem of Ecstasy*. Both developments climax with transformations of the main theme (although in the later work the theme is disguised at this point), and both recapitulations move toward a grand apotheosis of the same material. In fact, the orchestrational settings of the two apotheoses are remarkably similar. Both works end with an ascending arpeggiation beginning pianissimo and building to a sustained chord played with full force. If anything, the tripartite structure in *Prometheus* is even more definite than in the *Poem of Ecstasy*, largely because bold piano statements signal the beginning of each main section. However, the closing section of the exposition in *Prometheus* sets off the exposition from the development, in contrast to the transition between these sections in the *Poem of Ecstasy*. The most important difference between the two forms is the addition of a coda in the later work. Whereas the apotheosis is the grandiose conclusion of the *Poem of Ecstasy*, the process of transformation in *Prometheus* continues beyond the apotheosis, for the main subject is caught up in the delirious dance which follows. Dematerialization marks a significant development in Scriabin's technique of thematic transformation, and the resulting coda is the model for concluding sections in all of his later extended works (that is, the last five sonatas).

The unique exposition of theme D in the *Poem of Ecstasy* is perhaps a precedent for the treatment of d_1 in *Prometheus*. In both cases a fragment of an idea is presented initially and developed only later into a complete melodic thought. The process also applies to motives a_{1-3} in *Prometheus*, which are developed into a genuine melody in the conventional sense only in section E of the exposition. In general, however, the sequence of materials in the *Poem of Ecstasy* fits the conventions of nineteenth-century musico-dramatic structure, whereas the formal procedures in *Prometheus* are highly innovative.

From the beginning of *Prometheus*, the pacing and sequence of materials are extraordinary. Highly contrasting materials are paired and then freely alternated or repeated, creating momentum by the unpredictability of events. The succession of motives in mm. 21–25 is a case in point: b_1–c_2–b_1–b_2–b_1–b_2–b_2. At the root of structural contrasts in *Prometheus* is the concerto principle. In section B of the exposition, for example, the piano makes its first entrance with the imperious c_{2-3} motives sharply contrasted with the contemplative c_1 in the winds. However, there is something peculiar about the relation of these motives and their use in section B. When c_1 first occurs in mm. 26–30, it seems to culminate or continue the A section—an impression reinforced by the assertive piano entrance in m. 30, which would conventionally initiate a new section. The listener is thrown off balance when the succession c_{1-2-3} recurs beginning in m. 34. Because it is the incipit of a repeated pattern, c_1 must be reinterpreted as an antecedent, to which c_{2-3} is the consequent. This play with the listener's expectations is typical of the sequence of motives throughout the composition.

The unpredictable sequencing is especially important in the developmental extension of section C in the exposition (mm. 87–114). The mercurial nature of this passage is almost unprecedented in Scriabin's earlier works. (A rare example is a transitional episode in the development of the Fifth Sonata [mm. 281–89], where D and E materials are linked by alternating fragments of either theme. There is no equivalent passage in the *Poem of Ecstasy*.) In sections 3 and 4 of the development (mm. 223–60), the succession of materials is exceptionally erratic, concealing the conventional transpositional repetitions at T_5 in these measures.

Orchestration is clearly important in sequencing, for the materials which Scriabin juxtaposes are contrasted both in motivic content and in instrumentation and texture. Indeed, a given motive is often associated consistently with a particular setting, so that motive, texture, rhythm, and many other musical attributes are inseparable, as in section D. Scriabin's sequencing of materials thus juxtaposes discrete blocks of sound, each with an independent identity. (This procedure is an important precedent for similar techniques in works composed shortly after *Prometheus*, particularly *The Rite of Spring*.) Perhaps the most dramatic juxtaposition occurs in the development, beginning in m. 261. Here two motives are rapidly alternated in a sequential progression, depicting an extreme vacillation of emotion: terror (*déchirant, comme un cri* [piercing, like a cry])—a transformation of c_2—and bliss (*subitement très doux* [suddenly very sweet])—a brief fragment of section D.

Scriabin's orchestration in the *Poem of Ecstasy*, though brilliant and masterful in every respect, generally adheres to the conventions of Liszt, Tchaikovsky, and especially Wagner. Even those moments which are quintessentially characteristic of Scriabin, such as the dazzling buildup to the climax of the development beginning in m. 246, are rooted in the orchestration of *Der Ring des Nibelungen*, particularly such special effects as the Magic Fire Music at the end of *Die Walküre*. In his use of motivic recombination and superposition to create climaxes on a grand scale, Scriabin certainly aspires toward Wagner's contrapuntal achievements, epitomized in the prelude to *Die Meistersinger*. Nonetheless, there are gestures in the *Poem of Ecstasy* which are uniquely Scriabin's and which anticipate more original use in the *Poem of Fire*. For example, the piccolo in m. 232 and the flute and oboe in mm. 515–18, as well as the flutes and violins in mm. 177–80, are precedents for the widely used c_2 glissando motive first heard in section D of *Prometheus*. The horn glissandi in mm. 173–75 of the *Poem of Ecstasy* do not occur in *Prometheus* but may be a precedent for the more striking horn calls in the *orageux* (stormy) section in the development of the later work (mm. 235–42). The chromatic descents of augmented triads in the woodwinds beginning in m. 231 of the *Poem of Ecstasy* become quasi glissandi in the violins accompanying the piano entrance in mm. 305–08 of *Prometheus*. (Berg later used a similar device in depicting Wozzeck's watery death.) The extremely high first violin line, doubled an octave lower by the second violins, which reaches high F♯ at the climax of the development (m. 298) in the *Poem of Ecstasy* is paralleled in the corresponding section of *Prometheus*, where the violins reach the same high pitch at the climax in m. 363.

Example 134a *Poem of Ecstasy* Op. 54

In *Prometheus* Scriabin's orchestration is as original as his motivic, harmonic, and formal conceptions. A comparison of corresponding portions of the development sections of the *Poem of Ecstasy* (mm. 213–16) and *Prometheus* (mm. 237–42) (examples 134a–b) highlights the innovative orchestration and motivic procedures in the latter work. Both passages depict a tragic struggle, and thus both state main motivic material in the trombones in a stormy setting. In the *Poem of Ecstasy* this concept is handled conventionally, except for the extreme angularity of the trombone line. The melodrama here is almost pro forma; indeed, this is one of the few unconvincing moments in the work. This weakness results mostly from sequential repetition, in which the rumblings of sixteenth-note chromatic scales in the cellos and the lightning strokes in the violins and high woodwinds (involving b_2 in stretto) seem mechanical. Surprisingly, there is no percussion in this passage (though the gong is used in the preceding episode), and the accompaniment consists of sustained chords, played tremolo in the strings and low woodwinds.

In contrast, the *orageux* episode from *Prometheus* is stunningly effective. Great waves are created in the strings by the upward thrusts of c_2 in tremolo, which surge to a climax in m. 241. Cymbals, drums, and glissandi (ascending in the woodwinds, descending in the harp) complete the image. Scriabin's debt to Debussy is clear, although there is nothing quite like this string figuration in *La Mer*. The stroke of lightning in m. 235 is entirely original. A statement of b_1, this gesture doubles the high woodwinds with bright, percussive pizzicato chords in the high register of the violins. Except for this gesture, Scriabin does not use the high winds in this passage. Most astonishing are the echolike horn calls, alternately muted and unmuted, whose jagged rhythms seem independent of the other parts. These calls, with their ferocious glissandi, evoke primordial terror. The entire passage culminates victoriously with the f_1 fanfare played by three horns in mm. 239–41, answered by solo trumpet playing c_2 in mm. 241–42.

without mutes

Example 134b *Prometheus* Op. 60

Example 134b (cont.)

Many of these effects exemplify a new attention to detail which sets the orchestration of *Prometheus* apart from that of Scriabin's other works. His style here approaches the expressionism of his Viennese contemporaries, with individualized gestures often characterized by extreme changes of articulation and dynamics. Example 135 shows some of these novel gestures. The horns in mm. 213–14 play a single pitch embellished by grace notes in a rapid crescendo and decrescendo ranging from pianissimo to forte (example 135a). The trombone part beginning in m. 224 (example 135b) entails even greater dynamic extremes, from *ppp* to *f*. The delicate writing for harp and celesta in mm. 301–03 (*avec une joie éteinte* [with joy extinguished]) indicates a new style of minimal gestures highlighted by unique timbral combinations (example 135c). The strings in mm. 415–19 (*flot lumineux*) rapidly alternate pizzicato and tremolo articulations, and

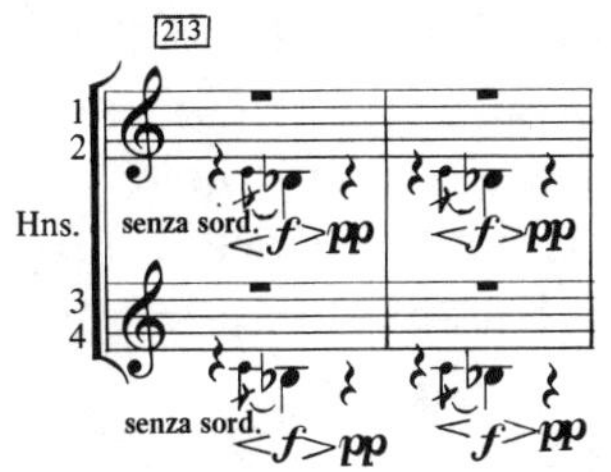

Example 135a *Prometheus* Op. 60

Example 135b *Prometheus* Op. 60

Example 135c *Prometheus* Op. 60

Example 135d *Prometheus* Op. 60

the parts interact with a complexity not found in Scriabin's earlier writing for strings (example 135d). Measures 231–33 (*avec un effroi contenu*) contain several sharply differentiated parts (example 135e). While the oboe plays a_1 legato, the clarinets and flutes play chattering, oscillating figures. The strings here are highly individualized. The cellos and basses double the bassoons with b_1, then continue with rapidly repeated spiccato chords. While the first violins play a sustained harmonic, the second violins play quick tremolo surges of c_2, punctuated by pizzicato chords in the violas.

Despite its innovative features, the orchestration of *Prometheus* was relatively conservative for its time. Apart from the highly specified dynamics and frequent alternations of plucked and bowed articulations, Scriabin does not indicate particular tone colors (for example, *col legno*) or bowings for strings. (The violin harmonics in example 135e are a rare occurrence.) Although Scriabin incorporates a large brass choir, his writing for brass is mostly sustained tones or simple, conventional rhythmic figures. His brass parts are devoid of rapid scalar runs and special tonguing effects, and horn glissandi are extremely rare. (A full-fledged horn glissando does not appear in *Prometheus*, but this effect does occur in m. 173 of the *Poem of Ecstasy*.)

Orchestration has special structural functions in Scriabin's two great poems. Timbral effects are never purely for the sake of color. On the contrary, orches-

Example 135e *Prometheus* Op. 60

tration always reinforces motivic development and, especially, counterpoint. Although the breadth and thematic complexity of the *Poem of Ecstasy* and *Prometheus* seem largely a function of a diverse orchestral palette, the reverse is equally true: the contrapuntal potential of Scriabin's materials and the grandeur of his formal conceptions demanded rich orchestral settings. The technical limitations of writing for solo piano prevented Scriabin from composing piano works as long as the orchestral poems chiefly because the piano did not afford him the means of creating the complex contrapuntal combinations so important in his developmental procedures. Splendid as the sonatas are, we must turn to the orchestral works for a full appreciation of Scriabin's genius in the art of counterpoint.

The addition of organ in the *Poem of Ecstasy* and organ, piano, and wordless chorus in *Prometheus* have a definite impact on musical structure. In each work the organ enters at the moment of apotheosis, reinforcing the culmination of the thematic transformation. The piano and chorus in *Prometheus* are of programmatic significance. The piano is clearly the protagonist in the musical drama and no doubt represents Prometheus; it is characteristically set against the orchestra, which is associated with elemental forces. After a titanic struggle in the development, the piano is victorious, at one with the orchestra. The chorus enters as the apotheosis approaches, representing the human race transfigured by the gift of fire.

Harmony and Structural Coherence

Prometheus has been universally recognized as having a revolutionary harmonic system. The basic component of this system is the mystic chord, 6–34, usually described as being constructed of superposed fourths. (In fact, 6–34 is presented in many ways in the piece, and we need not accept superposed fourths as the basic form of the chord. At the beginning of the piece, where it appears most conspicuously without other materials, 6–34 does not conform to this arrangement.) According to prevalent theories, the Prometheus chord is always present in the piece—although sometimes in incomplete form or with added "nonharmonic" tones—and it may be freely inverted.[5] No theory, however, has specified the laws of harmonic progression in *Prometheus*.

There can be no doubt that 6–34 is the primary chord in *Prometheus* and that it is almost always present. Example 136 lists normal-order forms of 6–34 in the

Example 136 Selected Forms of 6–34 in *Prometheus* Op. 60

	Measure	PC Content (Normal Order)
Exposition	1	6,7,9,11,1,3*
	29	3,4,*6*,8,10,0
	63	10,11,1,3,5,7
	69	3,4,*6*,8,10,0
	87	2,3,*5*,7,9,11
	111	2,3,*5*,7,9,11
	144	2,3,*5*,7,9,11
	184	9,*10*,0,2,4,6
Development	193	9,*10*,0,2,4,6
	203	5,*6*,8,10,0,2
	212	2,3,5,7,*9*,11
	223	6,7,*9*,11,1,3
	225	3,4,*6*,8,10,0
	231	2,3,5,7,*9*,11
	241	10,11,1,3,*5*,7

Example 136 (cont.)

	Measure	PC Content (Normal Order)
	243	7,8,10,0,*2*,4
	245	10,11,1,3,*5*,7
	247	7,8,10,0,*2*,4
	259	3,4,6,8,*10*,0
	261	6,*7*,9,11,1,3
	263	0,1,3,5,*7*,9
	271	3,4,6,8,*10*,0
	278	4,5,7,9,*11*,1
	282	1,2,*4*,6,8,10
	293	6,7,*9*,11,1,3
	301	2,3,5,7,*9*,11
	312	8,*9*,11,1,3,5
	323	6,7,*9*,11,1,3
	325	3,4,*6*,8,10,0
	330	8,9,*11*,1,3,5
	338	1,2,*4*,6,8,10
	343	3,4,*6*,8,10,0
	347	0,1,*3*,5,7,9
	351	3,4,*6*,8,10,0
	361	5,6,*8*,10,0,2
	364	2,*3*,5,7,9,11
Recapitulation	371	11,0,*2*,4,6,8
	390	5,6,*8*,10,0,2
	393	11,0,*2*,4,6,8
	425	10,11,*1*,3,5,7
	486	3,4,*6*,8,10,0
	492	11,0,*2*,4,6,8
	498	11,0,2,4,6,8†
	506	10,11,1,3,5,7‡
	564	3,4,*6*,8,10,0
	584	5,*6*,8,10,0,2
	595	5,*6*,8,10,0,2
	602	1,10,*6*

*The sounding bass note is italicized.
†G♮ in bass (anticipation).
‡Over tonic pedal (anticipation?).

piece. Von Gleich has noted a special relation between the part for color organ and the succession of forms of 6–34 throughout the piece. Despite flaws in his analysis, his thesis is correct: an element of each 6–34 is nearly always represented in the color organ.[6] This pitch class is almost invariably the third element in the normal-order form and is the element which von Gleich considers the root of the harmony. (This note appears in the bass if the chord is spelled as a series of superposed fourths.) Thus the color organ is a type of continuo, providing a fundamental-bass analysis for the entire work. In example 136, the actual pitch class in the bass of each set is italicized. In many cases the bass motion does not coincide with the "root" progressions, and thus even more questions arise about the logic of harmonic progression in this work.

Although the harmonic language of *Prometheus* is certainly innovative, its origins in the later tonal works are clear. The *Poem of Ecstasy* developed many of the important sonorities in the *Poem of Fire*, including the mystic chord. Examples 137a–b present analyses of set structure in the introductory passages of the *Poem of Ecstasy* and *Prometheus* respectively. Although boldly different in many respects, the introduction to *Prometheus* is strikingly similar to that of the *Poem of Ecstasy* in set content. In both the featured sets are 4–19, 5/7–21, and 6–34; all undergo similar processes of transposition. In the earlier work, a_1 forms 4–19, which is stated in sequence at T_0, T_5, and T_9. The first two 4–19s form 7–21, which is also the aggregate of all three forms, and the second and third together

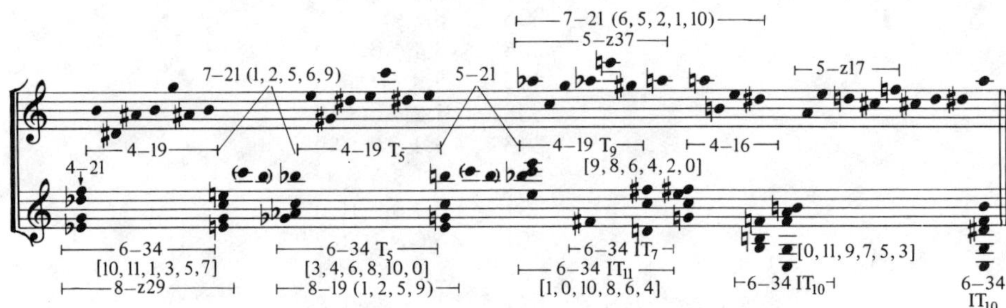

Example 137a *Poem of Ecstasy* Op. 54: Introduction

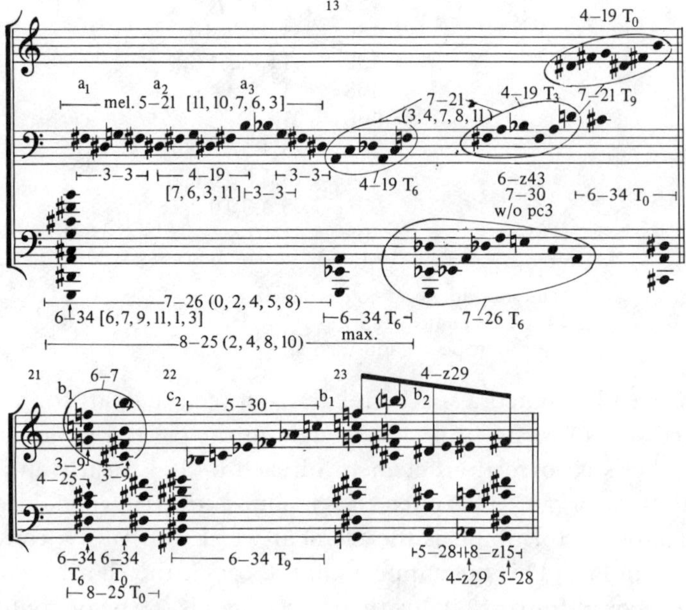

Example 137b *Prometheus* Op. 60: Introduction

form 5–21. The third statement of a_1 leads to the a_2 motive (4–16); these sets combine in a form of 7–21 which shares six pitch classes with the original. Set 6–34 is formed by motive a_1 and its accompanying whole-tone harmony. When 4–19 is transposed to T_5, 6–34 also appears at this level, but later this correspondence breaks down. With the third statement of 4–19, 6–34 occurs at IT_{11}, a form which shares five pcs with the preceding form at T_5. With the entrance of the trumpet in m. 12, the sequence is broken and tension mounts in anticipation of the *imperioso* motive (4–16). At this point (m. 12), 6–34 is stated at IT_7—the literal complement of the original presentation.

Not surprisingly, the introduction to *Prometheus* treats the most important sets in cycles of transposition more rigorously patterned than those in the *Poem of Ecstasy*. The basic intervals of progression, which consistently relate forms of 4–19, 5/7–21, and 6–34, are T_3 and its multiples, T_6 and T_9. Oddly enough, strict adherence to this pattern results in a much less thorough exploitation of the nontonal potential of these sets than in the introduction to the *Poem of Ecstasy*. No forms are related by inversion, and hence there is no literal complementation of the mystic chord (the literal complement occurs only through inversion). For sets 4–19 and 6–34, however, T_6 yields maximum invariance, which is important in the handling of both sets, particularly in the extremely condensed motive b_1 (m. 21).

Our analysis has not yet answered several important questions relating to overall coherence in *Prometheus*. Although the mystic chord permeates virtually the entire composition, we must nevertheless come to grips with the F♯ major chord reverberating in our ears and minds after the piece ends. Did the composer of the Fifth Sonata merely tack on the final chord as a concession to tradition? What is the meaning of F♯ major in this work? And what of the discrepancy between the actual bass progression throughout the piece and the succession of forms of 6–34, a problem observed in example 136? These crucial questions have not yet been addressed in the literature.

The parallels we have observed in the harmony of the two orchestral poems suggest that a closer comparison between *Prometheus* and the late tonal works—particularly with regard to bass progression—might lead toward solutions to these problems. The repetition of materials at T_5 in section E of *Prometheus* (m. 130) and at a larger level in the repetition of sections 3 and 4 (mm. 247–60) of the development are comparable to tonal sequences in earlier works (for instance, mm. 27–38 of the *Poem of Ecstasy* and especially mm. 27–42 and 317–28 in the Fifth Sonata). Moreover, Scriabin occasionally employs the circle-of-fifths progression in *Prometheus* (for example, mm. 277–85), which is used extensively in earlier works and in the development of the Fifth Sonata (example 111b, middleground sketch, mm. 207–51). The chromatic ascent in the turbulent episode in the development of *Prometheus* in mm. 261–71 (*déchirant, comme un cri—subitement très doux*) is analogous to the chromatic descent in the *tragico* section of the development in the *Poem of Ecstasy* (mm. 213–22).

In *Prometheus* the bass moves generally by tritone or descending fifth, and to

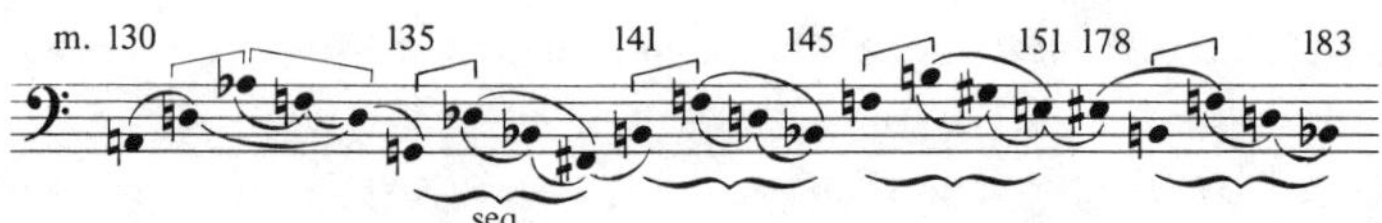

Example 138a *Prometheus* Op. 60

Example 138b *Poem of Ecstasy* Op. 54

a lesser degree by third. The resulting bass progressions are often similar to those in the *Poem of Ecstasy*. Compare, for instance, the bass line of section E, mm. 130–83 of *Prometheus* (example 138a), with that of section E, mm. 127–41 of the *Poem of Ecstasy* (example 138b). Of course, the tritone and fifth in succession are associated with the quintessential bass progression in Scriabin's tonal music: ♭II–V–I. In fact, the bass progression in mm. 135–39 of *Prometheus* (marked with a brace in example 138a) strongly resembles this cadential progression and seems to have tonal connotations. This progression is later repeated sequentially in a passage extending to the end of the exposition, leading the bass progression to B♭. Significantly, this motivic progression is equally important in mm. 498–506, just before the coda, when it progresses to F♯, which is effectively sustained for the rest of the piece.

Is this progression in some sense a cadence to F♯? If so, is F♯ then structurally significant? Because of the correspondences between bass progressions in *Prometheus* and the earlier tonal works, the implications of tonal structure in this work should be considered. Accordingly, a sketch of the bass progression of *Prometheus* is presented in example 139. As we have seen, parts of this bass progression correspond to those of the Fifth Sonata and the *Poem of Ecstasy*, but in *Prometheus* many of the harmonic and contrapuntal aspects considered in analyzing the earlier works are no longer in evidence. Nevertheless, using the conventions of bass progression in the tonal works as a guide, we can use Schenkerian techniques to determine underlying progressions at middleground and even background levels. These techniques reveal an astonishing feature of structure: *Prometheus* is constructed on a bass progression conforming in every respect to those of his late tonal pieces and in this sense is a tonal composition.

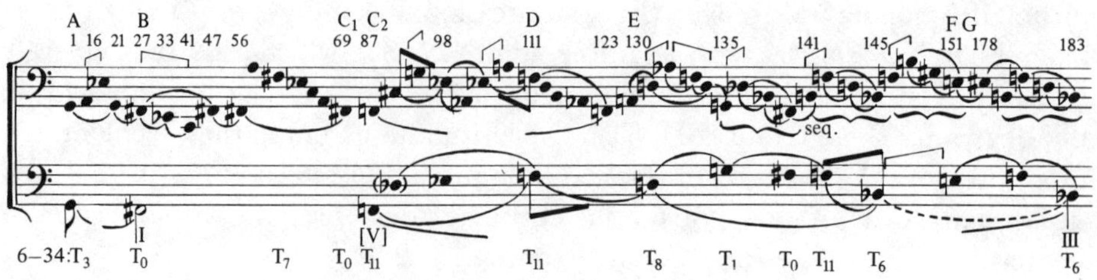

Example 139a *Prometheus* Op. 60: Exposition

In explicating the sketches in example 139, it is impossible to cite harmonic evidence for any particular analytical choice, for harmonic components are nontriadic throughout this piece. The bass is the primary agent of tonality, and only by implication. In an overview of the middleground sketch, the role of F♯ is clear: it is asserted as the tonic by a large-scale cadence from V, prolonged through the latter half of the recapitulation (mm. 425–505), to I (m. 506). The arrival of the tonic coincides almost exactly with the beginning of the coda. Not surprisingly, the piece has a nontonic beginning, but F♯ appears in the bass at the beginning of section B, recalling the tonic near the beginning of the *Poem of Ecstasy*. In fact, the arrival of the tonic in m. 19 of the latter work, coinciding with the exposition of a_3 (lento, *soavamente* [suave]), is strikingly similar to the bass progression to F♯ in *Prometheus* as the *contemplatif* material is first presented. The harmonic progression in the introductory section of *Prometheus* prolongs G♮, the upper auxiliary to the tonic. The tonic is prolonged throughout sections B and C1. With the sudden shift in mood in m. 87 (*voluptueux, presque avec douleur*), however, F♯ descends to F♮. This pitch is then prolonged throughout the developmental episode C2 as well as section D, where the prolongation is effected by an octave transfer arpeggiated through set 4–28. The long-range motion in section E is the unfolding from F♮ at the end of D, through D♮ at the beginning of E, to B♭ in m. 145, coinciding with a moment of repose (*limpide*). (The bass in mm. 144–45 reflects the same motion locally.) Section F is supported throughout by a pedal on E♮; the resulting tritone progression formed with B♭ (m. 145) prolongs B♭. In the closing section of the exposition, E♮ progresses to F♮, an applied dominant which returns to B♭ in m. 183 with the repetition (at T_0) of the *limpide* gesture. In the larger view, F♮ prolonged in the middleground in mm. 87–130 is the applied dominant of B♭ attained by the end of the exposition. (Because of the continuing sequence after m. 145 and the introduction of new material in section F, the earlier B♭ is an anticipation of the stronger B♭ in m. 183.) The overall harmonic motion in the exposition, then, is from F♯ to B♭, or more specifically from tonic to mediant (spelled more properly as A♯). The resemblance of this motion to the tonal plan of the exposition of the Fifth Sonata is startling. Both works, perhaps not coincidentally, are in the same key.

Attained only at the end of the exposition, the mediant is prolonged through the first five sections of the development (mm. 193–276) by a complex progression. Section 1 begins with the piano's fanfarelike cadenza supported by B♭ in the bass. The repetition of this passage at T_8 (mm. 202–12) occurs in conjunction with a consonant skip from B♭ to G♭. Section 2 prolongs A♮ in the bass by an unfolding through 4–28. Section 3 also is based on A♮, with a brief consonant skip to F♯ in mm. 225–26. Beginning on A♮ in m. 236, the bass in section 4 skips to F♮ in mm. 241–42. When sections 3 and 4 are repeated at T_5 in mm. 247–60, the resulting bass progresses from D♮ to B♭. Considering sections 3 and 4 (mm. 223–60) as a single gesture, the underlying progression moves from A♮ to B♭—a major seventh unfolded in descending thirds. The bass leaps to G♮ at the beginning of section 5 and then moves chromatically upward with the sequence, returning to B♭ in m. 271. At a deeper level, the A♮ prolonged from m. 212 until the arrival of B♭ in m. 259 is the lower auxiliary to the mediant.

At the beginning of section 6, the bass progresses to B♮ and from there quickly around the circle of fifths to A♮ (m. 285), the focal point through section 7. The B♮ at the beginning of section 6 (m. 277) anticipates a stronger B♮ in m. 330, the goal of the sequence in section 8. At this point the bass has progressed from the mediant to the subdominant, corresponding to the motion underlying the development of the Fifth Sonata. The subdominant is further prolonged by the complex sequence in mm. 341–59 of section 9. The passage involves a compound melodic structure which is a difficult progression to interpret. The pattern of repetition is broken immediately after the return of B♮ in m. 359. In the final measures of the development, the bass progresses to D♮, which carries over into the recapitulation, prolonged by the literal restatement of B1 at T_8.

At this point the background progression of *Prometheus* diverges for the first time from that of the Fifth Sonata. The modifications involved in the recapitulation of C material occur in conjunction with an ascending unfolding from D♮ to D♭ effected by transpositional repetition. The significance of this unfolding is concealed by spelling. In fact, D♭ is the enharmonic equivalent of C♯, the dominant of F♯ major. The arrival of the dominant is stressed here by association with the flamboyant passagework of the *flot lumineux* and *aigu, fulgurant* materials. The dominant is prolonged throughout the recapitulation of the rest of C and all of D. The recapitulation of section E, the apotheosis of the main theme, is based on a progression equivalent at T_8 to that in the original section E. This passage reaches a mighty climax in m. 498 with G♮ in the bass, sustained in subsequent measures as tension subsides. The recapitulation of E continues at

Example 139b *Prometheus* Op. 60: Development

Example 139c *Prometheus* Op. 60: Recapitulation

T_8 in mm. 504–06, allowing the sequence to reach the tonic. The purpose of this level of transposition is now clear: in the recapitulation of section E, the middleground bass progression which originally tonicized the mediant has been transposed to effect the structural cadence to the tonic closing the piece.[7]

Example 140 sketches the tonal progression at the background of *Prometheus*. The progression, although one not normally associated with sonata form, is strikingly conventional. The single bass arpeggiation from tonic to dominant, which spans almost all of the work, obviates the typical tonal "interruption form." (That is, in tonal terms the piece does not begin over again at the recapitulation, but rather continues to unfold.) The exposition is unconventional in its progression from tonic to mediant, although Scriabin set his own precedent for this procedure in the Fifth Sonata. The development prepares the dominant, introducing the passing subdominant note and the upper-auxiliary D♮, which is itself carried over into the recapitulation, a very unusual procedure. As a final innovation, Scriabin delays the cadence to the tonic until the coda.

The presence of a tonal bass progression in *Prometheus* creates a unique situation, for in a piece saturated with 6–34, this progression cannot in itself bring coherence to the composition. The structural function of this bass line is not immediately apparent. To interpret it as an independent stratum of the structure would seem to conflict directly with the overriding concern for coherence so evident in Scriabin's other works. If this bass progression has a bearing on the coherence of *Prometheus*, it must be related somehow to the use of the mystic chord.

Beneath the foreground sketch in example 139 are the levels of transposition of 6–34 at important points in the form. For this purpose, the form of 6–34 over the tonic bass note in m. 27—[3,4,6,8,10,0]—is assigned T_0. In the exposition, with only a few exceptions, the progression of forms of 6–34 parallels the tonal bass motion. For example, the progression from F♯ to F♮ in m. 87 corresponds to that from T_0 to T_{11} of 6–34. The exceptions to this pattern are notable. In the tonic prolongation in mm. 27–86, 6–34 occurs at T_7 in m. 63. This level should take place over the dominant note (as it does in the recapitulation in m. 425), and the fact that T_7 occurs here in a succession of 6–34s at T_0–T_7–T_0 suggests a circular progression prolonging the tonic, certainly appropriate to the context. In fact, the 6–34 at T_7 occurs over a tonic pedal in m. 63—one of the rare cases when the bass note is not an element of the set.

Another important exception is the 6–34 at T_3 in the introduction. (T_1 was expected.) The reason for choosing T_3 seems to be invariance, for the only two pcs shared by T_0 and T_3 are 3 and 6, important both in a_{1-3} and in c_1. (The

Example 140 *Prometheus* Op. 60: Underlying Bass Progression

pc 3–pc 6 dyad forms the endpoints of a_{1-3} and c_1.) The last important exception to the pattern is the use of T_6 (instead of T_4) with the mediant in mm. 145 and 183. Here the relation between T_6 and T_0 may have determined this choice; T_6 not only yields maximum invariance with T_0, it also strongly suggests Scriabin's quintessential tritone bass progression.

The development begins at the level with which the exposition ended (mediant with 6–34 at T_6). Beginning with section 2 (m. 212), however, the progression of 6–34 again parallels the tonal bass progression, though four half steps lower than expected. (For example, A♮ in m. 212 should occur with T_3 but instead supports T_{11}.) This pattern continues until m. 281, when the original parallelism is resumed for the rest of the development. Although the original parallelism is broken in sections 1–5 of the development, the progression of 6–34 is by no means independent of the tonal progression; rather, the interval of parallel motion has simply been changed. The general impact of this change is to support the prolongation of the mediant in mm. 193–276 with 6–34 at the "tonic" level of transposition, T_0. The tritone progression from T_6 to T_0 in mm. 193–225 is prolongational in this context.

In the recapitulation the progression of 6–34 parallels the tonal bass progression until the final cadence with no significant deviation. At the arrival of the tonic in m. 506, something unusual takes place: 6–34 continues at T_7, the level at which it occurs over the preceding dominant bass note, as if suspended in a conventional tonal gesture. The chord later "resolves" to T_0 (m. 564). While the tonic note is prolonged throughout the coda, 6–34 occurs in the final fanfare at the unexpected level of T_2 beginning in m. 584—[5,6,8,10,0,2]. This form probably results from voice leading, for it contains pc 6, the tonic pedal, as well as pcs 0, 2, 5, and 8, which are auxiliary notes to elements of the final F♯ major chord. In this way, T_2 may be understood as auxiliary to T_0, although T_0 itself is ultimately replaced by the consonant tonic triad.

To call *Prometheus* a tonal composition would be to oversimplify to the point of meaninglessness. Yet the piece is not purely atonal. The extraordinary melding of tonal and atonal procedures in this work is Scriabin's interim solution to a problem which many composers were confronting at the beginning of the twentieth century: how to compose an extended nontonal composition. Although the final F♯ major chord unlocks the puzzle of the structure, it lacks the inevitability of a genuine tonic. And although tonal relations are audible in short spans of the composition, even the most sensitive listener probably cannot perceive an overall tonal coherence. In the absence of triads at the surface of the music, it seems that the bass progression no longer fulfills a prolongational purpose. Rather, it is employed in the service of atonal relations, essentially as a means of formal organization. Clearly Scriabin shaped his composition in accordance with the sonata principle to ensure structural coherence. The bass line of the composition seems to be a vestige of traditional form.

Prometheus is the last of Scriabin's compositions to conclude with a consonant triad and his last work composed on a grand scale. We can only speculate how he would have organized the *Mysterium*, a work which, if completed, would surely have surpassed the *Poem of Fire* in breadth and scope. In the five remaining years of his life Scriabin consolidated his atonal craft in the last five piano sonatas and many shorter works, so it is doubtful that he would have resorted to tonal means for structural coherence. Indeed, *Prometheus* is a unique experiment in the history of music, for here Scriabin attains genuine atonality while expanding the tonal sonata form to its utmost limits.

AFTERWORD

Alexander Scriabin's transition to atonality took place gradually over the first decade of the twentieth century. Even though he was committed to innovation, he did not simply abandon tonality and the craft he had already mastered in order to experiment with atonal structural procedures. Instead, he devised a method of generating novel sonorities with interesting nontonal structures at the surface of a fundamentally tonal composition. The innovative procedures in Scriabin's transitional music involve two basic techniques: (1) omitting explicit endpoints of conventional unfoldings at any level, including the background; and (2) loosening traditional vertical strictures governing counterpoint so that lines which would ordinarily move in conjunction with traditional harmonic progressions are instead allowed to move out of synchrony. Scriabin quickly mastered these procedures so that he was able to control precisely the relations among the new foreground components.

In his transitional works, Scriabin generally chose sets in which most elements belong to a single whole-tone scale. (In this study these sets have been termed *predominantly whole-tone*.) Within an essentially tonal structure, Scriabin manipulated these sets to exploit their structural properties—especially their ability to hold elements of a whole-tone scale invariant under transposition or inversion. Later in his period of transition, he discovered other sets which, although not predominantly whole-tone, have invariance properties similar to those of the whole-tone scale.

Thus, in Scriabin's compositions dating from 1903 to 1909, tonal and atonal procedures—traditionally considered mutually exclusive—function inseparably within integral musical structures. Atonal procedures are used only at foreground levels, and overall coherence is guaranteed by the underlying tonal Ursatz. We might well question the term *atonal* for procedures used in tonal compositions, but because these procedures ultimately became the primary determinants of structure in the genuinely atonal works, the term is indeed appropriate. In fact, it was Scriabin's development of a method of melding tonal and atonal procedures that enabled him to progress gradually toward atonality without sacrificing the complexity and elegance of his conventional tonal structures.

In his tonal works, Scriabin never abandoned the I–V–I axis of conventional tonality. In analyzing his tonal works, therefore, we need not posit unusual background progressions, such as the contextually determined Ursatz structures involving "contrapuntal-structural" chords identified by Felix Salzer in his analyses of twentieth-century compositions. Scriabin's music does not represent the categories of "extended" or "hovering" tonality into which many twentieth-century works have been placed. Rather, his transitional works have real tonal foundations which are projected only implicitly.

Scriabin developed other tonal procedures which are original and idiosyncratic, if not unique. Perhaps the most important is the V–♭II–V progression which may be found at almost every level prolonging either primary or secondary dominant functions. (Often this progression occurs in conjunction with whole-tone invariance.) Another noteworthy achievement is the establishment of symmetrical Ursatz forms as the structural bases of such works as "Nuances" Op. 56/3. Thus, even while he was discovering the means to create nontonal musical structures, Scriabin was further refining the craft of tonal composition.

The study of the origins of atonality is just beginning. Although this book deals with one composer's evolution to atonality, the structure and methodology of the approach establish some guidelines for further research. The repertoire of compositions which represent a phase in the transition to posttonal music is so vast that no general analytical study has yet been written. From 1860 to 1920, many composers, like Scriabin, were experimenting independently with innovative procedures, often adopting idiosyncratic methods which seem unrelated to those of other composers. Because the paths to atonal music were many and diverse, transitional music continues to make extraordinary demands of the analyst.

Analysis of this music requires a command of late nineteenth- and early twentieth-century music, and an especially thorough knowledge of the transitional music of the composer being studied. It is impossible to analyze a transitional composition without understanding its place in the composer's evolution. At the outset of an analysis, therefore, it is essential to examine an adequate sample of works from every stage of the composer's development, and to determine the chronology of these compositions as well. One must then analyze each piece in terms of both its innovative components and procedures and its relation to conventional tonal structures.

Tonal compositions have a unique organic coherence resulting from relations among levels of structure. To analyze the tonal aspects of a transitional work, therefore, one must treat it as a unified structure. Judgments based on excerpts do not necessarily come to grips with the essential factor in tonal organization—structural coherence; it is not enough merely to point out tonal-like configurations, gestures, or progressions. To demonstrate the tonality of a composition, we must show that such components play precise roles within the conventional tonal hierarchy.

The important question for a composition on the borderline between tonality and atonality is not, Is it tonal or atonal? but rather, In what way is this piece tonal, and how do atonal procedures also determine its structure? Scriabin's transitional works have conventional Ursatz structures, but he developed procedures to avoid the explicit statement of these structures. No doubt other composers worked differently, perhaps even modifying the operations and functions of the tonal system. The analyst must discover and explain any such extensions of the system and thus relate the compositions to conventional tonal structures. The chapters dealing with tonality in Scriabin's music of 1903–10 have, I hope, demonstrated the types of specific comparison necessary in any study of transitional compositions.

This book also shows the applicability of set-complex theory to transitional music, even fundamentally tonal compositions. Further, in chapters 5 and 7 set-complex theory is the basis for a statistical survey of sonorities used in various phases of Scriabin's transition to atonality. Set nomenclature is ideally suited to the study of such an evolution, for it allows the precise classification and comparison of components according to structural properties. Before the development of set theory, analysts could only point out characteristic components in transitional music—for example, Wagner's "Tristan" chord or Scriabin's "Prometheus" chord—but they were unable to come to grips with the structural relations between these central harmonies and the multiplicity of harmonies in transitional music. A better understanding of novel structural components may be obtained within the framework of the set complex. The methods employed here may certainly be extended to other transitional music, and they may suggest other methodologies based on set-complex theory.

Alexander Scriabin will probably always be an enigmatic figure in the history of music. As we become more separated from the era in which he flourished, it is increasingly difficult to comprehend his grandiose self-image as high priest of an art which would bring about the end of the world, uniting all mankind in an ecstatic and all-consuming burst of energy. Although his visions were the primary motivation for his experimentation and innovation, what remains today is his music. Scriabin's art survives because he was a master of the craft of musical composition. Much as he might have been disappointed, it is through the study of his musical structures that we can best know him today.

Appendix
Terms Related to Set-Complex Theory

This appendix contains the briefest possible definitions and technical descriptions of components and operations relevant to the theory of pitch-class set relations. This theory has been set forth most comprehensively by Allen Forte in *The Structure of Atonal Music* (New Haven: Yale University Press, 1973). For an excellent introduction to this theory, see Forte's *Harmonic Organization of "The Rite of Spring"* (New Haven: Yale University Press, 1978), 1–17.

PITCH CLASS

A *pitch class* (*pc*) is "one of the 12 pitch classes designated by the integers 0 through 11. Pitch-class 0 refers to all notated pitches C, B-sharp, and D-double-flat. Pitch-class 1 refers to all notated pitches C-sharp, D-flat, B-double sharp, and so on" (Forte, *Atonal Music*, 210). In the pc integer system, 12 is equivalent to 0. (Such a system is called a *modulo12* system.) Thus the addition of 12 to a pc integer does not change its arithmetic value. A pc integer greater than or equal to 12 may occur. If we represent this integer by the variable j, its pitch class equals the remainder after j is divided by 12 (j mod 12).

PITCH-CLASS SETS AND SET NOMENCLATURE

A *pitch-class set* (*pc set*) is "a set of distinct integers representing pitch classes" (Forte, *Atonal Music*, 210). Forte lists pc sets by their prime forms and assigns a name to each (179–81), formed by two numbers separated by a hyphen. The first is the *cardinal number* of the set (the number of elements in the set), and the second is the *ordinal number*, indicating the position of the set in the list.

PRIME FORM AND NORMAL ORDER

To obtain the *prime form* of any collection of pc integers, we must first put the integers into *normal order*, determined as follows:

(1) Arrange the pc integers into ascending numerical order; for example, [2,0,5] becomes [0,2,5].

(2) Examine each circular permutation of the ordered set. (A circular permutation is obtained by placing the first element of a series last.) To maintain ascending numerical order, 12 must be added to each integer as it is shifted to the last position; for example, the first circular permutation of [0,2,5] is [2,5,12].

(3) Select as the normal order the permutation with the smallest difference between first and last elements. If this difference is the same for more than one permutation, select the one with the least difference between the first and second integers. If this is the same, choose the one with the smallest difference between the first and third, and so on.

Prime form is determined by transposing the normal-order form so that its first integer is 0 (see below for instructions on transposition). If the prime form does not occur in Forte's listing, it is necessary to invert that ordering (see below for instructions on inversion).

TRANSPOSITION

"Transposition of a pc set S consists of the addition . . . of some integer *t* [the *transposition operator*] to each element of S" (Forte, *Atonal Music*, 211). This addition sometimes produces a sum greater than or equal to 12. Because the largest pc integer is 11, it is necessary to replace any integer *j* greater than 11 by *j* mod 12. For example, if [7,8,10] is transposed up three half steps (that is, if t = 3), the result is [7 + 3, 8 + 3, 10 + 3] or [10,11,13]. The 13 must be replaced by its mod-12 equivalent, 1. Thus [10,11,1] is equivalent to [7,8,10] with t = 3 or, alternately, at T_3.

INVERSION

The inversion of a pc set is obtained by replacing each element of that set by its inverse. If b' is the inverse of a pc integer b, then $b' = 12 - b$ (mod 12). Thus 0 is the inverse of 0, 1 of 11, 2 of 10, and so on. In discussing the inversional equivalence of sets, it is always necessary to specify the level of transposition following inversion which produces identical pc contents. For example, we can establish that [7,9,10] is equivalent to [0,1,3] by inverting [7,9,10] to obtain [5,3,2] (or [2,3,5] in normal order). The level of transposition necessary to duplicate the pc content of [0,1,3] is t = 10. Thus [0,1,3] is equivalent to the inversion of [7,9,10] transposed with t = 10, or at IT_{10}.

Inversion in atonal music differs from inversion in twelve-tone theory, where orderings must be taken into account. The method described above is neutral with respect to order, a desirable feature in dealing with atonal works.

INTERVAL CLASS AND VECTOR

Forte provides a listing of the total interval content of a set in the *interval vector*. The interval between two pc integers a and b is the absolute value of $a - b$. (For example, the interval between pcs 8 and 10 is 2.) There are twelve possible intervals, from zero to eleven half steps. It is useful, however, to classify these intervals in seven *interval classes*, such that inverse-related intervals are members of the same interval class (*ic*). As with pc integers, if b' is the inverse of an interval b, then $b' = 12 - b$ (mod 12). Thus 0 is the inverse of 0, and both belong to ic 0; 1 is the inverse of 11, and both belong to ic 1; 2 is the inverse of 10, and both belong to ic 2; and so on. To construct the interval vector of a set, we must calculate the ic formed between every unordered pair of pc integers in the set. (Because the number of occurrences of ic 0 always equals the number of elements in the set, ic 0 is not included in the vector.) The total number of occurrences of ic 1 is recorded, then the total number of occurrences of ic 2, and so on. An ordered array of six digits results, and this array is enclosed in square brackets.

INVARIANCE

The interval vector of a set indicates the number of pcs which are retained when the set is transposed. For transposition up any interval except ic 6, the number in the column of any ic (its *vector entry*) corresponds to the number of pcs retained when a set is transposed up either interval of that ic. Thus, for set 6–34—whose vector is [142422], the minimum of one pc is held invariant when the set is transposed up 1 or 11 half steps (t = 1 or t = 11), and the maximum of four pcs under transposition with t = 2, t = 10, t = 4, and t = 8. For transposition of any set with t = 6, however, twice the number of pcs indicated by the vector entry for ic 6 will be retained. Thus, when 6–34 is transposed up six half steps, four pcs are retained.

Z-RELATION

Although sets are technically equivalent only through transposition or inversion, some pairs of sets are similar because they have identical interval contents, even though they are not reducible to a single prime form. The fact that a set shares the ic content (as listed in the interval vector) of a nonequivalent set is indicated by the letter Z before the ordinal number in the set name; for example, 4–Z15 and 4–Z29 have the same vector.

COMPLEMENTATION

The complement of a set A is the set of all pitch classes which are not members of A. (The complement of A is notated as $\overline{A}$.) A set and its complement have similar ic contents. "The arithmetic difference of corresponding vector entries for complement-related sets is the same as the difference *d* of the cardinal numbers of the sets, with the exception of the entry for ic 6, in which case *d* must be divided by 2 (since 6 is its own inverse mod 12)" (Forte, *Atonal Music*, 77). Therefore complements may be considered replicas of each other. Further, on the basis of similar ic content, any transpositional or inversional form of the complement of a set is also considered a complement, except in the case of non-Z-related hexachords, which are self-complementary. Forte's set names facilitate dealing with complementation in analysis. The cardinal numbers of complementary sets are inversely related (mod 12), and for all sets except hexachords, the ordinal numbers of complements correspond as well. There is no such correspondence for hexachords. Complementation for hexachords is complex because it is connected to the Z-relation. In twenty cases out of fifty, the complement of a six-note set forms the same set. In all other cases the complement is the Z-correspondent of the set.

SIMILARITY RELATIONS

Forte defines several relations by which the degree of similarity between two sets of the same cardinal number may be measured (*Atonal Music*, 46–49). If two sets of cardinal n contain at least one common subset of cardinal $n - 1$, they are said to be in R_p and are maximally similar in pitch class. Interval-class similarity may be measured by comparing the vectors of sets of the same cardinal number. Two sets are said to be in R_0 if no vector entries correspond and in R_1 if their vectors contain the same six integers and four entries correspond. Finally, two sets are in R_2 if their vectors do not contain the same six integers but four entries correspond. Two sets in R_0 are minimally similar in ic content, whereas R_1 and R_2 are relations of maximum similarity.

For purposes of gauging the similarity of sets according to Forte's relations, a set and its complement are considered equivalent so that, if a set A exists in R_0, R_1, or R_2 with a set B, then $\overline{A}$ exists in the same relation with B.

SET COMPLEX

A *set complex* is "a set of sets associated by virtue of the inclusion relation" (Forte, *Atonal Music*, 210). More particularly, a set S and its complement belong to the complex about a set T and its complement if and only if S contains or is contained in T, or if S contains or is contained in the complement of T. Membership in this complex is indicated by *K.* A special subcomplex of K is symbolized by *Kh.* For a set S to be in the subcomplex Kh about a set T, S must contain or be contained in both T and its complement. In these definitions, set T is the referential set for the complex and is frequently called the *nexus set.* If T is unrelated to some sets in a collection of sets, then a *secondary nexus set* W, related to all sets not related to T, must be selected. Otherwise the set-complex structure will not be *connected.* Further, if T and W are of the same cardinal number, then there must be a *tertiary nexus set* related to both T and W for the structure to be connected.

PREFACE

1. Alfred Swan points out that Scriabin did not conceive of his late music as divorced from his earlier compositions. As a recitalist, Scriabin often performed early and late works on the same program. See Alfred J. Swan, *Scriabin* (1923; reprint, New York: Da Capo, 1969), 67.

2. Leonid Leonidovich Sabaneiev, *Modern Russian Composers*, trans. Judah A. Joffe (1927; reprint, New York: Da Capo, 1975), 51.

3. Quoted in Faubion Bowers, *The New Scriabin: Enigma and Answers* (New York: St. Martin's Press, 1973), 134.

4. Ibid., 149.

5. In fact, he reneged on a promise to explain the system to Sergei Taneiev, the composer and systematic theorist, with whom he had studied counterpoint at the Moscow Conservatory. See ibid., 128–29.

6. The earliest works considered in this book date from 1903. In part because of a hiatus in Scriabin's composing during 1901–02, the works of 1903 are generally regarded as marking a new phase in his development, although even these compositions are well within the late romantic tradition.

7. In his essay "The Classical Concerto," Donald Francis Tovey explains the central premise of his analytical approach:

> But when I discuss music I shall speak of things musical . . . for it is these things . . . that make a concerto or a symphony what it is. And if it is objected that these things, as they occur in classical music, are non-poetical, or mere technical means of expressing some poetic idea that lies behind them, I can only reply that, so long as music remains music, this poetic idea will only be attainable through these musical phenomena. (*Concertos*, vol. 3 of *Essays in Musical Analysis* [London: Oxford University Press, 1936], 5)

I am fundamentally in sympathy with Tovey's outlook. It is understandable, however, that the extra-musical aspects of Scriabin's work have received more attention than the music itself. The philosophical, literary, and mystical associations of Scriabin's music are discussed in the following studies: Martin Cooper, "Aleksandr Skryabin and the Russian Renaissance," *Studi musicali* 1, no. 2 (1972): 327–55; Manfred Kelkel, *Alexandre Scriabine: Sa vie, l'ésotérisme et le langage musical dans son oeuvre* (Paris: Editions Honoré Champion, 1978); and Malcolm Brown, "Skriabin and Russian 'Mystic' Symbolism," *Nineteenth-Century Music* 3 (1979): 42–51. Hugh Macdonald's *Skryabin* (London: Oxford University Press, 1978) presents a fine overview of the composer's life and works.

8. For example Scriabin wrote the Poem Op. 32/2 as an aria for his uncompleted opera based on Nietzschean themes (see Bowers, *New Scriabin*, 47). The two *Danses* Op. 73 were intended for the *Mysterium* (see Bowers, *Scriabin: A Biography of the Russian Composer, 1871–1915*, 2 vols. [Tokyo: Kodansha International, 1969], 2:264).

9. Kurt Westphal, "Die Harmonik Scrjabins: Ein Versuch über ihr System und ihre Entwicklung in den Klavierwerken," *Musikblätter des Anbruch* 11 (1929): 64–69; and Paul Dickenmann, *Die Entwicklung der Harmonik bei A. Skrjabin*, vol. 4 of *Berner Veröffentlichungen zur Musikforschung* (Bern: P. Haupt, 1935).

10. Varvara Pavlovna Dernova, *Garmoniia Skriabina* (Leningrad: Muzyka, 1968). For a brief discussion of Dernova's theory, see chapter 1.

11. Zofia Lissa, "Zur Genesis des 'Prometheischen Akkords' bei A. N. Skrjabin," *Musik des Ostens* 2 (1963): 170–83.

12. According to Helga Boegner, for example, Scriabin's transitional harmonies function simultaneously as chords of thirds or fourths. See "Die Harmonik der späten Klavierwerke Alexander Skrjabins" (Ph.D. diss., Ludwig-Maximilians-Universität, Munich, 1955), 23–24. Gottfried Eberle attempts to trace the evolution of Scriabin's harmony from a chord-of-thirds structure to one of superposed fourths by extending the theories of Dickenmann and Lissa. See his *Zwischen Tonalität und Atonalität: Studien zur Harmonik Alexander Skrjabins*, vol. 14 of *Berliner Musikwissenschaftliche Arbeiten* (Munich: Musikverlag Emil Katzbichler, 1978).

13. For a survey and critique of attempts to extend Schenkerian techniques to posttonal music, see my article, "Schenkerian Analysis and Post-Tonal Music" in *Aspects of Schenkerian Theory*, ed. David Beach (New Haven: Yale University Press, 1983), 153–86.

14. Credit for this contribution must go to Helga Boegner and especially to Varvara Dernova. See notes 10 and 12 above.

15. Allen Forte, *The Structure of Atonal Music* (New Haven: Yale University Press, 1973).

CHAPTER 1

1. Scriabin's voice leading is characteristically complicated, generating many dissonant chords at the surface of the music. For purposes of commencing a description of Scriabin's harmony, the discussion is limited at first to the underlying harmony determined by bass progression. The methods for discerning harmony underlying the surface of the music are treated in later sections. For now, the reader should pay close attention to the progressions of low bass tones.

2. Throughout this book, a slash indicates a harmonic function within a particular tonal area. Thus "V/D" denotes the dominant in the tonal area of D and "V/II" denotes the dominant of the supertonic. On occasion, square brackets are an alternative means of indicating applied harmonic functions. In this notation, the function in square brackets applies to that immediately following. Thus, [V]–II is the same progression as V/II–II.

3. J. P. Kirnberger (1721–83) classified all dissonances which take the place of consonances in a harmony as "unessential." These ideally resolve before a change of harmony. The only essential dissonance, which resolves with a change of harmony, is the seventh. See David W. Beach, "The Origins of Harmonic Analysis," *Journal of Music Theory* 18 (1974): 283.

4. Henceforth, two symbolic notations for transposition are employed. The repetition of an element or component at T_n indicates that the repeated material is transposed up n half steps. Transposition with $t = n$ also indicates transposition up n half steps.

5. For a complete description of the linear $^4_2$ chord, see Allen Forte, *Tonal Harmony in Concept and Practice*, 3d ed. (New York: Holt, Rinehart and Winston, 1979), 358–60.

6. Varvara Pavlovna Dernova, *Garmoniia Skriabina* (Leningrad: Muzyka, 1968).

7. Although presumably the traditional tonal laws no longer completely pertain in the music governed by dual modality, Dernova retains roman and arabic numerals to designate basic sonorities. Thus the basic tetrachord G–B–D♭–F is labeled $V^{7}_{\flat 5}$/C. When transposed up a tritone and respelled C♯–E♯–G–B, the same four pitches are identified as $V^{7}_{\flat 5}$/F♯. Therefore the same sonority may be the dominant of either of two tonics separated by a tritone. These two versions of the same chord are labeled Da and Db. In pieces governed by dual modality, these chords may progress to their respective tonics, Ta and Tb, by bass progression of descending fifth (or ascending fourth). This tonal progression, however, is not the rule in Scriabin's later music, where the tonic is usually suppressed; instead, bass progression by tritone (which retains all pitches of the basic chord) is fundamental. According to Dernova, the next most common progression is up or down a major third. (At either level, the basic chord shares two pitches with the original.)

The relation of dual modality to conventional tonality is not clear in Dernova's study. Evidently the two are not mutually exclusive, for she explains some clearly tonal compositions in terms of Scriabin's new system (for example, her analysis of Op. 32/1, *Garmoniia Skriabina*, 31). Although the notion of levels of structure is implicit throughout Dernova's study, the operations making possible the distinction between tones of different structural weights are not stated and are not deducible from the analyses.

8. Paul Hindemith, *The Craft of Musical Composition*, trans. Arthur Mendel, 2 vols. (New York: Associated Music Publishers, 1942), 1:156; and Milton Babbitt, "The String Quartets of Bartók," *Musical Quarterly* 35 (1949): 380.

9. Although "Enigme" Op. 52/2 (composed in 1906) ends with a whole-tone chord, this etude and "Nuances" Op. 56/3 (both composed in 1907) are the first works to conclude with dissonant suspension chords.

10. In "Désir" Op. 57/1, a completed progression to the dominant is accomplished in m. 6 by the literal repetition of the opening material at T_7 (example 59). Because the original material opened to the dominant, a complete repetition at T_7 would lead to the dominant of the dominant, and motion around the circle of fifths could continue indefinitely. Therefore, as soon as Scriabin repeats the opening two-beat gesture at T_7 in m. 6, he deliberately shifts to T_5 for the rest of the literal repetition. He thereby obtains not only a progression tending toward the tonic, but also a poignant harmonic enhancement of the halting phrases which at the beginning were simply repeated exactly.

11. An exception is the opening of the "Feuillet d'album" Op. 45/1 (example 25), but even this work opens on a tonic unison, not a complete triad; the first complete tonic triad in the piece, the goal of the opening phrase, is the weakened first inversion. In fact, a complete root-position tonic chord is not heard until the end of the composition (m. 24). The Prelude Op. 51/2 is another exceptional piece; here the entire A minor tonic triad occurs at the beginning (example 28). However, the status of A minor as tonic is obfuscated by the continual presence of F♮. At the beginning, the underlying harmony seems to be an F major triad (in first inversion) with E♮ refusing to resolve. Only gradually does it become clear that the F♮ is auxiliary to E♮—and this is not certain until the end of the composition.

12. Interestingly, "Ironies" Op. 56/2 uses the same voice leading to conceal the tonic C major chord in m. 4 (example 11a). Late in the piece (m. 66) a pure tonic chord occurs briefly, but in first inversion and without the stabilizing effect of a cadence (example 39b). Only at the end is a firm tonic established by resolving A♭ and F♯ to G, a member of a root-position tonic triad. (The final progression to the tonic is not a cadence directly from the dominant but rather the resolution of an unessential neighbor chord.)

13. "Fragilité" Op. 51/1 features an adventurous progression to ♭II (m. 40), spelled as E major instead of F♭. The E♭ tonic (m. 44) returns via V/V (m. 41) and V (m. 42); the progression is made smooth by the retention of A♮ and D♯ (E♭) between V/♭II and V/V (the two aspects of a dual dominant function).

14. Dernova would argue that ♭II in these compositions is actually one form of the dual dominant, but a distinction between ♭II and V seems necessary. An argument for dual modality would be much stronger in Op. 56/4 (see the discussion of example 6). However, it is adequate to consider the chord on G♮ in mm. 5–6 an applied dominant of the C major chord which functions as ♭V in the key of G♭ (example 8).

15. Scriabin's basic phrases are usually four measures long, and two phrases are often balanced as antecedent and consequent ideas in an eight-measure period. In a rapid tempo, these units may comprise twice as many measures, as in "Caresse dansée" Op. 57/2, where a sixteen-measure periodic structure prevails (example 21).

CHAPTER 2

1. In many of the musical examples, analytical sketches are aligned beneath the music. Sketch numbers correspond to the examples they illustrate. Thus, sketches 15a–c are analyses of example 15.

2. For a detailed discussion of this passage, see my article "Scriabin's Implicit Tonality," *Music Theory Spectrum* 2 (1980): 8–9.

3. The lowering of the seventh scale degree poses a problem of harmonic closure. For a thorough consideration of this question see ibid., 12–14.

4. For a complete introduction to this phenomenon, see Allen Forte, *Tonal Harmony in Concept and Practice*, 3d ed. (New York: Holt, Rinehart and Winston, 1979), 363–76.

CHAPTER 3

1. Although the background and foreground are only the two extreme levels of a greatly stratified structure, it is conventional in graphic analysis to differentiate the foreground, middleground, and background with three staff systems, as in example 25. (The foreground and background systems usually contain elements from the nearest middleground levels.) I have condensed many graphic analyses in this book to two systems.

The first paragraph of this chapter is the briefest possible summary of the principle of structural levels developed by Heinrich Schenker and enunciated most clearly in his *Der freie Satz*, the third part of *Neue musikalische Theorien und Phantasien*, ed. Oswald Jonas, 2 vols., 2d ed. (Vienna: Universal Edition, 1956). This work is now available in an English translation by Ernst Oster (New York: Longman, 1979). An excellent introduction to Schenker's ideas may be found in Allen Forte, "Schenker's Conception of Musical Structure," *Journal of Music Theory* 3 (1959): 1–30.

2. As is customary in Schenkerian analysis, each scale degree of the Urlinie is designated by an arabic numeral with a circumflex.

3. William Austin, describing Op. 45/1, says that "no two listeners are likely to agree as to which notes are members of a chord and which are passing tones, appoggiaturas, cambiatas, and *échappés*" (*Music in the Twentieth Century: From Debussy through Stravinsky* [New York: W. W. Norton, 1966], 71). On the contrary, each pitch in this piece has a definite function in a coherent harmonic-contrapuntal structure enhanced by delicately varied repetitions of both bass progressions and melodic unfoldings. For the late tonal music of Scriabin—and probably for much of the highly chromatic music of the late nineteenth century—it is a mistake to equate unconventional voice leading and vague, dissonant harmonies at the foreground with real structural ambiguity.

4. The tonic in m. 12 arrives halfway through the main body of the piece, which extends only through m. 24 (after which the opening material is repeated as a coda). The completed prolongation of the tonic in m. 14 marks the exact midpoint of the piece (considered apart from the final cadence in mm. 29–30, appended after a fade-out in the preceding measures).

5. See Arnold Schoenberg, "Über schwebende und aufgehobende Tonalität," *Harmonielehre*, rev. 3d ed. (Vienna: Universal Edition, 1922), 459–60. Scriabin's reliance on a tonal framework during his period of experimentation is not surprising. Igor Stravinsky, writing of having gazed into the "abyss of freedom," states: "In art as in everything else, one can build only upon a resisting foundation: whatever constantly gives way to pressure constantly renders movement impossible" (*Poetics of Music*, trans. Arthur Knodel and Ingolf Dahl [New York: Vintage Books, 1947], 66, 68).

6. The F♭, if implicit in the dominant chord of m. 15, would complete a whole-tone aggregate in this measure. However, the formation of a whole-tone collection in no way affects the progress of the Urlinie. The G, the only non-whole-tone element here, is heard briefly and is actually a chromatic passing tone from A♭ in the previous measure to F♯. It anticipates a strong G in the final tonic triad, but G does not appear in the upper register in the final chord (m. 21).

7. The importance of the G♭ harmony in determining an exact structural symmetry in both the bass and the melody points to its precedence over the preceding D♭ harmony in the deep structure.

8. The title may well refer to Paul Verlaine's "Art poétique," written in 1874 as a declaration of the goals of the symbolist movement. The poem proclaims:

Cars nous voulons la Nuance encor,
Pas la Couleur, rien que la nuance!

[Never the Color, always the Shade,
always the nuance is supreme!]

These nuances are most fully realized through music:

De la musique avant toute chose,
Et pour cela préfère l'Impair,
Plus vague et plus soluble dans l'air,
Sans rien en lui qui pèse ou qui pose.

Il faut aussi que tu n'ailles point
Choisir tes mots sans quelque méprise:
Rien de plus cher que la chanson grise
Où l'Indécis au Précis se joint.

[You must have music first of all,
and for that a rhythm uneven is best,
vague in the air and soluble,
with nothing heavy and nothing at rest.

You must not scorn to do some wrong
in choosing the words to fill your lines:
nothing more dear than the tipsy song
where the Undefined and Exact combine.]

(Paul Verlaine, *Selected Poems*, trans. C. F. MacIntyre [Berkeley and Los Angeles: University of California Press, 1948], 180–83.) Scriabin's "Nuances" is one such merger, for indefinite foreground events are supported by a sound fundamental structure.

9. These connections are discussed in my article "Schenkerian Analysis and Post-Tonal Music" in *Aspects of Schenkerian Theory*, ed. David Beach (New Haven: Yale University Press, 1983), 179.

10. With the Etude Op. 56/4, Scriabin abandoned traditional key signatures for the rest of his career. Only the last piece of the Op. 56 set lacks a key signature, but the link between "Nuances" Op. 56/3 and this etude makes Scriabin's intent obvious. Op. 56/4 does in fact have a key signature, C major, which the listener accepts as the tonic at the beginning. This playful deception would be spoiled, at least in concept, if the key of G♭ were acknowledged by a key signature at the outset.

Excluding this special use of C major, Scriabin's first tonal composition without a key signature was the "Feuillet d'album" Op. 58 (perhaps composed as early as 1909), which may also be his last verifiably tonal work (see chapter 6).

11. Felix Salzer, *Structural Hearing: Tonal Coherence in Music*, 2 vols., rev. ed. (New York: Dover, 1962), 1:204.

CHAPTER 4

1. Allen Forte, *The Structure of Atonal Music* (New Haven: Yale University Press, 1973).

2. Ibid., 1.

3. Ibid., 5.

4. Conventional analysis does not attempt to deal with such large sonorities as 7–Z17, yet they are clearly significant in Scriabin's music.

5. For convenience, especially for comparison with the smaller complement, the pc content of a set with more than six elements is indicated by listing the pc content of its complement in parentheses instead of brackets. Thus the content of 7–13 is given in example 46 as (2,1,0,10,6), showing that it contains [3,4,5,7,8,9,11].

6. Unless otherwise stated, the invariance properties cited for any set refer to invariance under transposition, not under inversion.

7. See, for example, Leonid Leonidovich Sabaneiev, "Prometheus von Skrjabin," *Melos* 1.(1920): 481–82; and Alfred J. Swan, *Scriabin* (1923; reprint, New York: Da Capo, 1969), 87–100.

8. See, for example, Oliver Neighbour, "The Evolution of Twelve-Note Music," *Proceedings of the Royal Musical Association* 81 (1954): 56–57.

9. Another distinguishing feature of 6–34 is that, of these three similar chords, it alone minimizes ic 1. The importance of this property is discussed in the next chapter.

CHAPTER 5

1. For this survey, all complementary sets, including Z-related hexachords, are regarded as structurally equivalent. For convenience, complements of cardinals 4/8 or 5/7 are referred to by the lower cardinal number (that is, 4 or 5). In the case of Z-related hexachords, these sets are occasionally differentiated in the discussion. When interval content alone is considered, Z-related hexachords are of course equivalent. However, in counts of available six-element sets, it is advisable to consider sets in a Z-related pair individually, because they do not reduce to the same prime form by transposition or inversion.

2. Forte, *Atonal Music*, 37–38, 107.

3. Ibid., 37–38.

4. Ibid., 45.

5. Set 6–35 is completely invariant under both transposition and inversion, 6–30 only under transposition, and 6–32 only under inversion. For these sets the invariant subsets are improper, for the subset contains all of the elements of the superset. For a list of all sets with this property, see Forte, *Atonal Music*, 82.

6. Ibid., 78.

7. Ibid., 53–56.

8. For instance, Scriabin's sets cover almost the entire range of counts of basic interval patterns; ibid., 69.

CHAPTER 6

1. For a complete analysis of "Enigme" Op. 52/2, see my article "Schenkerian Analysis and Post-Tonal Music" in *Aspects of Schenkerian Theory*, ed. David Beach (New Haven: Yale University Press, 1983), 168–85. This work is one of Scriabin's furthest extensions of implicit tonality in his late tonal music (1903–10), which is surprising since it was composed in 1906, when most of his output was still fairly explicitly tonal. This piece is his first to close with a dissonant, nontriadic harmony. In fact, the final chord is 6–35, the whole-tone scale—an appropriate sonority because whole-tone invariance is one of the primary determinants of structure in the composition. Although the piece is considered by some to be atonal, my analysis demonstrates that tonal forces are largely responsible for its overall coherence.

2. Faubion Bowers, *Scriabin: A Biography of the Russian Composer, 1871–1915*, 2 vols. (Tokyo: Kodansha International, 1969), 2:210.

3. Compare my example 87 with the bottom sketch in Forte's example 110 (*Atonal Music*, 117), which contains an analysis of a three-measure passage from the beginning of Scriabin's Ninth Piano Sonata Op. 68.

CHAPTER 8

1. Hugh Macdonald advances the intriguing theory that the *Poem of Ecstasy* Op. 54 and the Fifth Sonata Op. 53 (in that order) are a diptych, a musical setting of Scriabin's original text "The Poem of Ecstasy." See "Words and Music by A. Skryabin," *Musical Times* 113 (1972): 22–27.

2. Oddly enough, the basic structure disclosed here resembles that of "Enigme" Op. 52/2 (see chapter 6, note 1), for if B major were the tonic of the Fifth Sonata, then the essential progression of the entire work would be V^7–I–V^7. There is no reason to choose this analysis, particularly in view of the key signature and because the minor seventh—an element of the F♯ harmony—is conventionally added to the tonic in Scriabin's tonal music.

3. In December 1907 Scriabin wrote to Margarita Morozova: "The *Poem of Ecstasy* took much of my strength and taxed my patience. So now are you imagining me giving myself over to rest, something I have wanted for so long? No, not at all! Today I have almost finished my 5th Sonata. It is a big poem for piano and I deem it the best piano composition I have ever written. I do not know by what miracle I accomplished it" (quoted in Faubion Bowers, *Scriabin: A Biography of the Russian Composer, 1871–1915*, 2 vols. [Tokyo: Kodansha International, 1969], 2:176).

4. Scriabin's dissatisfaction with the structural coherence of the Fourth Sonata did not cause him to drop the work from his performance repertoire. (In later years his recitals characteristically featured music both early and late, tonal and atonal.) For Scriabin the performer, the work continued to be an especially effective showpiece. In fact, the Fourth Sonata was the concluding piece of his last recital in Petersburg on 2 April 1915. Ibid., 2:270.

5. The precedent for this symmetrical progression may have been the tonal progression defining the latter portion of the development in the Fifth Sonata (mm. 281–328).

CHAPTER 9

1. Faubion Bowers, *Scriabin: A Biography of the Russian Composer, 1871–1915*, 2 vols. (Tokyo: Kodansha International, 1969), 2:130.

2. Under the influence of Georgy Plekhanov, Scriabin once considered posting the first lines of the "Internationale" as an epigraph to his work. Ibid., 2:95–96.

3. Ibid., 2:30.

4. The many relations between d_{1-2} and preceding materials indicate the difficulty in *Prometheus* of distinguishing genuine motives from derivative materials. In general, if an idea is distinct in rhythm, texture, orchestration, or other musical attributes, and if it occurs in more than one formal division of the piece, it is considered a motive and is listed in example 129.

5. See, for instance, Clemens-Christoph von Gleich, *Die sinfonischen Werke von Alexander Skrjabin* (Bilthoven, Holland: A. B. Creyghton, 1963), 68–69.

6. Ibid., 70–71. Von Gleich describes the upper voice of the two-voice part for color organ as containing the roots of the forms of 6–34 (arranged in superposed fourths). Scriabin's stemming does not confirm von Gleich's interpretation of the part writing, however.

7. The use of T_8 in the recapitulation of the Tenth Sonata may have its roots in *Prometheus*, although it serves no tonal function in the sonata.

Index

Selected pitch-class sets are listed by set name under "Pitch-class set." Harmonic functions are indexed under "Tonal function."